Programming
Time-Shared
Computers
in BASIC

Programming Time-Shared Computers in BASIC

Eugene H. Barnett

TRW Systems, Inc.
Redondo Beach, California

WILEY-INTERSCIENCE

a division of John Wiley & Sons, Inc.
New York · London · Sydney · Toronto

PREFACE

Time-shared computing was first introduced on a commercial scale in 1965. Since then many companies have offered the service to an expanding user market. Although several programming languages may be offered by any of these companies, the most universally available is BASIC (an abbreviation for Beginner's All-Purpose Symbolic Instruction Code language), and for good reason. One of the most valuable virtues of time-sharing is that it places enormous computing power into the hands of a wide assortment of individual engineers, managers, businessmen, accountants, and students. These users have one characteristic in common: They are *not* professional programmers. If the time-shared computer is to be an effective tool for these people in their normal work, it must demand as little of their time as possible to learn, leaving their energies and talents for more directly rewarding engineering or management enterprises. The language they use must serve them, not constrict them.

In this context, BASIC is an ideal language, for not only does it provide most of the capabilities available on more sophisticated computer systems, but it is also very easy to learn. This book intends to teach the newcomer to program in the latest versions of BASIC; in particular, on the time-shared computer. It presumes no prior programming experience by the reader.

Time-sharing companies provide some elementary manuals to get the new user started, but they are generally devoted to simply explaining the correct syntax of individual program statements and they do not adequately impart a cohesive approach to organizing that material into a successful programming talent. This text gives exhaustive treatment to both of these crucial subjects.

The sequence of presentation of some of the subject matter may seem a bit unorthodox to some experienced instructors. For example, I have put the material on LET and READ/DATA statements, INPUT statements, and INPUT data files into separate sections of the book, even though one might (indeed, reasonably!) argue that they are all of the same genre and therefore perhaps should be treated together. My intention in so arranging the text is not to separate statements possessing a common base, but to allow the introduction of other material in between them—a point which is much more than a mere semantical one. I have found that building a solid foundation of the fundamentals of programming is more crucial at first than is the exposure to all the language's "bells and whistles." Once those principles are learned well, perhaps at the cost of a little extra labor on the student's part, the numerous embellishments are easy to absorb and exploit. On the other hand, prematurely giving the student all the bells and whistles at once oftentimes causes confusion for him, while he is still trying to assimilate principles.

Recognizing that another instructor might prefer a different sequence, I have taken pains to organize the book in such a way that it simultaneously satisfies two teaching goals: first, to be patterned after the careful, selected, sequence of material presentation which I have found to be quite successful in my teachings of both BASIC and FØRTRAN; and second, to make various sections of the book sufficiently independent so that another instructor (or the aggressive reader) can judiciously assign (or study) selected parts of it out of sequence, thereby tailoring it to his specific needs.

It was an early myth that the time-sharing computer was designed for engineering problems and not for management or accounting applications. Today, however, an increasing proportion of the industry's advertising literature is addressed to nonengineering applications, and the author's experience in teaching this material and writing programs for a variety of users is conclusive. The time-sharing computer is a very valuable tool for nonengineering applications, too. After all, there are very few inherent limitations in time-sharing or in the BASIC language which would prohibit their use for many business problems, and most that did exist a short time ago have been eliminated by improvements in software (such as data files, alpha-numeric string capability and image printing). I believe that a tremendous potential exists for the person with nonengineering applications.

In accordance with this conviction, a fundamental question about structuring the book arises. If the language is going to be used by a diverse group of people, with an assortment of backgrounds, should not this book be written with that audience in mind? But, given that, who typifies the group; to whom should the book be oriented in its selection of example problems and other material? To the engineer? The chemist? The mathematician, businessman, accountant, sociologist? Or, to all of them? I have presumed the latter. This book gives equal attention to engineering and nonengineering applications. The examples usually involve problems that most persons can readily understand so that the reader's attention can be focused on programming and not be distracted by problems specialized beyond his technical comprehension. Some of the exercises are tailored to specific fields.

Chapters 2–5 are devoted to the examination of what, if it were not for possible semantic confusion, could best be called *basic* BASIC programming, including important aspects of using the computer hardware and a unique attempt at transmitting to the student the valuable confidence, techniques, and perception necessary to be self-sufficient in creating his own programs. The material presented in these chapters is generally applicable to all systems using the BASIC language, with very little modification.

In its original form, BASIC was satisfactory but lacked the depth, of say, modern FØRTRAN and CØBØL. But significant capabilities have been, and are still being, added by major suppliers of time-sharing services. They are usually combined with the original BASIC into "new" languages which each supplier gives his own trade name, such as EXTENDED BASIC* or SUPER BASIC.† Programmers are faced with the problem that these advancements are independently developed, resulting in significant differences between them. What one vendor feels is important to offer, others may feel should be subordinate to their own package of features. Common features sometimes take on differing characteristics in their implementation, most of them minor. It is not possible to cover all the variations in this book, and the student is left with a responsibility to research his computer company's manuals for the precise construction of various statements. On the other hand, the advancements in the language are far too important to simply ignore because of that inconvenience. Therefore Chapters 6–8, being an examination of those features which have been added to *basic BASIC*, are oriented toward teaching the student the principles behind the new features and giving him exposure to the most common, simplest, or illustrative versions. After understanding these chapters, the student should easily adjust to using the particular version available to him.

Many example problems are given to assist the reader in developing a consistent pattern of programming. The subject matter is further illustrated by specific exercises to be undertaken by the student. These are designed to solidify the student's approach to, and confidence in, his own programming techniques, and to illustrate more subtle points which may not be conveniently explained in the text. The student is thus able to develop

---

* General Electric Co., Bethesda, Md.
† Tymshare, Inc., Palo Alto, Ca.

personal approaches to defining his own programming requirements, to translating a generally defined task into a specific, organized, and logically flowing program.

Chapter 8 is of particular interest to the manager of an organization which engages in time-sharing programming. He must understand the exploitable capabilities available to him, and how to efficiently utilize this capability. That material is also pertinent to the time-sharing programmer, for the tools to implement the manager's objectives are also discussed.

Finally, the computer has been an excellent intellectual stimulator to me, often amazing me with its versatility and hidden secrets. Merely reading an obscure sentence in a manual, or accidentally making a mistake while typing a program, or being presented with some bizarre problem, has sent me whirling on a fascinating trip to learn to use some new tricks, like Monte Carlo, pattern recognition, matrix arithmetic, or solving logic and word-game puzzles. Yet the most fascinating part is learning that these tricks are very valuable tools for solving everyday financial, business, and engineering problems, as well as realizing that most of them can be learned quite easily by a high-school student if presented properly. I have tried to involve the reader in the same kind of adventure by carefully selecting interesting examples and explaining, on a very elementary level, those techniques with which he may not be familiar.

I hope that my readers experience the same pleasure from this book and their programming activities as I have.

I wish to express my gratitude to my wife Linda, whose patience and assistance in the preparation of the original manuscript have been monumental, and to Mr. Bernie Bergman of Tymshare, Inc. for providing a significant amount of computer time to write and debug many of the example programs in this book.

Torrance, California　　　　　　　　　　　　　　　Eugene H. Barnett
August 1971

CONTENTS

PROGRAM SUBJECTS

The following major subjects are illustrated by various examples and exercises through this text:

BUSINESS AND FINANCIAL
    Payroll
    Depreciation
    Return on investment
    Loan repayment
    Moving averages
    Inventory evaluation
    Billing discounts
    Make or buy calculations
    Commissions
    Matrix algebra
    Cost minimization
    Auditing and sampling
    Monte Carlo
    Sales analysis
    Simultaneous equations
    Curve plotting

SOCIOLOGY
    Benefits eligibility
    Teaching machines
    Survey analysis
    Mice in a maze

ENGINEERING
> Moving auto
> Trajectories
> Vectors
> Mass moments
> Volume determination
> Geometry
> Matrix algebra
> Quality control sampling
> Curve plotting
> Simpson's rule
> Spring vibration
> Truth tables
> Step functions
> Electronic circuits
> Orbital mechanics
> Complex numbers

MATHEMATICS AND OPERATIONS RESEARCH
> Queuing theory
> Linear regression
> Simultaneous equations
> Probability
> Numerical integration
> Common denominator
> Standard deviation
> Monte Carlo
> Binary numbers
> Newton–Raphson approximation

MISCELLANEOUS
> Recipes
> Acreage determination
> Roulette
> Children's game "BUZZ"
> Logic word games
> Library search
> Pattern recognition

Programming
Time-Shared
Computers
in BASIC

1 INTRODUCTION

Computer buffs ... have been likened to small boys who, given a hammer, suddenly find that everything needs pounding. The computer is a tool and a toy, but it is also a mistress of sorts.

—Readings in Psychology Today

To suggest that a computer has predicted an election or made an error in a customer's billing is akin to suggesting that the crayon, not the child, created a particularly endearing drawing. Neither device can do anything without direction and guidance from a human. Many people face the prospect of learning to program computers with a degree of uncertainty, near trepidation. The feeling is understandable but completely unnecessary. With advancements in time-sharing computing, and the BASIC language in which to instruct it, programming has become simple and enjoyable.

The language is at one time, so simple that a high school student can learn to use it, and so powerful that it is routinely used to plan buildings, bridges, and space flights, or to analyze corporate sales results. Generally speaking, the computer does just what a human does when working any arithmetic problem—it adds, subtracts, multiplies, divides, and writes answers on paper. Its principal virtue is its incredible speed at carrying out these operations—it can handle on the order of millions per second. The computer demands no more sophistication of its user than that he be able to work his own problem by hand if he were so inclined and had the energy, patience, and time to do so. This does not detract from the utility of the computer. It is the machine's dependency on a human to tell it what to do that makes it amenable to any problem. Its very speed often prompts us to

1

attempt extremely complex problems which would be far too tedious and time-consuming without the computer.

This book stresses how one goes about making the computer do the job he wishes it to do. As much as is possible, the book is complete and self-sufficient, but there is no substitute for actual experience on the computer for one to pick up the subtleties and nuances involved. In addition, progress will be accelerated if the reader has personal access to someone—a co-worker or an instructor—with some experience in the subject.

It is desirable at this point to skip ahead briefly and try programming a simple problem to give the reader the general flavor of the subject.

Example 1.1 The Family Homesite

A family wishes to purchase a plot at least one-third acre in size. The rectangular lots in Table 1.1 are available in their area. Write a program

Table 1.1 Available lots.

Lot	Length	Width
413	100	200
628	350	200
103	100	50
213	100	100

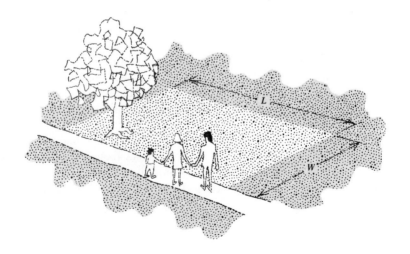

to determine which lots are acceptable (i.e., which are over one-third acre). The area of a lot is $A = L \times W$. An acre is 43,560 ft^2.*

DISCUSSION

Couldn't one sketch out some simple instructions for himself or another person, spelling out just how to go about the job? He might say something like this: "For each lot, calculate the area, using the length and the width. If the area is greater than 43,560/3, write down the number of the lot; if not, don't bother to write down the number. Repeat this for all four lots."

To formalize a bit, the **flowchart** in Figure 1.1 might be drawn to illustrate

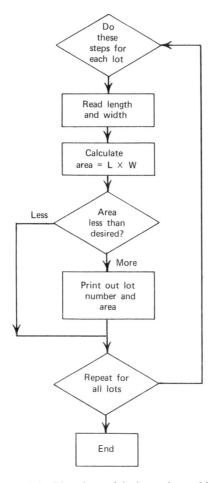

Figure 1.1   Flowchart of the homesite problem.

*Note that when data is put into a program all numbers should be written without commas, i.e., 43,560 should be written as 43560.

the steps and keep the logic straight. If one begins at the top and follows the arrows downward, he will see that the flowchart presents the same instructions in a very clear, concise and orderly manner.

After completing Chapter 2 and learning the necessary computer statements, we would write the series of computer instructions shown in Program 1.1. Each statement precisely duplicates one of the steps in the verbal and flowcharted procedures described above. The FØR/NEXT loop causes the computer to repeat a series of calculations for each lot; the READ statement causes the computer to retrieve DATA on each lot; if the area of the lot is less than one-third acre $[A < (43560/3)]$, the PRINT statement which writes out the lot number is bypassed. The computer's printout is shown immediately below the word RUN.

```
100 FØR I=1 TØ 4
200 READ N,L,W
300 LET A=L*W

400 IF A<(43560/3) THEN 600
500 PRINT "LØT #";N

600 NEXT I

700 DATA 413,100,200
800 DATA 628,350,200
900 DATA 103,100,50
1000 DATA 213,100,100
1100 END
 RUN

LØT #      413
LØT #      628
```

Program 1.1 Computerized solution to the homesite example.

This simple program illustrates the essential character of computer programming—define the problem, develop a concise procedure for solving it, and then duplicate that procedure in computer statements. Chapter 2 will explain the format and application of these statements in more detail.

1.1 THE FORMAT OF THE BOOK

For the convenience of the reader, the illustrative programs in this book are displayed with their principal sections set apart from each other, as shown in Program 1.1, where the program is broken into five parts. This makes the program easier to study. However, when actually putting a program into the computer, the parts are not so spaced.

We will often rewrite a given program to incorporate more features in it, as shown by the altered PRINT statement in Program 1.2. The unchanged parts of the program will be shaded out so that attention can be focused on the significant changes.

Usually, the computer's printout from each program is also shown. The reader would do well to compare the printouts to the statements in the program which produced them.

A number of exercises are given. Besides these, the reader is encouraged to formulate and solve problems of his own which he can tailor to his immediate problems in school or work.

```
100 FØR I=1 TØ 4
200 READ N,L,W
300 LET A=L*W

400 IF A<(43560/3) THEN 600
500 PRINT "LØT #";N,"AREA =";A

600 NEXT I

700 DATA 413,100,200
800 DATA 628,350,200
900 DATA 103,100,50
1000 DATA 213,100,100
1100 END
   RUN

LØT #     413   AREA =     20000
LØT #     628   AREA =     70000
```

Program 1.2   Illustrating a change in the first program.

ELEMENTARY BASIC PROGRAMMING

2

I think that I shall never see
A computer that was made for me.
A computer to a girl disposes
Hives and itch and runny noses.
Mastery of the tape and key
Is made for God and not for me.

—Geraldine Emmons

If the reader has any notion that computers are "smart" or that he will be at the mercy of a superintelligent mechanical monster, he should divorce himself of that opinion at the earliest possible moment. For, in this chapter, he shall learn that just the opposite is true—the computer is at the mercy of the student. It responds very precisely and predictably to every valid instruction the student gives it. The intention of this chapter, then, is to present elementary instructions which the computer will accept, and to discuss their implementation and the computer's response to each of them.

There is an aspect of computer programming which is not directly approached in this chapter. The programmer must develop a sense of programming creativity and intuition about how to organize individual instructions into a coherent program to solve any problem he desires. That subject is deferred to Chapter 3. However, while studying the examples given in this chapter, the student should give particular attention to the program strategies employed and to the conversion of problem requirements from the human language into computer statements.

2.1 PRINT STATEMENT

The PRINT statement is an ideal place to begin. The following message has been printed out by a time-sharing computer:

```
        WELCØME TØ THE WØRLD ØF
    TIME-SHARING CØMPUTNG.

        YØU WILL FIND IT VERY USEFUL,
    INTRIGUING AND REMARKABLY SIMPLE.
    GØØD LUCK!!
```

The question is this: "How did the computer 'know' to print out that message? How did it have the intelligence to assemble a conglomeration of individual letters into words, and those words into intelligible sentences and paragraphs?" Even more puzzling: "How did it chance to print out a message that was so appropriate to the beginning of this book?" The student will be a bit skeptical, thinking that no piece of machinery is this intelligent. And he will be right. The answers to these questions are: "It didn't do any of those things by itself. It was told to do them. It simply responded to instructions given by a programmer."

The mechanism by which the instructions were effected is revealed in Program 2.1. Observe that a set of seven statements has been constructed

```
100 PRINT "     WELCØME TØ THE WØRLD ØF"
200 PRINT "TIME-SHARING CØMPUTNG."
210 PRINT
300 PRINT "      YØU WILL FIND IT VERY USEFUL,"
400 PRINT "INTRIGUING AND REMARKABLY SIMPLE."
500 PRINT "GØØD LUCK!!"
600 END
```

Program 2.1 Program designed to print out a message of text.

by the programmer. Each one is an individual and specific instruction to the computer, which will be processed one at a time. For example, the first statement tells the computer to

PRINT the phrase "   WELCØME TØ THE WØRLD ØF"

When the computer begins to execute (or carry out) the instructions in the program, it first encounters statement 100, and responds by typing out (or printing on the teletype, see Section 2.3) the phrase "   WELCØME TØ THE WØRLD ØF", as instructed. Having executed this statement in its entirety, it proceeds to statement 200, which results in the printing of

"TIME-SHARING CØMPUTNG." The process is repeated until all statements have been executed, eventually resulting in the complete message being printed. Then the "END" statement tells the computer to terminate its execution of the program because there are no more instructions.

The assemblage of statements required to instruct the computer to do whatever the programmer desires is called a **program**. Programs are usually much more versatile than the one shown in Program 2.1; if this were the extent of a computer's capability, of course, it could be replaced by a typewriter. However, the program serves to illustrate several fundamentals of the computer's operation.

■ So far the computer's instructions have simply been written down, "on paper." Of course the computer cannot interpret them off the paper. Section 2.3 will address getting them into the computer's electronic processing devices and having them executed. But, for now, let us simply devise the instructions which are ultimately intended for the computer, and pretend that we know how to enter them.

■ Each statement (except RUN) is preceded and identified by a line number (i.e., 100, 200, 210, . . .). These line numbers serve two purposes. First, they tell the computer the order in which to execute the statements. Second, they delay the execution of each statement until the RUN statement is given, at which time the computer finds the lowest line number and begins execution. Therefore it is common to enter hundreds of lines, in any order one chooses, before beginning execution of any of them. The computer automatically sorts them into numerical order.

■ Line numbers can range from 0 to 999999. No fractional or negative line numbers are permitted. As illustrated by the example, the line numbers can be spaced as widely as desired. Spacing them in increments of 50–100 leaves adequate room in the numbering scheme to allow insertion of new lines (e.g., line 210 in Program 2.1) at a later time, as required by desired changes in the program.

■ The computer is not capable of "thinking." It has no knowledge of upcoming statements, and only a very limited ability to remember what it has done in the past. It always does exactly as it is instructed, and can never do anything else. If a statement given to the computer does not convey the programmer's true intentions, the computer has no way of knowing that an error has been made and will therefore go ahead and execute an "erroneous" statement. A simple example of this is obvious in Program 2.1. Notice that the word "CØMPUTING" is misspelled in line 200. The computer does not know that the intended word is CØMPUTING, and proceeds to print out, in the message, exactly what it is told to print, complete with spelling error.

■   There are certain mistakes which the computer *will* recognize. They are generally referred to as **grammatical** or **syntax errors**, and they result from giving an unintelligible instruction to the computer. For example, the statement

100   RINT "   WELCØME TØ THE WØRLD ØF"

cannot be executed at all, since the computer naturally cannot understand the instruction to "RINT." Such errors are usually rejected by the computer, giving a message called a **diagnostic**, informing the programmer of the computer's action. He must then correct the statement and reenter it (see Section 2.3).

A practical question arises. How can the computer interpret the instruction PRINT and, from that word, issue the electronic pulses required to achieve the printing? Or, if the computer is told to multiply two times three, how does it arrive at six? These things are made possible by the computer's **assemblers** and **compilers.** Their existence is the key to the operation of the computer, but the virtue of the BASIC language is that the programmer needs to know absolutely nothing of those very complicated devices. They are mentioned here only to make the new programmer appreciate their existence and to give him assurance that the computer will respond as instructed. No more will be said of them.

We shall now digress momentarily to study enough of the "LET" statement to give meaning to some variations of the PRINT statement.

VARIATIONS OF PRINTING

Let us say, briefly, that the statement

50   LET X = 2*3

results in setting the value of the variable X to six. Now consider these three statements

```
50 LET X=2*3
60 PRINT "ANSWERS","X";"Y"
70 PRINT "ANSWERS";X; 2*4
80 END
RUN
```

The computer's printout would be

```
ANSWERS        X       Y
ANSWERS    6       8
```

The points illustrated here are the following:

■ More than one desired phrase may be specified with each PRINT statement. The entries are separated by commas or semicolons (see line 60 above).

■ If the letters X and Y (or any others) are enclosed in quotation marks (as in line 60), they are printed out as letters. But if they are not enclosed in quotation marks (as in line 70), their **value** is printed.

■ When the printed messages are separated by commas, the computer automatically prints the outputs spaced fifteen horizontal spaces apart, measured from the beginning of each message. For example, from line 60, the "A" in "ANSWERS" is printed in the first horizontal space; the "X" is printed on the sixteenth. When the messages are separated by semicolons, the outputs are separated by three spaces; when they are separated by a colon, there is no spacing.

■ The spacing reserved for each message is called the **field**. If a message overspills its field, it takes up two or more whole fields.

Commas, semicolons, and colons permit some control over the horizontal format of the output. Using them, the printout can be spaced across the page as the programmer sees fit, forming columns and tables.

■ After printing a line of output, the computer automatically gives a carriage return and feeds the teletype paper one space so that two succeeding outputs do not overprint on the same line. Now observe line 210 of Program 2.1:

210   PRINT

Here the computer is instructed to "PRINT *nothing.*" And, after printing nothing on the line, it automatically executes a carriage return and line feed. The result is that one line in the printout is blank, effecting a vertical space between paragraphs. In this manner, vertical spacing on a page can be controlled. For example, to skip three lines between paragraphs, these statements would have been used:

210   PRINT
220   PRINT
230   PRINT

■ A comma or a semicolon can be used at the end of a print statement to suppress a carriage return and line feed. These statements:

200   PRINT "THE ANSWER IS"; "X";
210   PRINT "Y"

result in this output:

THE ANSWER IS X   Y

Some useful applications of this feature will be studied later.

■   The computer, when printing a value for X, prints out as many as eight digits. However, it does not print the "trailing zeros"* (see statement 58, below):

          57   LET X = 25.900
          58   PRINT X,10/3

results in this output:

          25.9   3.3333333

■   A numeric result can be calculated and printed out in the course of the print statement, as in lines 58 and 70 above.

■   The normal teletype carriage is 72 characters wide.

The reader should realize that any calculations made by the computer are stored inside it. It is only through the use of the PRINT statement that the results are made readable to the person at the keyboard.

This discussion exhausts the properties of the print statement as it is implemented on nearly every time-sharing system. However, some other very useful features are available on more advanced systems. They will be studied in Chapter 6.

For practice, the student should now try his hand at generating a message of his own design. Then he should devise the program required to generate the printout shown in Table 2.1, paying particular attention to horizontal and vertical spacing.

2.2 ASSIGNMENT STATEMENTS

An assignment statement is any one of several statements which assign a numerical value to a variable. The most commonly used are the LET and INPUT statements, and the READ/DATA combination of statements. The LET statement is discussed here, READ/DATA statements are covered in Section 2.6, and INPUT statements are discussed in Section 4.1.

VARIABLE NAMES

The **variable** is the vehicle whereby the computer "remembers" a calculated value from one line to another. There are 260 variable names available,

---

*Usually called "least significant zeros."

Table 2.1   Skeletal output of a Payroll Journal Program to be written by the student.

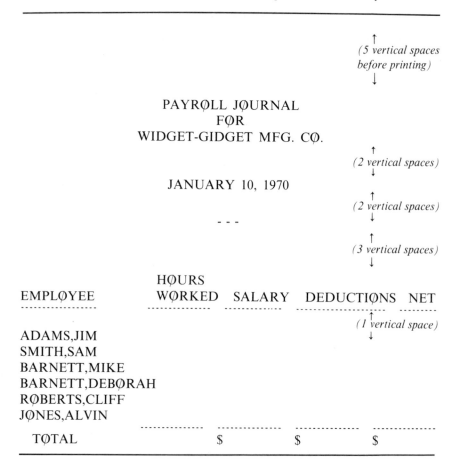

↑
*(5 vertical spaces
before printing)*
↓

PAYRØLL JØURNAL
FØR
WIDGET-GIDGET MFG. CØ.

↑
(2 vertical spaces)
↓

JANUARY 10, 1970

↑
(2 vertical spaces)
↓

- - -

↑
(3 vertical spaces)
↓

EMPLØYEE	HØURS WØRKED	SALARY	DEDUCTIØNS	NET
ADAMS,JIM				
SMITH,SAM				
BARNETT,MIKE				
BARNETT,DEBØRAH				
RØBERTS,CLIFF				
JØNES,ALVIN				
TØTAL	$	$	$	

↑
(1 vertical space)
↓

as shown in Table 2.2. They are designated by the letters A through Z, and by a letter combined with a one-digit number, such as X3, P2, etc. A variable name is usually chosen by the programmer to have some abbreviated relationship to the quantity it represents. For example, the number of hours an employee worked may be represented by H, and his salary by S. Furthermore, H1,S1 could be used for employee number one, H2,S2 for employee number two, etc.

To understand how and why variables and variable names are used in computing, imagine first that someone is working a problem by hand, and

Table 2.2 Allowable BASIC variables names. Variable names may be any letter, or any letter combined with a single digit 1–9.

A	A1	A2	A3	A4	A5	A6	A7	A8	A9
B	B1	B2	B3	B4	B5	B6	B7	B8	B9
C	C1	C2	C3	C4	C5	C6	·	·	·
D	D1	D2	D3	·	·	·	·	·	·
·	·	·	·	·	·	·	·	·	·
·	·	·	·	·	·	·	W7	W8	W9
·	·	·	·	X4	X5	X6	X7	X8	X9
Y	Y1	Y2	Y3	Y4	Y5	Y6	Y7	Y8	Y9
Z	Z1	Z2	Z3	Z4	Z5	Z6	Z7	Z8	Z9

that there are several steps to be executed. At one point, some complicated equation is evaluated. To keep from forgetting the answer, he writes it down in the corner of a piece of paper. The same thing is done with twenty or thirty other equations. Soon the paper looks like Figure 2.1a. When it comes time to use, say, the third answer calculated earlier, a problem arises. There is such a jumble of numbers scattered around the page that he cannot remember which one was the result of the third calculation.

To get a little more organized, he might decide to label each answer as it is written down, as shown in Figure 2.1b. The labels given each one have some bearing on their intrinsic meaning. For example, the number labeled "L" might represent the length of a box, "H" the height, "A" the surface area, etc. Now when the time comes to use "area" in another equation, he would simply refer back to the value labeled "A" on the paper!

The same principle is employed in programs. When a value is calculated

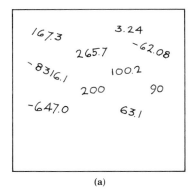

(a)

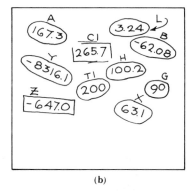

(b)

Figure 2.1 Keeping track of calculated values for later use.

and must be saved for future use, we tell the computer to save it in its memory, under a label (or name) which the programmer specifies. Imagine an area in the computer where answers may be written down, and that the area is divided into smaller parts, all reserved and prelabeled with names like A, A1, A2, A3, . . . , Z9, as shown in Figure 2.2. Whenever a statement like 100 LET A = 39.2 is given, one can imagine that the programmer is instructing the computer to put the value 39.2 into the space labeled A and save it there for future use. The statement 400 LET A5 = A + B1 instructs the computer to recall the previously saved values of A and B1, and to use them for calculating the value of A5.

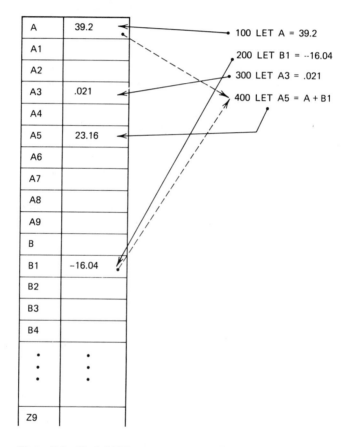

Figure 2.2 Each LET statement causes the computer to give a *variable name* to calculated values and store them for later retrieval.

LET STATEMENTS

The LET statement takes the form

```
100 LET X=3
200 LET Y=2*X+4
300 PRINT "X=";X;"Y=";Y
400 LET X=X+1
500 PRINT "X=";X;"Y=";Y
```

The computer is instructed to let (or set) X equal to the value of the algebraic expression given on the right-hand side of the equals sign. Any variable which is assigned a value (as in line 100) retains that value throughout the program until it is deliberately changed by another assignment statement (as in line 400). The output of the above statements is

```
X=      3    Y=      10
X=      4    Y=      10
```

Notice that X changes value between lines 300 and 500, because of line 400 which increases its value by one; Y does not change.

ARITHMETIC OPERATIONS

Two arithmetic operations—addition and multiplication—have already been inferred. Others—used to effect division, subtraction, and exponentiation—are shown in Table 2.3. In a statement containing several operations, the computer establishes a definite sequence for performing each one, as indicated by each operation's position in Table 2.3. (Those operations paired together with a brace share priority. Whenever they appear in the same line, the computer executes from left to right.) Parentheses are used to change the priorities as the programmer desires. Any operations inside parentheses are performed *before* any operations outside them, regardless of priorities. For example, the statement

$$100 \qquad \text{LET } X = 3 + 1/2$$

sets $X = 3\frac{1}{2}$, since the division operation is executed before addition. On the other hand, the statement

$$100 \qquad \text{LET } X = (3+1)/2$$

contains parentheses to indicate that the operation inside them should be performed first, regardless of the fact that the outside "/" normally has priority over the "+." This statement results in $X = 2$.

Table 2.3 Arithmetic symbols used in BASIC programming. Symbols are given in order of execution (priority). Parentheses serve to instruct the computer to use a different order of priority. Within parentheses, the established order given in this table still governs.

Priority	Arithmetic symbol	Use in a statement	Meaning
1	↑	LET X = A↑2	Square A, or A^2
		LET X = A↑B	Raise A to the B power
2	/	LET X = A/B	Divide A by B
	*	LET X = A*B	Multiply A times B
3	−	LET X = A − B	Subtract B from A
	+	LET X = A + B	Add A and B
	( )	LET X = (A + B)/C	Parentheses used to establish a different order of priority; here, A + B is calculated first; the result is then divided by C

NUMBERS

A few words are in order regarding the use of numbers in BASIC. The computer will accept positive and negative numbers. They may be whole (integer) or decimal numbers. Any variable can take on any numeric value.* The following are all acceptable BASIC numbers:

1.25	113.281
2.90	2568312.1
2.9	4
12.3	400
− 16.8294	− 24816328
	0.4

Any number given to the computer must be composed of fewer than eight digits. For numbers greater than eight digits, a special notation called *engineering notation* is adopted. In the beginner's terms, any number can be represented by another number between 1 and 10 if the computer is properly informed of the fact that the notation is being used as follows:

*Programmers experienced in the FØRTRAN language should dispense with the notion of fixed and floating decimal point numbers.

■   The number 2,340,000,000 can be written 2.34E9.* The notation "E9" means that the decimal point has been moved to the left nine positions. To get back—from 2.34E9 to 2,340,000,000—the decimal point should again be moved to the right nine places. The same number could be written as 23.4E8 or 0.0234E11.

■   If "E" is combined with a negative number (i.e., 1.18E − 3), it means that the decimal point has been moved to the right the indicated number of places. To get the original number back the decimal point should again be moved to the left (i.e., 1.18E − 3 = 0.00118).

Table 2.4 is included for illustration.

Table 2.4   Numbers represented by engineering notation. Either form can be used by the computer. Notice that any number can be represented by several forms of engineering notation, as illustrated with the number "63."

Number	Engineering notation
214.3	2.143E2
0.801	8.01E − 1
123,000	1.23E5
0.0032	3.2E − 3
63	6300E − 2
63	630E − 1
63	63E0
63	6.3E1
63	0.063E3

Example 2.1   A Recipe

The following recipe is used to make a single glass of pink lemonade:

> 2 TBSPNS LEMØN JUICE
> 2 TBSPNS SUGAR
> 1.5 TEASPNS CHERRY JUICE
> 1 GLASS WATER
>   ICE CUBES

Write a program to produce the recipe required for G glasses of lemonade, where G = 37. Then change the program to produce the recipe for G = 129.

*Equivalent to 2.34×10^9.

DISCUSSION

If two tablespoons of lemon juice are used for one glass, 2G tablespoons must be used for G glasses. Similar calculations must be made for the remaining ingredients. Program 2.2 presents a series of statements which will print out the recipe for G = 37 glasses. A few points deserve comment:

■   An assignment statement (line 200) must be employed to give G a value before the computer tries to use it in a calculation in line 300. Care must be used to ensure that information and instructions are given the computer in an orderly manner.

■   Lines 110 and 800 are placed in the program to provide an empty line immediately before and after the body of the recipe. This is done only for aesthetic purposes and printout readability.

■   The quantity of ice cubes is not specified for a single recipe, nor for that of larger quantities. However, line 700 should not be written 700 PRINT "ICE CUBES" for then the phrase would be printed in the same column on the page as the quantity of the other ingredients, a pictorially undesirable result. To avoid this, the computer is instructed to print a blank (i.e., "   ") in the first field so that the phrase "ICE CUBES" is placed in the second field, along with the other ingredients.

■   To produce a recipe for 129 glasses of lemonade, line 200 is simply changed to 200 LET G = 129.

```
100 PRINT "USE THESE INGREDIENTS"
110 PRINT
200 LET G=37
300 PRINT 2*G, "TBSPNS LEMØN JUICE"
400 PRINT 2*G, "TBSPNS SUGAR"
500 PRINT 1.5*G, "TEASPNS CHERRY JUICE"
600 PRINT 1*G, "GLASS WATER"
700 PRINT "     ", "ICE CUBES"
800 PRINT
900 PRINT "FØR"; G; "GLASSES ØF PERFECT LEMØNADE!"
1000 END
```

Program 2.2   A recipe for G glasses of lemonade. In this case, G is set equal to 37. For 129 glasses, change the third line to 200 LET G = 129.

2.3   ON THE COMPUTER

In the time-sharing situation, the programmer may be removed from the actual computer by several miles. He and the computer communicate with each other by means of ordinary telephone lines, as illustrated in Figure 2.3. A typical computer installation is shown in Figure 2.4.

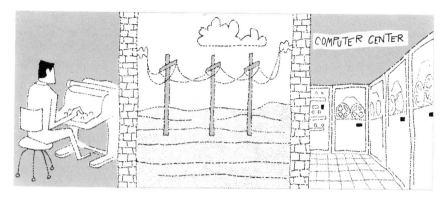

Figure 2.3 Illustrating the programmer's access to the computer through normal telephone service. The central computer can be a few blocks or many miles from the programmer.

The computer understands electronic pulses which are generated by the programmer typing on a standard teletype machine of the kind shown in Figure 2.5. More detail of the teletype's keyboard, paper tape punch, paper tape reader, and control console are shown in Figures 2.6–2.8.

A paper tape is usually created, with perforations in it corresponding to the letters, numbers, and other characters in the subject program (Fig. 2.9). There are several economical reasons for generating such a tape:

■ It can be generated **offline**, i.e., without establishing contact with the computer, so there are no charges incurred from the computing service.

■ It is possible to "save" a program in the computer's memory for reuse on some later day, but "storage charges" are usually assessed for the service. If the program is not going to be used very often, it can be saved on the tape instead.

■ The paper tape can be retained as back-up in case there is a malfunction of the computer which might result in loss of the program from the machine's memory.

CREATING A PAPER TAPE

The procedure for generating a paper tape begins with creating the program and writing it down on paper. From there the procedure is fairly standard on most computer systems. It is detailed in step-by-step fashion in Table 2.5. The student should use this procedure to generate paper tapes of his programs corresponding to Table 2.1 and Program 2.2, keeping the following points in mind:

Figure 2.4 Photograph of GE 635 Mark II time-sharing computer system. *(Courtesy General Electric Co.)*

■   There are no lowercase letters, only capital letters. Unlike a typewriter, the shift key is not used for capital letters.

■   A few of the keys have two symbols on them. The upper character is obtained by holding down the shift key; e.g., the # symbol results from striking the shift and "3" keys simultaneously.

■   The letters "O" and the number "zero" require the use of separate keys. Some teletypes distinguish one character from the other by a slash through one of them (Ø).

■   The letter "L" and the number "1" require the use of separate keys.

Figure 2.5 A typical teletype. *(Courtesy Vernitron Corporation.)*

Table 2.5 Instructions for generating a paper tape.

---

1. Turn on the control console and the tape punch device.
2. Simultaneously depress the "REPT" (or "REPEAT") key and the "RUBØUT" key until about 20 rubouts have been typed. The paper tape should feed through the punch device.
3. Type the program, one line at a time. End each line with this exact sequence of characters:

CARRIAGE RETURN	(or RETURN)
LINE FEED	(or LF)
RUBØUT	(or RØ)

4. If an error is made, simply retype the line at any later point. It does not matter if the lines are out of order. The computer automatically sorts them later.
5. Continue typing until all lines are completed.
6. When finished, again hold down the "REPT" and "RUBØUT" keys for 20 more rubouts.
7. Turn the tape punch ØFF.
8. Tear off the paper tape by pulling upward against the plastic wedge on the punch device.
9. Turn off the console.

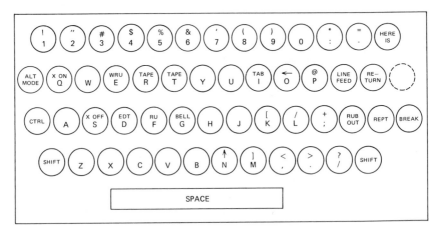

Figure 2.6 The teletype keyboard.

RUNNING THE COMPUTER

Before one can gain access to the computer he must establish a contract with a time-sharing service company which will then assign him a **user number** and provide the telephone number of the computer. Having done

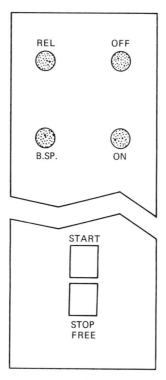

Figure 2.7 The paper tape punching and reading device.

that, and having generated a paper tape, the student is ready to run the program.

Unfortunately, the procedure is not uniform among all services but the differences are usually fairly easily accommodated by reference to the supplier's documentation and manuals, once the simple underlying principles are understood. The procedure outlined in Table 2.6 is typical and should be studied carefully. A session at the teletype is documented in Table 2.7 and the student should coordinate that example with the procedure. The typing which is done by the programmer is underlined for reference. The material which is not underlined in the example is typed by the computer.

A session can be broken into two phases. The first is a very structured period when the computer leads the programmer through a prescribed regime for identifying himself and establishing the language to be used. After that, the programmer is free to proceed with any legal instructions

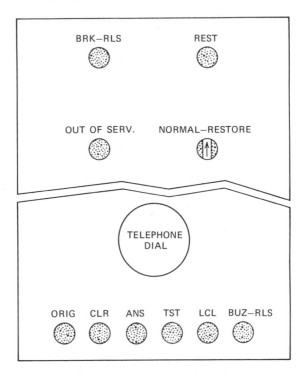

Figure 2.8 The control console.

(some of which are given in Table 2.8) he wishes, in any logical order. The example session should be considered illustrative, and not rigidly mandatory.

The outlined procedure is typical for running new programs or those which have not been previously saved in the computer's permanent memory. If one has been saved, the procedure shown in Example 2.2, coordinated with the documentation given in Table 2.9, may be used.

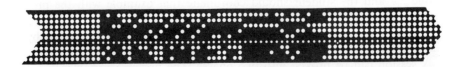

Figure 2.9 A perforated paper tape.

Table 2.6 Instructions for getting a program into the computer and running it.

1. At the teletype, depress the "ØRIG" button and dial the computer.
2. The computer should "beep" and then ask for the programmer's user number. Type the assigned number. End this (and all other) lines with a carriage return.
3. The computer then asks the programmer for the SYSTEM to be used. "System" is an unfortunate term meaning, simply, "Language" to the programmer. Type BASIC.
4. Now the computer asks if the program is going to be a "NEW" or an "ØLD" one. It is obviously a NEW program if it has not been saved in the computer's memory.
5. Give the computer a name for the new program.
6. At this point the computer types "READY," meaning it is prepared to accept any instructions the programmer gives it. The word "READY" might be called the "prompter," for it prompts the programmer that it is finished executing its last instruction and is requesting another one for execution. (Some computers give other prompting symbols, such as * or >.)
7. The programmer is now on his own and can give any of the commands listed in Table 2.8, in almost any logical sequence. The following sequence might be regarded as typical.
8. Instruct the computer that a paper tape is to be used for input by giving it the TAPE instruction. Insert the tape in the teletype's reader and push the button to START. The tape should begin feeding and typing on the teletype. When it finishes, instruct the computer that future instructions will again be entered from the keyboard by typing the word KEY.
9. Instruct the computer to RUN the program.
10. At this point the computer will make its first check of the syntax of the statements and it will make other preliminary checks of the integrity of the program. It will issue diagnostics to inform the programmer of its findings. If any errors are found, it will abort the run. The diagnostics in Table 2.7 are self-explanatory. The programmer can now inspect the erroneous statements and retype them one at a time.
11. The instruction "LIST" can be given at any time and the computer will list all the statements (including those changed) for the programmer's information.
12. When all the corrections have been made, retype RUN. The computer will again make its checks of the program and either give more diagnostics or attempt to execute. In Table 2.7, it executes properly on the second run.
13. If the program will be needed at another (later) session at the teletype, the computer must be instructed to permanently SAVE it in memory.
14. Now any line in the program can be changed by simply retyping the line, or it can be deleted by retyping the line number without an instruction. In Program 2.2, line 200 is changed to produce the recipe for G = 129. The program is then reexecuted.
15. If the latest version of the program is to be saved, the instruction REPLACE would now be given. (*It is not given in Table 2.7!*) Then the program with 200 LET G = 129 would have been saved for future use, replacing the original program.
16. When finished, type GØØDBYE and the computer will turn off.

Table 2.7   Documented session at the teletype.

```
USER NUMBER---3XA0132;BLAKE
SYSTEM---BASIC
NEW ØR ØLD---NEW
NEW PRØGRAM NAME---LMNADE

READY.
TAPE

READY.
100 PRINT "USE THESE INGREDIENTS
110 PRINT
200 LET G=37
300 PRINT 2*G,"TBSPNS LEMØN JUICE"
400 PRINT 2*G,"TBSPNS SUGAR"
500 PRINT 1.5G,"TEASPNS CHERRY JUICE"
600 PRINT 1*G,"GLASS WATER"
700 PRINT "  ","ICE CUBES"
800 PRIN
900 PRINT "FØR";G;"GLASSES ØF PERFECT LEMØNADE!"

KEY

READY.
RUN

LMNADE          9:20

MISSING " IN 100
ILLEGAL FØRMULA IN 500
ILLEGAL INSTRUCTIØN IN 800
NØ END INSTRUCTIØN

READY.

100 PRINT "USE THESE INGREDIENTS"
500 PRINT 1.5*G,"TEASPNS CHERRY JUICE"
800 PRINT
1000 END

LIST

100 PRINT "USE THESE INGREDIENTS"
110 PRINT
200 LET G=37
300 PRINT 2*G,"TBSPNS LEMØN JUICE"
400 PRINT 2*G,"TBSPNS SUGAR"
500 PRINT 1.5*G,"TEASPNS CHERRY JUICE"
600 PRINT 1.5*G,"GLASS WATER"
700 PRINT "  ","ICE CUBES"
800 PRINT
900 PRINT "FØR";G;"GLASSES ØF PERFECT LEMØNADE!"
1000 END
```

Table 2.7 (*continued*)

```
READY.

RUN

LMNADE     9:23
USE THESE INGREDIENTS

74              TBSPNS LEMØN JUICE
74              TBSPNS SUGAR
55.5            TEASPNS CHERRY JUICE
37              GLASS WATER
                ICE CUBES


FØR 37 GLASSES ØF PERFECT LEMØNADE!

READY.

SAVE

READY.

200 LET G=129
LIST 100-300

LMNADE     9:27

100 PRINT "USE THESE INGREDIENTS"
110 PRINT
200 LET G=129
300 PRINT 2*G,"TBSPNS LEMØN JUICE"

READY.

RUN

LMNADE     9:31
USE THESE INGREDIENTS

258             TBSPNS LEMØN JUICE
258             TBSPNS SUGAR
193.5           TEASPNS CHERRY JUICE
129             GLASS WATER
                ICE CUBES

FØR 129 PERFECT GLASSES ØF LEMØNADE!

READY.
GØØDBYE

ØFF AT 9:33
```

Table 2.8 Partial listing of control commands normally available on the time-sharing computer. The exact words to accomplish each command vary considerably from one computer to another. Refer to the time-sharing company's manuals.

Command	Meaning
NEW	Erases the program currently being worked and asks for a NEW PRØBLEM NAME
ØLD	Erases the program currently being worked and asks for an ØLD PRØBLEM NAME
SAVE	Saves the program intact for later use (to retrieve saved programs, type "ØLD")
UNSAVE	Erases a saved program from memory
RENAME	Changes the problem name of the program currently being worked, but does not destroy the program
CATALØG	The computer types a list of the names of all programs currently being saved in memory
SCRATCH	Erases the problem currently being worked on, but leaves the user number and problem name intact
RUN	Begins the execution of a program
STØP	Stops the computation at once; it can be typed even when the teletypewriter is typing at full speed (some computers use the "ALT MØDE" key instead of STØP)
LIST	Causes an up-to-date listing of the program to be typed
LIST XXX–YYY	Causes an up-to-date listing of the program to be typed out, beginning at line number XXX and continuing to line number YYY
RENUMBER	Tells the computer to renumber the program, beginning at line 100 and incrementing by ten
GØØDBYE	Used at the end of the session to tell the computer to terminate service

Example 2.2 Manipulating the Computer

Assume that the lemonade recipe was previously saved in the computer (say, as a result of having followed Table 2.7). Now, at a second session, retrieve the program and add the following line to it:

510   PRINT 1*G, "SPRIGS ØF MINT"

Renumber the program, list it, and save it (replacing the old program). Then give the computer a new program, namely the message in Program 2.1.

DISCUSSION

Review Table 2.9. In particular, notice that the ØLD lemonade program is the one with G = 37, since only that one was previously saved (in Table 2.7). At the end of the current session the saved LMNADE contains the line with "SPRIGS ØF MINT" and is renumbered, since the changes were followed by the REPLACE command. By giving the NEW command, another program can now be created, in this case MESGE.

■ **EXERCISES**

Answers to problems marked with an asterisk are given at the end of the book.

2.1   (a) What are line numbers and why are they used?

(b) Is it important for the programmer to understand how the computer manages to recognize and react to such statements as PRINT or LET?

(c) What are variables and why are they used?

(d) What happens if the computer is given an instruction that is legal but which is not the correct statement needed to fulfill the intention of the program?

(e) What is a "syntax error"? Give examples.

(f) What are the differences between 100 PRINT "X,Y,Z", 100 PRINT X,Y,Z, and 100 PRINT X;Y;Z?

(g) How many "trailing zeros" do each of the following numbers have? How would the computer print each number? 23.0400, 1.60000, 24,000, −16.02, 0.02.

(h) Explain what the "LET" statement tells the computer to do.

(i) If you have access to a computer, consult its manuals and identify the differences between the procedures described therein and those of Tables 2.5–2.9.

2.2   Write a program which prints this poem by Lewis Carroll:

> The time has come, the Walrus said,
> To talk of many things
> Of shoes—and ships—and sealing wax—
> Of cabbages—and kings.
> And why the sea is boiling hot—
> And whether pigs have wings.
>
> *Alice's Adventures in Wonderland*
> Chapter 4, The Walrus and the Carpenter

Table 2.9 A typical second session at the teletype.

```
USER NUMBER---3XA0132;BLAKE
SYSTEM---BASIC
NEW ØR ØLD---ØLD
ØLD PRØGRAM NAME---LMNADE

READY.

510 PRINT 1*G,"SPRIGS ØF MINT"
LIST

100 PRINT "USE THESE INGREDIENTS"
110 PRINT
200 LET G=37
300 PRINT 2*G,"TBSPNS LEMØN JUICE"
400 PRINT 2*G,"TBSPNS SUGAR"
500 PRINT 1.5*G"TEASPNS CHERRY JUICE"
510 PRINT 1*G,"SPRIGS ØF MINT"
600 PRINT 1*G,"GLASS WATER"
700 PRINT "   ","ICE CUBES"
800 PRINT
900 PRINT "FØR";G;"GLAASES ØF PERFECT LEMØNADE!"
1000 END

READY.
RENUMBER
READY.
LIST

100 PRINT "USE THESE INGREDIENTS"
110 PRINT
120 LET G=37
130 PRINT 2*G,"TBSPNS LEMØN JUICE"
140 PRINT 2*G,"TBSPNS SUGAR"
150 PRINT 1.5*G,"TEASPNS CHERRY JUICE"
160 PRINT 1*G,"SPRIGS ØF MINT"
170 PRINT 1*G,"GLASS WATER"
180 PRINT "   ","ICE CUBES"
190 PRINT
200 PRINT "FØR";G;"GLASSES ØF PERFECT LEMØNADE!"
210 END

READY.

RUN

LMNADE      2:06

USE THESE INGREDIENTS

74              TBSPNS LEMØN JUICE
74              TBSPNS SUGAR
55.5            TEASPNS CHERRY JUICE
37              SPRIGS ØF MINT
37              GLASS WATER
                ICE CUBES

FØR 37 GLASSES ØF PERFECT LEMØNADE!

READY.

REPLACE
```

Table 2.9 *(continued)*

```
READY.

SCRATCH

READY.

LIST
NØ PRØGRAM

READY.

NEW
NEW PRØGRAM NAME---MESGE
READY.

TAPE

READY.

100 PRINT "     WELCØME TØ THE WØRLD ØF"
200 PRINT "TIME-SHARING CØMPUTNG"
210 PRINT
300 PRINT "     YØU WILL FIND IT VERY USEFUL,"
400 PRINT "INTRIGUING AND REMARKABLY SIMPLE."
500 PRINT "GØØD LUCK!!"
600 END

KEY

READY.

RUN

MESGE      2:15
      WELCØME TØ THE WØRLD ØF
TIME-SHARING CØMPUTNG.

      YØU WILL FIND IT VERY USEFUL,
INTRIGUING AND REMARKABLY SIMPLE.
GØØD LUCK!!

READY.

SAVE

READY.

CATALØG

LMNADE
MESGE

READY.

GØØDBYE

ØFF AT 2:22
```

2.3 Write a program which prints out (a) Table 2.1, and (b) a message of your own choosing.

2.4 For programs indicated by each of the following phrases, adopt some typical variable names, and write PRINT statements to produce appropriate table headings and other phrases as you see fit:
(a) interest due on a loan at each of several payments;
(b) the number of days in each month of 1971 and 1972;
(c) the length of service of eight employees;
(d) the quantity of wigs of each color sold last month, the quantity in inventory, and the quantity on order;
(e) the altitude of a spacecraft at T minutes after launch.

2.5 Tell which of the following variable names are illegal: X3, G, 3G, DRESS, *3, V19, T1.5, L2/3.

*2.6 Some of the statements below contain errors. Identify them and write a correct version of each.
(a) 100 LET X$=3A+1$
(b) 100 G6$=A/B$
(c) 100 LET $-V=T3-1$
(d) 100 LET L19$=P**3+2$
(e) 201 LET Z$=A3+B2-6$
(f) 100 LET 3*Z$=2-A{\uparrow}(B-D)$
(g) 100 LET L$=(2+A*X*(4-A{\uparrow}2)$
(h) LET X$=2{\uparrow}Y-3$
(i) 100 SET Y/2$=Z/(4+B)$

*2.7 Write BASIC statements for each of the following expressions:
(a) Gross pay = (Number of hours) times (Hourly rate)
(b) $Y = X^3 + 2X^2 - X + 1/X$
(c) $t_1 = 301.28$
(d) $P = (X + Y)^{2.5}$
(e) $M = (P^2 + Q^2)^{1/2}$
(f) $X = (T - 1)^{g-1}$
(g) $X_1 = (x + Y)(M + N)/t^2$
(h) Equity = Payments − 6.3% of balance
(i) Inventory = (Initial quantity) − (Withdrawals) + (Replacements)
(j) Average = Sum divided by number of items

*2.8 In each case below, if the number is not written in E notation, convert it; if it is, change it back:

(a)	1.386E7	(d)	3.104×10^{-3}
(b)	.0141	(e)	.0086E3
(c)	308.1284	(f)	14.04E−10

2.9 Trace the program below by hand. Pretend you are the computer; calculate and jot down all variable values as they change. Follow all instructions as precisely as the computer must.

```
100     LET A=1
200     LET C=4
300     LET D=C/2+1
400     LET A=C+D+A
500     LET D=(D+6)↑.5
600     LET A=A-D
700     PRINT "THE ANSWER IS";A-2
800     END
```

*2.10 A student has F−$5 bills, Ø−$1 bills, Q quarters, D dimes, N nickels, and P pennies. Write a program which determines the value of those monies for any F,Ø,Q,D,N,P. Use the change in your pocket to test the program.

2.11 The author resides 6.3 miles from his place of business. Compute the round-trip distance in feet, yards, and inches (1 mile = 5280 ft).

2.12 Most of the industrialized world outside the United States uses the metric system of measurement. Write a program which does the following:
(a) converts these measurements to liters: 6.2 qt, 4.1 gal, and 13.1 qt (1 qt = 0.9463 liter, 1 gal = 4 qt);
(b) converts these measurements to centimeters: 136 inches, 25 inches, and 35.5 inches (1 inch = 2.54 cm).

2.13 A machine is purchased for $50,000 and depreciates at the rate of $4320 per year. Calculate the total depreciation and remaining value at the end of eight years.

2.14 A student has X dollars. He invests 30% of it at 8% interest and the rest at 5%. Compute his annual income. Let X = $1000 to run the program.

*2.15 A truck has dimensions $35 \times 9 \times 8$ ft. Calculate the weight and initial value of wheat the truck will hold if wheat weighs 10.3 lb/ft^3 and is initially worth $0.18/lb. The cost of loading, transporting, and unloading the entire shipment is $169. The program must also determine the "per pound" value added by shipping.

2.16 A building has sides $12 \times 30 \times 8$ ft. Boards are 6 inches wide and

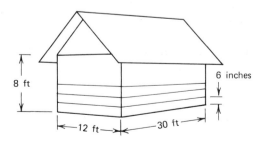

require thirty nails each, but an additional 10% of the nails are wasted. Boards cost $0.83/ft and nails cost $2.05/hundred. Compute the cost of materials for the walls.

*2.17 The floors of two rooms are to be covered at a cost of $8.32/yd^2. The bedroom and living-room are 9 × 20 ft and 15 × 20 ft, respectively. Print the area and cost of covering each room (1 yd^2 = 9 ft^2).

2.18 If money is invested at a nominal annual interest rate of r = 5%, but is compounded at shorter intervals (say m times per year) the effective rate is

$$i = \left(1 + \frac{r}{m}\right)^m - 1$$

Calculate i if r = 5% and the money is compounded semiannually, quarterly, monthly, or daily.

2.19 Units, which sell for $2.29 each, cost C = ($3000/n) + $1.50/unit to manufacture (where n is the number of units sold). Compute the total profit and the average profit per unit if 9826 units are sold.

2.20 Under certain conditions, the following problem can be formulated: A single line of people is waiting for service. People arrive at the mean rate a and are serviced at the mean rate s. Persons servicing the line are paid C_1$/hr; persons waiting are paid C_2$/hr, and the service facility is open h hr. Now the following quantities must be calculated:
(a) Average waiting time = $a/(s^2 - as)$
(b) Average length of the waiting line = a × (Average waiting time)
(c) Average time spent in waiting and service = $1/(s - a)$
(d) Number of arrivals = (Hours open) × (Arrival rate)
(e) Total waiting time = (Average waiting time) × (Number of arrivals)
(f) Idle time rate = 1 − a/s
(g) Cost of idle time = (Idle time rate) × (C_1) × (Hours open)
(h) Cost of waiting = (Total waiting time) × (C_2)
(i) Cost of service = C_1 × h
(j) Total cost = (Average time spent in waiting and service) × (Number of arrivals) × (Cost of waiting + Cost of service).
Write a program which calculates each of the above factors when a = 5 persons/hr, s = 6.1 persons/hr, C_1 = $3.12/hr, C_2 = $3.42/hr, and h = 12 hr.

*2.21 Water freezes at 32°F and boils at 212°F. Calculate those temperatures in °C, °K, and °R from the following equations:

°K = 273.16° + °C; °C = (5/9)(°F − 32°); °R = 460° + °F.

2.22 An angle, A_1 (= 30°) is given in degrees; convert it to radians. Another angle, A_2 (= 1.21 rad) is given in radians; convert it to degrees.

2.23   A capacitor is constructed of N ($= 200$) plates separated by S ($= 0.00012$ m) of glass ($\epsilon_r = 8.1$); each plate has area A $= 0.10 \times 0.20$ m. The total capacitance is

$$C = \frac{\epsilon_r(8.87 \times 10^{-12})A(N - 1)}{S}$$

Write a program to calculate C.

2.24   A bar is made of aluminum, radius r $= 10$ cm and length $l = 100$ cm. Calculate the volume V, weight W, moles M, and number of molecules N in the bar, using the following equations:

$$V = \pi r^2 l \qquad M = W/C$$
$$W = dV \qquad N = (A)(M)$$

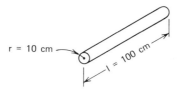

where $\pi = 3.14159$
$d =$ density of Al $= 2.7$ g/cm^3
$C =$ atomic weight of Al $= 13$
$A =$ Avogadro's number $= 6.023 \times 10^{23}$

2.25   In the right triangle shown, calculate Z, sine θ, cosine θ, tangent θ, secant θ, and sine 2θ using the following relationships:

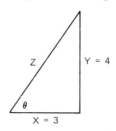

$$Z = \sqrt{X^2 + Y^2}$$

sine $\theta = Y/Z$ \qquad cosine $\theta = X/Z$ \qquad tan $\theta = \sin \theta/\cos \theta$

secant $\theta = \sqrt{(\tan \theta)^2 + 1}$ \qquad $\sin 2\theta = 2(\sin \theta)(\cos \theta)$

2.26   A spherical water tank, empty weight 2000 lb, radius r $= 8$ ft, is supported by three legs. The volume of the tank is $(4/3)\pi r^3$. Water weighs 62.4 lb/ft^3. Each leg carries one-third of the total weight of the structure. Compute each leg's load when the tank is full.

2.27 Two straight lines, with equations of the form $Y = m_iX + b_i$ intersect at the point

$$X = \frac{b_2 - b_1}{m_1 - m_2} \qquad Y = m_1X + b_1$$

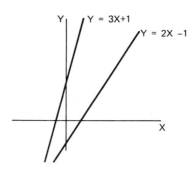

Compute the intersect point of the two lines $Y = 3X + 1$ and $Y = 2X - 1$.

*2.28 A straight line which passes through two points (X_1,Y_1) and (X_2,Y_2) is defined by the equation $Y = mX + b$, where

$$m = \frac{Y_2 - Y_1}{X_2 - X_1} \qquad b = Y_1 - mX_1$$

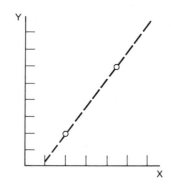

If $(X_1,Y_1) = (2,2)$ and $(X_2,Y_2) = (4,6)$, calculate m and b. Using m and b, calculate the value of Y when X = 3.

2.29 The resistance network shown has an equivalent resistance R. Compute R:

$$R = \frac{R_u \cdot R_5}{R_5 + R_u}$$

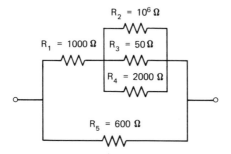

where

$$R_u = R_1 + \frac{R_2 R_3 R_4}{R_2 R_3 + R_3 R_4 + R_4 R_2}$$

2.30   A 100 lb weight is hung on the middle of a cable between two walls.
The rope sags 4 ft. Find the tension in each half of the rope. [*Hint:*
$T_1 = T_2$; $T_1 \sin \theta + T_2 \sin \theta = 100$.]

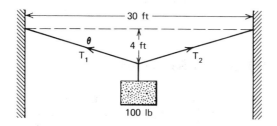

2.31   The volume expansivity coefficient of water is defined as

$$\beta = \frac{V_1 - V_0}{V_0 \Delta t}$$

where

V_0 = the initial volume at temperature T_0
V_1 = the new volume at temperature T_1
$\Delta t = T_1 - T_0$
$\beta_{H_2O} = 0.00037/°C$

A test tube of water, radius 1.5 cm, is filled to 10 cm at $T_0 = 25°C$.
Compute the height of the water when the tube is heated to 100°C.
[*Note:* The volume of a cylinder with radius r and height h is $\pi r^2 h$.]

2.32   A screw jack has a pitch p of 0.25, a lever arm l of 18 inches, and an
efficiency of 40%. Calculate the ideal and actual mechanical advantages. (See next page for illustration.)

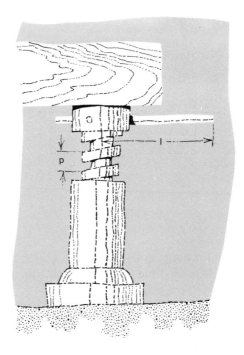

2.4 A COMPLETE PROGRAM

The student was requested to derive the program necessary to print out the skeletal table for a Payroll Journal shown in Table 2.1. Let us now expand the output, making calculations and filling in the table for each employee. The program will be very simple but, even by moderately advanced programming standards, quite cumbersome. There are some drawbacks which will be discussed later. In succeeding sections new tools will be developed to make the program much easier to write.

Suppose that, for each employee listed in Table 2.1 the personnel department of Widget-Gidget Mfg. Co. makes available the following pieces of information: the number of hours the employee worked during the week of January 10, 1970, his hourly rate, and the percentage of his salary to be deducted for taxes, as listed in Table 2.10. Now one can calculate the appropriate entries in Table 2.1 for each employee, using equations similar to those in Table 2.11.

Examine Program 2.3, where one version of an entire Payroll Journal Program is given, and Table 2.12, the printout of the program. Notice that the first 21 statements (lines 100–2100) simply accomplish the task set forth in Table 2.1, down to the underlined table headings. (The student should compare them with his own program). Beginning with the segment

Table 2.10 Payroll data on each employee listed in Table 2.1.

No.	Employee	Hours worked (H)	Hourly rate (R)	Tax rate (T)
1	ADAMS,JIM	40	3.32	0.103
2	SMITH,SAM	42	5.25	0.172
3	BARNETT,MIKE	38	4.28	0.145
4	BARNETT,DEBØRAH	40	2.13	0.085
5	RØBERTS,CLIFF	40	6.28	0.18
6	JØNES,ALVIN	41.5	5.03	0.163

of the program between lines 2200 and 2700, observe that statements
2200–2400 assign the values of H, R, and T for employee No. 1, Jim Adams.
A moment's reflection will make the student realize that these statements
are necessary because the computer does not "know," by itself, the par-
ticulars associated with Jim Adams. The programmer must give that data
to the computer through the LET statement.

Now that the computer has been given the values of H, R, and T, it can
be instructed to calculate the value of S (salary) and D (deductions), as
shown in lines 2500–2600, corresponding to the equations in Table 2.11.
Line 2700 accomplishes the printing of the employee's name and the other
values required by the output table: hours, salary, deductions, and net
(salary-deduction).

Using these six statements, the computer will successfully make the
calculations and print out the results for the first employee. Two notes are
in order: First, as written, the program does not actually employ the variables
H, R, and T; instead it uses H1, R1, and T1 for employee No. 1; H2, R2,
and T2 for employee No. 2; etc. Second, the NET was calculated during
the PRINT statement, and not in a unique assignment statement.* Study

Table 2.11 Word equations for a Payroll Journal, and the computer statements
required to implement them.

Word equation	Equivalent computer statement
Salary = (Hours worked) × (Hourly rate)	LET S = H*R
Deductions = (Salary) × (Tax rate)	LET D = S*T
Net = (Salary) − (Deductions)	LET N = S − D

*There is no reason not to use a LET statement, as shown in Table 2.11, for calculating the
NET, except to permit the author to make a point in later paragraphs.

```
100  PRINT
200  PRINT
300  PRINT
400  PRINT
500  PRINT
600  PRINT "                    PAYRØLL JØURNAL"
700  PRINT "                         FØR"
800  PRINT "                    WIDGET-GIDGET MFG. CØ."
900  PRINT
1000 PRINT
1100 PRINT "                    JANUARY 10, 1971"
1200 PRINT
1300 PRINT
1400 PRINT "                         ---"
1500 PRINT
1600 PRINT
1700 PRINT
1800 PRINT " ","HØURS"
1900 PRINT "EMPLØYEE","WØRKED","SALARY","DEDUCTIØNS","NET"
2000 PRINT "--------","------","------","----------","---"
2100 PRINT
2200 LET H1=40
2300 LET R1=3.32
2400 LET T1=.103
2500 LET S1=H1*R1
2600 LET D1=T1*S1
2700 PRINT "ADAMS,JIM",H1,S1,D1,S1-D1
2800 LET H2=42
2900 LET R2=5.25
3000 LET T2=.172
3100 LET S2=H2*R2
3200 LET D2=T2*S2
3300 PRINT "SMITH,SAM",H2,S2,D2,S2-D2
3400 LET H3=38
3500 LET R3=4.28
3600 LET T3=.145
3700 LET S3=H3*R3
3800 LET D3=T3*S3
3900 PRINT "BARNETT,MIKE",H3,S3,D3,S3-D3
4000 LET H4=40
4100 LET R4=2.13
4200 LET T4=.085
4300 LET S4=H4*R4
4400 LET D4=T4*S4
4500 PRINT "BARNETT,DEBØRAH",H4,S4,D4,S4-D4
4600 LET H5=40
4700 LET R5=6.28
4800 LET T5=.18
4900 LET S5=H5*R5
5000 LET D5=T5*S5
5100 PRINT "RØBERTS,CLIFF",H5,S5,D5,S5-D5
5200 LET H6=41.5
5300 LET R6=5.03
5400 LET T6=.163
5500 LET S6=H6*R6
5600 LET D6=T6*S6
5700 PRINT "JØNES,ALVIN",H6,S6,D6,S6-D6
5800 PRINT " ","--------","---------","---------","---------"

5900 PRINT "TØTAL",H1+H2+H3+H4+H5+H6,"$";S1+S2+S3+S4+S5+S6,"$";
5901 PRINT D1+D2+D3+D4+D5+D6,"$";(S1+S2+S3+S4+S5+S6)-(D1+D2+D3+D4+D5+D6)
6800 END
```

Program 2.3   A program for the Payroll Journal of Table 2.1.

Table 2.12 Printout of the Payroll Journal Program 2.3.

PAYRØLL JØURNAL
FØR
WIDGET-GIDGET MFG. CØ.

JANUARY 10, 1971

- - -

EMPLØYEE	HØURS WØRKED	SALARY	DEDUCTIØNS	NET
--------	------	------	----------	---
ADAMS, JIM	40	132.8	13.6784	119.1216
SMITH, SAM	42	220.5	37.926	182.574
BARNETT, MIKE	38	162.64	23.5828	139.0572
BARNETT, DEBØRAH	40	85.2	7.242	77.958
RØBERTS, CLIFF	40	251.2	45.216	205.984
JØNES, ALVIN	41.5	208.745	34.025435	174.71957
	--------	---------	----------	---------
TØTAL	241.5	$ 1061.085	$ 161.67063	$ 899.41437

lines 2800–5700, where identical programming statements are used to make the calculations and print the results on employees Sam Smith through Alvin Jones.

Finally, it is necessary to print out the totals of each column. The underlines are inserted by line 5800. The totals are calculated in lines 5900 and 5901, while printing. Observe that the total number of hours worked in the company is the sum of hours worked by each employee, i.e., $H1 + H2 + H3 + H4 + H5 + H6$. In a like manner, the total salary paid out is $S1 + S2 + S3 + S4 + S5 + S6$, and the total deductions are $D1 + D2 + D3 + D4 + D5 + D6$. The net would be $N1 + N2 + N3 + N4 + N5 + N6$; however, the variables $N1, N2, \ldots$ were never calculated in the program. The net for each employee was calculated in the PRINT statements, not in a statement like LET $N1 = \ldots$. Therefore it is necessary, in line 5901, to calculate the total NET as

$$\text{Total NET} = (S1 + S2 + S3 + S4 + S5 + S6) - (D1 + D2 + D3 + D4 + D5 + D6)$$

There are two more noteworthy points. First, we could have used only the variables H, R, T, S, and D, without a numerical combination, for all employees. We could simply assign the values for each variable in lines 2200 – 2600, and reassign them in 2800–3200, 3400–3800, 4000–4400, 4600–5000, and 5200–5600. However, in so doing, the previously assigned value would have been erased with each new employee. It is then obvious that, after printing out Alvin Jones in line 5700, only his data would be assigned to H, R, T, S, and D. The data on all other employees would have been "forgotten" by the computer, and it would have been impossible to calculate the company's totals in lines 5900 and 5901.

Second, all the totals are printed out on a single line, but the teletype carriage is simply not long enough to contain the required PRINT statement, and the program resorts to two print instructions, lines 5900 and 5901. To prevent splitting the output into two corresponding lines, a semicolon is used at the end of line 5900 to suppress the carriage return before continuing with line 5901.

2.5 CRITIQUE OF THE PAYROLL JOURNAL PROGRAM

There are a number of deficiencies in Program 2.3. For example, one would find this program extremely tedious if there were, say, several thousand employees. Then there would have to be six lines in the program for every employee. Every time a new employee was added to the payroll, another six lines would have to be added to the program; every time an employee left the company, his six lines would have to be deleted. The problem would be compounded if the program were also required to calculate overtime payments and Social Security tax (and check to see if the employee has reached the maximum amount deductible before so doing), deduct union dues and credit union monies, or a large variety of other payroll tasks. There could be dozens of lines for each employee.

And if there were thousands of employees, what variable names could be used? The variable H2138 for the 2138th employee is not permitted. These problems have solutions, but new BASIC statements must be learned.

2.6 READ/DATA STATEMENTS

The READ and DATA statements are always used together as a couplet. However, there may be more of one than another, and they need not be located in close proximity in the body of the program. In Program 2.4 READ/DATA statements replace lines 2200–2400 and all other corresponding lines for each employee of Program 2.3. All the data in Table 2.10 is entered in the program with the DATA statements of lines 6000–6700. The printout is identical to Table 2.12. Note the following:

```
100  PRINT
200  PRINT
300  PRINT
400  PRINT
500  PRINT
600  PRINT "                    PAYRØLL  JØURNAL"
700  PRINT "                        FØR"
800  PRINT "              WIDGET-GIDGET MFG. CØ."
900  PRINT
1000 PRINT
1100 PRINT "              JANUARY 10, 1971"
1200 PRINT
1300 PRINT
1400 PRINT "                    ---"
1500 PRINT
1600 PRINT
1700 PRINT
1800 PRINT " ","HØURS"
1900 PRINT "EMPLØYEE","WØRKED","SALARY","DEDUCTIØNS","NET"
2000 PRINT "--------","------","------","----------","---"
2100 PRINT
2400 READ H1,R1,T1
2500 LET S1=H1*R1
2600 LET D1=T1*S1
2700 PRINT "ADAMS,JIM",H1,S1,D1,S1-D1
3000 READ H2,R2,T2
3100 LET S2=H2*R2
3200 LET D2=T2*S2
3300 PRINT "SMITH,SAM",H2,S2,D2,S2-D2
3600 READ H3,R3,T3
3700 LET S3=H3*R3
3800 LET D3=T3*S3
3900 PRINT "BARNETT,MIKE",H3,S3,D3,S3-D3
4200 READ H4,R4,T4
4300 LET S4=H4*R4
4400 LET D4=T4*S4
4500 PRINT "BARNETT,DEBØRAH",H4,S4,D4,S4-D4
4700 READ H5
4800 READ R5,T5
4900 LET S5=H5*R5
5000 LET D5=T5*S5
5100 PRINT "RØBERTS,CLIFF",H5,S5,D5,S5-D5
5400 READ H6,R6,T6
5500 LET S6=H6*R6
5600 LET D6=T6*S6
5700 PRINT "JØNES,ALVIN",H6,S6,D6,S6-D6
5800 PRINT " ","--------","----------","----------"

5900 PRINT "TØTAL",H1+H2+H3+H4+H5+H6,"$":S1+S2+S3+S4+S5+S6,"$":
5901 PRINT D1+D2+D3+D4+D5+D6,"$":(S1+S2+S3+S4+S5+S6)-(D1+D2+D3+D4+D5+D6)

6000 DATA 40,3.32,.103
6100 DATA 42,5.25,.172
6200 DATA 38
6300 DATA 4.28,.145
6400 DATA 40,2.13,.085,40,6.28,.18
6500 DATA 41.5
6600 DATA 5.03
6700 DATA .163
6800 END
```

Program 2.4 Substitution of READ and DATA statements for the LET statements of Program 2.3.

■ If one begins at 6000 and reads the data horizontally, continuing on to 6100, 6200, etc., the data is arranged in exactly the same sequence as it appeared in Program 2.3.

■ Each data line must be identified with the word DATA.

■ As many, or as few, data can be included in each line as desired, as long as the order of the data is preserved.

■ When more than one data entry is given in each line, the entries are separated by commas.

The haphazard arrangement of data in Program 2.4 is used only to illustrate that it can be given in any arrangement, that only the order is important. The DATA statements are not usually this randomly constructed; either of the formats given in Table 2.13 are more typical, but nonetheless equivalent to that of Program 2.4. The format of Table 2.13b has a subtle, but valuable, advantage over Table 2.13a; each week the "hours worked" for each employee must be changed. In Table 2.13a, retyping "hours worked" also unnecessarily requires retyping the rate and deduction percentage.

Now let us review Program 2.4 more closely. The first 21 statements are unchanged from Program 2.3. Lines 2200 and 2300 have been deleted. Upon encountering 2400, the computer is instructed to READ the value of $H1$, $R1$, and $T1$ (rather than to LET $H1 = \ldots$, etc.); READ from where? From the DATA statements! In effect, the first READ statement encountered is instructing the computer to "go to the DATA statements, from them READ the first three elements (as indicated by the number of variables in the READ statement), and assign those values to $H1$, $R1$, and $T1$, respectively." And so, $H1$, $R1$, and $T1$ are assigned the values

Table 2.13 Two sets of DATA statements which are equivalent to the statements given in Program 2.4.

6000 DATA 40, 3.32, .103	6000 DATA 40
6100 DATA 42, 5.25, .172	6001 DATA 3.32, .103
6200 DATA 38, 4.28, .145	6100 DATA 42
6300 DATA 40, 2.13, .085	6101 DATA 5.25, .172
6400 DATA 40, 6.28, .18	6200 DATA 38
6500 DATA 41.5, 5.03, .163	6201 DATA 4.28, .145
	6300 DATA 40
(a)	6301 DATA 2.13, .085
	6400 DATA 40
	6401 DATA 6.28, .18
	6500 DATA 41.5
	6501 DATA 5.03, .163
	(b)

40, 3.32, and 0.103 from line 6000, just as they were assigned those values by the LET statements in Program 2.3.

An important aspect of the READ statement is that the computer has the ability to never read the same DATA entry twice.* Thus, when the second READ statement (3000) is encountered, the next three data entries (from line 6100) are read and assigned to H2, R2, and T2. The process is repeated with each READ statement. Review closely the remainder of the program and determine which data each READ statement retrieves. Table 2.14 is given for the student's convenience in understanding this important point.

Some final words about READ/DATA statements:

■   As may be inferred from the above examples, the READ statement can read as many variables simultaneously as desired.

■   DATA statements can be interspersed at any point in the program (except after the END statement). The computer will organize them into sequence according to the line number on the statements. However, it is convenient to organize the DATA statements as a group at the end of the main body of the program.

■   It is possible for the programmer to inadvertently leave out some data, or give more READ statements than there are data entries to be read. In such cases, the computer will continue to read and process the data until it expires, whereupon it will stop executing the program and print out a diagnostic on the teletype:

$$\text{ERR}\emptyset\text{R, }\emptyset\text{UT }\emptyset\text{F DATA IN LINE XXX,}$$

where XXX will be replaced by the line number in which the expired READ statement is given.

Table 2.14   Showing the source of DATA for each READ statement in Program 2.4.

READ statement line number	Resultant H, R, and T values	DATA statement line number
2400	40, 3.32, .103	6000
3000	42, 5.25, .172	6100
3600	38, 4.28, .145	6200, 6300
4200	40, 2.13, .085	6400
4700	H5 = 40	6400
4800	R5, T5 = 6.28, .18	6400
5400	41.5, 5.03, .163	6500, 6600, 6700

*Except under special conditions which are controlled by the programmer (see Section 4.6).

2.7 FØR/NEXT STATEMENTS

One of the unnecessary nuisances encountered in Programs 2.3 and 2.4 is the need to keep retyping the LET (or READ) statements, the calculations of S and D, and the PRINT statements. If there were several thousand employees, as already pointed out, it would be necessary to repeat these statements several thousand times. However, the similarities of these statements suggest that they might be reduced to a single set of statements which are repeated many times, once for each employee. The FØR/NEXT couplet of statements is specifically designed for this purpose.

First, for illustration, a simple program using the FØR/NEXT couplet is given in Table 2.15. The important thing to realize is that, with the FØR/NEXT statement, the execution of the program is no longer carried out in the same order as the line numbers indicate. Instead, the lines inside the FØR/NEXT couplet are repeated several times. The number of repetitions is actually dictated by the construction of the FØR statement. In Table 2.15a lines 300–400 are executed five times before the computer proceeds to line 600. The FØR statement instructs the computer to repeat all the statements between line 200 and the NEXT I, for all values of I from 1 to 3, in steps (or increments) of 0.5; e.g., for I = 1, 1.5, 2, 2.5, and 3.

Hence the computer, upon encountering the FØR statement, recognizes that a NEXT statement follows, and it prepares to repeat the intervening statements several times, once with each value of I indicated in the FØR statement. It then proceeds with those statements, using the first value of I. Upon reaching the NEXT I statement, it returns to the first intervening statement and again executes down to the NEXT I, using the second value of I. The process is repeated until the intervening statements have been executed for all values of I specified by the FØR statement.. For the student's reference, the order of execution of the program in Table 2.15a is illustrated in Table 2.15c.

Note that, in this example, the changing value of I is actually used within the intervening statements. This is very useful and is the normal procedure, but it is not necessary. For example, the following statements result in printing three blank lines:

$$
\begin{array}{ll}
100 & \text{FØR I} = 1 \text{ TØ } 3 \\
200 & \text{PRINT} \\
300 & \text{NEXT I}
\end{array}
$$

The repetition of the intervening statements is generally called **looping**, and the FØR/NEXT couplet is generally called a FØR/NEXT loop. Execution of one loop is called an **iteration**. The variable I is referred to as the **index** of the loop. There are some miscellaneous details about loops

Table 2.15 Illustration of the FØR/NEXT loop.

PRØGRAM	PRINTØUT
100 PRINT "STARTING"	STARTING
	I= 1
200 FØR I=1 TØ 3 STEP .5	STILL GØING
300 PRINT "I=";I	I= 1.5
400 PRINT "STILL GØING"	STILL GØING
500 NEXT I	I= 2
	STILL GØING
600 PRINT "FINISHED"	I= 2.5
700 END	STILL GØING
	I= 3
(a)	STILL GØING
	FINISHED
	(b)

(c) Order of execution of the program

Order	Line number	Value of I
1	100	None
2	200	I = 1
3	300	I = 1
4	400	I = 1
5	500	I = 1.5
6	300	I = 1.5
7	400	I = 1.5
8	500	I = 2
9	300	I = 2
10	400	I = 2
11	500	I = 2.5
12	300	I = 2.5
13	400	I = 2.5
14	500	I = 3
15	300	I = 3
16	400	I = 3
17	500	I = 3
18	600	I = 3
19	700	I = 3

which should be understood:

■ The index of the loop can be any variable A, B, C, . . . , Z7, Z8, Z9 (see Table 2.2). However, the same index variable must be used in both the FØR and the NEXT statements.

■   If the step size, or increment, is 1, the phrase "... STEP 1" may be eliminated from the FØR statement. In the statement 200 FØR I = 1 TØ 5, the variable I takes on values 1,2,3,4,5.

■   The increment may be negative, as in 200 FØR I = 10 to 5 STEP − 1. Then I begins at the largest value (10), and decreases in value by the increment indicated (i.e., I = 10,9,8,7,6,5).

■   Any of the numbers in the FØR statement may be negative, as in FØR I = − 3 TØ 1 STEP .5, where I = − 3, − 2.5, − 2, − 1.5, − 1, − 0.5,0,0.5,1.

■   Any of the numbers in the FØR statement may be variables, as in

```
100     LET  A = 1
200     LET  B = 5
300     FØR  I8 = A TØ B STEP A/B
             .
             .
             .
1000    NEXT  I8
```

In this case care should be taken that the step size is not inadvertently set to zero, for the computer would start at, say, I8 = 1. But then an increment of zero results in the second, third, fourth, . . . values of I8 = 1 also, and the loop will never be ended, for I8 will never get to the upper limit of the FØR statement.

USING FØR/NEXT IN PAYROLL JOURNAL PROGRAM

For the moment, ignore the printing of the employee's names; certain problems will temporarily be avoided so that study of the FØR/NEXT statement can proceed without obstruction. Just so the task of printing the employee's name is not overlooked, we shall temporarily use the dummy name XXX for every employee.

Part of a new version of the Payroll Journal Program, with the individual employee's calculations replaced by a single FØR/NEXT loop, is given in Program 2.5 (see also Fig. 2.10). If N is set equal to the number of employees (in line 2999), the FØR/NEXT loop between lines 3000 and 3400 will obviously be repeated a number of times equal to the number of employees. Each time the loop is executed, the first statement is 3100 READ H,R,T. On the first loop, the data entries 40, 3.32, 0.103 are read, and lines 3200–3400 are executed, using the data pertaining to ADAMS,JIM. On the second loop, the data entries 42, 5.25, 0.172 are read, and lines 3200–3400 are executed using the data pertaining to SMITH,SAM. The process is repeated for all six employees, and then execution proceeds to line 5800 and the beginning of the "TØTAL" printout.

```
100  FØR I=1 TØ 5
200  PRINT
300  NEXT I
600  PRINT "                           PAYRØLL  JØURNAL"
                               .
                               .
                               .
1900 PRINT "EMPLØYEE","WØRKED","SALARY","DEDUCTIØNS","NET"
2000 PRINT "--------","------","------","----------","---"
2100 PRINT
2999 LET N=6
3000 FØR I=1 TØ N
3100 READ H,R,T
3200 LET S=H*R
3300 LET D=T*S
3400 PRINT "XXX",H,S,D,S-D
4000 NEXT I

5800 PRINT " ","--------","----------","----------","----------"
5900 PRINT "TØTAL"," ","$","$","$"

6000 DATA 40,3.32,.103
6100 DATA 42,5.25,.172
6200 DATA 38
6300 DATA 4.28,.145
6400 DATA 40,2.13,.085,40,6.28,.18
6500 DATA 41.5
6600 DATA 5.03
6700 DATA .163
6800 END
```

Program 2.5   Use of the FØR/NEXT loop in the Payroll Journal Program.

A copy of the output using this program is given in Table 2.16. Notice that the body of the table—the calculations—is identical to that produced by the much longer Program 2.4.

Two things should now be obvious to the student. First, any number of employees can be processed automatically just by changing line 2999. For instance, to process 2138 employees line 2999 would be written

$$2999 \qquad \text{LET} \quad N = 2138$$

and the FØR/NEXT loop would be executed 2138 times. Now many statements need not be added for each additional employee, and there are no reservations about adding extra tasks (i.e., statements) for all employees.

Second, the same variables are reused for each employee—H, R, S, T, and D. Although the value of the index variable changes with each interation, the variable names in the READ and LET statements do not. But this poses a dilemna, for after finishing the loops the computer no longer has available the individual employee's data, so it cannot calculate the total of each column. The new programmer soon learns not to despair over getting backed into such corners. He invents a repertoire of tricks to save himself. The answer to this problem is deceptively simple. The clue is to create the

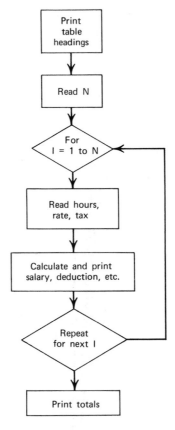

Figure 2.10 Flowchart for Program 2.5.

totals in a piecemeal fashion, with an important programming trick called an **accumulator**.

USING AN ACCUMULATOR IN THE PAYROLL JOURNAL PROGRAM

Consider, for now, only the problem of determining the total number of hours worked. If a technique can be found for accomplishing that task, the same technique can obviously be duplicated for the salary, deduction, and net totals.

Recognize that the total number of hours can be calculated equally well by either of two algorithms, illustrated in Tables 2.17a and b. The algorithm of Table 2.17a is equivalent to the statement

Table 2.16   Results of using the FØR/NEXT loops in Program 2.5.

```
                    PAYRØLL  JØURNAL
                          FØR
                WIDGET-GIDGET MFG.  CØ.


                    JANUARY 10,  1971


                          - - -
```

EMPLØYEE	HØURS WØRKED	SALARY	DEDUCTIØNS	NET
--------	------	------	----------	---
XXX	40	132.8	13.6784	119.1216
XXX	42	220.5	37.926	182.574
XXX	38	162.64	23.5828	139.0572
XXX	40	85.2	7.242	77.958
XXX	40	251.2	45.216	205.984
XXX	41.5	208.745	34.025435	174.71957
	--------	---------	----------	---------
TØTAL		$	$	$

$$\text{LET } H9 = H1 + H2 + H3 + H4 + H5 + H6$$

where H9 will be the total number of hours worked.

On the other hand, the algorithm of Table 2.17b is equivalent to the following set of programming statements, modifying Program 2.5:*

```
                     •
                     •
                     •
         2200 LET H9=0
         2999 LET N=6
         3000 FØR I=1 TØ N
         3100 READ H,R,T
                     •
                     •
                     •
         3500 LET H9=H9+H
         4000 NEXT I
                     •
                     •
                     •
         6000 DATA 40,3.32,.103
         6100 DATA 42,5.25,.172
                     •
                     •
                     •
```

*The summation process is sometimes noted by the shorthand expression

$$H9 = \sum_{i=1}^{n} H_i$$

meaning, H9 = sum of H_i for all i's, 1–n.

Table 2.17 Two methods of calculating the total number of hours worked by all employees. Algorithm (a) is equivalent to the method in Program 2.5. Algorithm (b) is equivalent to the accumulator discussed in this section.

(a) Add all numbers simultaneously	(b) Start with zero; add the first number for a partial total; then add another, etc.
$\begin{array}{r} 40 \\ +42 \\ +38 \\ +40 \\ +40 \\ +41.5 \\ \hline \end{array}$ Total 241.5	$\begin{array}{r} 0 \\ +40 \\ \hline 40 \\ +42 \\ \hline 82 \\ +38 \\ \hline 120 \\ +40 \\ \hline 160 \\ +40 \\ \hline 200 \\ +41.5 \\ \hline \end{array}$ Total 241.5

To simplify the discussion, line 3500 will be thought of as the verbal expression, "Let a new value of H9 be equal to its old value plus the current value of H." On the first iteration of the I loop, H = 40. Just before line 3500 is executed the first time, the "old value" of H9 is zero (from line 2200). After line 3500, its "new value" is equal to "its old value (0) plus H (= 40)," or H9 = 0 + 40 = 40. The first step of the algorithm in Table 2.17b is now accomplished.

On the second iteration of the loop, the "old value" of H9 is 40 because it was changed from zero on the previous pass, and was not reassigned since then. So, after the second execution of line 3500, the "new H9" is equal to its "old value (40) plus the current value of H(= 42)," or H9 = 40 + 42 = 82, accomplishing the second step of the algorithm. The process can be repeated many times, thereby accumulating the sum of all the Hs:

Third iteration	H9 = 82 + 38 = 120
Fourth iteration	H9 = 120 + 40 = 160
Fifth iteration	H9 = 160 + 40 = 200
Sixth iteration	H9 = 200 + 41.5 = 241.5

In a similar manner, accumulators can be used for salary (i.e., S9 =

```
100 FØR I=1 TØ 5
200 PRINT
300 NEXT I
600 PRINT "                        PAYRØLL JØURNAL"
                                  .
                                  .
                                  .
1900 PRINT "EMPLØYEE","WØRKED","SALARY","DEDUCTIØNS","NET"
2000 PRINT "--------","------","------","----------","---"
2100 PRINT

2200 LET H9=0
2300 LET S9=0
2400 LET D9=0
2500 LET N9=0

2999 LET N=6
3000 FØR I=1 TØ N
3100 READ H,R,T
3200 LET S=H*R
3300 LET D=T*S
3400 PRINT "XXX",H,S,D,S-D
3500 LET H9=H9+H
3600 LET S9=S9+S
3700 LET D9=D9+D
3800 LET N9=N9+(S-D)
4000 NEXT I

5800 PRINT " ","--------","----------","----------","----------"
5900 PRINT "TØTAL",H9,"$":S9,"$":D9,"$":N9

6000 DATA 40,3.32,.103
6100 DATA 42,5.25,.172
6200 DATA 38
6300 DATA 4.28,.145
6400 DATA 40,2.13,.085,40,6.28,.18
6500 DATA 41.5
6600 DATA 5.03
6700 DATA .163
6800 END
```

Program 2.6 Using an accumulator in the Payroll Journal Program to total all employees' data.

S9 + S), deductions (D9), and net salary (N9). Now examine their applications in the Payroll Journal Program by studying Program 2.6, Figure 2.11, and Table 2.18. The accumulator statements (including a statement like 2200 to give each accumulator an initial value!) are just slipped into the program at the end of the loop. Finally H9, S9, D9, and N9 can be printed as the total of each column after the I loop is finished (see line 5900).

Example 2.3   A Moving Auto

An auto is traveling at 30 mph. Determine the distance it has traveled after 0, 0.5, 1, 1.5, . . . , 3 hr. Arrange the printout in an attractive manner.

Table 2.18 Printout of the Payroll Journal as derived from Program 2.6.

```
                    PAYRØLL  JØURNAL
                          FØR
               WIDGET-GIDGET  MFG.  CØ.


                    JANUARY 10,  1971


                          - - -
```

EMPLØYEE	HØURS WØRKED	SALARY	DEDUCTIØNS	NET
--------	------	------	----------	---
XXX	40	132.8	13.6784	119.1216
XXX	42	220.5	37.926	182.574
XXX	38	162.64	23.5828	139.0572
XXX	40	85.2	7.242	77.958
XXX	40	251.2	45.216	205.984
XXX	41.5	208.745	34.025435	174.71957
	--------	---------	---------	---------
TØTAL	241.5	$ 1061.085	$ 161.67063	$ 899.41436

DISCUSSION

Program 2.7 and Table 2.19 are quite straightforward. Lines 700–1100 are
the heart of the program. A FØR/NEXT loop (with time being the index
of the loop) is used to change T in line 900 in the pattern described above.
Lines 100–600 construct presentable table headings.

Example 2.4   Hours on the Job, or Loops within Loops

Table 2.20 shows the number of hours each employee of Widget-Gidget
Mfg. Co. worked each day of the week. Write a program to determine the
sum of those numbers for each employee.

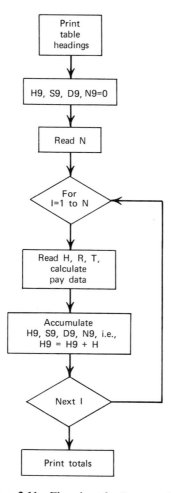

Figure 2.11 Flowchart for Program 2.6.

DISCUSSION

In Program 2.8 the loop between lines 300 and 1000 is executed once for each employee (see also Fig. 2.12). But what needs to be done for each one? To accumulate and print the total of six numbers representing hours worked on Monday, Tuesday, . . . , Saturday. Therefore an accumulator is installed with the J loop, lines 400–800. The resulting output is shown in Table 2.21.

The J loop is said to be **nested** inside the I loop. If desired, several other loops could be nested inside the J loop.

```
100 PRINT "    THE MØVING AUTØ PRØBLEM"
200 FØR I=1 TØ 3
300 PRINT
400 NEXT I
500 PRINT "HØURS","DISTANCE"
600 PRINT "-----","--------"

700 LET S=30
800 FØR T=0 TØ 3
900 LET D=S*T
1000 PRINT T,D
1100 NEXT T
1200 END
```

Program 2.7 Program to calculate the traveled distance of the moving auto.

Table 2.19   Printout from Program 2.7.

THE MØVING AUTØ PRØBLEM	
HØURS	DISTANCE
-----	--------
0	0
1	30
2	60
3	90

Table 2.20   Daily hours for each employee.

Employee	Monday	Tuesday	Wednesday	Thursday	Friday	Saturday
Adams, Jim	8.0	8.0	8.0	8.0	8.0	0.0
Smith, Sam	8.0	8.0	8.0	8.0	8.0	2.0
Barnett, Mike	8.0	7.0	8.0	7.0	8.0	0.0
Barnett, Deborah	0.0	8.0	8.0	8.0	8.0	8.0
Roberts, Cliff	8.0	8.0	8.0	8.0	8.0	0.0
Jones, Alvin	8.5	8.5	8.5	8.0	8.0	0.0

2.8   GØ TØ ... STATEMENT

The computer normally executes statements in the order indicated by their line numbers. The FØR/NEXT statements permit a temporary interruption of that sequence while some of the statements are repeated, but the

```
100  PRINT "EMPLØYEE","HØURS"
200  PRINT "--------","-----"

299  LET N=6
300  FØR I=1 TØ N

400  LET T=0
500  FØR J=1 TØ 6
600  READ H
700  LET T=T+H
800  NEXT J

900  PRINT I,T
1000 NEXT I

1100 DATA 8,8,8,8,8,0
1200 DATA 8,8,8,8,8,2
1300 DATA 8,7,8,7,8,0
1400 DATA 0,8,8,8,8,8
1500 DATA 8,8,8,8,8,0
1600 DATA 8.5,8.5,8.5,8,8,0
1700 END
```

Program 2.8 Adding the number of hours each employee worked during one week (Monday–Saturday).

Table 2.21 Printout from Program 2.8.

EMPLØYEE	HØURS
--------	-----
1	40
2	42
3	38
4	40
5	40
6	41.5

GØ TØ ... statement permanently interrupts the sequence. The format of the statement is

$$1001 \quad GØ \ TØ \ 3000$$

where 3000 is a line number in the program. To see how the statement is implemented, see Program 2.9, the output of which is

```
    WELCØME TØ THE WØRLD ØF
TIME-SHARING CØMPUTING.
GØØD LUCK!!
```

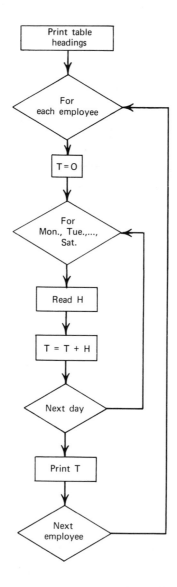

Figure 2.12 Flowchart for Program 2.8.

```
100 PRINT "     WELCØME TØ THE WØRLD ØF"
200 PRINT "TIME-SHARING CØMPUTING."
210 GØ TØ 600
300 PRINT
400 PRINT "YØU WILL FIND IT VERY USEFUL,"
500 PRINT "INTRIGUING AND REMARKABLY SIMPLE."
600 PRINT "GØØD LUCK!!"
700 END
```

Program 2.9 Use of the GØ TØ... statement in Program 2.1.


```
100 PRINT "     WELCØME TØ THE WØRLD ØF"
200 PRINT "TIME-SHARING CØMPUTING."
210 GØ TØ 200
300 PRINT
400 PRINT "YØU WILL FIND IT VERY USEFUL,"
500 PRINT "INTRIGUING AND REMARKABLY SIMPLE."
600 PRINT "GØØD LUCK!!"
700 END
```

Program 2.10 Misuse of the GØ TØ... statement.

Observe that the first two lines of the second paragraph were not printed because line 210 had been inserted. Upon encountering it, the computer is instructed to "GØ TØ 600," passing up lines 300–500.

It is permissible for the GØ TØ . . . statement to direct the computer to an earlier line number in the program, but care must be used. In Program 2.10 the GØ TØ . . . statement directs the computer back to line 200. This in itself, is permissible, but the design of the chosen example results in

```
     WELCØME TØ THE WØRLD ØF
TIME-SHARING CØMPUTING.
TIME-SHARING CØMPUTING.
TIME-SHARING CØMPUTING.
TIME-SHARING CØMPUTING.
TIME-SHARING CØMPUTING.
          .
          .
          .
```

Why? Upon being returned to line 200, the computer resumes sequential execution, i.e., after executing line 200 it proceeds to the next line—line 210! But line 210 sends it back to 200 again. It is clear, then, that the computer never proceeds beyond line 210 and, therefore, never finishes execution of the program. It goes on repeating lines 200–210 forever. Such traps are called **infinite loops**.

■ EXERCISES

When no data is given, make up your own.

*2.33 Mileage records were obtained on four automobiles, as shown below.

Car	Miles	Gallons consumed
1	302	21.3
2	418	25.0
3	192	15.1
4	225	14.8

(a) Write appropriate data statements to hold the information.
(b) Calculate each car's average mileage per gallon.
(c) Calculate total miles driven and total gasoline consumed.
(d) Calculate the average miles per gallon of all four cars.

*2.34 If $1000 is invested at 6% interest, compounded quarterly, its value at the end of t years will be

$$v = 1000*\left(1 + \frac{0.06}{4}\right)^{4t}$$

At 5.25%, compounded continuously, its value is

$$v = 1000*(2.71828)^{0.0525t}$$

Compute these values at t = 1, 2, 3, 4, . . . , 20 years.

2.35 Incorporate Table 2.20 and the principles described in Example 2.4 into the Payroll Journal Program. Each employee's data should look like this:

DATA 8,8,8,8,8,0,3.32,.18

where the first six numbers are "hours worked each day," 3.32 is the employee's hourly rate, and 0.18 is the deduction percentage.

2.36 There are 24 hours in a day, 7 days in a week, and 4.33 weeks (on the average) in a month. Compute the number of hours in 1, 2, 3, . . . , 24 months.

*2.37 A car travels east at 30 mph for 3 hours and then turns north for 5 hours. Calculate its easterly and northerly traveled distance (E and N) at half-hour intervals from 0 to 7 hours. Also, calculate the distance from its starting point at each interval by

$$D = \sqrt{E^2 + N^2}$$

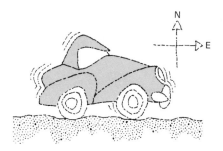

2.38   Write a program to add together all numbers 1,2,3,...,n. Set n = 39. Write another program to multiply together all n numbers. Write a third program to add all odd numbers 1,3,...,n.

2.39   A number of bonds, with $1000 face value, are purchased for a price other than the face value. The dividends on each bond are fixed. The effective interest rate of each, then, is

$$i = \text{Dividend}/\text{Price}$$

Write a program which reads data on several dozen bond purchases and prints out the purchase price, dividend, and interest rate on each. Also, print an appropriate table heading. Make up your own data. A typical purchase might be "3 bonds at $976.25, paying $6.25 each." At the end, print a summary of the number of bonds, the total purchase price, the total dividends, and the average effective interest rate.

2.40   Write a program to evaluate the curve

$$y = 12x^5 - 3x^4 - 2x^3 + 6.5x^2 + 2x + 0.5$$

for x = -2, -1.8, -1.6, ... , 9.6, 9.8, 10.0

2.41   Define and write at least three programs of your own choosing which involve DATA, FØR/NEXT, and nested loops.

2.42   Three tests are performed, with differing numbers, n, of readings in each one. The readings are given in the data statements below. Lines 10000, 20000, and 30000 give the value of n for each test. Using a nested loop, compute the total and average of each test.

```
10000     DATA 8
10100     DATA 93,62,78,100,98,88,87,93
20000     DATA 13
20100     DATA 30.5,28.4,31.3,20.9,24.4,21.6,24.6
20200     DATA 24.8,31.0,21.4,20.8,23.7,22.2
30000     DATA 6
30100     DATA -1.2,0,-.9,1.4,1.6,.2
```

2.43 A number of objects have masses $m_1, m_2, ..., m_n$. They are located at $x_1 y_1 z_1, x_2 y_2 z_2, ..., x_n y_n z_n$. The center of gravity of these masses is $\bar{x}, \bar{y}, \bar{z}$, where

$$\bar{x} = \frac{m_1 x_1 + m_2 x_2 + \cdots + m_n x_n}{m_1 + m_2 + \cdots + m_n}$$

$$\bar{y} = \frac{m_1 y_1 + m_2 y_2 + \cdots + m_n y_n}{m_1 + m_2 + \cdots + m_n}$$

$$\bar{z} = \frac{m_1 z_1 + m_2 z_2 + \cdots + m_n z_n}{m_1 + m_2 + \cdots + m_n}$$

Write a program to read data and determine $\bar{x}$, $\bar{y}$, and $\bar{z}$ when n = 4 and

$m_1 = 3.0$	$x_1, y_1, z_1 = -2, 1, 4$
$m_2 = 1.5$	$x_2, y_2, z_2 = 0, 0, 0$
$m_3 = 0.6$	$x_3, y_3, z_3 = 6, 1, -3$
$m_4 = 4.1$	$x_4, y_4, z_4 = 2, 2, 2$

2.44 There are 32 pairs of A and B data. Put them in data statements, and then compute

$$X = \sqrt{\sum_{i=1}^{32} (A_i \cdot B_i)^2}$$

*2.45 A force vector, illustrated by the arrow in Figure 2.13a, is represented by the complex number $v_1 = x_1 + y_1 i$, where x_1 is the projection of the vector onto the x axis, and y_1 is the projection onto the y axis. If several vectors act on an object at the origin, as shown in Figure

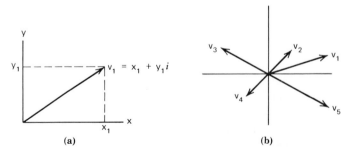

Figure 2.13

2.13b, the *resultant* vector is the sum of the original vectors, i.e.,
$v_r = x_r + y_r i = (x_1 + x_2 + \cdots + x_5) + (y_1 + y_2 + \cdots + y_5)i$.
Write data statements and compute x_r and y_r for the vectors indicated
below.

i	x	y
1	10	3
2	4	5
3	-5	4.5
4	-3	-4
5	10	-3

2.46 If $y = f(x)$ is a curve on a graph, as shown in Figure 2.14, where
$f(x) = (x^2/4) + 1$, the area under it between x_L and x_u (shown
shaded) can be approximately determined by the *trapezoidal rule*,
as follows: Divide the x interval into some number of points, say
$n = 25$, each equally spaced at $s = (x_2 - x_1)/(n - 1)$. The area
is then computed as

$$A = \frac{s}{2}(y_1 + 2y_2 + 2y_3 + \cdots + 2y_{24} + y_{25})$$

where $y_1 = (x_1^2/4) + 1$, $y_2 = (x_2^2/4) + 1$, etc. Using this rule,
calculate the area under the curve from $x_L = -2$ to $x_U = 3$, $n = 25$.

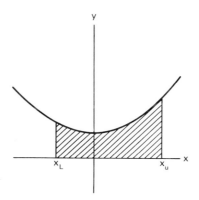

Figure 2.14

2.47 The equation $t = 3x^2 - 2xy + 3zx + 2yz - 4xyz + 3z^3$ must be computed for all combinations of x, y, and z where x goes from -2 to 1 in increments of 0.5, y goes from 0 to 3 in increments of 1.0, and z goes from 4.9 to 4.3 in increments of -0.3. Print the table below and count the number of t's which were computed.

x	y	z	t
-2	0	4.9	335.55
-2	0	4.6	276.46
-2	0	4.3	224.72
-2	1	4.9	388.54
-2	1	4.6	326.41
.			
.			
.			

2.48 An LC circuit of the design shown "resonates" at the frequency

$$f = \frac{1}{2\pi\sqrt{LC}}$$

Write a program which calculates the resonant frequency for L = 0.1–1 henrys (H), $\Delta L = 0.1$ H and C = $0.1 \times 10^{-6} - 0.5 \times 10^{-6}$ farads (F) in steps of 0.1×10^{-6} F.

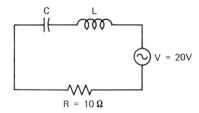

2.49 The circuit in Exercise 2.48 has an impedance

$$Z = \sqrt{R^2 + \left(2\pi fL - \frac{1}{2\pi fC}\right)^2}$$

The current flowing through it is I = V/Z. Calculate the impedance and the current at f = 100, 200, 300, 400, . . . , 1000 cycles/sec, if L = 0.5 H and C = 0.5×10^{-6} F.

2.50   Write a program to determine the standard deviation of $(n=)30x$ readings by

$$\text{Standard deviation} = \sqrt{\frac{\sum x^2 - (\sum x)^2/n}{n-1}}$$

2.9   IF . . . THEN . . . STATEMENT

The G∅ T∅ . . . statement causes the computer to automatically transfer to a new line number. The IF...THEN... statement may be used to impose selective conditions under which a transfer will be made. The conditions are stipulated by the programmer. If they are satisfied, the transfer is accomplished; if not, the computer proceeds to the next line. The form of the IF...THEN... statement is

100   IF X = 1 THEN 3000

In this example, the condition that is imposed before transfer can occur is that $X = 1$. The statement can be expressed verbally as the instruction: *"IF the value of X is 1, THEN go to 3000; if not, go on to the next line."* The program may also instruct the computer to transfer "if X is greater than 1" (i.e., the statement "100 IF X > 1 THEN 3000"), or "if X is less than 1" (i.e., the statement "100 IF X < 1 THEN 3000"). There are other allowable combinations of " =," " >," and " <," as shown in Table 2.22.

Table 2.22   Six combinations of symbols used in IF . . . THEN . . . statements.

Symbol	Use	Meaning
=	100 IF A = B THEN 3000	If A equals B . . .
>	100 IF A > B THEN 3000	If A is greater than B . . .
<	100 IF A < B THEN 3000	If A is less than B . . .
> =	100 IF A > = B THEN 3000	If A is greater than B . . . *or* If A equals B . . .
< =	100 IF A < = B THEN 3000	If A is less than B . . . *or* If A is equal to B . . .
< >	100 IF A < > B THEN 3000	If A is not equal to B . . .

Variables can be used in any combination of conditions in the IF...THEN... statement; i.e., any of the following statements are acceptable:

IF A=B THEN 3000
IF X<C+3 THEN 3000
IF X+2>A↑2+B↑2 THEN 3000

Variables cannot be used as the line number; i.e., the following IF...THEN... statement is illegal:

100   LET N=3000
200   IF X=A THEN N

The examples below are illustrations of the use of the IF...THEN... statement.

Example 2.5   Moving Auto

The moving auto of Example 2.3 was traveling at 30 mph. When it first passes 28 miles, the computer should type the message "JUST PASSED HØGWASH, PA."

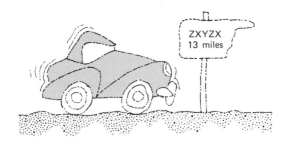

After it passes 54 miles, it should print "JUST PASSED ZXYZX, NY."

DISCUSSION

Each message obviously requires a PRINT statement, as shown in lines 1050 and 1080 of Program 2.11. But those statements should be bypassed if distance (D) is less than 28 and 54, respectively. Therefore IF...THEN... statements are installed in lines 1020 and 1070 to effect this requirement of the program. For example, if D < 28, then the computer is transferred from line 1020 to 1070, avoiding the first printout. But consider what happens when T = 1 hour, and D = 30. When the condition of line 1020 is checked, D is *not* less than 28, so the transfer is not made. As a result,

```
100 PRINT "     THE MØVING AUTØ PRØBLEM"
200 FØR I=1 TØ 3
300 PRINT
400 NEXT I
500 PRINT "HØURS","DISTANCE"
600 PRINT "-----","--------"

700 LET S=30
800 FØR T=0 TØ 3 STEP .5
900 LET D=S*T
1000 PRINT T,D

1020 IF D<28 THEN 1070
1050 PRINT "JUST PASSED HØGWASH, PA."

1070 IF D<54 THEN 1100
1080 PRINT "JUST PASSED ZXYZX, NY."

1100 NEXT T
1200 END
```

Program 2.11   IF...THEN... statements in the moving auto problem.

line 1050 is executed, accomplishing the appropriate printout. The same trick is used for the printout for ZXYZX, NY.

Now review the printout of Table 2.23. An unexpected error has been built into the program. The computer prints out "JUST PASSED HØG-WASH, PA." every iteration after D exceeds 28 miles. The same phenomena is exhibited with the ZYXZX printout. A close examination of the

Table 2.23   Erroneous printouts from Program 2.11.

THE MØVING AUTØ PRØBLEM

HØURS	DISTANCE
-----	--------
0	0
.5	15
1	30
JUST PASSED HØGWASH, PA.	
1.5	45
JUST PASSED HØGWASH, PA.	
2	60
JUST PASSED HØGWASH, PA.	
JUST PASSED ZXYZX, NY.	
2.5	75
JUST PASSED HØGWASH, PA.	
JUST PASSED ZXYZX, NY.	
3	90
JUST PASSED HØGWASH, PA.	
JUST PASSED ZXYZX, NY.	

program reveals the reason. The value of D is always increasing in magnitude; having passed 28 miles on the third iteration of the loop, it remains greater than 28 on all the succeeding iterations. Therefore, on the fourth, fifth, sixth, and seventh iteration, transfer is still not made from 1020 to 1070, resulting in the message being printed each time.

Another very valuable programming trick may now be introduced—the counter. Obviously, the messages should be printed only once, the first time that D is greater than the designated distance. So if there were some variable, say C1, which kept track of the number of times that the computer passed through line 1020, that variable could, in turn, be used in an IF/THEN statement to route the computer past 1050 if C1 was greater than one.

With that in mind, the program is rewritten as shown in Program 2.12 and Figure 2.15. Actually, two counting variables are used, C1 to keep track of the HØGWASH printouts and C2 to keep track of the ZXYZX printouts. Before the T loop is entered, the variables C1 and C2 are set to zero. Following only the behavior of C1 from now on, it remains zero until the third iteration, at which time transfer to 1070 does not occur. The variable C1 is immediately reset to 1 (i.e., $C1 = C1 + 1 = 0 + 1 = 1$). Then, since C1 is not greater than one, transfer is also not made from 1030 to 1070; instead, line 1050 is executed. On succeeding iterations, C1 is set to

```
100 PRINT "      THE MØVING AUTØ PRØBLEM"
200 FØR I=1 TØ 3
300 PRINT
400 NEXT I
500 PRINT "HØURS","DISTANCE"
600 PRINT "-----","--------"

700 LET S=30
710 LET C1=0
720 LET C2=0

800 FØR T=0 TØ 3 STEP .5
900 LET D=S*T
1000 PRINT T,D

1020 IF D<28 THEN 1070
1025 LET C1=C1+1
1030 IF C1>1 THEN 1070
1050 PRINT "JUST PASSED HØGWASH, PA."

1070 IF D<54 THEN 1100
1072 LET C2=C2+1
1074 IF C2>1 THEN 1100
1080 PRINT "JUST PASSED ZXYZX, NY."

1100 NEXT T
1200 END
```

Program 2.12 Using a counter to correct an error in the moving auto problem.

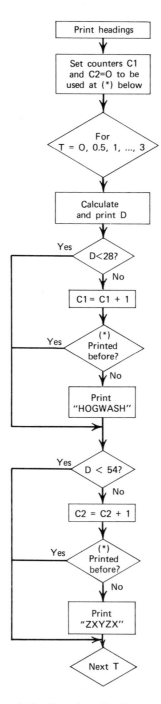

Figure 2.15 Flowchart for Program 2.12.

2, 3, 4, etc. Then C1 is greater than one and transfer away from line 1050 is accomplished. Study the program and Table 2.24 to see that an identical technique is used to limit the ZXYZX printout to one iteration.

Table **2.24** Corrected printout from Program 2.12.

```
                 THE MØVING AUTØ PRØBLEM


        HØURS                DISTANCE
        -----                --------
          0                     0
         .5                    15
          1                    30
        JUST PASSED HØGWASH, PA.
         1.5                   45
          2                    60
        JUST PASSED ZXYZX, NY.
         2.5                   75
          3                    90
```

USING THE IF ... THEN ... STATEMENT IN THE PAYROLL JOURNAL PROGRAM

Recall that Program 2.6 avoided printing the employee's name. The reason is obvious: There was no way to select the single name to be printed on each iteration of the I loop. The IF...THEN... statement can now be used to solve this problem. During the first iteration of the I loop (i.e., when I = 1), the computer must print "ADAMS,JIM"; on the second, when I = 2, it must print "SMITH,SAM"; etc. A PRINT statement is added (between lines 20000 and 20010) for each employee's name in Program 2.13. Now the computer must be given the ability to selectively print those names. First, line 3400 is inserted to cause the computer to temporarily exit from the I loop on every iteration. Second, at lines 10000–10005, the program utilizes the value of I (which corresponds to the number of iterations) to route the computer to the appropriate employee's name. Third, if the computer goes to, say line 20000, it should not be permitted to continue sequentially to 20002. Rather, it should be returned to the I loop and the print statement in line 3410, so lines 20001, 20003, . . . are added. Fourth, when the computer exits the I loop after six iterations, it should not be allowed to proceed further, eventually arriving at 10000 again. Therefore line 5901 is added to bypass the remainder of the program. The printout is given in Table 2.25.

```
                ⋮

1800 PRINT " ","HØURS"
1900 PRINT "EMPLØYEE","WØRKED","SALARY","DEDUCTIØNS","NET"
2000 PRINT "--------","------","------","----------","---"
2100 PRINT

2200 LET H9=0
2300 LET S9=0
2400 LET D9=0
2500 LET N9=0

2999 LET N=6
3000 FØR I=1 TØ N
3100 READ H,R,T
3200 LET S=H*R
3300 LET D=T*S
3400 GØ TØ 10000

3410 PRINT H,S,D,S-D
3500 LET H9=H9+H
3600 LET S9=S9+S
3700 LET D9=D9+D

3800 LET N9=N9+(S-D)
4000 NEXT I

5800 PRINT " ","--------","----------","----------","----------"
5900 PRINT "TØTAL",H9,"$":S9,"$":D9,"$":N9
5901 GØ TØ 30000

6000 DATA 40,3.32,.103
6100 DATA 42,5.25,.172
6200 DATA 38
6300 DATA 4.28,.145
6400 DATA 40,2.13,.085,40,6.28,.18
6500 DATA 41.5
6600 DATA 5.03
6700 DATA .163

10000 IF I=1 THEN 20000
10001 IF I=2 THEN 20002
10002 IF I=3 THEN 20004
10003 IF I=4 THEN 20006
10004 IF I=5 THEN 20008
10005 IF I=6 THEN 20010

20000 PRINT "ADAMS,JIM",
20001 GØ TØ 3410
20002 PRINT "SMITH,SAM",
20003 GØ TØ 3410
20004 PRINT "BARNETT,MIKE",
20005 GØ TØ 3410
20006 PRINT "BARNETT,DEBØRAH",
20007 GØ TØ 3410
20008 PRINT "RØBERTS,CLIFF",
20009 GØ TØ 3410
20010 PRINT "JØNES,ALVIN",
20011 GØ TØ 3410
30000 END
```

Program 2.13 Using IF...THEN... statements in the Payroll Journal Program.

Table 2.25 Printout that includes employee names by using IF . . . THEN . . . statements in Program 2.13.

```
                      PAYRØLL  JØURNAL
                           FØR
                 WIDGET-GIDGET MFG.  CØ.


                    JANUARY 10,  1971


                         - - -



                   HØURS
EMPLØYEE           WØRKED          SALARY          DEDUCTIØNS      NET
- - - - - - - -    - - - - - -     - - - - - -     - - - - - - - - - -   - - -

ADAMS,JIM            40            132.8           13.6784         119.1216
SMITH,SAM            42            220.5           37.926          182.574
BARNETT,MIKE         38            162.64          23.5828         139.0572
BARNETT,DEBØRAH      40             85.2            7.242           77.958
RØBERTS,CLIFF        40            251.2           45.216          205.984
JØNES,ALVIN          41.5          208.745         34.025435       174.71957
                   - - - - - - - - -  - - - - - - - - -  - - - - - - - - -  - - - - - - - - -
TØTAL               241.5        $ 1061.085      $  161.67063    $  899.41436
```

Two points deserve mentioning:

■   The existing value of the index is retained when the computer leaves the loop on each iteration. As long as I is not reassigned a new value outside the loop, all the iterations are carried out in the normal fashion.

■   Although two PRINT statements are executed for each employee, the comma at the end of each statement in 20000–20011 prevents a carriage return after the name is printed. Therefore the computer is tricked into printing the output of line 3410 on the same teletype line as the name.

2.10   COMMENTS ON THE PAYROLL JOURNAL PROGRAM

Before leaving the Payroll Journal Program, certain defects in it should be admitted. First, one of the obvious problems is that the computer prints out many decimal places. In most economic problems the output should be "rounded off" to two decimal places (i.e., to dollars and cents). Engineering problems usually require rounding off to some specific number of decimal places. Second, the tax deduction scheme is not very resourceful. In particular, the tax rate is normally not a fixed value. Instead, it usually depends on a number of factors—among them, the amount of salary an employee earns each week. A normal payroll program would have a complete tax table built into it, and the computer would automatically determine the tax rate on each employee. Third, the program has no capability for increasing the pay rate for overtime hours. Fourth, the construction of the program demands that the data for each employee be entered in exactly the order their names are listed in lines 20000–20011. Solutions for each of these problems will be examined in future chapters.

Fifth, handling the employee's name in Program 2.13 is very cumbersome, indeed. This is a good point for the reader to look at Section 6.1 and read the introductory material on **string** variables, which offers more convenience in problems of this sort. Briefly, on most computers, strings of alphabetic characters may be read from DATA and printed, similar to numerical variables. Variable names which will hold strings usually have a $ sign attached to them, i.e., B is a numeric variable, B$ is a string variable. With this simple introduction, review Program 2.14. The names of the employees are entered as DATA and read/printed as N$. The output is identical to Table 2.25, with a significant simplification to the program.

2.11 MORE SAMPLE PROBLEMS

Most of the examples so far have stressed only a few simple problems so that the rules for using each BASIC statement could be examined without the distraction of changing problem requirements. This section will feature a number of diverse problems dealing with real-life programs. The problems range from economics to simple engineering applications.

The reader may not have the technical background to completely understand every problem discussed here, but that should not trouble him, for he should be able to comprehend the programming implementations. It is the student's immediate task to

■ simply understand how each program does, in fact, implement each problem;

■ begin to appreciate some of the trickery, chicanery, and subterfuge generally used to accomplish real-life tasks; and

■ gain confidence that virtually any tasks or objectives can be accomplished by creative programming.

```
100 FØR I=1 TØ 5
200 PRINT
300 NEXT I
600 PRINT "                      PAYRØLL JØURNAL"
                      .
                      .
                      .
1900 PRINT "EMPLØYEE","WØRKED","SALARY","DEDUCTIØNS","NET"
2000 PRINT "--------","------","-------","-----------","---"
2100 PRINT

2200 LET H9=0
2300 LET S9=0
2400 LET D9=0
2500 LET N9=0

2999 LET N=6
3000 FØR I=1 TØ N
3100 READ N$,H,R,T
3200 LET S=H*R
3300 LET D=T*S
3400 PRINT N$,H,S,D,S-D
3500 LET H9=H9+H
3600 LET S9=S9+S
3700 LET D9=D9+D
3800 LET N9=N9+(S-D)
4000 NEXT I

5800 PRINT " ","--------","----------","----------","----------"
5900 PRINT "TØTAL",H9,"$":S9,"$":D9,"$":N9

6000 DATA "ADAMS,JIM",40,3.32,.103
6100 DATA "SMITH,SAM",42,5.25,.172
6200 DATA "BARNETT,MIKE",38,4.28,.145
6300 DATA "BARNETT,DEBØRAH",40,2.13,.085
6400 DATA "RØBERTS,CLIFF",40,6.28,.18
6500 DATA "JØNES,ALVIN",41.5,5.03,.163
6600 END
```

Program 2.14 Using string variables in the Payroll Journal Program.

Example 2.6   Even or Odd

Pick any three numbers between 1 and 100 and write a program to determine if they are even (2,4,6,8,...) or odd (1,3,5,7,...). Program 2.15 uses the
three numbers X = 3, 6, 53.

DISCUSSION

The fact that there are three values of X to evaluate suggests a FØR/NEXT
loop, FØR I=1 TO 3 (lines 100 and 1200). Within each iteration, one of
the values of X is read (line 200), a determination is made of whether the
value is even or odd (lines 300–700),* and an appropriate message is printed
(lines 800–1100).

*Although this is an ideal program to illustrate most of the statements learned so far, it can
be dramatically simplified by using the *integer function* in Section 4.2. The reader is invited
to look at that section.

Examine lines 300–700 more closely. The K Loop beginning in line 400 sets K equal to all even values between 1 and 100 (since it begins with 2 and is indexed in increments of two thereafter). Now consider one possible case, where X is even (say, X = 6). When K = 2, 4, 8, 10, . . . , K and X are unequal and therefore the computer will transfer from line 500 to line 700, bypassing line 600. But for one value of K (K = 6), transfer will not take place and line 600 will be executed, resulting in C being changed from its original value (0) to the value one. This change always occurs for one value of K when X is even.

Consider now the other case, when X is odd (say, X = 3). Since K is always even, K and X are never equal; transfer always occurs from line 500 to line 700, and C remains zero.

Therefore, after all NEXT Ks are executed (i.e., when the computer gets to line 800), the value of C will be either zero (if X was odd) or one (if X was even). If it is one, the computer will transfer from line 800 to line 1100 and print "EVEN"; if it is zero, the computer will proceed from line 800 to line 900, and print "∅DD."

Example 2.7 Interest on a Loan

A loan is executed in the amount (principal) of $72,000, for a period of 10 years. One payment is made each year. The payments on the principal are evenly spread over the 10 year period. However, at each payment,

```
100 FØR I=1 TØ 3
200 READ X

300 LET C=0
400 FØR K=2 TØ 100 STEP 2
500 IF K<>X THEN 700
600 LET C=C+1
700 NEXT K

800 IF C=1 THEN 1100
900 PRINT "THE NUMBER";X;"IS ØDD"
1000 GØ TØ 1200
1100 PRINT "THE NUMBER";X;"IS EVEN"

1200 NEXT I

1300 DATA 3,6,53
1400 END
RUN

THE NUMBER    3    IS ØDD
THE NUMBER    6    IS EVEN
THE NUMBER   53    IS ØDD
```

Program 2.15 Determining if an even number is even or odd.

interest of 8.5% of the previous year's unpaid balance is also paid. Write a program to determine these data for each of the ten payments: payment on the principal, interest charged, total payment, and the remaining unpaid balance.

DISCUSSION

The annual payment on the principal is obviously $72,000/10$, and this value is assigned to P in line 100 of Program 2.16. Then the "FØR Y = 1 TØ 10" loop will make the calculations for each of the 10 years. The unpaid balance each year is

$$\text{Principal} - \text{Annual payment} * \text{Number of payments}$$

or, "72000 − P*Y," as shown in line 400. Obviously, then, the previous year's unpaid balance is $72000 - P*(Y - 1)$, and the interest payment is therefore

$$(72000 - P*(Y - 1))*.085$$

as shown in line 300.

```
50 PRINT "YEAR","PAYMENT","INTEREST","TØTAL","REMAIN BAL."
100 LET P=72000/10

200 FØR Y=1 TØ 10
300 LET I=(72000-P*(Y-1))*.085
400 PRINT Y,P,I,P+I,72000-P*Y
500 NEXT Y

600 END
RUN
```

YEAR	PAYMENT	INTEREST	TØTAL	REMAIN BAL.
1	7200	6120	13320	64800
2	7200	5508	12708	57600
3	7200	4896	12096	50400
4	7200	4284	11484	43200
5	7200	3672	10872	36000
6	7200	3060	10260	28800
7	7200	2448	9648	21600
8	7200	1836	9036	14400
9	7200	1224	8424	7200
10	7200	612	7812	0

Program 2.16 Interest on a loan

Example 2.8 Largest Number

Given the numbers 40, −2, 106, 12, −3, 16, 12, 10, −6, 18, 14, write a program that will find, and print, the largest of them.

DISCUSSION

Use DATA statements to get the numbers into the computer. Use another one to tell the computer that there are 11 pieces of data (i.e., how many

```
100 READ N
200 READ L

300 FØR I=2 TØ N
400 READ X
500 IF X<L THEN 700
600 LET L=X
700 NEXT I

800 PRINT "LARGEST NØ. IS";L

900 DATA 11
1000 DATA 40,-2,106,12,-3,16,12
1001 DATA 10,-6,18,14
1200 END
RUN

LARGEST NØ. IS      106
```

Program 2.17 Finding the largest number in a
set of data.

items to read). Let the largest number be the variable "L." In Program 2.17,
lines 100–200 read the number (N) of datum and the first item in the list
(i.e., 40). The latter number is read as L because, being the first, it is obviously the largest item read so far.

Now there remain (N − 1) items to be read. After reading each, its value
should be compared to the value of L, and if it is larger, L should be reassigned that value. If it is smaller, L should not be reassigned, and the next
item should be read and evaluated. These things are accomplished in lines
300–700. The FØR statement specifies 10 loops (I = 2, 3, . . . , 11). In each,
X (i.e., the second, third, . . . , eleventh data item) is read at line 400. The
key statement is line 500: If the value of X is less than the value of L, transfer
is made to the NEXT I without reassigning L, and the loop is repeated with
the next data item. But if X is greater than L, the transfer is not made and
line 600 is executed, reassigning L with the larger value of X. So, at the
end of each iteration, L is assigned the largest value read so far. Each new X
is given the opportunity to be assigned to L if it is larger than the largest
number previously read.

Example 2.9 Calculating the Sum and Average of a Group of Numbers

Given three sets of numbers,

■   18.1, 19.2, 16.0, 12.8, 14.3, 20.9, 16.1, 11.9
■   100.3, 86.9, 143.8, 99.2, 109.6, 111.1, 97.0, 115.1, 121.9, 109.2, 109.2,
88.4, 89.1, 93.6, 108.2
■   −3.2, −0.5, 1.2, 0, 1.4, 1.5, 2.4, −1.5, 2.2, −2.1, −1.3

write a program which calculates the sum and the average of each group. (This problem is similar to Exercise 2.42. Compare your solution.)

DISCUSSION

The fact that there are three groups of data suggests a FØR/NEXT loop, "FØR I=1 TØ 3." The intervening statements would accomplish the summation and average of one group of data on each iteration. In Program 2.18 the loop is written "FØR I=1 TØ N1" (line 200). Then, by setting N1 = 3, the loop will be accomplished three times. This is done with statements 100 and 1100. The value of doing this is that a later application of this same program could automatically execute, say, six cases by simply changing line 1100 to "1100 DATA 6."

Now, within this loop another loop—an accumulator—is used (statements 500–800) to perform the summation of the values in each group. There is one problem—the computer must be told how many of these iterations to execute, that is, how many items there are in each group. But there are 8 data in the first group, 15 in the second, and 11 in the third. Thus, if the J loop were written "FØR J=1 TØ 8," it would be correct for the first data group, but wrong for the second. In fact, no matter what number were used

```
100  READ N1
200  FØR I=1 TØ N1
300  LET S=0

400  READ N2
500  FØR J=1 TØ N2
600  READ V
700  LET S=S+V
800  NEXT J

900  PRINT "TØTAL = ";S,"AVERAGE = ";S/N2
1000 NEXT I

1100 DATA 3

1200 DATA 8
1300 DATA 18.1,19.2,16,12.8,14.3,20.9,16.1,11.9

1400 DATA 15
1500 DATA 100.3,86.9,143.8,99.2,109.6,111.1,97
1600 DATA 115.1,121.9,109.2,109.2,88.4,89.1,93.6,108.2

1700 DATA 11
1800 DATA -3.2,-.5,1.2,0,1.4,1.5,2.4,-1.5,2.2,-2.1,-1.3
1900 END
RUN

TØTAL =      129.3         AVERAGE =      16.1625
TØTAL =      1582.6        AVERAGE =      105.50667
TØTAL =      1E-01         AVERAGE =      9.0909091E-03
```

Program 2.18 Calculating the sum and average of a group of numbers.

for the upper limit of the J loop, it would be the wrong one for some iterations.

Therefore, a scheme must be devised for varying the upper J limit within each iteration of the I loop. The one used here is to provide, as elements of data (lines 1200, 1400, 1700), the number of items in each group. Notice that they are located ahead of the DATA statements for each group. Notice also that line 400 has been included. Now if the student studies the program, he will realize that the logic is as follows:

■   Line 100 sets $N1 = 3$, and line 200 becomes, in effect, "Do lines 300–900, for $I = 1$ to 3."

■   On the first iteration of the I loop, line 400 sets $N2 = 8$, and the accumulator J loop becomes "Do lines 600–700, for $J = 1$ to 8." This, in turn, causes 8 data to be read as V and summed, e.g., the items 18.1–11.9.

■   On the second iteration, $N2 = 15$, and $V = 100.3 - 108.2$.

■   On the third iteration, $N2 = 11$, and $V = -3.2--1.3$.

Example 2.10   Depreciation

A machine cost $35,000. After 14 years, it will have a resale value of $550. Calculate the yearly depreciation by the method of the sum of the year's digits.

DISCUSSION

First, the sum of the year's digits must be calculated as $S = 1 + 2 + 3 + 4 + \cdots + 14$. Second, the depreciable amount must be calculated as $A = \$35,000 - \$550$. Then, in each of the 14 years, the depreciation will be

Year	Depreciation
1	(A∗14)/S
2	(A∗13)/S
3	(A∗12)/S
.	.
.	.
.	.
13	(A∗2)/S
14	(A∗1)/S

Observe that the multiplying term in each set of parentheses (i.e., 14, 13, 12, . . . , 1) is always (15 − the number of the year). This will play an im-

```
50 PRINT "YEAR", "DEPRECIATIØN"
100 LET Y1=14
200 LET S=0
300 LET A=35000-550

400 FØR Y=1 TØ Y1
500 LET S=S+Y
600 NEXT Y

700 FØR Y=1 TØ 14
800 LET D=A*(15-Y)/S
900 PRINT Y,D
1000 NEXT Y
1100 END
 RUN

YEAR                DEPRECIATIØN
 1                   4593.3333
 2                   4265.2381
 3                   3937.1429
 4                   3609.0476
 5                   3280.9524
 6                   2952.8571
 7                   2624.7619
 8                   2296.6667
 9                   1968.5714
10                   1640.4762
11                   1312.381
12                    984.28571
13                    656.19048
14                    328.09524
```

Program 2.19   Depreciation of a machine.

portant role in the design of Program 2.19. Lines 50 – 300 print the output table headings and initialize the values of Y1 (number of years), depreciable amount (A), and starting value of the sum of the digits (S). Lines 400–600 calculate the sum of the year's digits with an accumulator. Finally, S is used and lines 800–900 are executed repeatedly, once for each of the 14 years of depreciation. Line 800 calculates the year's depreciation, using $(15 - Y)$ as the multiplying factor in the above table.

Example 2.11 Three-Month Moving Average

The following data have been collected for 12 months:

January	112000	July	75800
February	24103	August	41000
March	81500	September	88000
April	153100	October	103100
May	90130	November	99000
June	201380	December	63100

Write a program which calculates the three-month moving averages, beginning with the period January–March and continuing through the period July–December as indicated in Table 2.26.

Table 2.26   Three-month moving average printout.

```
RUN

PERIØD ENDING   MARCH       AVERAGE IS    72534.333
PERIØD ENDING   APRIL       AVERAGE IS    86234.333
PERIØD ENDING   MAY         AVERAGE IS    108243.33
PERIØD ENDING   JUNE        AVERAGE IS    148203.33
PERIØD ENDING   JULY        AVERAGE IS    122436.67
PERIØD ENDING   AUGUST      AVERAGE IS    106060
PERIØD ENDING   SEPTEMBER   AVERAGE IS    68266.667
PERIØD ENDING   ØCTØBER     AVERAGE IS    77366.667
PERIØD ENDING   NØVEMBER    AVERAGE IS    96700
PERIØD ENDING   DECEMBER    AVERAGE IS    88400
```

DISCUSSION

A three-month moving average begins by calculating the average of the first three data (January, February, and March). The second average is for the data of February, March, and April. The data grouping continues to move on, one month at a time, until the period October, November, December is finally reached.

In Program 2.20 the variables M1, M2, and M3 contain the data for months 1, 2, and 3, respectively, of any given period. The program begins by reading M1 and M2 (data for January and February), and then it encounters a FØR/NEXT loop which instructs the computer to execute the intervening statements ten times (one for each period ending with months 3–12); those statements, of course, accomplish calculation of the moving averages.

Most of the statements are straightforward: line 300 causes March's data to be read; line 400 calculates the average of the three numbers; lines 600–1500 cause the computer to be diverted to the appropriate point in lines 1600–3400 to print the name of the last month in the period; line 3500 causes the average to be printed. Observe that punctuation is included after all the PRINT statements (except 3500) to suppress the line feed, thereby stringing all the printed words together on one line, even though three PRINT statements are used for each line. This avoids the need to have each month's PRINT statement contain the whole message. The alternative is to have the statements

1600 PRINT "PERIØD ENDING MARCH AVERAGE IS"; A
1700 GØ TØ 3600
1800 PRINT "PERIØD ENDING APRIL AVERAGE IS"; A

.
.
.

3400 PRINT "PERIØD ENDING DECEMBER AVERAGE IS"; A

```
100 READ M1,M2

200 FØR I=3 TØ 12
300 READ M3
400 LET A=(M1+M2+M3)/3
500 PRINT "PERIØD ENDING";

600 IF I=3 THEN 1600
700 IF I=4 THEN 1800
800 IF I=5 THEN 2000
900 IF I=6 THEN 2200
1000 IF I=7 THEN 2400
1100 IF I=8 THEN 2600
1200 IF I=9 THEN 2800
1300 IF I=10 THEN 3000
1400 IF I=11 THEN 3200
1500 IF I=12 THEN 3400

1600 PRINT "MARCH",
1700 GØ TØ 3500
1800 PRINT "APRIL",
1900 GØ TØ 3500
2000 PRINT "MAY",
2100 GØ TØ 3500
2200 PRINT "JUNE",
2300 GØ TØ 3500
2400 PRINT "JULY",
2500 GØ TØ 3500
2600 PRINT "AUGUST",
2700 GØ TØ 3500
2800 PRINT "SEPTEMBER",
2900 GØ TØ 3500
3000 PRINT "ØCTØBER",
3100 GØ TØ 3500
3200 PRINT "NØVEMBER",
3300 GØ TØ 3500
3400 PRINT "DECEMBER",

3500 PRINT "AVERAGE IS";A

3600 LET M1=M2
3700 LET M2=M3
3800 NEXT I

3900 DATA 112000,24103,81500,153100,90130,201380
4000 DATA 75800,41000,88000,103100,99000,63100
4100 END
```

Program 2.20 Three-month moving average.

The clever part of this program is lines 3600 and 3700. Before the NEXT I statement is executed and the loop is iterated, M1 is set equal to M2 (i.e., February's data), and M2 is set equal to M3 (i.e., March's data). At the beginning of the next loop M3 is given the value of April's data.

On the second iteration the "moving-up" process is repeated, and M1 = March's data, M2 = April's data, and M3 = May's data.

In this program, the relative placement of lines 300, 3600, and 3700 is important. The student should explain the reasons for the following:

■   Statement 300 is not placed near the NEXT I statement—say, at line 3750—so that all three variables are reassigned their proper values at one time, before the next iteration begins. [*Hint:* Consider the execution of line 400 on the first iteration if line 300 is moved to 3750.]

■   Statements 3600 and 3700 could not be interchanged. [*Hint:* Pretend that they are interchanged, and find the values of M1 and M2 after their execution on the first iteration.]

Example 2.12   Linear Regression

The height of twenty pairs of fathers and sons has been determined, as follows:

Pair	Father's height	Son's height	Pair	Father's height	Son's height
1	72.5	71.1	11	70.4	71.0
2	69.0	72.2	12	83.0	77.3
3	77.0	76.2	13	67.8	70.1
4	67.2	68.1	14	75.0	75.1
5	72.4	72.5	15	71.5	73.0
6	73.6	73.6	16	75.0	73.0
7	73.0	73.0	17	69.0	68.8
8	68.3	73.0	18	77.6	74.8
9	84.0	79.4	19	83.0	80.5
10	70.4	71.0	20	78.0	77.3

The data is plotted in Figure 2.16, where an approximate straight line through it is also shown. Write a program to determine the "best" such straight line by the standard method of least squares. That is, the equation of the best line is

$$Y = MX + B$$

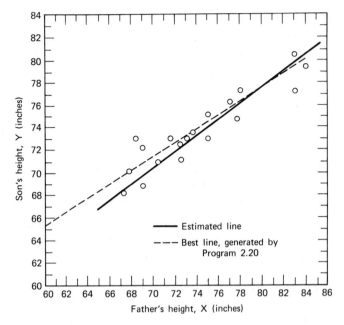

Figure 2.16 Son's height versus father's height for linear regression program.

where

$$M = \frac{(\sum YX)n - (\sum Y)(\sum X)}{(\sum X^2)n - (\sum X)(\sum X)}$$

$$B = \frac{(\sum Y)(\sum X^2) - (\sum YX)(\sum X)}{(\sum X^2)n - (\sum X)(\sum X)}$$

$$n = 20$$

$$\sum Y = Y_1 + Y_2 + Y_3 + \cdots + Y_{20}$$

$$\sum X = X_1 + X_2 + X_3 + \cdots + X_{20}$$

$$\sum YX = Y_1 X_1 + Y_2 X_2 + Y_3 X_3 + \cdots + Y_{20} X_{20}$$

$$\sum X^2 = X_1^2 + X_2^2 + X_3^2 + \cdots + X_{20}^2$$

DISCUSSION
In Program 2.21 the accumulators X1, X2, Y1, and Y2 start with a value

of zero. As the I loop is executed 20 times, (X,Y) pairs are read and the accumulations

$$X1 = \sum X \qquad X2 = \sum X^2 \qquad Y1 = \sum Y \qquad Y2 = \sum XY$$

```
100 READ N
200 LET X1=0
300 LET X2=0
400 LET Y1=0
500 LET Y2=0

600 FØR I=1 TØ N
700 READ X,Y
800 LET X1=X1+X
900 LET X2=X2+X↑2
1000 LET Y1=Y1+Y
1100 LET Y2=Y2+X*Y
1200 NEXT I
1300 PRINT "M=";(Y2*N-Y1*X1)/(X2*N-X1*X1)
1400 PRINT "B=";(Y1*X2-Y2*X1)/(X2*N-X1*X1)

1500 DATA 20
1600 DATA 72.5,71.1,  69.0,72.2,  77.0,76.2,  67.2,68.1
1700 DATA 72.4,72.5,  73.6,73.6,  73.0,73.0,  68.3,73.0
1800 DATA 84.0,79.4,  70.4,71.0,  70.4,71.0,  83.0,77.3
1900 DATA 67.8,70.1,  75.0,75.1,  71.5,73.0,  75.0,73.0
2000 DATA 69.0,68.8,  77.6,74.8,  83.0,80.5,  78.0,77.3
2100 END
 RUN

M=      .59359316
B=      29.692369
```

Program 2.21   Linear regression program.

are made. After completing all summations, the slope (M) and the Y intercept (B) may be calculated and printed (lines 1300 and 1400).

Example 2.13   A Rising Balloon

A rock is dropped from a balloon at a height of 500 ft. Thereafter the balloon rises, and the rock falls until it hits the ground. The height of the balloon increases according to $H_1 = 500 + 10t$ (ft). The rock falls until $H2 = 0$ according to $H2 = 500 - 16t^2$ (ft), after which H2 remains at zero. The distance between the balloon and the rock is $D = H1 - H2$ (ft). The rate of change of distance between the two is $R = 10 + 32t$ (ft/sec) until $H2 = 0$, and $R = 10$ (ft/sec) after $H2 = 0$. Write a program to calculate (a) the height of the balloon, (b) the height of the rock, (c) the distance between them, and (d) the rate of change of the distance for time = 0, 1, 2, 3, ... , 8 sec.

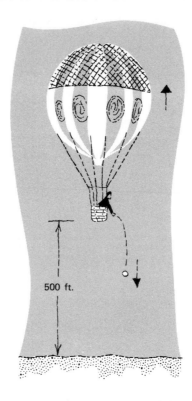

DISCUSSION

The expression for the height of the rock results in H2 being negative after about 5–6 sec. This is interpreted as "below ground" if the ground had not stopped it. Program 2.22 calculates H1 and H2, the heights of the balloon and the rock, respectively. If H2 is negative at any instant in time, its value

```
50 PRINT "TIME","BALLØØN","RØCK","DISTANCE","RATE"
60 PRINT "----","--------","----","--------","----"
70 PRINT

100 FØR T=0 TØ 8
200 LET H1=500+10*T
300 LET H2=500-16*T↑2
400 IF H2>=0 THEN 900

500 LET H2=0
600 LET D=H1
700 LET R=10
800 GØ TØ 1000
900 LET R=10+32*T
910 LET D=H1-H2

1000 PRINT T,H1,H2,D,R
1100 NEXT T
1200 END
```

Program 2.22   Program for the rising balloon problem.

Table 2.27   Printout from the rising balloon problem.

RUN

TIME	BALLOON	ROCK	DISTANCE	RATE
0	500	500	0	10
1	510	484	26	42
2	520	436	84	74
3	530	356	174	106
4	540	244	296	138
5	550	100	450	170
6	560	0	560	10
7	570	0	570	10
8	580	0	580	10

is changed to zero by the combined effect of lines 400 and 500. In a like manner, the values of D and R are calculated differently when H2 ≤ 0, i.e., the rock is on the ground, again because of line 400. The printout is shown in Table 2.27.

Example 2.14   Quadratic Equations

Write a program to solve for two values of x in

$$ax^2 + bx + c = 0$$

Use the expressions

$$x_1 = \frac{-b + \sqrt{b^2 - 4ac}}{2a} \qquad x_2 = \frac{-b - \sqrt{b^2 - 4ac}}{2a}$$

If $b^2 - 4ac < 0$, then print "SOLUTION IS IMAGINARY" instead. Use the program to solve $-2x^2 - 3x + 4 = 0$ for x.

DISCUSSION

The term $b^2 - 4ac$ must be used three times; first to decide if $b^2 - 4ac < 0$, and then once in each calculation of x_1 and x_2. To economize in Program 2.23 it is calculated only once, and assigned to the variable S. Thereafter, S is used in lieu of the more cumbersome $b^2 - 4ac$. In lines 400 and 500, raising S to the 0.5 power is equivalent to $\sqrt{S}$ and therefore to $\sqrt{b^2 - 4ac}$. Line 300 prevents execution of lines 400–700 when x is imaginary.

```
100 READ A, B, C
110 DATA -2, -3, 4

200 LET S= B↑ 2- 4*A*C
300 IF S<0 THEN 800

400 LET X1=(-B+S↑.5)/(2*A)
500 LET X2=(-B-S↑.5)/(2*A)
600 PRINT "X1=";X1, "X2=";X2
700 GØ TØ 900

800 PRINT "SØLUTIØN IS IMAGINARY"
900 END
RUN

X1=   -2.3507811          X2=     .85078106
```

Program 2.23   Quadratic equations.

Example 2.15   Binary Numbers

Write a program which will print out all binary numbers from 0000 to 1111, and their decimal (base 10) equivalent:

Binary	Decimal
0000	0
0001	1
0010	2
0011	3
0100	4
.	.
.	.
.	.
1111	15

DISCUSSION

In Program 2.24 four nested FØR/NEXT loops are used (one for each digit of the binary number). The value of each digit alternates between 0 and 1. Study the value of I, J, K, and L printed by line 600 on each iteration. Furthermore, if I, J, K, and L are the digits of the binary number, from left to right, the decimal equivalent number is

$$D = I \cdot 2^3 + J \cdot 2^2 + K \cdot 2^1 + L \cdot 2^0$$

This equation is implemented in line 500 of Program 2.24.

```
50 PRINT " I      J      K      L      D"
100 FØR I=0 TØ 1
200 FØR J=0 TØ 1
300 FØR K=0 TØ 1
400 FØR L=0 TØ 1
500 LET D=I*2↑3+J*2↑2+K*2↑1+L*2↑0
600 PRINT I;J;K;L;D
700 NEXT L
800 NEXT K
900 NEXT J
1000 NEXT I
1100 END
RUN
```

I	J	K	L	D
0	0	0	0	0
0	0	0	1	1
0	0	1	0	2
0	0	1	1	3
0	1	0	0	4
0	1	0	1	5
0	1	1	0	6
0	1	1	1	7
1	0	0	0	8
1	0	0	1	9
1	0	1	0	10
1	0	1	1	11
1	1	0	0	12
1	1	0	1	13
1	1	1	0	14
1	1	1	1	15

Program 2.24 Generating binary numbers from 0000 to 1111.

Example 2.16 Binomial Probability

Write a program which calculates the binomial probabilities

$$P = \binom{10}{x}(0.87)^x(0.13)^{10-x}$$

where

$$\binom{10}{x} = \frac{10!}{x!(10-x)!}$$

$$0! = 1$$

for $x = 0,1,2,...,10$. Also construct the total of all the Ps, which should equal one.

DISCUSSION
In Program 2.25 the parameters of the problem are treated as variables; i.e., line 1700 could have been written as

$$P = F2*(.87)\uparrow X*(.13)\uparrow(10-X)$$

where
$$F2 = \binom{10}{x}$$

Instead, variables are used for the values 0.87, 0.13, 10, and 0. Then, by making simple changes in lines 100–400, the program could be reused for another set of values in the same problem.

The quantity "ten-factorial" (i.e., $10 \cdot 9 \cdot 8 \cdots 1$) is used for all values of x. It is calculated once, at the beginning of the program (lines 500–800), and thereafter it is simply called the variable F1.

```
1 LET T=0
100 LET P1=.87
200 LET P2=.13
300 LET U=10
400 LET L=0
500 LET F1=1

600 FOR I=1 TO U
700 LET F1=F1*I
800 NEXT I

900 FOR X=L TO U
1000 LET F2=F1
1100 FOR J=1 TO X
1200 LET F2=F2/J
1300 NEXT J

1400 FOR J=1 TO U-X
1500 LET F2=F2/J
1600 NEXT J

1700 LET P=F2*P1↑X*P2↑(U-X)
1701 LET T=T+P
1800 PRINT X;P
1900 NEXT X
1999 PRINT "TOTAL =";T
2000 END
RUN

0        1.3785849E-09
1        9.2259145E-08
2        2.7784196E-06
3        4.9584104E-05
4        5.8070614E-04
5        4.663517E-03
6        2.6008076E-02
7        9.9459454E-02
8        .24960498
9        .3712074
10       .24842341
TOTAL =  1
```

Program 2.25 Generating binomial probabilities.

The x loop between lines 900 and 1900 performs the evaluation of P for each value of x. It begins by setting $F2 = F1 = 10!$; line 1200 is then executed for $J = 1,2,3,...,x$, thereby setting

$$F2 = \left(\frac{10!}{x!}\right)$$

Finally, line 1500 is evaluated for $J = 1,2,3,...,(10 - x)$, thereby setting

$$F2 = \frac{10!}{x!(10 - x)!}$$

From this point, the program is quite simple. Observe that in this example, the x loop (lines 900–1900) has *two* J loops nested within it.

■ **EXERCISES**

2.51 Program statements to fulfill the following intentions:
 (a) If $x^2 - 3x$ is negative, transfer to line 2100.
 (b) If $x^2 - 3x = 0$, transfer to line 2199.
 (c) If $x^2 - 3x$ is positive, transfer to line 3993.

2.52 Write statements to transfer as follows:

To line 1500	if $x \leqslant 0$
To line 1600	if $0 < x \leqslant 1$
To line 1700	if $1 < x \leqslant 2$
To line 1800	if $2 < x \leqslant 3$
To line 1900	if $3 > x$

2.53 A vote is taken on a certain issue and recorded in DATA as 0s and 1s: $1 = $ YES, $0 = $ NØ. As a result, 4212 1s and 0s are contained in data statements. Count the number of YES and NØ votes and print either "YES VØTES WIN" or "NØ VØTES WIN," or "TIE," as appropriate.

2.54 Alter Program 2.17 to find the *smallest* number in the list.

2.55 Read X, Y, and Z from DATA. Set S equal to the smallest of them, L equal to the largest, and M equal to the middle value.

2.56 Trace through the following program by hand, showing the printout:

```
100 LET N=7
200 LET N1=0
300 FØR I=1 TØ N
400 READ X1,X2
500 IF X1>=50 THEN 900
600 IF X2<50 THEN 900
700 LET N1=N1+1
800 PRINT X1,X2
900 NEXT I
1000 PRINT "I PRINTED";N; "PAIRS"
1100 DATA 53,16.28
1200 DATA 38.1,62.4
1300 DATA 10.13,41.08
1400 DATA 50,76.11
1500 DATA 49.9,50.1
1600 DATA 28.14,61.2
1700 DATA 28.14,50
1800 DATA 39,99
1900 END
```

[*Note:* Caution! As written, the program produces an error. Be sure to follow the program very precisely. This is a very important habit to develop.]

*2.57 A carton whose length plus girth (girth = distance around the carton) exceeds 72 inches cannot be mailed. A manufacturer has five styles of cartons whose dimensions are the following:

Style	Length (inches)	Width (inches)	Height (inches)
2044	36	$2\frac{1}{2}$	8
128	12	12	12
1611	$40\frac{1}{4}$	15	16
9021	28	9	12
4144	30	9	12

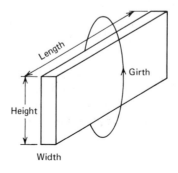

Write a program which reads the above information from data statements and prints out the style number of all boxes which cannot be mailed.

2.58   A company offers its clients a discount if their bills are paid promptly. If they are paid within 10 days, the discount is 5%; if within 30 days, 2%; and after 30 days, no discount. Several lines of data contain the following information:

AMT ⌀F BILL	DATE DUE	YEAR DUE	DATE PAID	YEAR PAID

The dates are recorded as the number of days in the year; i.e., January 1 = Day 1, December 31 = Day 365. Compute and print the bill, discount, and net from each line, and the company's total billings, total discounts, and total net.

2.59   Modify Program 2.8 so that "straight time" and "overtime" are calculated separately for each employee. All hours on Saturday, and any over eight on the other days of the week, are considered overtime.

2.60   Social Security withholding is paid at the rate of 4.8% of the first $7800 earned in a calendar year. Read, for N employees (1) the number of hours each worked this week; (2) the hourly pay rate; (3) the year-to-date earnings prior to this week. Compute and write the salary this week, withholding, net, and new year-to-date. When calculating withholding, account for the following three cases:
(a) Year-to-date exceeds $7800 before this week. Set withholdings to zero.
(b) Year-to-date plus this week's pay do not exceed $7800. The entire week's earnings are taxed.
(c) This week's wages puts them over $7800. Only that part up to $7800 is taxed.

*2.61   The DATA contains the number of checks written against, and monthly minimum balance of, several checking accounts:

Number of checks	Minimum balance ($)
3	96.00
10	112.00
23	16.00
6	422.00

Compute each entry's service charge by this rule: If minimum balance is more than $100, there is no charge. If the balance is less than $100, the charge is $0.04/check, or $0.50 minimum.

2.62 Each employee's hours and pay rate are in data statements and his salary must be computed and printed. If any employee's pay is over $400, an "*" must be printed beside his line.

*2.63 A resistor is supposed to measure 10 ± 0.2 ohms. Voltage (V) and current (I) measurements are taken on thirty resistors, from which the resistance can be calculated as R = V/I. Write a program to read data from each experiment and print

"RESISTØR # IS ØUT ØF SPEC"

if R is outside the range 9.8–10.2 ohms.

2.64 Compute y for x = −3 to 6 in increments of 0.5 by

$$y = -0.6x + 1 \quad \text{if } x < 0$$
$$y = 0.8x + 1 \quad \text{if } x \geq 0$$

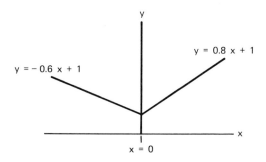

2.65 In engineering and mechanics, a step function is a variable, $u(t_1)$, which has value $u = 0$ until, say, t_1 but value $u = 1$ after that, as shown in Figure 2.17a. If u is then multiplied by another function, say, $y = (t^3/3) - 3$, as shown in Figure 2.17b, the resultant function $y = u(t_1)[(t^3/3) - 3]$, shown in Figure 2.17c, has a value $y = 0$ when $t < t_1$ and $y = (t^3/3) - 3$ when $t \geq t_1$. Compute $u(t_1)[(t^3/3)-3]$ for $t = 0,0.5,1.0,...,10$ when $t_1 = 4.5$.

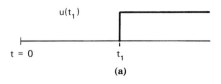

Figure 2.17

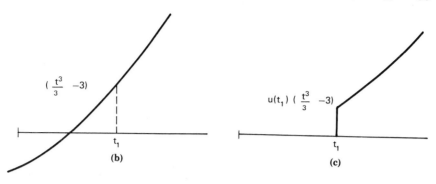

Figure 2.17   (*continued*)

2.66   Read, from DATA, x_1, x_2, and x_3. Then compute

$$y = 3x^2 + 2x - \frac{1}{\sqrt{1 + x}} \qquad \text{if } x \geqslant 0$$

$$y = 3x^2 + 2x - \frac{1}{\sqrt{1 - x}} \qquad \text{if } x < 0$$

for $x = x_1$ to x_2, in increments of x_3. At the end of the printout, print the largest value of y calculated.

2.67   Write a program to solve two simultaneous equations of the form

$$a_1 x + b_1 y = c_1$$
$$a_2 x + b_2 y = c_2$$

for x and y, where

$$x = \frac{c_1 b_2 - c_2 b_1}{a_1 b_2 - a_2 b_1} \qquad y = \frac{c_1 a_2 - c_2 a_1}{b_1 a_2 - b_2 a_1}$$

There is no solution if

$$\frac{a_1}{b_1} = \frac{a_2}{b_2}$$

Use the program to decide if the following equations have solutions, and if so, what they are:

(a) $3x + 2y = 5$ (b) $2x + 4y = 6$
     $4x - 2y = 6$ $-3x - 6y = -5$

3 PROGRAMMING HINTS

The conceptions I have summarized here I first put forward only tentatively, but in the course of time they have won such a hold over me that I can no longer think in any other way.

—*Sigmund Freud*

A number of programming statements were introduced in Chapter 2, and their meanings to the computer are fairly easy to comprehend. Several examples were also given, in a rather "cookbook" fashion, to show applications of those statements. But more is required; the student will probably not often need to program problems exactly like those described in this book. He must, therefore, develop a degree of intuition for formulating his own problems, and creativity in translating them into coherent and logical computer statements.

In all things, such intuitive and creative thought processes are difficult to teach. However, this chapter will offer the student some guidelines for developing self-sufficiency in programming.

3.1 PRACTICE AND EXPERIMENT

Practice and experimentation are keys to the mastery of programming. The new programmer should capitalize on every opportunity to practice, to discover, and to retain the innuendos and tricks of formulating and constructing programs. He should begin with simple problems and then continually attack others which are a bit beyond his current capability. In this sense, the particular problems are not important. In fact, if they are a bit zany—doing odd or clever things—they can be more challenging, enjoyable, and educational.

3.2 FLOWCHARTS

Most programs are long and moderately complicated—perhaps comprised of hundreds of lines and dozens of tasks, decisions, and loops. To manage such a formidable aggregate of details simultaneously is a task which stretches the capability of the average human mind! Actually, there is no need to contend with all the details simultaneously. All programs can be reduced to a group of smaller, manageable, parts or modules comprised of 10–20 statements which are created more or less independently but which are all eventually fitted together into the final product. Furthermore, these modules can be represented in very general terms on a **flowchart**, or a pictorial diagram which allows the programmer to organize his overall programming strategy. Flowcharts are simply pictorial displays of the sequence of operations and the logic of a computer program. In the context discussed here, they are formulated before actually writing the program to assist the programmer in clarifying his mental image of the program.

An example flowchart, which is really too simple to have any practical value, is shown in Figure 3.1. Observe that it is composed of several boxes, each representing some particular computer activity as described therein,

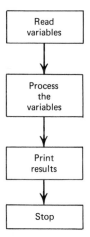

Figure 3.1 A simple flowchart.

and arrows to designate the logical progression of the program; i.e., from READ to STØP. The boxes and arrows are called flowcharting **symbols**. There are many symbols in common usage but only two, other than those shown, are of importance here. They are the diamond and circular shapes shown and described in Figure 3.2.

Example 3.1   A Flowchart

Five hundred positive and negative numbers are randomly arranged in DATA statements. Compose a flowchart to depict a program which will count the number of positive values in the data.

DISCUSSION

Each of the 500 data statements must be read and analyzed to determine if it is positive or negative. Whenever one is positive, the computer should execute a counting statement of the form "LET C = C + 1."

Study Figure 3.3a. Proceeding from the top of the diagram, the variable C

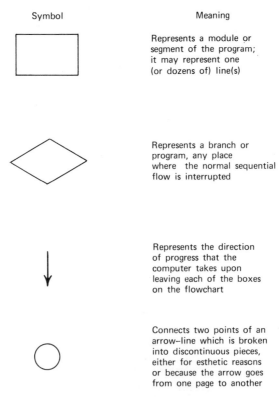

Symbol	Meaning
	Represents a module or segment of the program; it may represent one (or dozens of) line(s)
	Represents a branch or program, any place where the normal sequential flow is interrupted
	Represents the direction of progress that the computer takes upon leaving each of the boxes on the flowchart
	Connects two points of an arrow-line which is broken into discontinuous pieces, either for esthetic reasons or because the arrow goes from one page to another

Figure 3.2   Flowcharting symbols

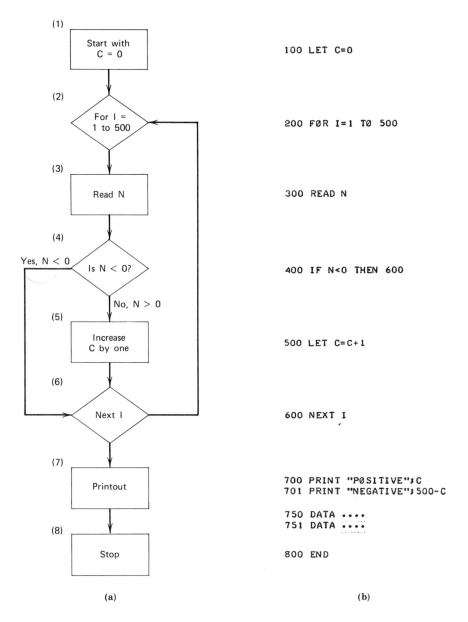

(1) Start with C = 0 — 100 LET C=0

(2) For I = 1 to 500 — 200 FØR I=1 TØ 500

(3) Read N — 300 READ N

(4) Is N < 0? — 400 IF N<0 THEN 600
Yes, N < 0
No, N > 0

(5) Increase C by one — 500 LET C=C+1

(6) Next I — 600 NEXT I

(7) Printout — 700 PRINT "PØSITIVE"; C
701 PRINT "NEGATIVE"; 500-C

750 DATA ....
751 DATA ....

(8) Stop — 800 END

(a)   (b)

Figure 3.3 A flowchart and the corresponding program for counting positive numbers from the data.

is set equal to zero, to give it an initial value for use later in box 5. Next an I loop is established so that the intervening statements may be repeated 500 times, i.e., once for each data item. Inside the loop, a data value is read and a check is made to determine if the number is negative (box 4); if so, the computer must bypass the counting statement and go on to the NEXT I statement, iterating the loop with a new data item. If the value is positive, the computer must pass to box 5, where C is incremented. When the computer arrives at box 7, then, the value of C corresponds to the number of positive values found in the data.

TRANSLATING A FLOWCHART INTO A PROGRAM

The flowchart of Figure 3.3a is quite lucid in its presentation of the logic of the program required to accomplish the subject problem, but there is a bonus. There is a direct correlation between each box in the diagram and the programming statements required to accomplish it, as shown in Figure 3.3b. Every box is precisely and simply transformable into one or two BASIC statements, completing the program.

The level of detail of a flowchart is the personal prerogative of the programmer. It is usually preferable to arrange the boxes into modules of 10–20 statements each, with only a few of them—particularly decision points—representing smaller groups of statements. Of course, Example 3.1 is such a simple problem that small groups for each box are almost unavoidable.

It is sometimes convenient to draw a simple flowchart to describe the overall program and then, on another sheet of paper, expand certain of the boxes into more detailed presentations if they are elaborate or tricky, or if they involve several loops and branches.

3.3 LEARN TO "THINK" LIKE THE COMPUTER

The programmer must always bear in mind that the innate ability of the computer to contemplate, reason, infer, presume, and research for additional data is critically limited. The most common mistake the new programmer makes is to presume that the computer will automatically do the same thing he would if he had the same job to do, and the same program by which to do it. As testimony to this claim, the author has observed numerous programs which appear completely reasonable to their novice creators but, even by a casual review, are a shambles to a more seasoned programmer; the computer could not possibly produce correct answers. Yet if the programmer is asked to produce the answers manually by following the instructions he can usually do so. The fact that he can, while the computer cannot, dismays him.

Invariably, the problem in these cases is that the student fails, in fact, to obey the programmed instructions in the same precise and meticulous manner as the computer must. Instead, he capitalizes on the ability of the human mind to organize all the instructions at once, understand the program's objectives, and assimilate miscellaneous background information into a coherent approach, regardless of how muddled they may be arranged before him. Sometimes he even draws on outside knowledge from his own experience or he brushes lightly over the individual steps which get him to the final results.

The computer can do none of these things. Its only knowledge and capabilities are those specifically given it by the grace of the programmer. So, the most common mistake is failure to adopt the same cold, unemotional obedience to the program that the computer must. The human must learn to think just like the computer *does not* think.

A simple example illustrates the errors made by a typical beginner. A student was asked to write a program to produce the squares of the numbers from 1 to 5 in the output of Figure 3.4. He wrote Program 3.1 which, of course, produced the results shown in Figure 3.5. When asked to explain the logic of the program he replied "First, the computer should print the

```
RUN

A          A-SQUARED
1          1
2          4
3          9
4          16
5          25
```

Figure 3.4   Desired printout.

```
100 PRINT "A          A-SQUARED"
200 FØR A=1 TØ 5
300 LET X=A↑2
400 NEXT A
500 PRINT A
600 PRINT X
700 END
```

Program 3.1   A student's attempt to produce Figure 3.4.

```
RUN

A          A-SQUARED
5
25
```

Figure 3.5   The erroneous output from Program 3.1.

table heading. Then it should set A = 1, 2, 3, 4, and 5, and set X equal to the square of all those numbers. Finally, in lines 500 and 600, it should print out those As and Xs."

But that is not what the computer did. The programmer obviously missed the essential nature of the computer's operation, overlooking the fact that it has no idea of what it is *supposed* to do, and can do only what it is *told* to do. The way to avoid this error is to trace through the program by hand, being extremely careful to obey exactly each individual instruction given as it occurs, never succumbing to the temptation to look forward or backward in the program or violating any instruction in even the smallest detail. Had the programmer taken a sheet of paper in hand, imagined himself as the computer, and proceeded through the program in this manner, he might have produced Figure 3.6. When the program told him to PRINT, he would have printed, as shown on the right side of Figure 3.6. Every time the program told him to "NEXT A" or "LET X=," he would have obediently reset A or X as instructed, forgetting whatever he was previously told about the values of those variables, as symbolically represented by crossing out (or erasing) expired values of A and X in Figure 3.6. When he

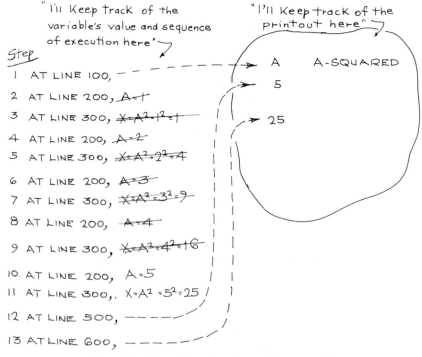

Figure 3.6 Manually tracing through Program 3.1.

finally arrived at line 500 he would have printed the only value of A he had left—the last one—and, just as the computer would, he would have begun the printout from line 600 on a new line.

Now that the programmer has followed the program and produced the same errors the computer did, he is allowed to put on his "thinking cap" and realize he had not printed each value of A and X as they became available to him, and that two PRINT statements caused A and X^2 to be placed on two different lines rather than adjacent to each other. Then he might have changed the program as shown in Program 3.2.

Admittedly, writing down each step and calculation that the computer makes can become quite tedious as one develops proficiency and writes longer and longer programs. The student will probably soon give up the practice, but even the most experienced programmer mentally goes through the same exercise, keeping in mind those lessons learned by the more tedious procedures. Once in a while, on particularly difficult problems, he may still have to resort to the manual method.

```
100 PRINT "A       A-SQUARED"
200 FØR A=1 TØ 5
300 LET X=A↑2
400 PRINT A;X
500 NEXT A
600 END
```

Program 3.2   Corrected version of Program 3.1.

■ EXERCISES

3.1   Compose flowcharts representing Program 2.15 and your solution to Exercises 2.60 and/or 2.65.

*3.2   Compose a flowchart for the following problem and then write the program accordingly: Read the sales and expenses of the company from DATA. Calculate profit as sales − expenses. Calculate the company's tax by this rule: If profit is \$25,000 or less, the tax is 30% of profit; if profit is greater than \$25,000, the tax is 30% of \$25,000 plus 52% on the profit above \$25,000; if profit is negative (i.e., expenses are greater than sales), the tax is zero. Print profit, effective tax rate (total tax/profit), and net tax.

3.3   Compose a flowchart for the following problem and then write the program accordingly: There are an unknown number of lines of data, each containing two values which are read as X and Y. The last data line contains 0,0. Count the number of pairs which have $X > Y$, $X = Y$, $X < Y$. Determine the average amount by which X exceeds Y, or Y exceeds X in the first and last cases, respectively.

3.4 One method of finding the area between X = 0 and X = 2 under the curve Y = 4 − X² in Figure 3.7 is known as *Simpson's rule.* Divide the X interval into an even number of segments (say 10) and number each point as follows:

$$\text{Point } 0, \quad X = 0$$
$$\text{Point } 1, \quad X = 0.2$$
$$\text{Point } 2, \quad X = 0.4$$

. .

. .

. .

$$\text{Point } 10, \quad X = 2.0$$

Determine Y_0, Y_1, Y_2, ... , Y_{10} corresponding to each X. The approximate area, then, is

$$A = \frac{h}{3}(Y_0 + 4Y_1 + 2Y_2 + 4Y_3 + 2Y_4 + 4Y_5 + 2Y_6 + 4Y_7$$
$$+ 2Y_8 + 4Y_9 + Y_{10})$$

where h = 0.2. Draw a flowchart representing a program to apply Simpson's rule to the above problem. Write the program. [*Hint:* An accumulator should be used to add the terms in parentheses; if i = 0,10, the term Y_i is multiplied by one; if i = 1, 3, ... , 9 (i.e., odd), the term Y_i is multiplied by four; and if i = 2, 4, ... , 8 (i.e., even), the term Y_i is multiplied by two.]

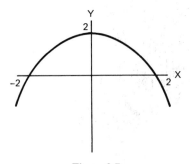

Figure 3.7

*3.5 Businesses often value their inventory by rather complex rules. Draw a flow chart and write a program which reads the following data: inventory number, number of units on hand, selling price, cost, normal profit, replacement value, and completion cost. Print these quantities:

inventory number, in-inventory value and writedown on each item, and total value and writedown on all items combined. Use the following rules:

■   Determine a market value, as follows:

(a) Calculate "net realizable value," V = selling price minus completion cost.

(b) Calculate X = net realizable value minus normal profit.

(c) If replacement value lies between V and X, the market value is set equal to the replacement value.

(d) If replacement value exceeds V, market value is set equal to V.

(e) If replacement value is less than X, market value is set equal to X.

■   The per-unit value is the lower of market value and cost. The in-inventory value is the per-unit value times the number of units on hand.

■   If the per-unit value is reduced from cost to market value, the reduction in in-inventory value is termed the writedown; otherwise the writedown is set equal to zero.

3.4   A BAG OF TRICKS

Consciously develop a standard bag of tricks. All programmers have favorite little gimmicks which they find peculiarly applicable to a wide variety of problems. Is part of a program required to find the employee with the highest gross salary this year? The highest point in a rocket's trajectory? The tallest person? Then, figuratively speaking, reach into your bag of favorite tricks and pull out Example 2.8,* for it works for all these jobs. Change the "<" in Example 2.8 to ">," and use it for finding the shortest person.

Does another part of the program require ascertaining whether a given number is even or odd? Then dig into the bag and find Example 2.6. Use it as a small part of the larger program.

There are many similarities among various kinds of programs. The programmer would be well-advised to absorb the techniques he uses for one program and retain them for use on future programs, so it will not be necessary to reinvent the technique each time. This is not meant to imply that the bag can be so extensive that it will solve all facets of every program. Far from it. It is always necessary to invent new techniques for complex problems, but standard tricks can simplify the overall task.

*The program which finds the largest of a group of numbers.

This section will discuss a number of convenient and frequently used tricks. As new statements are learned in subsequent chapters, they will lead to more. All the tricks mentioned in this book do not nearly cover those that the student can eventually develop for himself.

ACCUMULATORS

The accumulator is, in the author's opinion, the most important single trick in computer programming. There are several variations, some of which have been discussed earlier but still deserve closer examination here.

The Adding Accumulator

An adding accumulator is one which constructs the summation of several numeric values in a piecemeal fashion. It is used when all the summed elements are not in the computer's memory (i.e., are not assigned to a variable) at any one instant when the computer should perform the summation. A typical adding accumulator is illustrated in Program 3.3. The accumulator has three components: the line which performs the summation (line 500); a mechanism for varying the value of X in preparation for each execution of the accumulating statement (in this case the READ and I loop); and a statement giving the variable T an initial value.

Program 3.4 expands the concept a bit, the summed terms being more complex. In this case the value of T, after exiting from the loop, is

$$T = \left(0 - \frac{1^2}{4}\right) + \left(2 - \frac{3^2}{4}\right) + \left(0 - \frac{1^2}{4}\right) + \left(1 - \frac{1^2}{4}\right)$$

All examples of the adding accumulator shown so far have the initial value set to zero. Consider now the following problem: A bank account begins with $10,920 in it, and then has deposits of $3120.09, $614.11, $1210.82, and $88.63 made to it. What is the value of the account afterward? Program 3.5 solves this problem by reading T in line 100 thereby giving it an initial value of $10,920, rather than zero, before entering the loop.

```
100 LET T=0
200 LET N=6
300 FØR I=1 TØ N
400 READ X
500 LET T=T+X
600 NEXT I
650 PRINT "TØTAL IS ";T
700 DATA 3,2,1,0,1,2
800 END
   RUN

TØTAL IS      9
```

Program 3.3   An adding accumulator.

```
100 LET T=0
200 LET N=4
300 FOR I=1 TO N
400 READ X,Y
500 LET T=T+(Y-X↑2/N)
600 NEXT I
650 PRINT "TOTAL IS ";T
700 DATA 1,0,2,3,1,0,1,1
800 END
RUN
```

```
TOTAL IS     2.25
```

Program 3.4 A more sophisticated adding accumulator.

```
100 READ T
200 LET N=4
300 FOR I=1 TO N
400 READ X
500 LET T=T+X
600 NEXT I
610 PRINT "CURRENT BALANCE =";T
700 DATA 10920.00,3120.09,614.11,1210.82,88.63
800 END
RUN
```

```
CURRENT BALANCE =     15953.65
```

Program 3.5 An adding accumulator with a nonzero initial value.

The Subtracting Accumulator

Obviously, a subtracting accumulator can be constructed by simply writing a statement like

$$\text{LET } T = T - X$$

For example, suppose a bank teller begins the day with $50,000 cash, and then dispenses the following amounts during the day: $123.10, $6144.82 and $13,800. Program 3.6 determines the amount the teller has on hand at the end of the day by initializing C to $50,000 and then subtracting one payout at a time from it.

The Multiplier

It is sometimes necessary, particularly in engineering and mathematical applications, to accumulate the product of a series of numbers. For example, if the probabilities of three events occurring are

Event 1	A flipped coin comes up heads, $P = 0.5$
Event 2	A rolled die comes up 3, $P = 0.1667$
Event 3	A ball drawn from an urn is red, $P = 0.2$

```
100 READ C
200 FØR I=1 TØ 3
300 READ P
400 LET C=C-P
500 NEXT I
600 PRINT "CASH ØN HAND AT END ØF DAY";C
700 DATA 50000,123.10,6144.82,13800
800 END
RUN
```

CASH ØN HAND AT END ØF DAY   29932.08

Program 3.6   A subtracting accumulator.

then the probability that, in one experiment, all three events happen simultaneously is

$$P_{all\ three} = P_{heads} \times P_3 \times P_{red}$$
$$= 0.5 \times 0.1667 \times 0.2$$
$$= 0.01667$$

Program 3.7 reads three appropriate data items and multiplies them together. Make this important observation: Unlike the previous accumulators, this one starts with an initial value of 1; multiplying (or dividing) accumulators should not start with zero. Why not?

The Divider

A dividing accumulator can be devised in much the same manner as the previous accumulator. For example, a program to determine the value

$$V = \frac{1}{1 \times 2 \times 3 \times 4 \times 5 \times 6}$$

is shown in Program 3.8.

```
100 LET P=1
200 LET N=3
300 FØR I=1 TØ N
400 READ X
500 LET P=P*X
600 NEXT I
610 PRINT "PRØDUCT =";P
700 DATA .5,.1667,.2
800 END
RUN
```

PRØDUCT =   1.667E-02

Program 3.7   A multiplying accumulator.

```
100 LET V=1
200 LET N=6
300 FØR I=1 TØ N
400 LET V=V/I
500 NEXT I
600 PRINT "VALUE ="JV
700 END
RUN

VALUE =    1.3883889E-03
```

Program 3.8 A dividing accumulator.

COUNTERS

Counters are a special variety of accumulator in that they simply "accumulate" a fixed value on each execution:

$$100 \quad \text{LET} \quad C = C + 1$$

or

$$200 \quad \text{LET} \quad X = X + 2$$

The first statement above counts by one; the last, by two. It may be strategically placed in a program so that, in fact, it is executed once each time a particular point is passed. The counting variable, C or X, can start the program with any appropriate value. It usually starts with zero, but not necessarily so. Furthermore, a counter may start with some value (for example, to represent the number of can openers in inventory) and then count downward every time one is sold. Such a counter would be constructed as 100 LET $C = C - 1$.

Example 3.2   A Resettable Counter

Write a program which prints the sequence of days of the week, beginning with Wednesday and continuing for fourteen consecutive days.

DISCUSSION

In Program 3.9 each weekday is given in a separate print statement. The variable D (for day) begins at four, to represent Wednesday. Lines 300–900 route the computer to the appropriate printout. Afterward, line 2300 increments D so that the next day is printed on the succeeding iterations. The process repeats until $D = 8$. There being no eighth day of the week (instead the eighth day restarts the week with Sunday), lines 2400 and 2500 act together to reset D to value one whenever it reaches eight. Then the succeeding iteration begins a new week, as required.

```
100 LET D=4
200 FØR I=1 TØ 14
300 IF D=1 THEN 1000
400 IF D=2 THEN 1200
500 IF D=3 THEN 1400
600 IF D=4 THEN 1600
700 IF D=5 THEN 1800
800 IF D=6 THEN 2000
900 IF D=7 THEN 2200

1000 PRINT "SUNDAY"
1100 GØ TØ 2300
1200 PRINT "MØNDAY"
1300 GØ TØ 2300
1400 PRINT "TUESDAY"
1500 GØ TØ 2300
1600 PRINT "WEDNESDAY"
1700 GØ TØ 2300
1800 PRINT "THURSDAY"
1900 GØ TØ 2300
2000 PRINT "FRIDAY"
2100 GØ TØ 2300
2200 PRINT "SATURDAY"

2300 LET D=D+1
2400 IF D<8 THEN 2600
2500 LET D=1
2600 NEXT I
2700 END
RUN

WEDNESDAY
THURSDAY
FRIDAY
SATURDAY
SUNDAY
MØNDAY
TUESDAY
WEDNESDAY
THURSDAY
FRIDAY
SATURDAY
SUNDAY
MØNDAY
TUESDAY
```

Program 3.9 A resettable counter designed to count off days of the week.

ITERATIVE TECHNIQUES

A variety of problems require that the computer make some calculation to arrive at the value of a variable, make some sort of check to determine the acceptability of the value, and if the answer is unacceptable, repeat (or iterate) the calculations with a prescribed, controlled change in the conditions, thus looking for a "correct" answer. Example 3.3 illustrates this procedure.

Example 3.3   Percent Return on an Investment

A company has $100,000 to invest, and wishes to receive at least $56,000 return after five years. The total value of the investment at that time will be $156,000. The equation

$$P = \left(1 + \frac{I}{4}\right)^{(4*5)} 100,000$$

determines the value, P, of the $100,000 if it is invested at an annual interest rate I, compounded quarterly. Using it, write a program which "finds" the value of I required.

DISCUSSION
Although there is a more direct way to solve this problem, the following method illustrates the iterative technique being discussed: Begin by setting I = 0.01 and calculating P accordingly (lines 200–300, Program 3.10). If a satisfactory value is not attained (i.e., if P is not at least $156,000), the computer must be returned to line 200 and the process repeated with I increased by 0.01.

USE OF NUMBERS TO REPRESENT WORDS

It is common practice to use numbers as codes for words, names, and other alphabetic phrases. This sometimes eliminates a lot of unnecessary statements. For example, referring back to the Payroll Journal Program of Program 2.13, suppose that each employee were assigned a number, Table 3.1 (as indeed they are in most companies).

Now the DATA of Program 2.13 may be rewritten; the original lines 3410, 10000–10005, 20000–20011 of the program may be eliminated, and lines 3100, 3400, and 6000–6500 may be modified in Program 3.11, with the resultant output shown in Table 3.2.

The author suggests that this is a convenient point to look up Section 6.1

```
100 LET I=0
200 LET I=I+.01
300 LET P=(1+I/4)↑(20)*100000
400 IF P<156000 THEN 200
500 PRINT "REQUIRED INTEREST RATE =";I*100;" PERCENT"
600 END
    RUN

REQUIRED INTEREST RATE =     9     PERCENT
```

Program 3.10   Iteration technique for finding acceptable interest rate.

Table 3.1 Employee's numbers.

Number	Name
40312	ADAMS,JIM
08140	SMITH,SAM
31402	BARNETT,MIKE
12440	BARNETT,DEBØRAH
21443	RØBERTS,CLIFF
41102	JØNES,ALVIN

```
        •
        •
        •
1700 PRINT
1800 PRINT " ","HØURS"
1900 PRINT "EMPLØYEE","WØRKED","SALARY","DEDUCTIØNS","NET"
2000 PRINT "--------","------","------","----------","---"
2100 PRINT

2200 LET H9=0
2300 LET S9=0
2400 LET D9=0
2500 LET N9=0

2999 LET N=6
3000 FØR I=1 TØ N
3100 READ N1,H,R,T
3200 LET S=H*R
3300 LET D=T*S
3400 PRINT N1,H,S,D,S-D
3500 LET H9=H9+H
3600 LET S9=S9+S
3700 LET D9=D9+D
3800 LET N9=N9+(S-D)
4000 NEXT I

5800 PRINT " ","--------","---------","---------","---------"
5900 PRINT "TØTAL",H9,"$";S9,"$";D9,"$";N9

6000 DATA 40312,40,3.32,.103
6100 DATA 08140,42,5.25,.172
6200 DATA 31402,38,4.28,.145
6300 DATA 12440,40,2.13,.085
6400 DATA 21443,40,6.28,.18
6500 DATA 41102,41.5,5.03,.163
6800 END
```

Program 3.11 Using employee numbers rather than names.

Table 3.2 Printout from Program 3.11.

PAYRØLL JØURNAL
FØR
WIDGET-GIDGET MFG. CØ.

JANUARY 10, 1971

- - -

EMPLØYEE	HØURS WØRKED	SALARY	DEDUCTIØNS	NET
--------	------	------	----------	---
40312	40	132.8	13.6784	119.1216
8140	42	220.5	37.926	182.574
31402	38	162.64	23.5828	139.0572
12440	40	85.2	7.242	77.958
21443	40	251.2	45.216	205.984
41102	41.5	208.745	34.025435	174.71957
	--------	----------	----------	----------
TØTAL	241.5	$ 1061.085	$ 161.67063	$ 899.41436

to discover string variables, which may offer even more convenience than the numerical substitution discussed here.

Example 3.4 Geometrical Shapes

For another example of coded entries, write a program which will accept, as data, the measurements on eight physical objects and calculate their volume from one of the equations shown in Figure 3.8. The data is to be presented to the computer in the order shown in Table 3.3.

DISCUSSION

The data is actually given the computer as shown in Program 3.12. The first entry in each DATA line is a numerical code to indicate the shape of the object: code 1 = brick, code 2 = cone, etc. A flowchart, exploiting the presence of this code, is given in Figure 3.9. Observe that the code, C1, is read from DATA, and then used in IF...THEN... statements to route the computer to an appropriate equation. From there, the program is self-explanatory.

Code	Volume	Illustration	Code	Volume	Illustration

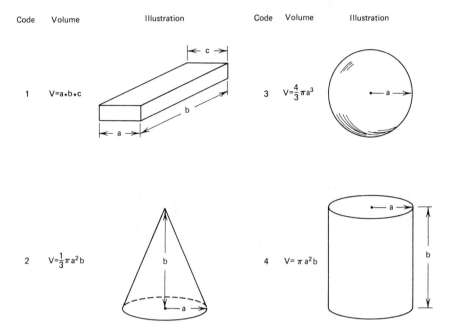

| 1 | $V = a*b*c$ | | 3 | $V = \frac{4}{3}\pi a^3$ | |
| 2 | $V = \frac{1}{3}\pi a^2 b$ | | 4 | $V = \pi a^2 b$ | |

Figure 3.8 Geometrical objects and their volume equations.

Table 3.3 Data for Example 3.4.

Object	A	B	C
Brick	5	6	3
Brick	5	3	8
Cylinder	10	6	0
Cone	1	1	0
Cylinder	3	2	0
Sphere	6	0	0
Sphere	4	0	0
Brick	6	1	1

PROGRAMMED ERROR DETECTION

Suppose the data in Example 3.4 were erroneously entered in some way. For simplicity, suppose that the person using the program misunderstood and added a data item with code 5 (admittedly an unlikely event in this case, but a serviceable one for discussion).

```
  50 PRINT "NUMBER", "SHAPE", "VØLUME"
 100 READ N
 200 FØR I=1 TØ N

 300 READ C1, A, B, C
 400 IF C1=1 THEN 1300
 500 IF C1=2 THEN 1100
 600 IF C1=3 THEN 900

 700 LET V=3.1416*A↑2*B
 800 GØ TØ 1500
 900 LET V=4*3.1416*A↑3/3
1000 GØ TØ 1500
1100 LET V=3.1416*A↑2*B/3
1200 GØ TØ 1500
1300 LET V=A*B*C
1400 GØ TØ 1500

1500 PRINT I, C1, V
1600 NEXT I

1700 DATA 8
1800 DATA 1, 5, 6, 3
1900 DATA 1, 5, 3, 8
2000 DATA 4, 10, 6, 0
2100 DATA 2, 1, 1, 0
2200 DATA 4, 3, 2, 0
2300 DATA 3, 6, 0, 0
2400 DATA 3, 4, 0, 0
2500 DATA 1, 6, 1, 1
2600 END
  RUN
```

NUMBER	SHAPE	VØLUME
1	1	90
2	1	120
3	4	1884.96
4	2	1.0472
5	4	56.5488
6	3	904.7808
7	3	268.0832
8	1	6

Program 3.12   Using a numerical code for selected shapes in Example 3.4.

Review the flowchart in Figure 3.9 and recognize that if $C1 = 5$, the computer will employ the equations relating to cylinders. Unless the five is a simple typing error, substituted for a four, the computer produces an erroneous result. By simply adding a decision point to specifically route the computer to line 700 when $C1 = 4$ (Fig. 3.10 and Program 3.13) it becomes impossible for the computer to advance to the PRINT in line 620 if $C = 1, 2, 3, 4$. Any other (illegal) value of C will result in the error message being printed. This technique is often used to prevent execution of errors in the data.

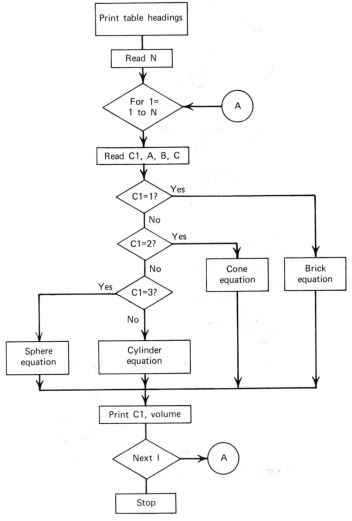

Figure 3.9 Flowchart for the problem of geometrical shapes.

USE OF "FILLING" DATA

Program 3.13 illustrates another standard "trick." Observe that the data for all bricks must contain, besides the coded number designating the shape, three dimensions of the brick (A, B, and C). Therefore the computer must read three variables (line 300). Now note that the cylindrical and cone shapes only utilize two variables, A and B. The sphere utilizes only one, A.

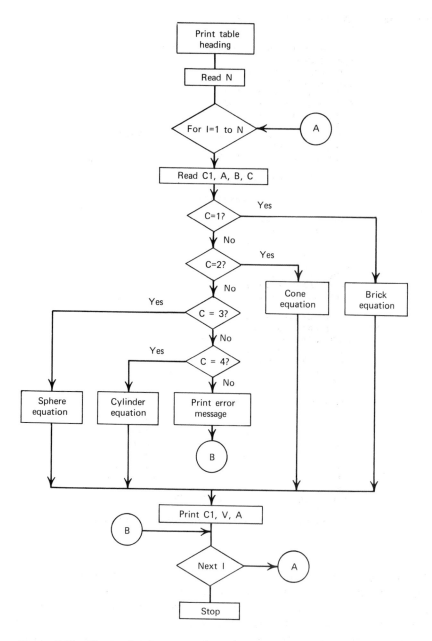

Figure 3.10 Change in the geometrical shapes flowchart to protect against inadvertent error in the data.

```
 50 PRINT "NUMBER", "SHAPE", "VØLUME"
100 READ N
200 FØR I=1 TØ N
300 READ C1,A,B,C
400 IF C1=1 THEN 1300
500 IF C1=2 THEN 1100
600 IF C1=3 THEN 900
610 IF C1=4 THEN 700
620 PRINT "THE CØDE ";C1;" IS NØT VALID"
630 GØ TØ 1600
700 LET V=3.1416*A↑2*B
800 GØ TØ 1500
900 LET V=4*3.1416*A↑3/3
1000 GØ TØ 1500
1100 LET V=3.1416*A↑2*B/3
1200 GØ TØ 1500
1300 LET V=A*B*C
1400 GØ TØ 1500
1500 PRINT I,C1,V
1600 NEXT I
1700 DATA 9
1800 DATA 1,5,6,3
1900 DATA 1,5,3,8
2000 DATA 4,10,6,0
2100 DATA 2,1,1,0
2200 DATA 4,3,2,0
2300 DATA 3,6,0,0
2400 DATA 3,4,0,0
2500 DATA 1,6,1,1
2600 DATA 5,3,3,3
2700 END
RUN
```

NUMBER	SHAPE	VØLUME
1	1	90
2	1	120
3	4	1884.96
4	2	1.0472
5	4	56.5488
6	3	904.7808
7	3	268.0832
8	1	6

THE CØDE   5   IS NØT VALID

Program 3.13 Automatic error detection in Example 3.4.

However, one READ statement is used for reading all shapes, and the computer will thus attempt to read three values, whether three are given in the DATA or not. Therefore it behooves the programmer to add sufficient filling data (in this case the extra zeros in many of the lines) to give the computer something to READ as C when it is processing the cylinder or cone, or to read as B and C when it is processing the sphere.

An alternate strategy is to arrange several READ statements so that the number of dimensions actually read is three when $C1 = 1$, two when $C1 = 2$ or $C1 = 4$, and one when $C1 = 3$. That can obviously be done as shown in Program 3.14. Only N1 is read at first, and the transfer is made to the appropriate shape equations. At that point, the statements

1300	READ A,B,C
1100	READ A,B
900	READ A
700	READ A,B

are added, causing the computer to read the correct number of dimensions, no more and no less, for each shape. Then the extra zeros in lines 1800–2600 are deleted.

```
  50 PRINT "NUMBER", "SHAPE", "VØLUME"
 100 READ N
 200 FØR I=1 TØ N

 300 READ C1
 400 IF C1=1 THEN 1300
 500 IF C1=2 THEN 1100
 600 IF C1=3 THEN 900
 610 IF C1=4 THEN 700

 700 READ A,B
 701 LET V=3.1416*A↑2*B
 800 GØ TØ 1500

 900 READ A
 901 LET V=4*(3.1416)*A↑3/3
1000 GØ TØ 1500

1100 READ A,B
1101 LET V=3.1416*A↑2*B/3
1200 GØ TØ 1500

1300 READ A,B,C
1301 LET V=A*B*C
1400 GØ TØ 1500

1500 PRINT I,C1,V
1600 NEXT I
1700 DATA 8
1800 DATA 1,5,6,3
1900 DATA 1,5,3,8
2000 DATA 4,10,6
2100 DATA 2,1,1
2200 DATA 4,3,2
2300 DATA 3,6
2400 DATA 3,4
2500 DATA 1,6,1,1
2600 END
```

Program 3.14 Eliminating "filling zeros" from Program 3.13.

RECOGNIZING THE END OF DATA

If there are a certain number of data entries, the computer must be told how many items there are so that it does, in fact, read them all, but does not try to read too many. There are two conventional ways of so instructing the computer. One is to count the number of read statements required (say, N), and give the computer a statement like FØR I = 1 TØ N. This is what was done in Program 3.14.

But if, for any reason at all, it is inconvenient to manually count the number of READ statements required, an alternate method is to put a phony value at the end of the data—one which is known in advance to be an impossible legitimate datum. Then the computer can READ an entry and immediately check to see if it is the phony one. If not, it can process it in the normal fashion and return for more data. But if it is the appropriate value, it can detect that the reading and processing should be terminated. The example below illustrates this method.

Example 3.5   Detecting the End of the Data in the Payroll Journal Program

Suppose that the Payroll Journal Program (starting from the version in Program 3.11) contains data for hundreds of employees, and the operator cannot be burdened with counting them each week when the program is run. Then the statements

```
2999     LET  N=6
3000     FØR  I=1 TØ  N
                 .

                 .

                 .

4000     NEXT  I
```

in Program 3.11 cannot be employed. Modify the program so that the computer detects the end of the data by itself.

DISCUSSION

It seems reasonably safe to assume that no employee will ever be assigned the employee number "0." Therefore, that value can be used as the cue that no more data is available—in Program 3.15, the line 99998 DATA 0,0,0,0 is added at the end.

The FØR/NEXT loop in lines 2999, 3000, and 4000 in Program 3.11 must be removed from Program 3.15 because the upper limit of the loop index is not available to the computer. In their place, lines 3110 and 4000 are added. Now, the computer will read the first line of data. Since N1 of

```
                  .
                  .
                  .
1800  PRINT " ","HØURS"
1900  PRINT "EMPLØYEE","WØRKED","SALARY","DEDUCTIØNS","NET"
2000  PRINT "--------","-------","-------","-----------","---"
2100  PRINT

2200  LET H9=0
2300  LET S9=0
2400  LET D9=0
2500  LET N9=0

3100  READ N1,H,R,T
3110  IF N1=0 THEN 5800
3200  LET S=H*R
3300  LET D=T*S
3400  PRINT N1,H,S,D,S-D
3500  LET H9=H9+H
3600  LET S9=S9+S
3700  LET D9=D9+D
3800  LET N9=N9+(S-D)
4000  GØ TØ 3100
5800  PRINT " ","--------","----------","----------","----------"
5900  PRINT "TØTAL",H9,"$";S9,"$";D9,"$";N9

6000  DATA 40312,40,3.32,.103
                  .
                  .
                  .
6500  DATA 41102,41.5,5.03,.163
99998 DATA 0,0,0,0
99999 END
```

Program 3.15   Program self-detects the end of the DATA.

that line is not zero, the computer will continue to line 3200 and begin processing that employee's data. The GØ TØ... statement in line 4000 will return the computer to READ another line of data. Again, N1 is not zero, so again the data will be processed. This procedure continues until all the "legitimate" data has been consumed. Eventually, though, the computer reads the last line of data, i.e., the phony data, where N1 = 0. This prompts the computer to stop repeating the regime, since line 3110 directs it to line 5800 and the printout.

STEP FUNCTIONS

Step functions often occur in engineering, payroll, billing, and taxation problems. They are characterized by the existence of three or more possible program modules which the computer should undertake, depending upon several steps in value which a variable can assume. The example below illustrates these functions.

Example 3.6   Salesmen's Commissions

Salesmen for the Widget-Gidget Mfg. Co. are paid monthly. The pay plan is comprised of a fixed amount ($500) plus a percentage which varies in steps as the sales increase. A graph of the commission schedule is given in Figure 3.11, and is detailed further in Table 3.4. Write a program to calculate a salesmen's pay based on his sales dollars.

DISCUSSION

The program must have the ability to route the computer to the proper equation indicated by Table 3.4, depending on the value of D. Note, too, that the computer must print out an error message if, by mistake, D is less than zero. A flowchart to accomplish this problem is given in Figure 3.12.

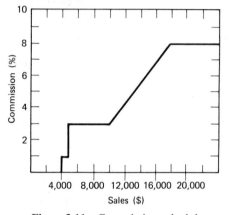

Figure 3.11   Commission schedule.

Table 3.4   Salesmen's commissions schedule.

Sales dollars (D)		Commissions	
From	To	Fixed amount	Percent of sales
(Less than 0)		(Not possible, print error message)	
0	4,000	500	0
4,000	5,000	500	1
5,000	10,000	500	3
10,000	18,000	500	$\left(\dfrac{5D - 26,000}{8,000}\right)$
18,000	(and over)	500	8

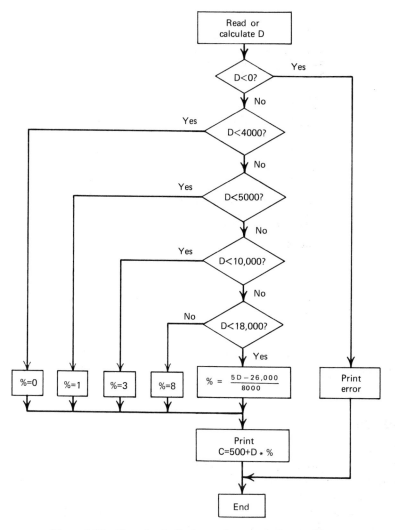

Figure 3.12 Flowchart of salesmen's commission problem.

After reading D from DATA, or calculating it by some earlier statements, the computer encounters a decision point. If D is less than $4000, the second decision point intercepts the computer and sends it to the equation C = 500 + .01D. If D is greater than $4000, the process continues until the computer eventually is routed to the appropriate equation.

Program 3.16 is designed exactly as inferred in the flowchart. Typically, such programs are written with one branch point for each breakover point

```
100 READ D
200 IF D<0 THEN 1700
300 IF D<4000 THEN 1500
400 IF D<5000 THEN 1300
500 IF D<10000 THEN 1100
600 IF D<18000 THEN 900

700 LET P=8
800 GØ TØ 1900
900 LET P=(5*D-26000)/8000
1000 GØ TØ 1900
1100 LET P=3
1200 GØ TØ 1900
1300 LET P=1
1400 GØ TØ 1900
1500 LET P=0
1600 GØ TØ 1900
1700 PRINT "ERRØR: NEGATIVE D"
1800 GØ TØ 2100
1900 PRINT "CØMMISSIØN =";500+D*(P/100)
2000 DATA 8431.21
2100 END
  RUN

CØMMISSIØN =     752.9363
```

Program 3.16 Salesmen's commissions; step functions.

in the variable D (i.e., at D = 0, 4000, 5000, 10000). The first decision point is made on the lowest breakover value; the second decision point is made on the second lowest, etc.

AND, ØR

It often occurs that one wishes a certain portion of a program to be executed only if two (or more) conditions hold simultaneously. For example, consider a payroll problem where an unmarried man (represented by M = 1) with taxable income (I) between \$169 and \$340 is taxed according to the equation T = 30.10 + 0.25(I − 169). If that equation is inserted into a program, it may only be executed when M = 1 AND I > 169 AND I < 340. Does not Program 3.17 prevent execution if any of the AND conditions do not hold? The trick here is to have one IF...THEN... statement for each condition, and each one, if satisfied, sends the computer on to the next. They must all be satisfied before the equation is executed. If any are not satisfied, the computer incurs a GØ TØ... statement which bypasses the equation.

On the other hand, a portion of the program could be executed if either of two (or more) conditions hold simultaneously. For example, a person is eligible for certain benefits if he is either under 18 years ØR over 60 years

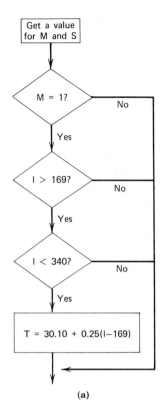

(a)

```
1300 IF M=1 THEN 1500
1400 GØ TØ 2000
1500 IF I>169 THEN 1700
1600 GØ TØ 2000
1700 IF I<340 THEN 1900
1800 GØ TØ 2000
1900 LET T=30.10+.25*(I-169)
2000       •
            •
            •
```

(b)

Program 3.17 (a) Flowchart for, and (b) program of a problem which executes line 1900 only if three simultaneous conditions hold (i.e., an AND-logic program).

of age. Program 3.18 produces the required result. If line 1300 does not cause the PRINT to be executed, line 1400 has an opportunity. Either of them divert the computer to line 1600.

These program segments might be called AND and ØR tricks. They can obviously include as many conditions as desired.

ONE MORE TRICK—JUST FOR FUN

Suppose the data in Program 3.15—i.e., employee number, hours, etc.—will be used in a program, but for one reason or another it is necessary or convenient to have the data arranged in ascending order of the employee number. How can the data be so arranged without actually forcing the typist to put them in order beforehand? One possibility is to use the employee numbers as line numbers for corresponding data statements:

```
40312 DATA 40312, 40, 3. 32, . 103
08140 DATA 08140, 42, 5.25, . 172
31402 DATA 31402, 38, 4.28, . 145
12440 DATA 12440, 40, 2.13, .085
21443 DATA 21443, 40, 6.28, . 18
41120 DATA 41120, 41.5, 5.03, . 163
```

What does this accomplish? When these statements are given to the computer, it automatically sorts them into line-number order, which corresponds exactly to putting them into employee-number order!

One would quite likely never invent this trick on his own. While it has some usefulness in its own right, it is included in this book primarily for the purpose of illustrating the part that ingenuity, imagination, and creativity play in computer programming.

Other very valuable tricks have been discussed—although not identified

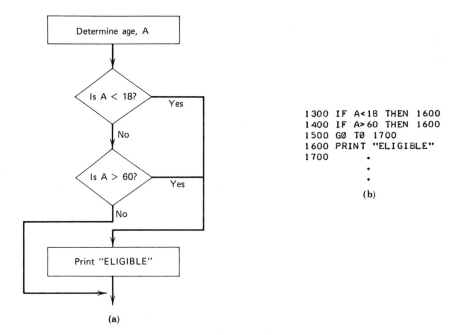

(a)

```
1300 IF A<18 THEN 1600
1400 IF A>60 THEN 1600
1500 GØ TØ 1700
1600 PRINT "ELIGIBLE"
1700        .
             .
             .
```

(b)

Program 3.18 (a) Flowchart for, and (b) program of a problem which executes line 1600 if either of two conditions hold (i.e., an ØR-logic program).

as such—in Chapter 2. The student is invited to adopt others he has read about, or others he may invent himself.

3.5 THINKING IN COMPUTEREZE

In a very real way, this recommendation ties closely to the bag of tricks discussion. Students of foreign languages are always advised to think in the new language instead of undertaking word-for-word translation. Programming is a new language, and the student must learn to think in a blend of English and *computereze*. He can do this by developing a repertoire of catch phrases which bridge the small, but sometimes troublesome, gap between the mental conception of a problem and the on-paper realization of its programmed solution. For example, one might dispense with the phrase "even or odd" to express the problem of Example 2.6, for in the most elemental analysis it can just as easily be described as "determining whether or not a number is divisible by two." If the latter phrase is adopted, it is but a small step to convert the original procedure to one which determines whether a number is divisible by five, seven, or a hundred.

As another example, instead of describing a payroll program as determining all employe s' paychecks, one might equally easily describe it as "calculating the gross and net pay, once for each employee." The difference is that the latter statement directly infers the organization of the program into a series of simple statements which calculate the subject values, and a FØR/NEXT loop which causes their execution once for I = 1 TØ "the number of employees."

Similarly, instead of thinking "A married person uses this tax equation" the statement can be profitably rephrased as "IF the person is married, THEN this equation is used." It is clear that the latter phrase is interpretable in both English and BASIC.

3.6 ONE THING AT A TIME

A lengthy and complex program should be divided into a number of smaller, more manageable parts. There are always one or two threads which can serve as the nucleus upon which to build other parts of the program. Construct those threads first, and then add other parts, *one at a time*. The program described in Example 3.7 will serve as an illustration of this principle, although the author does not necessarily recommend that the program be rerun after each addition, as it is in the example.

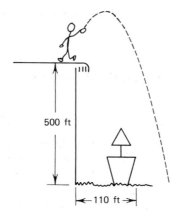

Example 3.7   The Dominator

A man is standing on the top of a hill which is 500 ft high and overlooks the ocean. One hundred and ten feet out in the water lies the shipwrecked Dominator. The man tosses a rock upward and seaward with the following speeds:

Vertical velocity	50 ft/sec
Horizontal velocity	13 ft/sec

After any time, t, the vertical position is given by $V = 500 + 50t - 16t^2$. The horizontal distance is $H = 13t$. Addressing only one of these tasks at a time, develop a program which does the following: (1) calculates and prints the horizontal and vertical distance for values $t = 0, 0.5, 1, 1.5, \ldots,$ 10 sec; (2) prints the highest point of the projectile which was calculated above; and (3) prints the message "THE RØCK MADE IT ØVER THE DØMINATØR" if the rock hits the water more than 110 ft from the shore, and prints "DIDN'T MAKE IT" if it hits the water less than 110 ft from the shore. [*Hint:* The rock "hits the water" when $V \leqslant 0$. Since time increments of 0.5 sec are being considered, it may happen that V will never exactly equal zero (that is, the rock might hit the water at, say, 6.2 sec, while the computer is evaluating only $\ldots, 5, 5.5, 6, 6.5, \ldots$ sec). Therefore, consider the first negative value of V to be the occurrence of the rock striking the water.]

DISCUSSION
See the remainder of this section.

CALCULATING V, H

The entire program discussed in Example 3.7 obviously hinges on the calculation of vertical and horizontal distance for each t. The phrase "for values t = 0, 0.5, 1, . . ." in the problem should immediately suggest the programming statement "FØR T=0 TØ 10 STEP .5," and its associated "NEXT T." Therefore, a T loop is established between lines 300 and 1900 in Program 3.19. On each iteration of the loop, appropriate values of V and H are calculated and printed. The first task of the program is thus accomplished, with no consideration at all given to the second or third tasks.

FINDING THE HIGHEST POINT OF THE PROJECTILE

The phrase "highest point of the projectile" can be thought of as *finding the largest value of V*, which, in turn, should suggest the use of the technique illustrated in Example 2.8. As in the earlier example, L is initially set to

```
100 PRINT "TIME","VERT","HØRIZ"
200 PRINT "----","----","-----"
300 FØR T=0 TØ 10 STEP .5

400 LET V=500+50*T-16*T↑2
500 LET H=13*T
501 PRINT T,V,H

1900 NEXT T
2500 END
    RUN
```

TIME	VERT	HØRIZ
----	----	-----
0	500	0
.5	521	6.5
1	534	13
1.5	539	19.5
2	536	26
2.5	525	32.5
3	506	39
3.5	479	45.5
4	444	52
4.5	401	58.5
5	350	65
5.5	291	71.5
6	224	78
6.5	149	84.5
7	66	91
7.5	-25	97.5
8	-124	104
8.5	-231	110.5
9	-346	117
9.5	-469	123.5
10	-600	130

Program 3.19 First stage of the Dominator program.

the first value of V (i.e., when T = 0); this is accomplished by adding lines 1100–1300, Program 3.20. On succeeding iterations (i.e., when T > 0), lines 1400–1500 cause L to be set equal to the latest value of V, but only if V > L (since line 1400 causes line 1500 to be bypassed if V < L). Finally, the value of L is printed after all the NEXT Ts have been completed.

PRINTING THE MESSAGE

There are two possible messages to be printed, requiring two lines of program, namely lines 800 and 1000, Program 3.21. Either of them should only be executed if the rock hits the water (i.e., V ⩽ 0), so line 600 is interjected to route the computer around the print statements when V > 0. When V ⩽ 0, the computer proceeds from line 600 to line 700 where the decision is made whether to print "THE RØCK MADE IT ØVER THE DØMINATØR" or to print "DIDN'T MAKE IT." That is, as stipulated in the problem, if, at that point H < 110, line 1000 is printed. If H ⩾ 110, line 800 is printed.

```
100 PRINT "TIME","VERT","HØRIZ"
200 PRINT "----","----","-----"
300 FØR T=0 TØ 10 STEP .5

400 LET V=500+50*T-16*T↑2
500 LET H=13*T
501 PRINT T,V,H

1100 IF T>0 THEN 1400
1200 LET L=V
1300 GØ TØ 1900
1400 IF V<L THEN 1900
1500 LET L=V

1900 NEXT T
2100 PRINT "HIGHEST PØINT =";L
2500 END
RUN
```

TIME	VERT	HØRIZ
0	500	0
.5	521	6.5
1	534	13
1.5	539	19.5
2	536	26
:	:	
9.5	-469	123.5
10	-600	130
HIGHEST PØINT =	539	

Program 3.20 Second stage of the Dominator program.

```
100 PRINT "TIME","VERT","HØRIZ"
200 PRINT "----","----","-----"

300 FØR T=0 TØ 10 STEP .5
400 LET V=500+50*T-16*T↑2
500 LET H=13*T
501 PRINT T,V,H

600 IF V>0 THEN 1100
700 IF H<110 THEN 1000
800 PRINT "THE RØCK MADE IT ØVER THE DØMINATØR"
900 GØ TØ 1100
1000 PRINT "DIDN'T MAKE IT"

1100 IF T>0 THEN 1400
1200 LET L=V
1300 GØ TØ 1900
1400 IF V<L THEN 1900
1500 LET L=V
1900 NEXT T
2100 PRINT "HIGHEST PØINT =";L
2500 END
RUN

TIME            VERT            HØRIZ
----            ----            -----
 0              500             0
 .5             521             6.5
                 •
                 •
                 •

 7              66              91
 7.5            -25             97.5
DIDN'T MAKE IT
 8              -124            104
DIDN'T MAKE IT
 8.5            -231            110.5
THE RØCK MADE IT ØVER THE DØMINATØR
 9              -346            117
THE RØCK MADE IT ØVER THE DØMINATØR
 9.5            -469            123.5
THE RØCK MADE IT ØVER THE DØMINATØR
 10             -600            130
THE RØCK MADE IT ØVER THE DØMINATØR
HIGHEST PØINT =     539
```

Program 3.21   Third stage of the Dominator program.

The program is nearly complete, but one thing remains to be done. Observe the output from Program 3.21. Once V has gone negative, it remains negative for all the following values of t. Therefore lines 700–1000 are repeated on every iteration after t = 7.5 sec, and the message is printed many times; however, the original problem is such that this message should only be printed when the rock hits the water, or only the *first time* V ⩽ 0. This suggests that one should keep count of the number of times V ⩽ 0 and bypass the PRINT statements on the second, and succeeding, incidences of a negative V. A counter, the variable C, is used in Program 3.22. Its value starts at zero (line 50), and is incremented by one every time line 610 is executed, which is, in fact every time $V \leq 0$. Then an IF...THEN... statement is added in 620 to route the computer to, or away from, the print statements. The first time that $V \leq 0$, C is set to value $C = 1$ and the computer passes from line 620 to line 700, printing the appropriate statement. However, the second, third, ... time that $V \leq 0$, $C = 2, 3, \ldots$, and line 620 routes the computer around the message statements.

```
 50 LET C=0
100 PRINT "TIME","VERT","HØRIZ"
200 PRINT "----","----","-----"
300 FØR T=0 TØ 10 STEP .5

400 LET V=500+50*T-16*T↑2
500 LET H=13*T
501 PRINT T,V,H

600 IF V>0 THEN 1100
610 LET C=C+1
620 IF C>1 THEN 1100
700 IF H<110 THEN 1000
800 PRINT "THE RØCK MADE IT ØVER THE DØMINATØR"
900 GØ TØ 1100
1000 PRINT "DIDN'T MAKE IT"

1100 IF T>0 THEN 1400
1200 LET L=V
1300 GØ TØ 1900
1400 IF V<L THEN 1900
1500 LET L=V

1900 NEXT T
2100 PRINT "HIGHEST PØINT =";L
2500 END
     RUN
```

TIME	VERT	HØRIZ
----	----	-----
0	500	0
.5	521	6.5
.		
.		
.		
7	66	91
7.5	-25	97.5
DIDN'T MAKE IT		
8	-124	104
8.5	-231	110.5
9	-346	117
9.5	-469	123.5
10	-600	130
HIGHEST PØINT =	539	

Program 3.22 Fourth and final stage of the Dominator program.

3.7 DEBUGGING

It is almost axiomatic that no program runs properly the first time. It is always necessary to change statements or alter whole sections of the program after a, or, usually several, trial run(s). In the programming vernacular, program errors are called **bugs**, and the process of getting them out is called **debugging**. Even experienced programmers realize that they will inevitably have to devote some (perhaps a good deal of) time to correcting and verifying the integrity of their programs.

Debugging can often demand as much ingenuity as did construction of the original program. The new student should strive to become efficient and imaginative at it. There are a number of good principles and techniques which he should adopt. Completely successful implementation of them at first requires practice and concentration.

DETECTING ERRORS

The presence of bugs is sometimes immediately obvious from visual observation of defects in the printout. However, many errors are very subtle and are detectable only after a close examination of the printout; others lie in waiting, ready to come back and haunt the user at a later time. Several steps may be taken to insure against such errors.

Never presume that the program is correct simply because, on the surface, it produces seemingly reasonable results. Instead, carefully scrutinize the printout to see if there are any anomalies amongst its various parts. Make checks and crosschecks. Do columns of numbers add up properly? Does the value of one parameter grow—or decrease—in magnitude as it should? Do the answers *look* right? Or is the office boy being paid $400/week? Is he getting 60% of his salary deducted for taxes? It usually helps to take the same data that was given to the computer and work through it by hand, generating the results which the computer should match. Having satisfied oneself that the program produces an appropriate printout, there are still other hazards.

Sometimes a particular set of data which the computer is processing is too complicated to evaluate manually. In such cases, one should give the computer *phony* data, for which the answer is known, or calculatable, in advance. The program should be expected to produce the correct answer for that data. For example, the author has a probability-related program which he knows should, if given appropriate data, produce a series of ones as answers; if given other data, it should produce a series of zeros. Or, given a third set of data, it should produce the answers given in an example problem from a certain textbook on the subject.

Often, a lengthy program will have many loops and branch points in it. Literally dozens of different paths through the program are possible, so that any given set of data may or may not exercise each one of them. If it does not, there is obviously a potential for some future execution of the program to come up with the proper circumstances which lead to incurring that error by executing the faulty branch. Therefore, it is advisable to make several trial runs, varying the conditions in the data so that all the possible paths are exercised at least once.

TRACING

After the error is apparent, there remains the task of identifying its cause in the program. Depending on the circumstances, the cause may be obvious. If not, there are a number of techniques one can use to uncover the cause.

Many times, the program may have several mistakes in it. Efficient debugging requires attention be focused on one of them at a time. To the extent possible, a very complex program might be executed after each module is added to it, as was done in the Dominator problem, so that errors can be uncovered and isolated early, before they propagate their effects into other parts of the program and confuse matters.

The most effective debugging technique is one called *tracing*. To see how it is used, consider Program 3.23, whose objective is to read the data as X1, and to separately add the positive and negative numbers. The sum of negative numbers is obviously wrong. The reason for the error may not be so obvious (at least, for illustration, pretend it is not). The problem with analyzing the behavior of the computer which leads to the error is that we see printed out only the results of its final calculation, and not those inter-

```
100 LET T1=0
200 LET T2=0
300 FØR I=1 TØ 10
400 READ X1
500 IF X1<0 THEN 800
600 LET T1=T1+X1
700 GØ TØ 900
800 LET T2=T2+T1
900 NEXT I
1000 PRINT "SUM ØF + NUMBERS ="; T1
1100 PRINT "SUM ØF - NUMBERS ="; T2

1200 DATA 50,-16,23,14,-22
1300 DATA 5,-6,0,14,-2
1400 END
     RUN

SUM ØF + NUMBERS =      106
SUM ØF - NUMBERS =      335
```

Program 3.23   Program with an error.

mediate calculations where the error is made. To get around this difficulty, extra print statements are added to trace the value of pertinent variables as the computer progresses through the program, as shown in Program 3.24.

```
100 LET T1=0
200 LET T2=0
300 FØR I=1 TØ 10
400 READ X1

401 PRINT "I=";I;"X1=";X1
500 IF X1<0 THEN 800
600 LET T1=T1+X1
700 GØ TØ 898
800 LET T2=T2+T1
898 PRINT "T1=";T1;"T2=";T2
899 PRINT

900 NEXT I
1000 PRINT "SUM ØF + NUMBERS =";T1
1100 PRINT "SUM ØF - NUMBERS =";T2
1200 DATA 50,-16,23,14,-22
1300 DATA 5,-6,0,14,-2
1400 END
 RUN

I=      1    X1=      50
T1=    50    T2=       0

I=      2    X1=    -16
T1=    50    T2=      50

I=      3    X1=      23
T1=    73    T2=      50

I=      4    X1=      14
T1=    87    T2=      50

I=      5    X1=    -22
T1=    87    T2=     137

I=      6    X1=       5
T1=    92    T2=     137

I=      7    X1=     -6
T1=    92    T2=     229

I=      8    X1=       0
T1=    92    T2=     229

I=      9    X1=      14
T1=   106    T2=     229

I=     10    X1=     -2
T1=   106    T2=     335

SUM ØF + NUMBERS =     106
SUM ØF - NUMBERS =     335
```

Program 3.24 Addition of variable tracing.

The printout from the altered program makes it obvious from the first negative value of X1 where the error lies; T1, rather than X1, is being accumulated into T2.

Sometimes it is also difficult to determine the exact course the computer took as it progressed through the program, particularly if there are a large number of intricate decision points in it. The problem can be solved by inserting other tracing statements of the form shown in Program 3.25, so

```
     100 LET T1=0
     200 LET T2=0

     300 FØR I=1 TØ 10
  ✓  399 PRINT "NØW AT 399"
     400 READ X1
  ✓  401 PRINT "I=";I;"X1=";X1

     500 IF X1<0 THEN 800
  ✓  501 PRINT "NØW AT 501"
     600 LET T1=T1+X1      .
  ✓  700 GØ TØ 897

     800 LET T2=T2+T1
  ✓  897 PRINT "NØW AT 897"
  ✓  898 PRINT "T1=";T1;"T2=";T2
     899 PRINT

     900 NEXT I
    1000 PRINT "SUM ØF + NUMBERS =";T1
    1100 PRINT "SUM ØF - NUMBERS =";T2
    1200 DATA 50,-16,23,14,-22
    1300 DATA 5,-6,0,14,-2
    1400 END
    RUN

    NØW AT 399
    I=        1      X1=      50
    NØW AT 501
    NØW AT 897
    T1=      50      T2=       0

    NØW AT 399
    I=        2      X1=     -16
    NØW AT 897
    T1=      50      T2=      50

    NØW AT 399
    I=        3      X1=      23
    NØW AT 501
    NØW AT 897
    T1=      73      T2=      50
              •
              •
              •
```

Program 3.25   Addition of statements to trace the progress of the computer.

that the computer will keep the programmer informed of its maneuvers. He can later study them at his own leisure.

The tracing procedure can be used very effectively on programs of any size, but it can be a bit tedious to implement. In Program 3.25 all the statements marked with a check have to be either inserted in, or changed from, the original program. After debugging, they must again be deleted. This can be very bothersome and time-consuming. The technique is so valuable, however, that most computers permit automatic tracing with simple insertion of a statement like

100   TRACE

whereupon the computer automatically traces through the program. Implementation of this single statement in Program 3.26 produces exactly the same information as did the more extensive changes in the previous program, and it is much easier to add and delete.

```
50 TRACE
100 LET T1=0
200 LET T2=0
300 FOR I=1 TO 10

400 READ X1
500 IF X1<0 THEN 800
600 LET T1=T1+X1
700 GO TO 900
800 LET T2=T2+T1

900 NEXT I
1000 PRINT "SUM OF + NUMBERS =";T1
1100 PRINT "SUM OF - NUMBERS =";T2
1200 DATA 50,-16,23,14,-22
1300 DATA 5,-6,0,14,-2
1400 END
 RUN

AT 100,  T1=0
AT 200,  T2=0
AT 300,  I=1
AT 400,  X1=50
AT 600,  T1=50
AT 300,  I=2
AT 400,  X1=-16
AT 800,  T2=50
AT 300,  I=3
AT 400,  X1=23
AT 500,  T1=73
       .
       .
       .
```

Program 3.26 Substituting the TRACE statement for those in Program 3.25.

OTHER DEBUGGING HINTS

When there are errors in the program, one must often rerun it several times. It can be distracting and time-consuming to sit watching many lines of printout before coming to the point of the error. Take Program 3.27a as a simple example. Suppose the error is somewhere between lines 600 and 9999. The I loop (lines 200–600) obviously causes one hundred lines of print-out before the error is encountered. To prevent rerunning that part of the program many times, line 450 is inserted in Program 3.27b. That GØ TØ statement bypasses the PRINT statement, reducing the execution of that part of the program from several minutes to a few seconds at most. Similarly, if appropriate, whole segments of the program can be bypassed at once.

While debugging, it is very important to have a current copy of the program at hand to review in coordination with the printout. After every few changes, one should get another copy. However, it is very inefficient to keep relisting the whole program each time. Instead, it is better to relist only those statements in the vicinity of the changes or near the suspected location of the error.

Often, the program hits an unexpected error and it would be extremely helpful to be able to tell what value certain variables (say, for example, the index of a loop) had at the instant something went wrong. Some com-

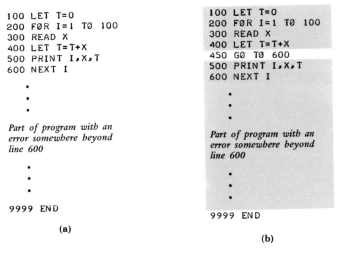

```
100 LET T=0
200 FØR I=1 TØ 100
300 READ X
400 LET T=T+X
500 PRINT I,X,T
600 NEXT I
        .
        .
        .

Part of program with an
error somewhere beyond
line 600
        .
        .
        .

9999 END
        (a)
```

```
100 LET T=0
200 FØR I=1 TØ 100
300 READ X
400 LET T=T+X
450 GØ TØ 600
500 PRINT I,X,T
600 NEXT I
        .
        .
        .

Part of program with an
error somewhere beyond
line 600
        .
        .
        .

9999 END
        (b)
```

Program 3.27 (a) Program which produces 100 lines of printouts before it gets to the erroneous segment. (b) Insertion of a GØ TØ statement which, until removed again, causes the PRINT statement to be bypassed so that the program immediately moves to the offending segment.

puter systems permit the programmer to type "PRINT I" (or any other variables) *without any line number,* and its value at the time of interruption will be displayed.

3.8 A FINAL EXAMPLE

The following problem is an excellent illustration of most of the concepts discussed in this chapter. A computerized game of roulette is certainly of little importance in comparison with programs which process corporate payrolls or solve space shot problems, but one of the guidelines mentioned earlier was to practice and experiment with zany programs.

Example 3.8 Roulette

A roulette roll may result in any one of 38 possible numbers, from 0 to 36 and double 0 (00). Bets can be placed on

■   individual numbers;
■   even or odd;
■   red or black (1, 3, 5, 7, 9, 12, 14, 16, 18, 19, 21, 23, 25, 27, 30, 32, 34, 36 are red; 2, 4, 6, 8, 10, 11, 13, 15, 17, 20, 22, 24, 26, 28, 29, 31, 33, 35 are black; 0 and 00 are colorless);
■   whether the number is in the first half (1–18) or the second half (19–36) of possible values;
■   whether the number is in the low (1–12), middle (13–24), or high (25–36) group of values.

Write a program to "play" roulette. Read any number in the range 0–37 (37 represents 00) from DATA, and determine its characteristics. An example printout from the program is shown below:

```
32    RED        EVEN     SECØND HALF    HIGH
00    CØLØRLESS
2     BLACK      EVEN     FIRST HALF     LØW
```

Use the following numbers as test DATA: 15, 37, 8, 21, 26, 12, 0.

THE FLOWCHART

A simplified flowchart describing the necessary program for Example 3.8 is given in Figure 3.13. In the example printout given above, there is only one line of printing for each number. But the line is most conveniently printed in fragments; that is, the computer should print "RED" or "BLACK" before proceeding to determine (and then printing) whether the number is in the first or second half. Therefore, the trick described in Section 2.1 will be used, employing a comma after each PRINT statement to suppress the carriage return. Box 8 of Figure 3.13 determines whether the chosen number is even or odd. This, too, is now a familiar trick.

It might be desirable to expand the block diagram now to present more clarification of the logic being used. The reader should carefully study the expanded flowchart given in Figure 3.14. For reference, each box retains a numbered identification relating to its original position in Figure 3.13. For example, box 1 has been expanded into boxes 1a and 1b. Boxes 2, 3, 9, 10, and 11 are so simple that they need no elaboration. Box 5 will become absorbed into box 4. Box 8, being a known technique, will not be expanded in detail. The flowchart has been expanded considerably, but there still remain several boxes which involve a number of statements each.

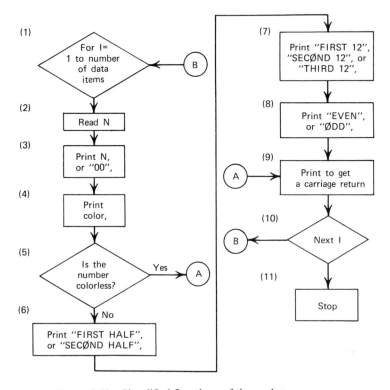

Figure 3.13 Simplified flowchart of the roulette program.

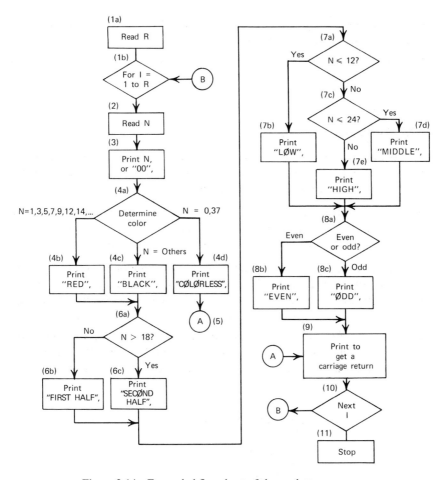

Figure 3.14 Expanded flowchart of the roulette program.

TRICKS FROM THE BAG

A number of standard tricks become obvious from the expanded flowchart:

■ Fragmentation of the printout.

■ The determination of the evenness or oddness of N (box 8).

■ Making the upper limit of the I loop a variable to be read from the data (box 1) permits simple changes in the program at a later date in order to include processing of more or fewer data.

■ ∅R-logic, executing a particular set of statements when any one of a number of conditions hold (box 4).

■ Selectively routing the computer to various modules of the program, where the variable N is a "step function" (boxes 4, 6, and 7).

ONE THING AT A TIME

It is now possible to write the program in several steps. At each one, it will be run on the computer to make sure that the added statements properly perform their function before continuing to the next function.

■ *Step 1* (Program 3.28). Boxes 1, 2, 3, 9, 10, and 11 are really the minimal activities which contain the single thread of the program. As a result, they will constitute the first writing of the program.

Ordinarily, the program should proceed from line 420 to the beginning of the module which prints the color. However, that module is not yet installed in the program, so the line (line 10000) which gives a carriage return is a convenient place to temporarily direct the computer.

■ *Step 2* (Program 3.29). First, line 420 must be changed to direct the computer to the beginning of the "Color" module (line 500). From there, any one of the lines between 500 and 517 will direct the computer to line 560.

```
100 READ R
200 FØR I=1 TØ R
300 READ N
400 IF N=37 THEN 430
410 PRINT NJ
420 GØ TØ 10000
430 PRINT " 00"J
10000 PRINT
10100 NEXT I
11000 DATA 7
11100 DATA 15,37,8,21,26,12,0
12000 END
 RUN

 15
 00
 8
 21
 26
 12
 0
```

Program 3.28 Reading and printing the roulette number, including converting "37" to "00."

```
100 READ R
200 FØR I=1 TØ R
300 READ N

400 IF N=37 THEN 430
410 PRINT N;
420 GØ TØ 500
430 PRINT " 00";

500 IF N=1 THEN 560
501 IF N=3 THEN 560
502 IF N=5 THEN 560
503 IF N=7 THEN 560
504 IF N=9 THEN 560
505 IF N=12 THEN 560
506 IF N=14 THEN 560
507 IF N=16 THEN 560
508 IF N=18 THEN 560
509 IF N=19 THEN 560
510 IF N=21 THEN 560
511 IF N=23 THEN 560
512 IF N=25 THEN 560
513 IF N=27 THEN 560
514 IF N=30 THEN 560
515 IF N=32 THEN 560
516 IF N=34 THEN 560
517 IF N=36 THEN 560
518 IF N=0 THEN 570
521 IF N=37 THEN 570

550 PRINT "BLACK",
551 GØ TØ 10000
560 PRINT "RED",
561 GØ TØ 10000
570 PRINT "CØLØRLESS",
571 GØ TØ 10000

10000 PRINT
10100 NEXT I

11000 DATA 7
11100 DATA 15,37,8,21,26,12,0
12000 END

RUN

15      BLACK
00      CØLØRLESS
8       BLACK
21      RED
26      BLACK
12      RED
0       CØLØRLESS
```

Program 3.29 Printing the colors.

If N is 0 or 37, lines 518 and 521 will direct the computer to line 570. If the computer is not sent to either line 560 or 570, it will proceed to line 550. Thus the appropriate color will be printed.

■ *Step 3* (Program 3.30). Observe that lines 551 and 561 are changed to "GØ TØ 600" to ensure that the "HALF" module will be incurred, but line 571 is not changed. This is in accordance with the condition in the problem which infers that the remaining printouts are bypassed if the number is "colorless."

```
100 READ R
200 FØR I=1 TØ R
300 READ N

400 IF N=37 THEN 430
410 PRINT NJ
420 GØ TØ 500
430 PRINT " 00"J

500 IF N=1 THEN 560
          •
          •
          •
521 IF N=37 THEN 570

550 PRINT "BLACK",
551 GØ TØ 600
560 PRINT "RED",
561 GØ TØ 600
570 PRINT "CØLØRLESS",
571 GØ TØ 10000

600 IF N>18 THEN 630
610 PRINT "FIRST HALF",
620 GØ TØ 10000
630 PRINT "SECØND HALF",

10000 PRINT
10100 NEXT I

11000 DATA 7
11100 DATA 15,37,8,21,26,12,0
12000 END
RUN

15    BLACK       FIRST HALF
00    CØLØRLESS
8     BLACK       FIRST HALF
21    RED         SECØND HALF
26    BLACK       SECØND HALF
12    RED         FIRST HALF
0     CØLØRLESS
```

Program 3.30 Printing the position of the number in the first or second half of the numbers.

■   *Step 4* (Program 3.31). A step function determines if the roulette number is in the lowest, middle, or highest third of all numbers.

■   *Step 5* (Program 3.32). This module is quite similar to the sequence given in Example 2.6 and determines if the number is even or odd. Line 50 is added to initialize C = 0; it will be changed to a one (line 820) if N is even.

A review of the output in Program 3.32 reveals that an error has developed! The computer properly determines that the numbers 15 and 8 are odd and

```
100  READ R
200  FØR I=1 TØ R
300  READ N

400  IF N=37 THEN 430
410  PRINT N;
420  GØ TØ 500
430  PRINT " 00";

500  IF N=1 THEN 560
         •
         •
         •
600  IF N>18 THEN 630
610  PRINT "FIRST HALF",
620  GØ TØ 700
630  PRINT "SECØND HALF",

700  IF N<=12 THEN 740
710  IF N<=24 THEN 730
720  PRINT "HIGH",
721  GØ TØ 10000
730  PRINT "MIDDLE",
731  GØ TØ 10000
740  PRINT "LØW",

10000  PRINT
10100  NEXT I

11000  DATA 7
11100  DATA 15,37,8,21,26,12,0
12000  END

RUN

15   BLACK       FIRST HALF      MIDDLE
00   CØLØRLESS
8    BLACK       FIRST HALF      LØW
21   RED         SECØND HALF     MIDDLE
26   BLACK       SECØND HALF     HIGH
12   RED         FIRST HALF      LØW
0    CØLØRLESS
```

Program 3.31   Determining the position of the number in the first, second, or third portion of the range of numbers.

```
 50 LET C=0
100 READ R
200 FØR I=1 TØ R
300 READ N

400 IF N=37 THEN 430
410 PRINT NJ
420 GØ TØ 500
430 PRINT " 00"J
         .
         .
         .
700 IF N<=12 THEN 740
710 IF N<=24 THEN 730
720 PRINT "HIGH",
721 GØ TØ 800
730 PRINT "MIDDLE",
731 GØ TØ 800
740 PRINT "LØW",
800 FØR K=2 TØ 36 STEP 2
810 IF K<>N THEN 830
820 LET C=C+1
830 NEXT K

840 IF C=1 THEN 870
850 PRINT "ØDD",
860 GØ TØ 10000
870 PRINT "EVEN",

10000 PRINT
10100 NEXT I

11000 DATA 7
11100 DATA 15,37,8,21,26,12,0
12000 END
 RUN
```

15	BLACK	FIRST HALF	MIDDLE	ØDD
00	CØLØRLESS			
8	BLACK	FIRST HALF	LØW	EVEN
21	RED	SECØND HALF	MIDDLE	EVEN
26	BLACK	SECØND HALF	HIGH	ØDD
12	RED	FIRST HALF	LØW	ØDD
0	CØLØRLESS			

Program 3.32 Determining if the number is even or odd. An error develops!

even, respectively. But it erroneously calls 21 even and 26 and 12 odd. How could the computer make such a mistake on those numbers when it operates correctly on the previous numbers? If this "bug" can be worked out, the program will be completed.

DEBUGGING THE PROGRAM

The variable C is the key to printing the correct message, so a moment's reflection will lead one to suspect the manipulation of C. To investigate this aspect, a few lines are added to the program which cause the computer to print out information about the behavior of C as the program progresses (Program 3.33). But first, line 420 is altered to temporarily bypass the uninteresting lines between 500 and 740. The most important additions to the program are lines 799 and 831 which trace the value of C for us.

Running the program with these changes results in the printout shown in Program 3.33. It is enlightening to observe that, when N = 26 and 12, C = 2 and 3. This is certainly an unexpected development for, remembering Example 2.6, C is supposed to take on only the values 0 and 1. Tracing back further in the printout, it can be seen that, when N = 21, C had value one *before* entering the K loop. Although C was not changed (to one) in that

```
50 LET C=0

100 READ R
200 FØR I=1 TØ R
300 READ N

400 IF N=37 THEN 430
410 PRINT N;
420 GØ TØ 799
430 PRINT " 00";
            .
            .
            .
799 PRINT "AT LINE 799, C=";C;
800 FØR K=2 TØ 36 STEP 2
810 IF K<>N THEN 830
820 LET C=C+1
830 NEXT K

831 PRINT "AT LINE 831, C=";C;
840 IF C=1 THEN 870
850 PRINT "ØDD",
860 GØ TØ 10000
870 PRINT "EVEN",

10000 PRINT
10100 NEXT I

11000 DATA 7
11100 DATA 15,37,8,21,26,12,0
12000 END
   RUN
```

15	AT LINE 799, C=	0	AT LINE 831, C=	0	ØDD
00	CØLØRLESS				
8	AT LINE 799, C=	0	AT LINE 831, C=	1	EVEN
21	AT LINE 799, C=	1	AT LINE 831, C=	1	EVEN
26	AT LINE 799, C=	1	AT LINE 831, C=	2	ØDD
12	AT LINE 799, C=	2	AT LINE 831, C=	3	ØDD
0	AT LINE 799, C=	3	AT LINE 831, C=	3	ØDD

Program 3.33 Trying to find out (debug) what went wrong with Program 3.32.

K loop, it still had value one when the loop was finished. Therefore, line 840 directed the computer to 870, even though 21 was odd.

When N = 26, C has the value of one at line 799. Line 820 sets C = 2, and line 840 does not direct the computer to 860, even though 26 is even. The problem now becomes obvious: C is not reset to zero before entering the K loop. The only point at which C is set equal to zero is line 50, *outside the I loop.* It should be reset at line 800 instead.

Moving the statement "FØR I = 2 TØ 36 STEP 2," and changing line 800 to "LET C=0" corrects this bug. Then, after the debugging statements are removed, the corrected Program 3.34 results in the proper output, and the program is completed.

```
100 READ R
200 FØR I=1 TØ R
300 READ N

400 IF N=37 THEN 430
410 PRINT NJ
420 GØ TØ 500
430 PRINT " 00"J

500 IF N=1 THEN 560
501 IF N=3 THEN 560
502 IF N=5 THEN 560
503 IF N=7 THEN 560
504 IF N=9 THEN 560
505 IF N=12 THEN 560
506 IF N=14 THEN 560
507 IF N=16 THEN 560
508 IF N=18 THEN 560
509 IF N=19 THEN 560
510 IF N=21 THEN 560
511 IF N=23 THEN 560
512 IF N=25 THEN 560
513 IF N=27 THEN 560
514 IF N=30 THEN 560
515 IF N=32 THEN 560
516 IF N=34 THEN 560
517 IF N=36 THEN 560
518 IF N=0 THEN 570
521 IF N=37 THEN 570

550 PRINT "BLACK",
551 GØ TØ 600
560 PRINT "RED",
561 GØ TØ 600
570 PRINT "CØLØRLESS",
571 GØ TØ 10000

600 IF N>18 THEN 630
610 PRINT "FIRST HALF",
620 GØ TØ 700
630 PRINT "SECØND HALF",

700 IF N<=12 THEN 740
710 IF N<=24 THEN 730
720 PRINT "HIGH",
721 GØ TØ 800
730 PRINT "MIDDLE",
731 GØ TØ 800
740 PRINT "LØW",
```

Program 3.34 Complete, corrected roulette program. (*Continued on next page.*)

```
800 LET C=0
801 FOR K=2 TO 36 STEP 2
810 IF K<>N THEN 830
820 LET C=C+1
830 NEXT K

840 IF C=1 THEN 870
850 PRINT "ODD",
860 GO TO 10000
870 PRINT "EVEN",

10000 PRINT
10100 NEXT I

11000 DATA 7
11100 DATA 15,37,8,21,26,12,0
12000 END

RUN
15    BLACK    FIRST HALF    MIDDLE          ODD
00    COLORLESS
8     BLACK    FIRST HALF    LOW             EVEN
21    RED      SECOND HALF   MIDDLE          ODD
26    BLACK    SECOND HALF   HIGH            EVEN
12    RED      FIRST HALF    LOW             EVEN
0     COLORLESS
```

Program 3.34 *(continued)*

■ EXERCISES

In each exercise requiring a program, follow good debugging procedures. Use the "tricks" liberally.

3.6   If the following data were given to the computer in Program 3.13 (i.e., omitting the filling zeros), show the values of C1, A, B, C that the computer would read on each loop:

2000	DATA	1,5,6,3
2100	DATA	1,5,3,8
2200	DATA	4,10,6
2300	DATA	2,1,1
2400	DATA	4,3,2
2500	DATA	3,6
2600	DATA	3,4
2700	DATA	1,6,1,1
2800	DATA	5,3,3,3

3.7   Install a counter in Program 3.15 and, at the end of the program, print out the number of employees actually having data submitted.

3.8   A poll of 5000 persons is taken on a particular issue, and their positions are recorded as FOR, AGAINST, and UNDECIDED. Choose numbers to represent each vote. Doing one thing at a time.

- read and count the number of each response;
- print the percentage of votes in each response;
- print YES (or NØ) VØTES LEAD, as appropriate.

Strategically place PRINT statements for debugging.

3.9 What phony test case data would you use to debug the following programs: Program 3.16, Exercise 3.4, and Exercise 3.5.

3.10 An angle A, expressed in degrees, may be larger than 360° (e.g., 520°, 1024°, 729°, etc.), but it is always equivalent to one between 0° and 360°. The equivalent angle is found by subtracting an integer number of 360° increments from A:

$$370° \quad \text{is equivalent to} \quad 370° - 1(360°) = 10$$
$$829° \quad \text{is equivalent to} \quad 829° - 2(360°) = 109$$

Write a program which reads A and (a) prints A; (b) converts A to the equivalent angle less than 360°; (c) prints the new angle; and (d) counts and prints the number of increments which were subtracted.

*3.11 Write a program which "gives change." It should read some amount in the range $0–100.00 and print out the number of $5 bills, $1 bills, quarters, nickels, dimes, and pennies corresponding to that amount. Put twenty amounts in the data and have the computer repeat for each one. Let the twenty first data be a zero, meaning that upon reading it the program should terminate its iterations and print out the sum of all data, and the total number of fives, ones, and each coin issued. Strategically place PRINT statements for debugging.

3.12 Many invoices come to the computer with the following information listed as data:

INVØICE NUMBER, ITEM I.D., QUANTITY, PRICE/UNIT

One invoice may be constituted by several lines. The program should read each data line and, if the invoice number is the same as the number on the previous line, accumulate the total value of the invoice. Whenever a new invoice number is encountered, the computer should print the following information for the previous number:

INVØICE NUMBER, TØTAL CHARGES, DISCØUNT,
BILLABLE AM'T

where the discount is calculated by the schedule below.

Total charges ($)	Discount (%)
0–1,000	None
1,000.01–3,000	1
3,000.01–8,000	2.5
Above 8,000	5

3.13 For accounting and taxing purposes, the value of a machine may be depreciated by either (a) the "straight-line," or (b) the "sum-of-the-year's-digits" method. There are a number of machines, and for each one, a line of data is given containing these facts:

■ machine i.d. number;
■ depreciation code: 1 if the machine is on straight-line depreciation,
2 if the machine is on sum-of-the-year's digits depreciation,
0 if the data is exhausted;
■ original value of the machine, in dollars;
■ scrap value at end of depreciable life, in dollars;
■ purchase year of the machine (i.e., 1963, 1964, etc.);
■ the depreciable life (i.e., 8 years, 11 years, etc.).

For each machine, calculate the depreciation for 1972. Use these procedures:

■ Straight-line:
Depreciable amount = Original value − Scrap value

$$1972 \text{ Depreciation} = \left(\frac{\text{Depreciable amount}}{\text{Life}} \right)$$

■ Sum-of-the-year's-digits:
Depreciable amount = Original value − Scrap value

$$\text{Sum of digits} = \sum_{i=1}^{\text{Life}} i = 1 + 2 + 3 + \cdots + \text{Life}$$

$$1972 \text{ Depreciation} = \left(\frac{\text{Depreciable amount}}{\text{Sum of digits}} \right)$$
$$\times (\text{Life} - \text{No. years since purchase})$$

■   If the depreciable life has expired, print out the error message "PLEASE REMØVE MACHINE XXX FRØM DATA. IT HAS BEEN FULLY DEPRECIATED."

3.14 A company sells products to three types of customers which are designated by number. Each type gets a certain discount:

Type 1,   General public, no discount
Type 2,   Retailers, 10% discount
Type 3,   Manufacturers, 15% discount
Type 0,   Indicates end of data (not a customer)

An additional discount is given for large purchases, as follows:

Total ($)	Discount (%)
0–1,000	0
1,000.01–3,000.00	1
3,000.01–8,000.00	2.5
8,000.01–15,000.00	5.0
15,000.01–30,000.00	8.0
Above 30,000	10.0

In no event shall the discount from both factors exceed 18.5%. Invoices are prepared for each sale. Each invoice has a unique number. Each line of data represents one sales entry on the invoice; there may be many data lines for each invoice. You may presume that all lines for each invoice are grouped together. The following are typical data lines:

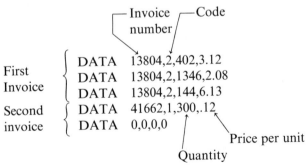

Read and accumulate gross billable ($= \sum$ quantity*prices) until a new invoice number is discovered. At that time, compute and print

Invoice number, Gross billable, Discount, Net(= Gross − Discount), Tax(=5% Net), and Net+Tax. At the end, print out the company's totals in each category above (except, of course, invoice number) for all invoices.

3.15 Facts concerning students enrolled in a college are entered into DATA statements; a typical one is shown below:

$$498,44,9218,0,3,2,4,0,0,0,0,0$$

■   The first three entries are the student's social security number (i.e., 498,44,9218 is equivalent to 498 − 44 − 9218). Why is it not entered as 498449218? [*Hint:* Consider the number of digits.]

■   The 0 in the fourth location indicates that the student is from out-of-state; a 1 in that position would indicate that he was from in-state; a 2 would indicate that he was from a foreign country.

■   The remaining nine entries give the credit hours earned for each class in which the student is enrolled (up to nine classes).

Tuition is as follows:

Code 0 students:	$30/credit hour; $360 maximum
Code 1 students:	$25/credit hour; $300 maximum
Code 2 students:	$40/credit hour; $480 maximum

Calculate and print each student's tuition.

*3.16 The population of the world today is estimated at 3.7 billion. Each year, it increases by 1.9% over the previous year. Iteratively, compute the years in which it will double and triple its current level.

3.17 A company is concerned about its rising overhead costs and wishes to analyze data to determine which departments have the highest costs per employee. Fifty data lines are given the computer:

Department number	Number of employees	Overhead dollars
8122.2	36	48264.10
1603.1	29	36142.80
4028.9	156	190281.44
.	.	.
.	.	.
.	.	.

Write a program which calculates and prints (a) for each department, the overhead per employee (OPE); (b) the average and standard deviation of OPE (see Exercise 2.50); and (c) the linear regression curve with number of employees on the horizontal axis versus overhead costs on the vertical axis (see Example 2.12).

3.18 A company uses Q gears/year. A supplier charges $10 each for the first 1000 gears, and $8 each for any over 1000. The company could make its own gears at a cost of $10,000 + $4.50/gear. Given Q, draw a flowchart for a program which will determine the cost of (a) making and (b) buying the gear, and print whether the company should make or buy to achieve the lowest cost. Write the program. Use Q = 2000/year.

3.19 Three production machines are tested. The probabilities that each will be successful are $P_1 = 0.9$, $P_2 = 0.8$, $P_3 = 0.7$; that each will be a failure is $Q_i = 1 - P_i$. There are eight (2^3) combinations (states of) success/failure conditions which might occur. If one lets the number zero represent a success condition and the number one represent a failure condition, the eight states can be produced by generating a three-digit binary table, Table 3.5. Therefore state 3, for example, represents that condition where machine 1 is successful *and* machine 2 is a failure *and* machine 3 is a failure. Since those conditions are mutually exclusive events, the probability that state 3 will, in fact, occur is $P_{s3} = P_1 Q_2 Q_3$. Similar equations can be generated for other states.

Write a program which will (a) generate the state numbers, the success/failure conditions of each state, and the probability of each state; (b) print out the truth table but substitute the letters "S" (meaning success) for zero and "F" (meaning failure) for one in the

Table 3.5 Truth table.

	Machine			
State	1	2	3	Probability
0	0	0	0	$P_1 P_2 P_3$
1	0	0	1	$P_1 P_2 Q_3$
2	0	1	0	$P_1 Q_2 P_3$
3	0	1	1	.
4	1	0	0	.
5	1	0	1	.
6	1	1	0	
7	1	1	1	

body of the table; (c) print out the probability of each state occurring; (d) print an asterisk beside each state which has at least two successful machines; (e) add up state probabilities of all asterisked states; and (f) print out the message "THE PRØBABILITY ØF TWØ ØR MØRE MACHINES ØPERATIVE IS X.XXX," where X.XXX represents the calculated sum.

3.20 The Newton–Raphson approximation is often used to determine the roots of an equation, $f(x) = 0$. To implement the method, the derivative $f'(x)$ is first determined. Then an arbitrary value for x (one thought to be near the real root) is chosen. Call it x_1. A new approximation for x is determined by

$$x_2 = x_1 - \frac{f(x_1)}{f'(x_1)}$$

The value of x_2 is substituted into the right side of the equation to determine x_3; x_3 determines x_4; etc. Eventually, the difference between succeeding approximations of x becomes acceptably small, and the latest approximation is used as the root. Program the computer to calculate the real root of $x^3 + 2x^2 + 4x - 24 = 0$.

3.21 A sheet of metal measures 10×20 inches. A box-shaped container

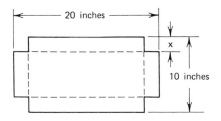

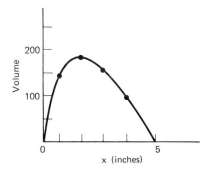

Figure 3.15

must be formed from it by cutting squares of length x from the corners and folding the tabs upward. The volume of such a box is

$$V = (L)(W)(H)$$
$$= (20 - 2x)(10 - 2x)x$$

The minimum value of x is obviously 0 inch; the maximum is one-half the width of the sheet, or 5 inches. Within the range $0 \leqslant x \leqslant 5$, the above equation has the curve shown in Figure 3.15. The volume is maximized at approximately x = 2 inches. Use an iterative technique to determine the value of x which maximizes volume. Begin with x = 0; increase it in 0.5 inch increments until the volume begins to decrease. Then begin decreasing x, with $\Delta x = 0.05$, moving leftward on the graph; V should begin increasing again for a time. When it first decreases, repeat the rightward movement once more, with $\Delta x = 0.005$ inch. Print both the value of x and the maximum volume.

3.22 If e is the base of the natural logarithm (e = 2.718 . . .), e^x can be approximated by

$$e = 1 + \frac{x^1}{1!} + \frac{x^2}{2!} + \frac{x^3}{3!} + \cdots + \frac{x^i}{i!} + \left(\frac{x^i}{i!} \cdot \frac{x}{i+1}\right) + \cdots$$

The series goes on infinitely. Write a program to iteratively calculate $e^{0.5}$. Successively add terms to an accumulator until the increase in the sum is less $1E - 5$. Print out $e^{0.5}$ and the number of iterations required. [*Hint:* Note that each term is created by multiplying the previous term by x/(i + 1). This suggests a multiplying accumulator.]

4 MATRICES, INPUT, RANDOM NUMBERS, AND OTHER GOOD FEATURES

There remain a number of very important BASIC statements and concepts which the student will probably find available on his time-sharing computer.

4.1 INPUT STATEMENT

This statement is another in the series of "assignment statements" begun earlier with the LET and READ statements. Upon encountering an INPUT statement of the form

$$100 \quad \text{INPUT A,X1,Y}$$

the computer actually interrupts execution of the program and requests that the person at the teletype present it with the values to use for the prescribed variables. The user simply types them at the appropriate time. When they are received by the computer, program execution resumes at the next statement and the variable is thereafter treated exactly as any other which might have been given a value by LET or READ statements.

To signify that it is ready to accept values from the teletype, the computer prints a question mark when it arrives at the INPUT statement. One important programming "trick" is to combine PRINT and INPUT statements into pairs which cause the computer to appear to be asking a grammatically correct, intelligent, English-structured question.

Example 4.1 Illustrating the Input Statement

Write a program which simply adds together "n" numbers, but in this case the values of n and each of the added numbers must be entered by the user through the keyboard in response to an INPUT statement. Use the program to add the following numbers: 3, 2, -1, 0.2, 0, 4.

DISCUSSION
A simple flowchart of the required program is shown in Figure 4.1; Program 4.1 implements the problem. The output of the program, as it looks after a RUN, is also shown in Program 4.1. The PRINT and INPUT statements are phrased and arranged to give the appearance that the computer is actually questioning the person at the teletype. In the printout, the user's typed responses are underscored for illustration.

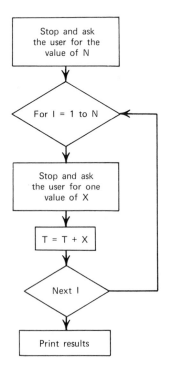

Figure 4.1 Flowchart illustrating the INPUT statement in a program.

```
100 LET T=0
200 PRINT "HØW MANY VALUES DØ YØU WISH TØ ADD";
300 INPUT N
400 PRINT

500 FØR I=1 TØ N
600 PRINT "NUMBER";
700 INPUT X
800 LET T=T+X
900 NEXT I

1000 PRINT
1100 PRINT "THE SUM ØF THØSE NUMBERS IS";T
1200 END
 RUN

HØW MANY VALUES DØ YØU WISH TØ ADD   ? 6

NUMBER    ? 3
NUMBER    ? 2
NUMBER    ? -1
NUMBER    ? .2
NUMBER    ? 0
NUMBER    ? 4

THE SUM ØF THØSE NUMBERS IS    8.2
```

Program 4.1 Illustrating the use of the INPUT statement
to assign the variable values from the keyboard. The under-
scores indicate the parts which the user types.

NOTES ON INPUT STATEMENTS

There are a few simple rules which must be followed when using INPUT
statements:

■   Any number of variables can be requested with one INPUT statement. The number of values typed after the question mark must exactly
equal the number of variables in the INPUT statement.

■   Each value typed at the keyboard must be separated by a comma.

■   After all values are entered for one INPUT statement, a "carriage
return" must be given to indicate the termination of the list, and to instruct
the computer to resume program execution.

■   To prevent a carriage return after the question's verbage is printed,
before the INPUT statement is executed, punctuation is usually placed at
the end of the PRINT statement, as shown by the semicolons in lines 200
and 600 of Program 4.1. Had such punctuation not been inserted each
question would have been printed in this manner:

HØW MANY VALUES DØ YØU WISH TØ ADD
? 6

because a carriage return would have automatically been given after the message was printed.

There are several programming situations where the INPUT statement can be conveniently exploited. For example, a program may be written by a programmer but intended for use by another person, one less sophisticated in dealing with the computer or one who is unfamiliar with the mechanics of the particular program. The phrasing of questions and use of this statement may serve to prompt the user or give him guidance. Example 4.2, below, illustrates the simple principles involved.

Or, a program may be designed for running many times and the presumption is made that the user will wish to specify changes in certain of the variables to tailor each run to his immediate interest. Typically, the computer might ask such questions as:

HØW MANY EMPLØYEES ARE THERE THIS WEEK?
WHAT IS THE CURRENT INTEREST RATE?
WHAT TEMPERATURE RANGE ARE YØU CØNSIDERING?
WHAT IS THE INITIAL VELØCITY?
WHAT ARE THE CENTER-ØF-GRAVITY'S CØØRDINATES?

Examples 4.2 and 4.3 also illustrate this application of the INPUT statement.

Finally, a generalized program may contain several optional routines which the user is allowed to select for execution during each running. Example 4.3 is designed to show this principle by asking the user which of several recipes to use at the time of each execution.

Example 4.2 Helping the User

Suppose a program has been written to calculate the true annual interest rate being charged for a loan. That program, by itself, is not of particular interest here. However, it should include instructions for its use and ask the user to give it the principal, number of payments, and other details about the loan.

DISCUSSION
The segment of the program which is of interest here is given in Program 4.2. The main body of the program—that which calculates the answer—is presumed to follow line 226. Instructions are given in the form of PRINT statements between lines 106 and 113. The program begins by asking the user if he wants instructions. If he answers "No" (by typing a zero), line 104 diverts the computer around the instructions. The user is thus permitted to avoid a lengthy and (possibly, if he is already familiar with the program) boring printout each time he uses the program.

```
100 PRINT "TYPE A ØNE IF YØU THINK YØU NEED"
101 PRINT "HELP WITH THIS PRØGRAM.   TYPE A ZERØ"
102 PRINT "IF YØU DØN'T";
103 INPUT A
104 IF A=0 THEN 2000

105 PRINT
106 PRINT "THIS PRØGRAM CALCULATES THE TRUE ANNUAL"
107 PRINT "INTEREST RATE BEING PAID ØN A LØAN.   ALL"
108 PRINT "PAYMENTS BUT THE LAST ARE ASSUMED EQUAL."
109 PRINT "IF THE LAST PAYMENT IS UNEQUAL,"
110 PRINT "YØU MUST ANSWER 'YES' TØ A QUESTIØN"
111 PRINT "I WILL LATER ASK ABØUT BALLØØN"
112 PRINT "PAYMENTS.       ...NØW...."
113 PRINT

200 PRINT "WHAT IS THE PRINCIPAL ØF THE LØAN";
201 INPUT P
205 PRINT "HØW MANY PAYMENTS ARE TØ BE MADE";
206 INPUT N
210 PRINT "IS THE LAST ØNE A BALLØØN PAYMENT?  ANSWER"
211 PRINT "ØNE IF YES, AND ANSWER ZERØ IF NØ";
212 INPUT B
215 IF B=0 THEN 225
220 PRINT "HØW MUCH IS THE BALLØØN PAYMENT";
221 INPUT B1
225 PRINT "HØW MUCH ARE THE EQUAL PAYMENTS";
226 INPUT P1
  RUN

TYPE A ØNE IF YØU THINK YØU NEED
HELP WITH THIS PRØGRAM.   TYPE A ZERØ
IF YØU DØN'T   ? 1

THIS PRØGRAM CALCULATES THE TRUE ANNUAL
INTEREST RATE BEING PAID ØN A LØAN.   ALL
PAYMENTS BUT THE LAST ARE ASSUMED EQUAL.
IF THE LAST PAYMENT IS UNEQUAL,
YØU MUST ANSWER 'YES' TØ A QUESTIØN
I WILL LATER ASK ABØUT BALLØØN
PAYMENTS.       ...NØW....

WHAT IS THE PRINCIPAL ØF THE LØAN    ? 1055
HØW MANY PAYMENTS ARE TØ BE MADE     ? 25
IS THE LAST ØNE A BALLØØN PAYMENT?  ANSWER
ØNE IF YES, AND ANSWER ZERØ IF NØ    ? 1
HØW MUCH IS THE BALLØØN PAYMENT  ? 95
HØW MUCH ARE THE EQUAL PAYMENTS  ? 46.25
```

Program 4.2 Illustrating the principles of prompting and instructing the user, and asking him to tailor the program to his immediate needs.

Example 4.3 Recipes

Using the recipes in Table 4.1, write a program to ask the user if he would like a recipe for pink lemonade, eggnog, or beer, and the quantity of the chosen product that he wishes to make. After printing a selected recipe, ask the user if he would like another recipe.

Table 4.1   Recipes for Example 4.3

PINK LEMONADE (Serves 1)
2 tbspns lemon juice
2 tbspns sugar
1 teaspn maraschino cherry juice
1 glass water
  ice cubes

EGGNOG (Serves 18)
6 eggs
.5 cups sugar
2 cups milk
2 cups heavy cream, whipped
2 cups brandy
  dash salt

BEER (Makes 50 gallons)
45 gallons water
75 pounds malt
25 pounds corn
 8 pounds hops
 1 pound yeast

DISCUSSION

The listing in Program 4.3 accomplishes the required tasks.

The printout, in Table 4.2, illustrates the interactive nature of the computer and the user engaged in "talking" to each other. The key statements are lines 500–600, 1001–1100, 2001–2100, 3001–3010, and 5100–5300. The program is also endowed with the ability to sense an invalid response from the user and coach him to give an acceptable answer (see lines 700–920 and 5400–5700).

TEACHING MACHINES

A teaching concept currently enjoying experimental popularity is individual tutoring of students by computers. In an elemental sense it is the INPUT statement which makes the technique possible when the teaching computer is programmed in BASIC, for it can be programmed with statements like

```
100 PRINT "WHAT IS 4+2";
101 INPUT A
102 IF A=6 THEN 110

103 PRINT "TRY AGAIN...HERE ARE FOUR X'S AND"
104 PRINT "TWO MORE X'S...."
105 PRINT "     XXXX   XX"
106 PRINT "COUNT THEM ALL, AND THEN TELL ME"
107 GO TO 100

110 PRINT "CORRECT!!   NOW FOR ANOTHER ONE..."
111 REM       .
112 REM       .
113 REM--- CONTINUE IN THIS WAY WITH MORE
114 REM       QUESTIONS
    RUN

WHAT IS 4+2    ? 5
TRY AGAIN...HERE ARE FOUR X'S AND
TWO MORE X'S....
     XXXX   XX
COUNT THEM ALL, AND THEN TELL ME
WHAT IS 4+2    ? 6
CORRECT!!   NOW FOR ANOTHER ONE...
```

The questions, of course, could be as complex as appropriate—questions on physics, medicine, or history. In fact, at least one computer company has developed tutorial programs to teach students the rudimentary principles of computer programming.

4.2   MATHEMATICAL FUNCTIONS

For the programmer's convenience, the computer is able to recognize and evaluate certain mathematical functions. Examples with general utility are given in Table 4.3. More specialized functions—used widely in engineering, mathematics, and science—are given in Table 4.4.

Functions are designated by a three-letter "name" and an "argument," the latter being enclosed in parentheses. In Tables 4.3 and 4.4 the arguments of the functions are represented by a ($\cdot$). The dot is, of course, not actually typed when using the function. It is used here only to mean that any value or mathematical expression can be used where the dot appears. The computer first evaluates the mathematical expression and then performs the specified function. Discussion of a few of the functions will illustrate all of them.

SQR ($\bullet$)

The expressions on p. 166 illustrate the use of the SQR function. Observe that functions can be used as any other variable—they can be added, multiplied together, or used in other mathematical expressions.

```
50 PRINT
100 PRINT "THE CHØICES FRØM WHICH YØU MAY SELECT ARE:"
200 PRINT "    1. PINK LEMØNADE"
300 PRINT "    2. EGGNØG"
400 PRINT "    3. BEER"
500 PRINT "WHICH WØULD YØU PREFER";
600 INPUT A

700 IF A=1 THEN 1000
800 IF A=2 THEN 2000
900 IF A=3 THEN 3000
910 PRINT "YØU MAY ØNLY ANSWER 1,2 ØR 3.  TRY AGAIN..."
920 GØ TØ 600

1000 PRINT
1001 PRINT "HØW MANY GLASSES WØULD YØU LIKE TØ MAKE";
1100 INPUT Q
1300 PRINT "THEN USE THESE QUANTITIES ØF EACH INGREDIENT"
1400 PRINT 2*Q,"TBSPNS LEMØN JUICE"
1500 PRINT 2*Q,"TBSPNS SUGAR"
1600 PRINT 1*Q,"TEASPNS MARASCHINØ CHERRY JUICE"
1700 PRINT 1*Q,"GLASSES WATER"
1800 PRINT " ","ICE CUBES"
1900 PRINT "AND YØU WILL HAVE ";Q;" PERFECT GLASSES ØF PINK LEMØNADE."
1910 GØ TØ 5000

2000 PRINT
2001 PRINT "HØW MANY SERVINGS WØULD YØU LIKE TØ MAKE";
2100 INPUT Q
2200 PRINT
2300 PRINT "THEN USE THESE QUANTITIES ØF EACH INGREDIENT"
2400 PRINT 6*Q/18,"EGGS"
2500 PRINT .5*Q/18,"CUPS SUGAR"
2600 PRINT 2*Q/18,"CUPS MILK"
2700 PRINT 2*Q/18,"CUPS HEAVY CREAM, WHIPPED"
2800 PRINT 2*Q/18,"CUPS BRANDY"
2900 PRINT " ","DASH SALT"
2910 PRINT "AND YØU WILL HAVE ";Q;" PERFECT SERVINGS ØF EGGNØG."
2920 GØ TØ 5000

3000 PRINT
3001 PRINT "HØW MANY GALLØNS WØULD YØU LIKE TØ MAKE";
3010 INPUT Q
3100 PRINT
3200 PRINT "THEN USE THESE QUANTITIES ØF EACH INGREDIENT"
3300 PRINT Q*45/50,"GALLØNS WATER"
3400 PRINT Q*75/50,"PØUNDS MALT"
3500 PRINT Q*25/50,"PØUNDS CØRN"
3600 PRINT Q*8/50,"PØUNDS HØPS"
3700 PRINT Q/50,"PØUNDS YEAST"
3800 PRINT
3900 PRINT "AND YØU WILL HAVE ";Q;" GALLØNS ØF PERFECT BEER."

5000 FØR I=1 TØ 3
5010 PRINT
5020 NEXT I
5100 PRINT "WØULD YØU LIKE ANØTHER RECIPE (ANSWER 0. IF NØ,"
5200 PRINT "AND ANSWER 1. IF YES.)";
5300 INPUT A1
5400 IF A1=0 THEN 6000
5500 IF A1=1 THEN 500
5600 PRINT "PLEASE ANSWER ØNLY 0 ØR 1.  TRY AGAIN...";
5700 GØ TØ 5300
6000 PRINT
6100 PRINT "THEN WE ARE FINISHED."
6200 END
```

Program 4.3 Recipes.

Table 4.2 Output from the recipe program.

```
RUN


THE CHØICES FRØM WHICH YØU MAY SELECT ARE:
    1. PINK LEMØNADE
    2. EGGNØG
    3. BEER
WHICH WØULD YØU PREFER   ? 2

HØW MANY SERVINGS WØULD YØU LIKE TØ MAKE   ? 12

THEN USE THESE QUANTITIES ØF EACH INGREDIENT
    4            EGGS
    .33333333    CUPS SUGAR
    1.3333333    CUPS MILK
    1.3333333    CUPS HEAVY CREAM, WHIPPED
    1.3333333    CUPS BRANDY
                 DASH SALT
AND YØU WILL HAVE      12     PERFECT SERVINGS ØF EGGNØG.



WØULD YØU LIKE ANØTHER RECIPE (ANSWER 0. IF NØ,
AND ANSWER 1. IF YES.)   ? 2
PLEASE ANSWER ØNLY 0 ØR 1.   TRY AGAIN...   ? 1
WHICH WØULD YØU PREFER   ? 1

HØW MANY GLASSES WØULD YØU LIKE TØ MAKE   ? 100
THEN USE THESE QUANTITIES ØF EACH INGREDIENT
    200          TBSPNS LEMØN JUICE
    200          TBSPNS SUGAR
    100          TEASPNS MARASCHINØ CHERRY JUICE
    100          GLASSES WATER
                 ICE CUBES
AND YØU WILL HAVE      100     PERFECT GLASSES ØF PINK LEMØNADE.



WØULD YØU LIKE ANØTHER RECIPE (ANSWER 0. IF NØ,
AND ANSWER 1. IF YES.)   ? 1
WHICH WØULD YØU PREFER   ? 1

HØW MANY GLASSES WØULD YØU LIKE TØ MAKE   ? 150
THEN USE THESE QUANTITIES ØF EACH INGREDIENT
    300          TBSPNS LEMØN JUICE
    300          TBSPNS SUGAR
    150          TEASPNS MARASCHINØ CHERRY JUICE
    150          GLASSES WATER
                 ICE CUBES
AND YØU WILL HAVE      150     PERFECT GLASSES ØF PINK LEMØNADE.



WØULD YØU LIKE ANØTHER RECIPE (ANSWER 0. IF NØ,
AND ANSWER 1. IF YES.)   ? 0

THEN WE ARE FINISHED.
```

Basic statement	Meaning
100 LET M = SQR(5)	$M = \sqrt{5}$
903 LET C = SQR(A↑2 + B↑2)	$C = \sqrt{a^2 + b^2}$
120 LET X1 = 3*SQR(2*L + 1)	$X1 = 3\sqrt{2L + 1}$
140 LET Y = SQR((A + B)*(2 + C))	$Y = \sqrt{(a + b)*(2 + c)}$

INT (•)

The computer first evaluates the argument and then gives the integer value of it. If the argument is positive, the decimal part of the argument is dropped, leaving only the whole number of the argument; i.e., INT (16.06) = 16. In fact, the integer function actually determines "the greatest whole number which is smaller than the argument." Indeed, 16 is the greatest whole number less than 16.05.

Care must be used if the argument is negative, for it should be recognized that the integer of, for example, -16.05 is -17, the latter number being the greatest whole number which is smaller than -16.05.

The integer function is further illustrated by the examples below. Note that in some of these the argument contains another function.

Basic statement	Meaning
100 LET X = INT(21.03)	X = INT(21.03)
100 LET Y = INT(2*L)	Y = INT(2L)
100 LET Z = INT(21.03) + INT(1.4)	Z = INT(21.03) + INT(1.4)
100 LET A = INT(SQR(M↑2 + N↑2))	$A = INT(\sqrt{M^2 + 2^2})$

The integer function has two special applications which are not immediately obvious. One is to round off variables to a specified number of decimal places; the other is to determine if a number is evenly divisible by two (i.e., even or odd) or any other number.

Rounding Off

Suppose X = \$12.287, and it is desirable to set Y = X, rounded off to the nearest cent (i.e., Y = 12.29). The following statement may be used:

$$100 \quad LET \quad Y = INT(100*X + .5)/100$$

To observe how this statement results in the appropriate round off of X, let us trace the processing of the statement through the computer. The following steps are undertaken:

First,   evaluate 100∗X   ($= 1228.7$)
Second, add 0.5   ($= 1229.2$)
Third,   take integer of 100∗X + 0.5   ($= 1229$)
Fourth, divide by 100   ($= 12.29$)
Fifth,   set Y equal to number derived in the fourth step ($Y = 12.29$)

   To round off to some other number of decimal places the quantities (100) in the expression are changed. To investigate, try rounding X = 1.28443 to three decimal places (i.e., change 100s to 1000 and repeat steps 1–5 above).
   Program 4.4 applies the technique to the Payroll Journal Program so

Table 4.3   General utility functions.

Statement	Examples	Meaning
LET X = INT(·)	X = INT(2.8) = 2 A = INT(−1.2) = −1 A = INT(.2) = 0 C = INT(A+B)	Set X = the largest whole number not greater than the value in parentheses
LET X = ABS(·)	X = ABS(−3) = 3 Y = ABS(2−3) = 1 Y = ABS(3∗C)	Let X = the number in the parentheses, ignoring the sign.
LET X = SQR(·)	X = SQR(25) = 5 X1 = SQR(3↑2 + 4↑2) = 5 T = SQR(2∗B + 3)	Let X = the square root of the value in parentheses
LET X = MAX(·, ·, ·)	X = (−3,A,B↑2)	Sets X = largest value among −3, A, B^2
LET X = MIN(·, ·, ·)	X = (3∗Y, X + 2, Z/3)	Sets X = smallest value among 3∗Y, X + 2, Z/3
LET X = CØMP (A,B)	X = CØMP(3,5) = −1 X = CØMP(5,3) = +1 X = CØMP(3,3) = 0	If A < B, sets X = −1 If A > B, sets X = +1 If A = B, sets X = 0
LET X = DATE	X = DATE = 41372	Sets X = today's date,* as April 13, 1972
LET X = TIME	X = TIME = 1345	Sets X = the time of day* at the instant the statement is executed, as 1:45 pm

*These functions have no arguments.

Table 4.4 Mathematical functions.

Statement	Examples	Meaning
LET X = SIN(·)	X = SIN(1.28) S1 = SIN(T + .32)	Set X = sine of 1.28 radians
LET X = CØS(·)	X = CØS(1.28) A = CØS(90/57.269)	Set X = cosine of 1.28 radians
LET X = TAN(·)	A = TAN(1.28)	Set X = tangent of 1.28 radians
LET X = CØT(·)	T3 = CØT(1.28)	Set X = cotangent of 1.28 radians
LET X = ATN(·)	X = ATN(.304)	Set X = angle whose tangent is 0.304, or X = $\tan^{-1}$ (0.304)
LET X = EXP(·)	X = EXP(−0.01) E1 = EXP(−L*T)	Set X = $e^{-0.01}$, or X = $(2.718)^{-0.01}$
LET X = LØG(·)	X = LØG(0.408) X = LØG(2*T + 2 − 1)	Set X = $\log_e(0.408)$ = ln(0.408)
LET X = PI	X = 3.14159	Let X = π*

*Pi requires no argument.

that the employee's payroll amounts are appropriately rounded to two decimal points. The result is shown in Table 4.5.

Divisible By . . .

A method for determining the evenness or oddness of a given number was given in Example 2.6. That procedure was very awkward by comparison with the one below:

```
100 READ X
200 IF X/2=INT(X/2) THEN 500

300 PRINT "ØDD"
400 GØ TØ 600
500 PRINT "EVEN"
550 DATA 14
600 END
RUN

EVEN
```

Examining line 200, suppose X = 14 (i.e., an even number). Then X/2 = 7 and INT(X/2) = 7. Therefore, X/2 = INT(X/2) and the computer is appropriately diverted to line 500. On the other hand, suppose

```
100 FØR I=1 TØ 5
200 PRINT
300 NEXT I
600 PRINT "               PAYRØLL JØURNAL"
700 PRINT "                  FØR"
800 PRINT "            WIDGET-GIDGET MFG. CØ."
900 PRINT
1000 PRINT
1100 PRINT "            JANUARY 10, 1971"
1200 PRINT
1300 PRINT
1400 PRINT "               ---"
1500 PRINT
1600 PRINT
1700 PRINT
1800 PRINT "  ","HØURS"
1900 PRINT "EMPLØYEE","WØRKED","SALARY","DEDUCTIØNS",'NET"
2000 PRINT "--------","------","------","----------","---"
2100 PRINT

2200 LET H9=0
2300 LET S9=0
2400 LET D9=0
2500 LET N9=0

2999 LET N=6
3000 FØR I=1 TØ N
3100 READ N1,H,R,T
3200 LET S=INT(100*H*R+.5)/100
3300 LET D=INT(100*T*S+.5)/100
3400 PRINT N1,H,S,D,S-D
3500 LET H9=H9+H
3600 LET S9=S9+S
3700 LET D9=D9+D
3800 LET N9=N9+(S-D)
4000 NEXT I

5800 PRINT "  ","--------","----------","----------","----------"
5900 PRINT "TØTAL",H9,"$";S9,"$";D9,"$";N9

6000 DATA 40312,40,3.32,.103
6100 DATA 08140,42,5.25,.172
6200 DATA 31402,38,4.28,.145
6300 DATA 12440,40,2.13,.085
6400 DATA 21443,40,6.28,.18
6500 DATA 41102,41.5,5.03,.163
6800 END
```

Program 4.4 Incorporating rounding off into the Payroll Journal Program.

$X = 31$ (i.e., an odd number). Then $X/2 = 15.5$, but $INT(X/2) = 15$. Since $X/2$ and $INT(X/2)$ are not equal, the computer proceeds from line 200 to line 300, printing "ØDD."

Obviously, line 200 can be changed to determine if X is divisible by any other number. Example 4.4, below, is a most useful problem illustrating the INT function.

Table 4.5 Payroll Journal Program printout with rounding off included.

```
                         PAYRØLL  JØURNAL
                               FØR
                     WIDGET-GIDGET MFG.  CØ.


                         JANUARY 10,  1971


                             ---
```

EMPLØYEE	HØURS WØRKED	SALARY	DEDUCTIØNS	NET
--------	------	------	----------	---
40312	40	132.8	13.68	119.12
8140	42	220.5	37.93	182.57
31402	38	162.64	23.58	139.06
12440	40	85.2	7.24	77.96
21443	40	251.2	45.22	205.98
41102	41.5	208.74	34.02	174.72
	--------	---------	---------	---------
TØTAL	241.5	$ 1061.08	$ 161.67	$ 899.41

Example 4.4   Skipping Lines in the Printout

Programs often involve many lines of printout, and it is desirable to leave a blank every five (or some other number of) lines to make the output more readable. Install this feature in the Payroll Journal problem.

DISCUSSION
Lines 3900 and 3901 have been added to Program 4.5. Whenever I is not divisible by five (i.e., on employees number 1, 2, 3, 4, 6, 7, . . .) line 3901 is bypassed. But on every fifth iteration I is divisible by five, and the extra PRINT statement is executed, as shown in Table 4.6.

4.3   PROGRAMMER-DEFINED FUNCTIONS

Section 4.2 discussed functions which were preprogrammed into the computer. If it is convenient to him, the programmer can also create his own functions for the computer to evaluate. Like the previous ones, these functions are given a three-letter name and an argument. In this case, all functions are given a name beginning with the letters "FN". The third letter is at the programmer's discretion. It may be A through Z. A function named "FND" is called "function D."

Programmer-defined functions are used to shorten and simplify the programming and typing tasks when either (a) the same mathematical expression is used several places in the program; or (b) essentially the same mathematical expression, but with one (or more) of the variables changed, is used several places in the program.

The first step is to "define" the desired function for the computer with a DEF statement similar to

$$101 \quad \text{DEF FND(X)} = X{\uparrow}3 - 3{*}Y{*}SQR(X+Y) - A1/3$$

Of course, the expression on the right side of the equals sign can be any expression the programmer chooses. As shown, it can (a) contain constants; (b) contain any variables, whether they are the same as the argument or not; and (c) contain other functions described in Section 4.2.

When the computer encounters the DEF statement it does nothing except

```
                  •
                  •
                  •
1800 PRINT " ","HØURS"
1900 PRINT "EMPLØYEE","WØRKED","SALARY","DEDUCTIØNS","NET"
2000 PRINT "---------","-------","-------","-----------","---"
2100 PRINT

2200 LET H9=0
2300 LET S9=0
2400 LET D9=0
2500 LET N9=0

2999 LET N=6
3000 FØR I=1 TØ N
3100 READ N1,H,R,T
3200 LET S=INT(100*H*R+.5)/100
3300 LET D=INT(100*T*S+.5)/100
3400 PRINT N1,H,S,D,S-D
3500 LET H9=H9+H
3600 LET S9=S9+S
3700 LET D9=D9+D
3800 LET N9=N9+(S-D)
3900 IF INT(I/5)<>I/5 THEN 4000
3901 PRINT
4000 NEXT I

5800 PRINT " ","---------","---------","---------","---------"
5900 PRINT "TØTAL",H9,"$":S9,"$":D9,"$":N9

6000 DATA 40312,40,3.32,.103
6100 DATA 08140,42,5.25,.172
6200 DATA 31402,38,4.28,.145
6300 DATA 12440,40,2.13,.085
6400 DATA 21443,40,6.28,.18
6500 DATA 41102,41.5,5.03,.163
6800 END
```

Program 4.5 Altering the Payroll Journal Program to leave a blank every fifth line in the printout.

Table 4.6 Result of change in the Payroll Journal Program to leave blank spacing every fifth line.

```
                        PAYRØLL  JØ URNAL
                              FØ R
                   WIDGET-GIDGET MFG.  CØ.


                       JANUARY  10,  1971


                             - - -



                   HØ URS
EMPLØYEE           WØ RKED          SALARY          DEDUCTIØNS        NET
- - - - - - - -    - - - - - -      - - - - - -     - - - - - - - -   - - -

  40312               40            132.8             13.68          119.12
  8140                42            220.5             37.93          182.57
  31402               38            162.64            23.58          139.06
  12440               40             85.2              7.24           77.96
  21443               40            251.2             45.22          205.98

  41102               41.5          208.74            34.02          174.72
                   - - - - - - - - -  - - - - - - - - -  - - - - - - - - -  - - - - - - - -
TØ TAL               241.5       $ 1061.08        $ 161.67        $ 899.41
```

to remember its meaning for use in later statements, as in line 1510 below:

   101   DEF FND(X) = X$\uparrow$3 − 3$*$X$*$Y$*$SQR(X + Y) − A1/3

       .

       .

       .

   1509   LET X = .2
   1510   LET T3 = 4 + FND(X)

The computer then refers back to the DEF statement and recognizes that it should evaluate line 1510 as

$$T3 = 4 + X\uparrow3 − 3*Y*SQR(X + Y) − A1/3$$

or in this case,

$$T3 = 4 + .2\uparrow3 − 3*Y*SQR(.2 + Y) − A1/3$$

Although the same variable, X, is used for the argument in line 1510 as was used in line 101, one of the principal advantages of the programmer-defined function is that this is not necessary. For example, had line 1510 been written

   1510   LET T3 = 4 + FND(J)

the computer would have substituted the argument variable J for the original variable X in the function, in effect resulting in the following statement being evaluated:

$$T3 = 4 + J\uparrow3 - 3*Y*SQR(J + Y) - A1/3$$

Some computer systems have the ability to accept two or more arguments in the DEF statement:

101   DEF FND(X,Y) = X↑3 − 3*Y*SQR(X+Y) − A1/3

It follows, then, that line 1510 above would also specify two arguments:

1510   LET T3 = 4 + FND(J,K)

meaning

$$T3 = 4 + J\uparrow3 - 3*K*SQR(J + K) - A1/3$$

That is, J is substituted for X, and K is substituted for Y.

Example 4.5   Programmer-Defined Function in the Payroll Journal Program

In Program 4.5 the round off function was utilized twice, in lines 3200 and 3300. Had the function been used several dozen times in the program, it would have been quite tedious to implement. Use the programmer-defined function to simplify the implementation.

DISCUSSION
The installation of line 50 in Program 4.6 and the alteration of lines 3200 and 3300 obviously produce the desired results.

The rounding off technique can now be used very effectively in any elaborate program. The programmer-defined functions are obviously not confined to this single application. They should always be considered when the same mathematical expression is used several times in a program.

4.4   REMARK STATEMENT

The REMARK statement provides a means for inserting explanatory text in the middle of the program. It is convenient for documenting the meaning of parts of the program. This is helpful when one tries to recall the intention of those parts at some later date, or when someone else attempts to read the program. It can also give instructions for using the program.

```
  50 DEF FNR(X)=INT(100*X+.5)/100
          :
          :
          :
1800 PRINT " ","HØURS"
1900 PRINT "EMPLØYEE","WØRKED","SALARY","DEDUCTIØNS","NET"
2000 PRINT "--------","------","------","----------","---"
2100 PRINT

2200 LET H9=0
2300 LET S9=0
2400 LET D9=0
2500 LET N9=0

2999 LET N=6
3000 FØR I=1 TØ N
3100 READ N1,H,R,T
3200 LET S=FNR(H*R)
3300 LET D=FNR(T*S)
3400 PRINT N1,H,S,D,S-D
3500 LET H9=H9+H
3600 LET S9=S9+S
3700 LET D9=D9+D
3800 LET N9=N9+(S-D)
3900 IF INT(I/5)<>I/5 THEN 4000
3901 PRINT
4000 NEXT I

5800 PRINT " ","--------","---------","---------","---------"
5900 PRINT "TØTAL",H9,"$";S9,"$";D9,"$";N9

6000 DATA 40312,40,3.32,.103
6100 DATA 08140,42,5.25,.172
6200 DATA 31402,38,4.28,.145
6300 DATA 12440,40,2.13,.085
6400 DATA 21443,40,6.28,.18
6500 DATA 41102,41.5,5.03,.163
6800 END
```

Program 4.6   Programmer-defined function for rounding off.

REMARK statements are shown in Program 4.7. The computer simply ignores the text on a line beginning with the phrase REMARK.*

4.5   STØP STATEMENT

There can only be one END statement in a program, and it must be the last line. It often happens that the program is finished when any of a number of branches are completed; i.e., there are several places where the computer could stop. In such cases, it would be necessary to have a series of statements like

---

*Actually, most computers permit use of the three characters REM, as well as the full word:

—REM   THIS LØØP IS DØNE ØNCE FØR EACH EMPLØYEE

.
.
.

150   GØ TØ 30000

.
.
.

600   GØ TØ 30000

.
.
.

30000   END

A STØP statement at lines 150 and 600 is equivalent:

.
.
.

150   STØP

.
.
.

600   STØP

.
.
.

30000   END

4.6   RESTØRE STATEMENT

Occasionally a program requires that the DATA be read and reused more than once. Whenever the RESTØRE statement is encountered, the computer again begins reading the data from the beginning. The following simple program illustrates:

```
100 FØR I=1 TØ 3
110 READ X
120 PRINT X
130 NEXT I

200 RESTØRE
300 FØR I=1 TØ 6
310 READ X
320 PRINT X
330 NEXT I

400 DATA 10,-1,112
401 DATA 16,14,33
500 END
```

The printout from this program is

```
                        RUN

                         10
                        -1
                         112
                         10
                        -1
                         112
                         16
                         14
                         33
```

```
  50 DEF FNR(X)=INT(100*X+.5)/100
  99 REMARK-BEGINNING ØF TABLE HEADING
             .
             .
             .
1800 PRINT " ","HØURS"
1900 PRINT "EMPLØYEE","WØRKED","SALARY","DEDUCTIØNS","NET"
2000 PRINT "--------","------","------","-----------","---"
2100 PRINT

2199 REMARK-INITIALIZE ACCUMULATØR
2200 LET H9=0
2300 LET S9=0
2400 LET D9=0
2500 LET N9=0

2999 LET N=6
3000 FØR I=1 TØ N
3001 REMARK-THIS LØØP IS DØNE ØNCE FØR EACH EMPLØYEE
3100 READ N1,H,R,T
3200 LET S=FNR(H*R)
3300 LET D=FNR(T*S)
3400 PRINT N1,H,S,D,S-D
3500 LET H9=H9+H
3600 LET S9=S9+S
3700 LET D9=D9+D
3800 LET N9=N9+(S-D)
3900 IF INT(I/5)<>I/5 THEN 4000
3901 PRINT
4000 NEXT I

5799 REMARK-PRINT TØTALS
5800 PRINT " ","--------","----------","----------","----------"
5900 PRINT "TØTAL",H9,"$";S9,"$";D9,"$";N9

5998 REMARK-DATA IS:EMP NØ.;HRS WRKD;SALARY/HR.;TAX RATE
5999 REMARK-EMPLØYEES MAY BE IN ANY ØRDER
6000 DATA 40312,40,3.32,.103
6100 DATA 08140,42,5.25,.172
6200 DATA 31402,38,4.28,.145
6300 DATA 12440,40,2.13,.085
6400 DATA 21443,40,6.28,.18
6500 DATA 41102,41.5,5.03,.163
6800 END
```

Program 4.7 Illustrating the REMARK statement.

4.7 GØ SUB/RETURN

The GØ SUB statement initiates an action quite like that caused by the GØ TØ statement. The statement

1000   GØ SUB 9000

causes the computer to *temporarily* abandon the normal sequence at line 1000 and go immediately to the **subroutine** beginning in line 9000. The difference between GØ SUB and GØ TØ lies in the way the computer returns to the original program sequence. Imagine, for a moment, that there exist at several points in the program identical sets of statements of considerable complexity, and it is desirable to isolate and retain only one set for programming and typing ease. The GØ TØ statement presents some problems which GØ SUB eliminates, as shown in Example 4.6.

Example 4.6   *Greatest Common Denominator*

Given three numbers, say 60, 90, and 120, the largest number which will divide into all of them without remainders [i.e., the greatest common denominator (GCD)] can be found by use of the Euclidean algorithm. Understanding that algorithm is not important here. Suffice it to say that Program 4.8 is suitable to finding the GCD. Note that the series of statements in lines 2000–3000 must be employed twice—once when the computer reaches line 500, and again when it reaches line 800. Rather than duplicating those statements at each location it has been decided to keep them at the end of the program and simply use GØ TØ statements at lines 500 and 800 to divert the computer to them. Lines 2000–3000 are called a "subroutine."

But now a dilemma has been created. After executing the subroutine, the computer must be instructed to return to its original point in the program and resume execution. That is the initial intention of line 3100, but the dilemma is this: If the computer is in the subroutine as a result of line 500, line 3100 should read GØ TØ 600; but if it is in the subroutine as a result of line 800, line 3100 should read GØ TØ 900. Alas, the line cannot be written both ways. A GØ SUB/RETURN combination of statements can be used, as shown in Program 4.9.

Upon encountering the GØ SUB statements, the computer goes to line 2000, as before. However, when it gets to line 3100 and encounters the RETURN statement, it automatically returns just beyond the statement which sent it to the subroutine; i.e., the first time it encounters line 3100, it returns to line 600. The second time it returns to line 900, solving the problem.

```
100 PRINT " A        B        C        G"
200 READ A,B,C
300 LET X=A
400 LET Y=B
500 GØ TØ 2000

600 LET X=G
700 LET Y=C
800 GØ TØ 2000
900 PRINT A;B;C;G
1000 STØP

2000 LET Q=INT(X/Y)
2100 LET R=X-Q*Y
2200 IF R=0 THEN 3000
2300 LET X=Y
2400 LET Y=R
2500 GØ TØ 2000

3000 LET G=Y
3100 GØ TØ   ????

3200 DATA 60,90,120
3300 END
```

Program 4.8 Erroneous GØ TØ statements in
the Euclidean algorithm solution to Example 4.6.

```
100 PRINT " A        B        C        G"
200 READ A,B,C
300 LET X=A
400 LET Y=B
500 GØ SUB 2000

600 LET X=G
700 LET Y=C
800 GØ SUB 2000
900 PRINT A;B;C;G
1000 STØP

2000 LET Q=INT(X/Y)
2100 LET R=X-Q*Y
2200 IF R=0 THEN 3000
2300 LET X=Y
2400 LET Y=R
2500 GØ TØ 2000

3000 LET G=Y
3100 RETURN

3200 DATA 60,90,120
3300 END
   RUN
```

A	B	C	G
60	90	120	30

Program 4.9 Illustrating the use of GØ SUB/
RETURN statements in Example 4.6.

One subroutine can send the computer into another one, if desired; however, each subroutine must have its own RETURN statement.

■ EXERCISES

4.1 Write program segments which ask the user the following questions and accept values for appropriately named variables:

- What value of alpha and beta should be used?
- How long will the fuel supply last?
- What is the average production of this machine?
- What are the dimensions of the room?
- How many boxes are on order?
- What is the gear ratio of the first stage?

*4.2 A program is capable of determining the depreciation of a machine by (1) the straight-line, (2) sum-of-the-year's digits, and (3) declining balance methods. Pretend that method 1 starts in line 1000, method 2 in line 2000, and method 3 in line 3000. Program the statements necessary to ask the user for the depreciable value and useful life of the machine, and by which method he wishes to depreciate. Include the statements necessary to route the computer to the selected method's calculations and to protect against an erroneous entry when specifying the method.

4.3 The strength, elasticity, and other properties of a drive shaft depend on the material of which it is made. Presume that a program has the individual modules to calculate these characteristics for the following materials: steel (starting at line 1000), aluminum (at line 2000), brass (at line 3000), and fiberglass (at line 4000). Designate the materials 1, 2, 3, 4, respectively. Program the statements necessary to ask the user for the material and dimensions (x, y, and z) of his drive shaft, and route the computer to the appropriate module.

*4.4 A certain kind of satellite is launched in pairs aboard a Titan III C booster. A program should ask the user how many satellities are being launched. If the response is not an even number, the computer should explain that an error has been made and ask for a new answer.

*4.5 Given two numbers, say X and Y, the smaller (or larger) one can be found by

$$\text{smaller} = \frac{X + Y - |X - Y|}{2}$$

$$\text{larger} = \frac{X + Y + |X - Y|}{2}$$

Where $|n|$ = absolute value of n. Write programmer-defined func-
tions FNA and FNB to effect these equations. Use them to find the
largest and smallest of the following pairs of numbers: $(3, -1)$,
$(12, 2.1)$, $(\sin(30°), \cos(30°))$. Also, use them to find the largest and
smallest of these *triplets* of numbers: $(6, -16, 8.2)$, $(0.102, -0.102,
1.80)$.

4.6　Write statements to GØ SUB to line 1628 if $X + Y$ is negative; otherwise GØ SUB to line 1930.

4.7　A certain part of a program should be executed only during quarterly
months of the year—i.e., March (month 3), June (month 6), etc.
Using the DATE and INT functions, determine the month. If it is a
quarterly month, execute an appropriate subroutine.

*4.8　Using the INT function, print out the number of $5 bills, $1 bills,
quarters, dimes, nickels, and pennies to be given in change for a
$20 bill when the sale is for $3.68. [*Hint:* In, say, $12.15, there are an
integer number of $5 bills, plus an integer number of remaining $1
bills, etc.]

4.9　An angle A is read from data. Convert it to an equivalent angle
between 0° and 360° by subtracting an integer number of 360°
increments.

4.10　An employee receives life insurance in an amount equal to three
times his yearly salary, to the next highest $1000. Using the INT
function, write the statement to determine the amount of policy for
an employee whose salary is $243.16/week.

4.11　The number N of decibels (db) by which P_2 exceeds P_1 is defined by
$N = \log_{10}(P_2/P_1)$. Calculate decibels for the following pairs of
P_2, P_1: $3.04, 2.81$; $10.0, 1$; $6.3, 4.2$; and $6.3, 8.2$.

4.12　Once stage of a cascaded amplifier has a gain of $A_1 \angle \theta_1$, the other has
a gain of $A_2 \angle \theta_2$. The resultant gain of both stages is $A_1 A_2 \angle \theta_1 + \theta_2$.
"A" is called the magnitude, and "θ" is called the phase shift. Cal-
culate the resultant magnitude and phase shift if $A_1 = 1.3$, $\theta_1 =
\tan^{-1} 1.0$, $A_2 = 2.4$, $\theta_2 = \tan^{-1} 0.53$. Be sure the phase shift is
printed in degrees.

*4.13　The arguments of the sine and cosine functions must be expressed in
radians. If the angle is given in degrees, write programmer-defined
functions FNS and FNC to convert it to radians and take the sine
and cosine (radians = π*angle/180). Use them to evaluate

$$y = \sin 30° \sin 60° - \cos 30° \cos 60°$$

$$z = \sin 30°/\cos 30°$$

4.14　Construct programmer-defined functions to represent sinh x and

cosh x, where

$$\sinh x = \frac{e^x - e^{-x}}{2} \qquad \cosh x = \frac{e^x + e^{-x}}{2}$$

4.15 When the switch in Figure 4.2 is closed, the following equations define the current flowing in the circuit:

$$I = \frac{E}{w_1 L} e^{-bt} \sin(\omega_1 t) \qquad \text{if } \omega_1{}^2 = \frac{1}{LC} - \frac{R^2}{4L^2} > 0$$

$$I = \frac{E}{kL} e^{-bt} \sinh(kt) \qquad \text{if } k^2 = \frac{R^2}{4L^2} - \frac{1}{LC} > 0$$

where $b = R/2L$ and ω_1 is in rad/sec. Program to calculate I for $t = 0, 10, 20, \ldots, 900$ milliseconds (msec). Use the following data: $E = 100$ V, $R = 100\ \Omega$, $L = 10$ H, $C = 50 \times 10^{-6}$ F.

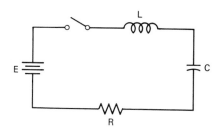

Figure 4.2

4.16 If $m_1 = m_2 = 0.25$ slugs, $k_1 = 16$ lb/ft, $k_2 = 24$ lb/ft, $w^2 = k_2/m_2$, $F_0 = 5$lb, and $F = F_0 \sin \omega t$, the displacement of m_1 in Figure 4.3 is

$$x(t) = \frac{F_0}{15k_2} [12\sqrt{2} \sin(\omega t/\sqrt{2}) + \sqrt{3} \sin(\omega t/\sqrt{3}) - 15 \sin(\omega t)]$$

Find x(t) for $t = 0, 0.01, 0.02, \ldots, 1.0$ sec.

Figure 4.3

4.17 A force vector, illustrated by the arrow in Figure 4.4a, is represented by the complex number $v_1 = x_1 + y_1 i$, where

$$x_1 = \text{magnitude } (v_1) \cdot \cos \phi$$

$$y_1 = \text{magnitude } (v_1) \cdot \sin \phi$$

If several vectors act on an object at the origin, as shown in Figure 4.4b, the resultant vector is the sum of the original vectors, i.e.,

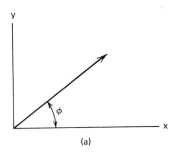

(a)

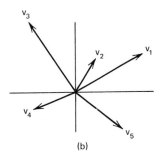

(b)

Figure 4.4

$v_r = x_r + y_r i = \Sigma x_i + \Sigma y_i i$. Write data statements and compute x_r and y_r for these vectors. Also, convert the resultant vector back to *polar* notation with this expression: $\overline{v}_r = \text{mag}(v_r)$ at the angle θ, where

$$\text{mag}(v_r) = \sqrt{x_r^2 + y_r^2} \qquad \theta = \tan^{-1}(y_r/x_r)$$

i	Magnitude (v)	$\phi(°)$
1	14.2	32
2	6.8	73
3	16.1	130
4	8.8	210
5	13.3	312

4.18 Write a multiple choice program to test students in United States geography, history, or some other subject. Ask ten questions. If necessary, the student should be allowed two attempts to answer properly. If he fails, give him the correct answers. Print his score, i.e., the number he gets correct on the first attempt, the number on the second attempt, and the number he does not get at all.

4.19 A thin white plate located in space, at an angle θ from the sun line absorbs thermal energy so that its temperature is

$$T = \sqrt[4]{\frac{Q_s \alpha \sin \theta}{2\epsilon\sigma}} + 460 \ (°F)$$

where

Absorvity $\alpha = 0.3$

Emissivity $\epsilon = 0.7$

$Q_s = 440 \ \text{Btu/hr/ft}^2$

$\sigma = 0.1713 \times 10^{-8} \ \text{Btu/hr/ft}^2$

Calculate T as a function of $\theta = 0\text{--}90°$, $\Delta\theta = 1°$.

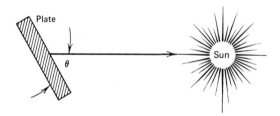

4.20 The children's game "buzz" goes something like this: All people sit in a circle and begin counting 1, 2, 3, ... Whenever a number either contains a seven or is divisible by seven, the child says "buzz," rather than the number. If the number meets both conditions, he says "buzzbuzz." Program the computer to play buzz while counting to 200.

4.21 A simple model of a satellite whirling about the earth incorporates the following parameters:

a = semimajor axis of the orbital trace
i = orbit's angle of inclination from the equator
e = eccentricity of the orbit
ω = argument of perigee
Ω = right ascension of the ascending node
t = elapsed time since the satellite passed perifocal

$$n = \frac{0.743657}{(a/6371)^{3/2}}$$

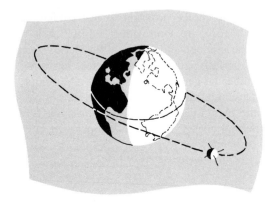

At $t = 0, 1, 2, \ldots, 30$ min, compute the (x,y,z) position of a satellite with $a = 100000$ km, $i = 5°$, $e = 0.05$, $\omega = 0$, $\Omega = 35°$, using

$$E - e\sin(E) - nt = 0 \qquad \text{(solve for E by a Newton–Raphson iteration, Exercise 3.20)}$$

$$x(t) = a(\cos E - e)(\cos \omega \cos \Omega - \sin \omega \sin \Omega \cos i)$$
$$+ (a\sqrt{1 - e^2} \sin E)(-\sin \omega \cos \Omega - \cos \omega \sin \Omega \cos i)$$

$$y(t) = a(\cos E - e)(\cos \omega \sin \Omega + \sin \omega \cos \Omega \cos i)$$
$$+ (a\sqrt{1 - e^2} \sin E)(-\sin \omega \sin \Omega + \cos \omega \cos \Omega \cos i)$$

$$z(t) = a(\cos E - e)(\sin \omega \sin i) + (a\sqrt{1 - e^2} \sin E)(\cos \omega \sin i)$$

4.8 SINGLY SUBSCRIPTED VARIABLES

Until now this book has dealt with only those variable names composed of a single letter, or of one letter adjoining a number. The following sections introduce an extremely important concept—the **subscripted variable.***†
Here, business problems are used for illustration. Engineering and mathematical problems are offered in the exercises and in selected case studies in Chapter 5.

Subscripted variables make it possible to use numbers in the variable name which exceed ten (a significant property, but there are many others which are even more important). The subscript numbers are enclosed in parentheses: $A(1), A(9), A(12), B(16), K(33)$.

---

*So named from the mathematical notation $v_1, v_2, v_3, \ldots, v_i$, etc.—i.e., "v-subscript-one."
†Sometimes called an "array" or a "matrix."

Before using these variables the computer must be informed of the maximum number of subscripts which will be required by the program. This is called **dimensioning** the variable, and it is accomplished with the DIM statement*:

$$50 \quad DIM \ A(50), X(22), P(13)$$

In the illustration, the DIM statement permits the subscript to be as high as 50 for variable **A**,† as high as 22 for variable **X**, and as high as 13 for variable **P**. Such variables are often regarded as representing a whole **table** of values, as shown in Example 4.7.

Example 4.7   A Price List

A clothing wholesaler lists thirteen products, at prices shown in Table 4.7. Using subscripted variables, write a program which calculates the average price of the wholesaler's products.

DISCUSSION
Such a program is given in Program 4.10. It is an introduction to the use of subscripted variables and does not fully exploit them, but it does illustrate the principles of subscripting.

Table 4.7   Prices of thirteen products being sold by a company.

Item number	Product name	Variable	Price ($)
1	Shirts, boys'	P(1)	2.39
2	Shirts, men's	P(2)	3.04
3	Blouses	P(3)	2.88
4	Skirts	P(4)	6.09
5	Trousers	P(5)	8.33
6	Belts	P(6)	1.88
7	Shoes	P(7)	12.16
8	Sandals	P(8)	1.19
9	Slacks, girls'	P(9)	2.14
10	Slacks, women's	P(10)	3.98
11	Jacket, sports	P(11)	6.93
12	Coat, summer	P(12)	9.82
13	Coat, winter	P(13)	21.04

*Most computers do not require dimensioning if the maximum subscript does not exceed 10; however, there is no risk in dimensioning anyway.

†This book adopts the convention that subscripted variables, such as **A**, **X** and **P**, will be written in boldface type when all elements are referred to simultaneously.

```
100 DIM P(13)

200 LET P(1)=2.39
201 LET P(2)=3.04
202 LET P(3)=2.88
203 LET P(4)=6.09
204 LET P(5)=8.33
205 LET P(6)=1.88
206 LET P(7)=12.16
207 LET P(8)=1.19
208 LET P(9)=2.14
209 LET P(10)=3.98
210 LET P(11)=6.93
211 LET P(12)=9.82
212 LET P(13)=21.04

300 LET T1=P(1)+P(2)+P(3)+P(4)+P(5)+P(6)+P(7)+P(8)
301 LET T1=T1+P(9)+P(10)+P(11)+P(12)+P(13)
400 PRINT "AVERAGE PRICE =";T1/13
500 END
 RUN

AVERAGE PRICE =    6.2976923
```

Program 4.10 A simple example of the use of subscripted variables.

VARIABLES AS THE SUBSCRIPT

The most powerful feature of these variables is the ability to refer to the subscript by another variable, as in

210   READ P(I)

The variable in the parentheses is called the **index**. In Program 4.11 the multitude of LET statements between lines 200 and 212 in Program 4.10

```
100 DIM P(13)

200 FØR I=1 TØ 13
201 READ P(I)
202 NEXT I

300 LET T1=0
301 FØR J=1 TØ 13
302 LET T1=T1+P(J)
303 NEXT J

400 PRINT "AVERAGE PRICE =";T1/13

500 DATA 2.39,3.04,2.88,6.09,8.33,1.88,12.16
501 DATA 1.19,2.14,3.98,6.93,9.82,21.04
600 END
RUN

AVERAGE PRICE =    6.2976923
```

Program 4.11 A more elegant example of the use of subscripted variables.

are replaced with an I loop containing the statement 201 READ P(I). When I = 1, line 201 refers to P(1) and the first data entry is assigned to P(1); when I = 2, P(2) = 3.04, etc. The process is repeated for each I.

The variables P(1),...,P(13) can now be used elsewhere in the program. For example, lines 301–303 use an accumulator to calculate the sum of the prices of the thirteen items. Observe that the variable J is used as the index in the second loop, although I was used in the original READ statement. This is done here only to illustrate that any variable can be used as the index, and different variables can be used throughout the program. It is the value, not the letter, of the index that is important. For instance, if I = 6, J = 6, K3 = 6, and L = 5, then

$$
\begin{array}{ll}
400 & \text{LET } A = P(I) \\
401 & \text{LET } B = P(J) \\
402 & \text{LET } C = P(K3) \\
403 & \text{LET } D = P(L+1)
\end{array}
$$

set A, B, C, and D = P(6) = 1.88.

Example 4.8   Wholesaler's Sales

The wholesaler described in Example 4.7 makes sales to three retailers during the month of March, as shown in Table 4.8. Write a program to determine the total billings accrued to each retailer and the wholesaler's total billings.

Table 4.8   Quantities of each product sold to three retailers.

Item number	Name	Retailer 1	Retailer 2	Retailer 3
1	Shirts, boys'	100	288	0
2	Shirts, men's	144	288	0
3	Blouses	82	432	500
4	Skirts	300	432	300
5	Trousers	50	88	0
6	Belts	25	18	0
7	Shoes	62	0	200
8	Sandals	300	0	100
9	Slacks, girls'	150	144	144
10	Slacks, women's	144	144	144
11	Jacket, sports	38	50	0
12	Coat, summer	6	15	0
13	Coat, winter	59	0	0

DISCUSSION

The DATA of Program 4.12 (lines 700–900) is an exact replica of that in Table 4.8. The quantities pertaining to each item are entered in the same order as the prices. The subscripted variable **R** represents the billable amount to each of the three retailers; **N** represents the quantity of each product sold to a retailer.

For each retailer (i.e., FØR I = 1 TØ 3 in line 300), the computer executes the inside J loop thirteen times, thereby reading, as N(1),N(2),...,N(13), the data pertaining to the *I*th retailer's sales. The total billing to each re-

```
100 DIM P(13),R(3),N(13)
200 FØR I=1 TØ 13
210 READ P(I)
220 NEXT I

250 FOR I=1 TØ 3
260 LET R(I)=0
270 NEXT I

300 FØR I=1 TØ 3
320 FØR J=1 TØ 13
330 READ N(J)
340 LET R(I)=R(I)+P(J)*N(J)
350 NEXT J
360 NEXT I

400 FØR I=1 TØ 3
410 PRINT "BILLINGS TØ RETAILER #";I,R(I)
420 NEXT I

500 PRINT
510 LET T1=0
520 FØR I=1 TØ 3
530 LET T1=T1+R(I)
540 NEXT I
550 PRINT "TØTAL, ALL RETAILERS ";T1

599 REMARK-PRICE DATA
600 DATA 2.39,3.04,2.88,6.09,8.33,1.88,12.16
601 DATA 1.19,2.14,3.98,6.93,9.82,21.04

699 REMARK-MARCH'S DATA
700 DATA 100,144,82,300,50,25,62,300,150,144
701 DATA 38,6,59
800 DATA 288,288,432,432,88,18,0,0,144,144
801 DATA 50,15,0
900 DATA 0,0,500,300,0,0,200,100,144,144,0,0,0
1000 END
  RUN

BILLINGS TØ RETAILER #    1     6772.08
BILLINGS TØ RETAILER #    2     7580.84
BILLINGS TØ RETAILER #    3     6699.28

TØTAL, ALL RETAILERS     21052.2
```

Program 4.12   Wholesaler's sales to several retailers.

tailer is obviously $R(I) = P(1)*N(1) + P(2)*N(2) + \cdots + P(13)*N(13)$. Or, more elegantly, the accumulator in line 340 performs the addition of $P(J)*N(J)$ terms, for $J = 1, 2, \ldots, 13$. For example, when $I = 2$,

$$R(2) = 2.39*288 + 3.04*2.88 + \cdots + 21.04*0$$

Lines 400–420 effect the printing of $R(1)$, $R(2)$, and $R(3)$. It is left to the student to examine lines 510–550, convincing himself that they generate the wholesaler's total billings.

Example 4.9 Several Months' Sales

Now suppose that a given execution of the computer program is required to process three months' worth of data for each retailer and that the data in lines 1000–1500, Program 4.13, are applicable to April's and May's sales. It is left to the student to determine that the addition of the K loop around lines 300–360 causes the repetition of the I and J loops, once for each month, resulting in continued accumulation into the variables $R(1)$, $R(2)$, or $R(3)$ until all months are completed.

VARIATIONS OF SINGLY SUBSCRIPTED VARIABLES

Before concluding the discussion on singly subscripted variables, a few words are in order about some of the variations which may be encountered. The reader is advised to consult programming manuals on the system he uses to resolve any questions. In particular, the following variations should be noted:

■ The dimension statement ordinarily infers that variables will take on subscripts from one to the maximum value in the dimension statement. On some computers, it may infer that the lowest subscript can be zero, rather than one.

■ On some computers, variables may be used to specify the maximum value in the DIM statement. This is a highly useful capability* for an INPUT statement may then be used to inquire of the operator regarding how the variables should be dimensioned on each run. For example, in Example 4.9, it is very likely that, on some future run, there will be more than three retailers to account for, and the beginning of the program might well be rewritten as shown in Program 4.14.

*This book will presume, in future examples, that this capability is available.

```
100 DIM P(13),R(3),N(13)
200 FØR I=1 TØ 13
210 READ P(I)
220 NEXT I

250 FØR I=1 TØ 3
260 LET R(I)=0
270 NEXT I

299 FØR K=1 TØ 3
300 FØR I=1 TØ 3
320 FØR J=1 TØ 13
330 READ N(J)
340 LET R(I)=R(I)+P(J)*N(J)
350 NEXT J
360 NEXT I
370 NEXT K

400 FØR I=1 TØ 3
410 PRINT "BILLINGS TØ RETAILER #";I,R(I)
420 NEXT I

500 PRINT
510 LET T1=0
520 FØR I=1 TØ 3
530 LET T1=T1+R(I)
540 NEXT I
550 PRINT "TØTAL, ALL RETAILERS ";T1

599 REMARK-PRICE DATA
600 DATA 2.39,3.04,2.88,6.09,8.33,1.88,12.16
601 DATA 1.19,2.14,3.98,6.93,9.82,21.04

699 REMARK-MARCH'S DATA
700 DATA 100,144,82,300,50,25,62,300,150,144
701 DATA 38,6,59
800 DATA 288,288,432,432,88,18,0,0,144,144
801 DATA 50,15,0
900 DATA 0,0,500,300,0,0,200,100,144,144,0,0,0

999 REMARK-APRIL'S DATA
1000 DATA 200,63,100,100,50,25,100,250,300,144,60,10,100
1100 DATA 112,112,500,500,12,50,50,25,144,200,50,0,20
1200 DATA 0,100,200,115,18,25,100,50,72,144,0,0,0

1299 REMARK- MAY'S DATA
1300 DATA 60,120,100,80,50,25,125,210,144,144,80,15,110
1400 DATA 300,200,400,450,20,100,100,100,100,200,100,0,50
1500 DATA 30,110,240,230,50,50,200,100,80,100,0,0,0
1600 END
  RUN

BILLINGS TØ RETAILER #    1      21562.9
BILLINGS TØ RETAILER #    2      25039.27
BILLINGS TØ RETAILER #    3      16607.97

TØTAL, ALL RETAILERS      63210.14
```

Program 4.13 Several months' data being combined.

```
 50 PRINT "HØW MANY RETAILERS ARE THERE THIS MØNTH";
 60 INPUT X
 70 PRINT "HØW MANY MØNTH'S DATA ARE THERE";
 80 INPUT X1

100 DIM P(13),R(X),N(13)
200 FØR I=1 TØ 13
210 READ P(I)
220 NEXT I

250 FØR I=1 TØ X
260 LET R(I)=0
270 NEXT I

299 FØR K=1 TØ X1
300 FØR I=1 TØ X
320 FØR J=1 TØ 13
330 READ N(J)
340 LET R(I)=R(I)+P(J)*N(J)
350 NEXT J
360 NEXT I
370 NEXT K

400 FØR I=1 TØ X
410 PRINT "BILLINGS TØ RETAILER #";I,R(I)
420 NEXT I

500 PRINT
510 LET T1=0
520 FØR I=1 TØ X
530 LET T1=T1+R(I)
540 NEXT I
550 PRINT "TØTAL. ALL RETAILERS ";T1

599 REMARK-PRICE DATA
600 DATA 2.39,3.04,2.88,6.09,8.33,1.88,12.16
601 DATA 1.19,2.14,3.98,6.93,9.82,21.04

699 REMARK-MARCH'S DATA
700 DATA 100,144,82,300,50,25,62,300,150,144
701 DATA 38,6,59
800 DATA 288,288,432,432,88,18,0,0,144,144
801 DATA 50,15,0
900 DATA 0,0,500,300,0,0,200,100,144,144,0,0,0

999 REMARK-APRIL'S DATA
1000 DATA 200,63,100,100,50,25,100,250,300,144,60,10,100
1100 DATA 112,112,500,500,12,50,50,25,144,200,50,0,20
1200 DATA 0,100,200,115,18,25,100,50,72,144,0,0,0

1299 REMARK- MAY'S DATA
1300 DATA 60,120,100,80,50,25,125,210,144,144,80,15,110
1400 DATA 300,200,400,450,20,100,100,100,100,200,100,0,50
1500 DATA 30,110,240,230,50,50,200,100,80,100,0,0,0
1600 END
RUN

HØW MANY RETAILERS ARE THERE THIS MØNTH    ? 3
HØW MANY MØNTH'S DATA ARE THERE   ? 3
BILLINGS TØ RETAILER #   1      21562.9
BILLINGS TØ RETAILER #   2      25039.27
BILLINGS TØ RETAILER #   3      16607.97

TØTAL, ALL RETAILERS      63210.14
```

Program 4.14 Showing variable sizing of the dimensioned variable.

■ Some computers permit dimensioning to specify, at the programmer's will, the lower (as well as the upper) limit of the subscript. This is accomplished by a DIM statement of the form

100   DIM Q(20:30)   meaning   Q(20),Q(21),...,Q(30)

or

100   DIM Z(−3:2)   meaning Z(−3),Z(−2),Z(−1),Z(0),Z(1),Z(2)

■ Some computers require that the DIM statement be given as the first statement in the program.

4.9 DOUBLY SUBSCRIPTED VARIABLES

Doubly subscripted variables are quite similar to single subscripted variables. However, they represent two-dimensional tables, rather than one-dimensional tables; that is, they represent several columns and rows. Such variables are designated by using two subscripts in the DIM statement:

$$100 \quad \text{DIM} \ X(3,4),A(3,3),Z(N,3)$$

meaning, for example, that **X** is dimensioned as a table which has three rows and four columns, or is constructed "three-down by four-across." Such tables are used when data entries are correlatable to two characteristics at once; i.e., shoes sold to retailer 1, shirts sold to retailer 3, etc.

The gross sales of three departments in a store during the months January–June 1969 could be represented by a two-dimensional table:

Month	Department A	Department B	Department C
January	10309.23	82040.09	16204.22
February	8214.14	68092.28	14186.79
March	10021.00	68092.28	13486.79
April	8268.11	83142.08	12459.10
May	9388.29	85086.14	17208.11
June	11328.46	86411.83	16143.28

A program that reads a doubly subscripted variable S to represent the above sales might look like this:

```
100 DIM S(6,3)
200 FØR I=1 TØ 6
300 FØR J=1 TØ 3
400 READ S(I,J)
500 NEXT J
600 NEXT I

700 DATA 10309.23,82040.09,16204.22
710 DATA  8214.14,68092.28,14186.79
720 DATA 10021.00,68092.28,13486.79
730 DATA  8268.11,83142.08,12459.10
740 DATA  9388.20,85086.14,17208.11
750 DATA 11328.46,86411.83,16143.28
800 END
RUN
```

The I and J loops are so constructed that the following sequence of reading takes place: S(1,1),S(1,2),S(1,3),S(2,1),S(2,2),...,S(6,3), and the body of the subscripted variable is exactly equal to the numerical values in the body of the table.

Example 4.10   Using Doubly Subscripted Variables

In Program 4.14 the quantity of each item sold to the retailers can obviously be described as a doubly subscripted variable. Rewrite the program accordingly.

DISCUSSION

In Program 4.15, N has been dimensioned $(X,13)$, or X-down (one for each retailer, in this case 3) by 13-across (one for each product line). When $X = 3$, there are 39 elements in N. Lines 299–303 initialize all of them to 0, progressing across each row of the variable.

Lines 304–311 result in the piecemeal generation of N by reading the "unsubscripted N" in line 307 and accumulating its value into the previously derived $N(I,J)$, which is zero the first month (when $K = 1$), but nonzero for $K = 2$ or 3. To assist the reader, Figure 4.5 is provided to show the development of N through the loops of lines 304–311. When the computer reaches line 320, N has the value shown in Figure 4.5e.

The reader should study lines 320–360 carefully to see that they cause the following accumulation into $R(1)$:

$$R(1) = 360{*}2.39 + 327{*}3.04 + 282{*}2.88 + \cdots + 269{*}21.04$$

Similar accumulations of $R(2)$ and $R(3)$ result when $I = 2$ and 3, respectively.

```
50 PRINT "HOW MANY RETAILERS ARE THERE THIS MONTH";
60 INPUT X
70 PRINT "HOW MANY MONTH'S DATA ARE THERE";
80 INPUT X1

100 DIM P(13),R(X),N(X,13)
200 FOR I=1 TO 13
210 READ P(I)
220 NEXT I

250 FOR I=1 TO X
260 LET R(I)=0
270 NEXT I

299 FOR I=1 TO X
300 FOR J=1 TO 13
301 LET N(I,J)=0
302 NEXT J
303 NEXT I

304 FOR K=1 TO X1
305 FOR I=1 TO X
306 FOR J=1 TO 13
307 READ N
308 LET N(I,J)=N(I,J)+N
309 NEXT J
310 NEXT I
311 NEXT K

320 FOR I=1 TO X
330 FOR J=1 TO 13
340 LET R(I)=R(I)+N(I,J)*P(J)
350 NEXT J
360 NEXT I

400 FOR I=1 TO X
410 PRINT "BILLINGS TO RETAILER #";I,R(I)
420 NEXT I
```

Program 4.15 Double subscripting of N. (*Continued on next page.*)

MULTIDIMENSIONAL MATRICES

A singly subscripted variable may be regarded as a column of data. A doubly subscripted variable may be regarded as a two-dimensioned table. Some computers permit three, four-, or five-dimensioned variables. Confining attention to the triply subscripted variable, which is dimensioned DIM X(4,3,6), the analogy to columns and tables is simple; the added dimension may be loosely regarded as the number of rows "deep" in the matrix. In the above statement, **X** may be envisioned as four 3 × 6 matrices stacked up on each other. Or more alliteratively, each 3 × 6 matrix is a table on a separate piece of paper and there are four sheets of paper. The added subscript (i.e., the first one in the DIM statement) identifies which sheet of paper contains the element. On that sheet, the second subscript tells in which row, and the third tells in which column the element is located.

```
500 PRINT
510 LET T1=0
520 FØR I=1 TØ X
530 LET T1=T1+R(I)
540 NEXT I
550 PRINT "TØTAL, ALL RETAILERS ";T1

599 REMARK-PRICE DATA
600 DATA 2.39,3.04,2.88,6.09,8.33,1.88,12.16
601 DATA 1.19,2.14,3.98,6.93,9.82,21.04

699 REMARK-MARCH'S DATA
700 DATA 100,144,82,300,50,25,62,300,150,144
701 DATA 38,6,59
800 DATA 288,288,432,432,88,18,0,0,144,144
801 DATA 50,15,0
900 DATA 0,0,500,300,0,0,200,100,144,144,0,0,0

999 REMARK-APRIL'S DATA
1000 DATA 200,63,100,100,50,25,100,250,300,144,60,10,100
1100 DATA 112,112,500,500,12,50,50,25,144,200,50,0,20
1200 DATA 0,100,200,115,18,25,100,50,72,144,0,0,0

1299 REMARK- MAY'S DATA
1300 DATA 60,120,100,80,50,25,125,210,144,144,80,15,110
1400 DATA 300,200,400,450,20,100,100,100,100,200,100,0,50
1500 DATA 30,110,240,230,50,50,200,100,80,100,0,0,0
1600 END
  RUN

HØW MANY RETAILERS ARE THERE THIS MØNTH   ? 3
HØW MANY MØNTH'S DATA ARE THERE   ? 3
BILLINGS TØ RETAILER #   1      21562.9
BILLINGS TØ RETAILER #   2      25039.27
BILLINGS TØ RETAILER #   3      16607.97

TØTAL, ALL RETAILERS      63210.14
```

Program 4.15 *(continued)*

For example, imagine a chain of three department stores, each having the same four departments. Figure 4.6 illustrates the nature of a three-dimensioned table, dimensioned (3,12,4), to hold the monthly sales of each store's individual departments.

4.10 MATRIX ALGEBRA

Subscripted variables naturally lead to the use of matrix algebra for many types of business and engineering problems. At first the subject may seem a bit alien to the average reader, but this section describes, in simple terms, the mechanics and applications of matrix operations. The concept is quite easily understood.

For the purpose of this book, any subscripted variable may be called a

$$N = \begin{bmatrix} 0 & 0 & 0 & 0 & 0 & 0 & 0 & 0 & 0 & 0 & 0 & 0 & 0 \\ 0 & 0 & 0 & 0 & 0 & 0 & 0 & 0 & 0 & 0 & 0 & 0 & 0 \\ 0 & 0 & 0 & 0 & 0 & 0 & 0 & 0 & 0 & 0 & 0 & 0 & 0 \end{bmatrix}$$

(a)

$$N = \begin{bmatrix} 100 & 144 & 82 & 300 & 0 & 0 & 0 & 0 & 0 & 0 & 0 & 0 & 0 \\ 0 & 0 & 0 & 0 & 0 & 0 & 0 & 0 & 0 & 0 & 0 & 0 & 0 \\ 0 & 0 & 0 & 0 & 0 & 0 & 0 & 0 & 0 & 0 & 0 & 0 & 0 \end{bmatrix}$$

(b)

$$N = \begin{bmatrix} 200 & 144 & 82 & 300 & 50 & 25 & 62 & 300 & 150 & 144 & 38 & 6 & 59 \\ 288 & 288 & 432 & 432 & 88 & 18 & 0 & 0 & 144 & 144 & 50 & 15 & 0 \\ 0 & 0 & 500 & 300 & 0 & 0 & 200 & 100 & 144 & 144 & 0 & 0 & 0 \end{bmatrix}$$

(c)

$$N = \begin{bmatrix} 200 & 207 & 182 & 400 & 100 & 50 & 162 & 550 & 450 & 288 & 98 & 16 & 159 \\ 400 & 400 & 932 & 932 & 100 & 68 & 50 & 25 & 288 & 344 & 100 & 15 & 20 \\ 0 & 100 & 700 & 415 & 18 & 25 & 300 & 150 & 216 & 288 & 0 & 0 & 0 \end{bmatrix}$$

(d)

$$N = \begin{bmatrix} 360 & 327 & 282 & 480 & 150 & 75 & 287 & 760 & 594 & 432 & 178 & 31 & 269 \\ 700 & 600 & 1332 & 1382 & 120 & 168 & 150 & 125 & 388 & 544 & 200 & 15 & 70 \\ 30 & 210 & 940 & 645 & 68 & 75 & 500 & 250 & 296 & 388 & 0 & 0 & 0 \end{bmatrix}$$

(e)

Figure 4.5 (a) The value of N after line 303 has been executed for all values of I. (b) The value of N after line 308 has been executed for K = 1, I = 1, J = 4. (c) The value of N after line 308 has been executed for April's data, K = 1, I = 3, J = 13. (d) The value of N after line 308 has been executed for April's and May's data, K = 2, I = 3, J = 13. (e) The value of N after line 308 has been executed for all months' data, K = 3, I = 3, J = 13.

matrix.* There are a number of special BASIC statements which are specifically designed for efficient manipulation of matrices. They require the use of the word MAT in the statement to signify a matrix operation to the computer.

In previous statements involving subscripted variables, only one element of the variable was processed by a single statement (i.e., READ P(I) reads only one—the ith—element of the variable). However, the important point

*Traditionally, mathematicians refer to doubly subscripted variables as "matrices," and singly subscripted variables as "vectors." They may continue to do so when reading this chapter, but the distinction is not important here.

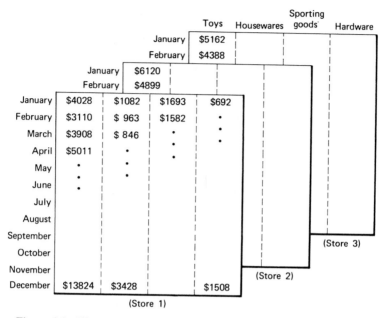

Figure 4.6 Illustration of data stored in a three-dimensional matrix.

to remember now is that MAT statements imply identical operations on all elements of the matrix simultaneously.

MAT READ

The MAT READ statement causes a previously dimensioned variable to have all its elements read from data. For example, the programs

```
100 DIM M(5)
200 FØR I=1 TØ 5
201 READ M(I)
202 NEXT I
300 DATA 5,3,1
301 DATA 6,2,-1,-3
400 END
   RUN
```

```
100 DIM M(5)
200 MAT READ M
300 DATA 5,3,1
301 DATA 6,2,-1,-3
400 END
   RUN
```

are exactly equivalent. In the case illustrated on the right, the statement MAT READ M implies that the computer should read the first data item, and assign its value to $M(1)$; then it should read the second item and assign its value to $M(2)$, and so on, until all elements (in this case five) have been read. Note that, in either program the values -1 and -3 are not read at all. Only the first five items are read because of the dimension of **M**.

Example 4.11 MAT READ in the Retailer's Problem

Rewrite Programs 4.15 to use a MAT READ statement for **N** and **P**.

DISCUSSION

In this case, **N** is a doubly subscripted variable, of dimension "3-down and 13-across." In Program 4.16 note that the variables **P** and **N** are read from the same statement in the program. Since **P** is mentioned first, the computer reads the first 13 data entries and assigns them to **P**. It then proceeds to read

```
100 DIM P(13),R(13),N(3,13)
200 MAT READ P,N

250 FØR I=1 TØ 3
260 LET R(I)=0
270 NEXT I

300 FØR I=1 TØ 3
320 FØR J=1 TØ 13
330 REMARK -DELETED
340 LET R(I)=R(I)+P(J)*N(I,J)
350 NEXT J
360 NEXT I

400 FØR I=1 TØ 3
410 PRINT "BILLINGS TØ RETAILER #";I,R(I)
420 NEXT I

500 PRINT
510 LET T1=0
520 FØR I=1 TØ 3
530 LET T1=T1+R(I)
540 NEXT I
550 PRINT "TØTAL, ALL RETAILERS ";T1

599 REMARK-PRICE DATA
600 DATA 2.39,3.04,2.88,6.09,8.33,1.88,12.16
601 DATA 1.19,2.14,3.98,6.93,9.82,21.04

699 REMARK-MARCH'S DATA
700 DATA 100,144,82,300,50,25,62,300,150,144
701 DATA 38,6,59
800 DATA 288,288,432,432,88,18,0,0,144,144
801 DATA 50,15,0

900 DATA 0,0,500,300,0,0,200,100,144,144,0,0,0
1000 END
```

```
    RUN

BILLINGS TØ RETAILER #    1      6772.08
BILLINGS TØ RETAILER #    2      7580.84
BILLINGS TØ RETAILER #    3      6699.28

TØTAL, ALL RETAILERS      21052.2
```

Program 4.16 Using the MAT READ statement.

the next 39 entries (3 × 13) and assigns them to **N**. Had the letters **P** and **N** been reversed in line 200, the data would have been scrambled in the matrices—the first 39 items in **N** and the last 13 in **P**.

It is also important to realize that the computer, when reading **N**, proceeds in a "rowwise fashion"; e.g., it reads and assigns first the complete top row of the matrix, from left to right, and then proceeds to assign the second and succeeding rows, also from left to right.*

MAT INPUT

As the ordinary INPUT statement causes the computer to stop execution and solicit a value for a variable from the user at the terminal, so does the MAT INPUT statement. However, the user must now type in all the matrix elements, as in this abbreviated example:

```
100 DIM V(5)
200 PRINT "WHAT ARE THE FIVE VALUES ØF V";
300 MAT INPUT V

400 LET T=0
500 FØR I=1 TØ 5
600 LET T=T+V(I)
700 NEXT I
800 PRINT "TØTAL IS";T
900 END
    RUN
```

This printout results at the terminal:

```
WHAT ARE THE FIVE VALUES ØF V    ?  1,8,2,6,3
TØTAL IS      20
```

MAT PRINT

As might be presumed, the MAT PRINT statement causes the entire matrix to be printed out on the teletype. The program

```
100 DIM X(2,3),Y(3,2)
200 MAT READ X,Y
300 PRINT "THE MATRIX X IS"
400 MAT PRINT X
500 PRINT "THE MATRIX Y IS"
600 MAT PRINT Y
700 DATA 1,2,3,4,5,6
800 DATA 10,20,30,40,50,60
900 END
    RUN
```

*Some computers read in a "columnwise" fashion, reading the left column first, from top to bottom and then proceeding to the second column, again top to bottom. In this event, the DATA must be rearranged to accommodate the computer.

results in the following printout:

```
THE MATRIX X IS
  1              2              3
  4              5              6

THE MATRIX Y IS
  10            20
  30            40
  50            60
```

MAT X=CØN

A statement of the form 100 MAT X = CØN is used to set all elements in the matrix equal to the value "1." It is useful for certain of the matrix algebra statements discussed later. The following program illustrates the statement:

```
100 DIM X(2,3)
200 MAT X=CØN
300 PRINT "MAT X IS "
400 MAT PRINT X;
500 END
    RUN
```

The resulting printout is

```
MAT X IS
  1     1     1
  1     1     1
```

MAT X=ZER

A statement of the form 100 MAT X=ZER is used to set all elements of the matrix equal to the value "0." It too is useful for certain of the matrix algebra statements discussed later.

MAT X=IDN

From this point on, all variables used in MAT statements must be doubly subscripted. If one wishes to have a matrix with only one row, it should be dimensioned X(1,N); for one column, the variable should be dimensioned X(N,1).

Certain restrictions must be placed on the dimensions of the variable used in the remaining MAT statements. These restrictions are not on the value of the maximum subscript, but on their relationship to the dimensions of other variables in the statement. For example, to use the MAT X=IDN statement, the number of rows in **X** must be equal to the number of columns in **X**.* Only matrices that have been dimensioned in the manner

$$\text{DIM } X(5,5)A(3,3),B(N,N)$$

are eligible for use of the IDN statement. The following matrices are not:

$$\text{DIM } Y(2,3),X(1,4),B(Z,N)$$

The MAT X = IDN statement sets the diagonal elements (from upper left corner to lower right corner) equal to one, and all the other elements equal to zero. The program

```
100 DIM X(3,3)
200 MAT X=IDN
300 PRINT "MAT X IS"
400 MAT PRINT X;
500 END
```

results in the printout

```
RUN

MAT X IS
 1     0     0
 0     1     0
 0     0     1
```

The abbreviation IDN results from such matrices being called "identity matrices".

The dimensioning rules for this and all succeeding MAT statements are given in Table 4.9.

MAT C = A + B AND MAT D = A − B

One matrix can be "added to" or "subtracted from" another. The operation may result in another matrix, as in

$$100 \qquad \text{MAT } C = A + B$$
$$200 \qquad \text{MAT } D = A - B$$

or in altering the value of one of them, in the sense of an accumulator, as in

$$100 \qquad \text{MAT } A = A + B$$

To utilize these statements,† **A**, **B**, **C**, and **D** must all have the same dimen-

---

*Such a matrix is called a "square" matrix.

†Only one matrix operation can be performed at a time—i.e., 100 MAT A = B + C − D is not permissible.

Table 4.9 Dimensioning restraints for matrix operations.

Matrix statement	Example dimension statement	Restrictions on dimensions of X, Y, and Z
MAT X = IDN	DIM X(N1,N2)	N1 = N2
MAT X = Y + Z	DIM X(N1,N2),Y(N3,N4),Z(N5,N6)	N1 = N3 = N5, N2 = N4 = N6
MAT X = Y − Z	DIM X(N1,N2),Y(N3,N4),Z(N5,N6)	N1 = N3 = N5, N2 = N4 = N6
MAT X = Y*Z	DIM X(N1,N2),Y(N3,N4),Z(N5,N6)	N1 = N3, N2 = N6, N4 = N5
MAT X = INV(Y)	DIM X(N1,N2),Y(N3,N4)	N1 = N2 = N3 = N4
MAT X = TRN(Y)	DIM X(N1,N2);Y(N3,N4)	N1 = N4, N2 = N3
MAT X = CØN	DIM X(N1,N2)	None
MAT X = ZER	DIM X(N1,N2)	None
MAT PRINT X	DIM X(N1,N2)	None
MAT READ X	DIM X(N1,N2)	None
MAT INPUT X	DIM X(N1,N2)	None
MAT X = (A)*Y	DIM X(N1,N2),Y(N3,N4)	N1 = N3, N2 = N4

sions. For the purpose of investigating the manipulation of matrices, it is convenient to adopt this notation: If **A** is a doubly subscripted variable, a lowercase **a** will be used to denote one of its elements. Furthermore, the notation a_{23} infers the particular element that is located at "2-down and 3-across." Figures 4.7a and b depict the notation for two 3 × 4 matrices, **A** and **B**. The element a_{23} is circled for reference.

When **A** and **B** are added, the corresponding elements of **A** and **B** are summed together to yield the value of the same element in **C**: $c_{ij} = a_{ij} + b_{ij}$. Likewise, when **B** is subtracted from **A**, each element in **B** is subtracted from the corresponding value in **A** to yield the value of the same element of **D**: $d_{ij} = a_{ij} - b_{ij}$. Figures 4.7c and d depict the addition and subtraction of matrices in terms of the elements. It is obvious, now, that **A**, **B**, **C**, and **D** must all be of the same dimension, for there must be a corresponding element in each matrix.

To confirm the addition of matrices in the reader's mind, numerical

$$A = \begin{bmatrix} a_{11} & a_{12} & a_{13} \\ a_{21} & a_{22} & \boxed{a_{23}} \\ a_{31} & a_{32} & a_{33} \\ a_{41} & a_{42} & a_{43} \end{bmatrix}$$

(a)

$$B = \begin{bmatrix} b_{11} & b_{12} & b_{13} \\ b_{21} & b_{22} & b_{23} \\ b_{31} & b_{32} & b_{33} \\ b_{41} & b_{42} & b_{43} \end{bmatrix}$$

(b)

$$C = A + B = \begin{bmatrix} a_{11} + b_{11} & a_{12} + b_{12} & a_{13} + b_{13} \\ a_{21} + b_{21} & a_{22} + b_{22} & a_{23} + b_{23} \\ a_{31} + b_{31} & a_{32} + b_{32} & a_{33} + b_{33} \\ a_{41} + b_{41} & a_{42} + b_{42} & a_{43} + b_{43} \end{bmatrix}$$

(c)

$$D = A - B = \begin{bmatrix} a_{11} - b_{11} & a_{12} - b_{12} & a_{13} - b_{13} \\ a_{21} - b_{21} & a_{22} - b_{22} & a_{23} - b_{23} \\ a_{31} - b_{31} & a_{32} - b_{32} & a_{33} - b_{33} \\ a_{41} - b_{41} & a_{42} - b_{42} & a_{43} - b_{43} \end{bmatrix}$$

(d)

Figure 4.7

$$A = \begin{bmatrix} 3 & 5 & 6 \\ 2 & 0 & ③ \\ 8 & 4 & -2 \\ 4 & -2 & 1 \end{bmatrix}$$

(a)

$$B = \begin{bmatrix} 2 & 1 & -7 \\ 4 & 2 & 6 \\ 4 & 4 & 0 \\ 4 & 3 & 0 \end{bmatrix}$$

(b)

$$C = \begin{bmatrix} 5 & 6 & -1 \\ 6 & 2 & 9 \\ 12 & 8 & -2 \\ 8 & 1 & 1 \end{bmatrix}$$

(c)

$$D = \begin{bmatrix} 1 & 4 & 13 \\ -2 & -2 & -3 \\ 4 & 0 & -2 \\ 0 & -5 & 1 \end{bmatrix}$$

(d)

Figure 4.8

examples are given in Figure 4.8. However, for a practical application recall Example 4.9 and suppose that two 3×13 matrices N and M represent the quantity of each item sold to each retailer during March and April, respectively. That is,

$$N = \begin{bmatrix} 100 & 144 & 82 & 300 & 50 & 25 & 62 & 300 & 150 & 144 & 38 & 6 & 59 \\ 288 & 288 & 432 & 432 & 88 & 18 & 0 & 0 & 144 & 144 & 50 & 15 & 0 \\ 0 & 0 & 500 & 500 & 0 & 0 & 200 & 100 & 144 & 144 & 0 & 0 & 0 \end{bmatrix}$$

$$M = \begin{bmatrix} 200 & 63 & 100 & 100 & 50 & 25 & 100 & 250 & 300 & 144 & 60 & 10 & 100 \\ 112 & 112 & 500 & 500 & 12 & 50 & 50 & 25 & 144 & 200 & 50 & 0 & 20 \\ 0 & 100 & 200 & 115 & 18 & 25 & 100 & 50 & 72 & 144 & 0 & 0 & 0 \end{bmatrix}$$

The matrix statement

$$100 \quad MAT \ Q = N + M$$

will then set Q equal to the total quantities sold over the two-month period; i.e.,

$$Q = N + M = \begin{bmatrix} 300 & 207 & 182 & 400 & 100 & 50 & 162 & 550 & 450 & 288 & 98 & 16 & 159 \\ 400 & 400 & 932 & 932 & 100 & 68 & 50 & 25 & 288 & 344 & 100 & 15 & 20 \\ 0 & 0 & 700 & 415 & 18 & 25 & 300 & 150 & 216 & 288 & 0 & 0 & 0 \end{bmatrix}$$

Example 4.12   MAT ADD in the Retailers Problem—
a Matrix Accumulator

Use matrix statements to accumulate the total sales for each retailer, using the data shown in Program 4.15.

DISCUSSION

The above technique would require that a third matrix for May's data (say $\emptyset$) be read and added to **Q** to attain a matrix representing all three months' sales. More matrices would be needed if there were many sets of data. A more attractive process is illustrated in Program 4.17, where an accumulator in the FØR/NEXT loop is used to read an entire month's data (MAT M) at once and add it to a previously accumulated MAT N. As many months of data as desired can be accumulated by simply changing the value of X1 in response to line 80.

MAT A=B∗C

Two matrices can be "multiplied together," within a special—and most useful—context of multiplication. First consider three matrices: **B**, which is a one-row matrix, of DIM B(1,4); **C**, which is a one-column matrix, of DIM C(4,1); and **A**, which is a one-element matrix, of DIM A(1,1). The mathematical interpretation of the statement **B∗C** may be illustrated as follows:

$$\mathbf{B*C} = [b_{11}\ b_{12}\ b_{13}\ b_{14}] * \begin{bmatrix} c_{11} \\ c_{21} \\ c_{31} \\ c_{41} \end{bmatrix} = [(b_{11}*c_{11}) + (b_{12}*c_{11}) + (b_{13}*c_{31}) \\ + (b_{14}*c_{41})]$$

The first elements of **B** and **C** are multiplied together; this value is added to the product of the second elements, the third elements, etc.

For further illustration, suppose **B** represents the quantity of four items, for example, $\mathbf{B} = [10 \quad 20 \quad 25 \quad 15]$, and **C** represents the price of each item,

$$\mathbf{C} = \begin{bmatrix} 2.50 \\ 3.00 \\ 2.00 \\ 1.00 \end{bmatrix}$$

The net value of all the items, then, is obviously

$$10*2.50 + 20*3.00 + 25*2.00 + 15*1.00 = 150.00$$

But fortunately, matrix multiplication produces exactly the same result, for

$$\mathbf{A} = \mathbf{B*C} = [10 \quad 20 \quad 25 \quad 15] * \begin{bmatrix} 2.50 \\ 3.00 \\ 2.00 \\ 1.00 \end{bmatrix}$$

$$= [10*2.50 + 20*3.00 + 25*2.00 + 15*1.00] = [150]$$

```
50 PRINT "HØW MANY RETAILERS ARE THERE THIS MØNTH";
60 INPUT X
70 PRINT "HØW MANY MØNTH'S DATA ARE THERE";
80 INPUT X1

100 DIM P(13),R(X),N(X,13),M(X,13)
200 MAT READ P
250 MAT R=ZER

299 MAT N=ZER
300 FØR I=1 TØ X1
301 MAT READ M
302 MAT N=N+M
303 NEXT I

320 FØR I=1 TØ X
330 FØR J=1 TØ 13
340 LET R(I)=R(I)+N(I,J)*P(J)
350 NEXT J
360 NEXT I

400 FØR I=1 TØ X
410 PRINT "BILLINGS TØ RETAILER #";I,R(I)
420 NEXT I

500 PRINT
510 LET T1=0
520 FØR I=1 TØ X
530 LET T1=T1+R(I)
540 NEXT I
550 PRINT "TØTAL, ALL RETAILERS ";T1

599 REMARK-PRICE DATA
600 DATA 2.39,3.04,2.88,6.09,8.33,1.88,12.16
601 DATA 1.19,2.14,3.98,6.93,9.82,21.04

699 REMARK-MARCH'S DATA
700 DATA 100,144,82,300,50,25,62,300,150,144
701 DATA 38,6,59
800 DATA 288,288,432,432,88,18,0,0,144,144
801 DATA 50,15,0
900 DATA 0,0,500,300,0,0,200,100,144,144,0,0,0

999 REMARK-APRIL'S DATA
1000 DATA 200,63,100,100,50,25,100,250,300,144,60,10,100
1100 DATA 112,112,500,500,12,50,50,25,144,200,50,0,20
1200 DATA 0,100,200,115,18,25,100,50,72,144,0,0,0

1299 REMARK- MAY'S DATA
1300 DATA 60,120,100,80,50,25,125,210,144,144,80,15,110
1400 DATA 300,200,400,450,20,100,100,100,100,200,100,0,50
1500 DATA 30,110,240,230,50,50,200,100,80,100,0,0,0
1600 END
 RUN

HØW MANY RETAILERS ARE THERE THIS MØNTH    ? 3
HØW MANY MØNTH'S DATA ARE THERE    ? 3
BILLINGS TØ RETAILER #    1      21562.9
BILLINGS TØ RETAILER #    2      25039.27
BILLINGS TØ RETAILER #    3      16607.97

TØTAL, ALL RETAILERS     63210.14
```

Program 4.17 A matrix accumulator.

Suppose now, that **B** contains three rows of data, as follows:

$$\mathbf{B} = \begin{bmatrix} 10 & 20 & 25 & 15 \\ 6 & 25 & 15 & 10 \\ 12 & 30 & 10 & 15 \end{bmatrix}$$

Then

$$\mathbf{A} = \mathbf{B} \ast \mathbf{C} = \begin{bmatrix} 10 & 20 & 25 & 15 \\ 6 & 25 & 15 & 10 \\ 12 & 30 & 10 & 15 \end{bmatrix} \ast \begin{bmatrix} 2.50 \\ 3.00 \\ 2.00 \\ 1.00 \end{bmatrix}$$

$$= \begin{bmatrix} 10 \ast 2.50 + 20 \ast 3.00 + 25 \ast 2.00 + 15 \ast 1.00 \\ 6 \ast 2.50 + 25 \ast 3.00 + 15 \ast 2.00 + 10 \ast 1.00 \\ 12 \ast 2.50 + 30 \ast 3.00 + 10 \ast 2.00 + 15 \ast 1.00 \end{bmatrix}$$

$$= \begin{bmatrix} 150 \\ 130 \\ 155 \end{bmatrix}$$

That is, each row of **B** is individually multiplied by the column of **C**, resulting in one row for **A**.

For another example, suppose one desires to simply add up the quantity in each row of **B**, and then consider these equations:

$$\mathbf{C} = \mathbf{C \emptyset N} = \begin{bmatrix} 1 \\ 1 \\ 1 \\ 1 \end{bmatrix}$$

$$\mathbf{A} = \mathbf{B} \ast \mathbf{C} = \begin{bmatrix} 10 & 20 & 25 & 15 \\ 6 & 25 & 15 & 10 \\ 12 & 30 & 10 & 15 \end{bmatrix} \ast \begin{bmatrix} 1 \\ 1 \\ 1 \\ 1 \end{bmatrix}$$

$$= \begin{bmatrix} 10 \ast 1 + 20 \ast 1 + 25 \ast 1 + 15 \ast 1 \\ 6 \ast 1 + 25 \ast 1 + 15 \ast 1 + 10 \ast 1 \\ 12 \ast 1 + 30 \ast 1 + 10 \ast 1 + 15 \ast 1 \end{bmatrix}$$

$$= \begin{bmatrix} 70 \\ 56 \\ 67 \end{bmatrix}$$

To illustrate one more variation of matrix multiplication, suppose **C** is composed of two rows; the first represents the price of the items, while the second column represents the profit from each item:

$$
C = \begin{bmatrix} 2.50 & 0.20 \\ 3.00 & 0.30 \\ 2.00 & 0.20 \\ 1.00 & 0.15 \end{bmatrix}
$$

Then, two rows are created for **A**, as follows:

$$
A = B*C = \begin{bmatrix} 10 & 20 & 25 & 15 \\ 6 & 25 & 15 & 10 \\ 12 & 30 & 10 & 15 \end{bmatrix} * \begin{bmatrix} 2.50 & 0.20 \\ 3.00 & 0.30 \\ 2.00 & 0.20 \\ 1.00 & 0.15 \end{bmatrix}
$$

$$
= \begin{bmatrix} (10*2.50 + 20*3.00 + 25*2.00 + 15*1.00) \\ \qquad (10*0.20 + 20*0.30 + 25*0.20 + 15*0.15) \\ (6*2.50 + 25*3.00 + 15*2.00 + 10*1.00) \\ \qquad (6*0.20 + 25*0.30 + 15*0.20 + 10*0.15) \\ (12*2.50 + 30*3.00 + 10*2.00 + 15*1.00) \\ \qquad (12*0.20 + 30*0.30 + 10*0.20 + 15*0.15) \end{bmatrix}
$$

$$
= \begin{bmatrix} 150 & 15.25 \\ 130 & 13.20 \\ 155 & 15.65 \end{bmatrix}
$$

Now the first column of **A** represents the net value of each row of **B**, and the second column of **A** represents the profit from each row of **B**.

Example 4.13   *Using Matrix Multiplication*

Using matrix multiplication and other matrix statements as much as possible, rewrite Program 4.17.

DISCUSSION

To use the features of matrix multiplication in Program 4.18

■   **P** and **R** are doubly subscripted, $P(X,1)$ and $R(X,1)$;

■   T1 is changed to a subscripted variable with one element, $T(1,1)$;

■   A matrix **C**, is added to accommodate constants for summing together the values in the **R** matrix.

The mechanics of Program 4.18 are self-explanatory in the context of the statements already discussed in this section. To assist the reader, Figure 4.9 is provided, detailing the meaning, in numerical terms, of each of the added matrix statements.

```
50 PRINT "HØW MANY RETAILERS ARE THERE THIS MØNTH";
60 INPUT X
70 PRINT "HØW MANY MØNTH'S DATA ARE THERE";
80 INPUT X1

100 DIM P(13,1),R(X,1),N(X,13),M(X,13),C(1,X),T(1,1)
200 MAT READ P

299 MAT N=ZER
300 FØR I=1 TØ X1
301 MAT READ M
302 MAT N=N+M
303 NEXT I

320 MAT C=CØN
330 MAT R=N*P
340 MAT T=C*R
400 FØR I=1 TØ X
410 PRINT "BILLINGS TØ RETAILER #";I,R(I,1)
420 NEXT I

500 PRINT
510 PRINT "TØTAL, ALL RETAILERS ";T(1,1)

599 REMARK-PRICE DATA
600 DATA 2.39,3.04,2.88,6.09,8.33,1.88,12.16
601 DATA 1.19,2.14,3.98,6.93,9.82,21.04

699 REMARK-MARCH'S DATA
700 DATA 100,144,82,300,50,25,62,300,150,144
701 DATA 38,6,59
800 DATA 288,288,432,432,88,18,0,0,144,144
801 DATA 50,15,0
900 DATA 0,0,500,300,0,0,200,100,144,144,0,0,0

999 REMARK-APRIL'S DATA
1000 DATA 200,63,100,100,50,25,100,250,300,144,60,10,100
1100 DATA 112,112,500,500,12,50,50,25,144,200,50,0,20
1200 DATA 0,100,200,115,18,25,100,50,72,144,0,0,0

1299 REMARK- MAY'S DATA
1300 DATA 60,120,100,80,50,25,125,210,144,144,80,15,110
1400 DATA 300,200,400,450,20,100,100,100,100,200,100,0,50
1500 DATA 30,110,240,230,50,50,200,100,80,100,0,0,0
1600 END
  RUN

HØW MANY RETAILERS ARE THERE THIS MØNTH   ? 3
HØW MANY MØNTH'S DATA ARE THERE   ? 3
BILLINGS TØ RETAILER #   1      21562.9
BILLINGS TØ RETAILER #   2      25039.27
BILLINGS TØ RETAILER #   3      16607.97

TØTAL, ALL RETAILERS      63210.14
```

Program 4.18 Using matrix multiplication.

$$P = \begin{bmatrix} 2.39 \\ 3.04 \\ 2.88 \\ 6.09 \\ 8.33 \\ 1.88 \\ 12.16 \\ 1.19 \\ 2.14 \\ 3.98 \\ 6.93 \\ 9.82 \\ 21.04 \end{bmatrix}$$

$$C = \begin{bmatrix} 1 & 1 & 1 \end{bmatrix}$$

(b) The value of **C** after line 320 is executed.

(a) The value of **P** after line 200 is executed.

$$R = \begin{bmatrix} 360 & 327 & 282 & 480 & 150 & 75 & 287 & 760 & 594 & 432 & 178 & 31 & 269 \\ 700 & 600 & 1332 & 1382 & 120 & 168 & 150 & 125 & 388 & 544 & 200 & 15 & 70 \\ 30 & 210 & 940 & 645 & 68 & 75 & 500 & 250 & 296 & 388 & 0 & 0 & 0 \end{bmatrix} \begin{bmatrix} 2.39 \\ 3.04 \\ 2.88 \\ 6.09 \\ 8.33 \\ 1.88 \\ 12.16 \\ 1.19 \\ 2.14 \\ 3.98 \\ 6.93 \\ 9.82 \\ 21.04 \end{bmatrix}$$

$$= \begin{bmatrix} 21562.90 \\ 25039.27 \\ 16607.97 \end{bmatrix}$$

(c) The value of **R** after line 330 is executed.

$$T = \begin{bmatrix} 1 & 1 & 1 \end{bmatrix} \begin{bmatrix} 21562.90 \\ 25039.27 \\ 16607.97 \end{bmatrix} = \begin{bmatrix} 63210.14 \end{bmatrix}$$

(d) The value of **T** after line 340 is executed.

Figure 4.9   The value of subscripted variables as Program 4.18 progresses.

SCALAR MULTIPLICATION

The remaining matrix operations are especially useful in applications of engineering, mathematics, and physics.

Each element of the matrix can be simultaneously multiplied by a constant* with an expression of the form

$$100 \quad \text{MAT } B=(2) *A$$

or

$$200 \quad \text{MAT } B=(X+1) *A$$

The quantity in parentheses is a single number, not a matrix. Suppose, for example,

$$\mathbf{A} = \begin{bmatrix} 3 & 2 \\ 1 & 4 \end{bmatrix}$$

Then

$$\mathbf{B} = (0.5) *\mathbf{A} = \begin{bmatrix} 1.5 & 1 \\ 0.5 & 2 \end{bmatrix}$$

MATRIX TRANSPOSITION

The statement

$$100 \quad \text{MAT } A=\text{TRN}(B)$$

causes **A** to be set equal to the *transpose* of **B**, in this manner:

$$\mathbf{A} = \begin{bmatrix} 1 & 4 & 0 \\ 2 & 6 & 9 \\ -1 & 12 & -3 \end{bmatrix}$$

$$\mathbf{B} = \text{TRN}(\mathbf{A}) = \begin{bmatrix} 1 & 2 & -1 \\ 4 & 6 & 12 \\ 0 & 9 & -3 \end{bmatrix}$$

More formally, the elements of **A** and **B** relate in this manner: $b_{ij} = a_{ji}$.

*Called a "scalar" in mathematical jargon.

MATRIX INVERSION

The inverse of a matrix is computed by the statement

$$100 \quad \text{MAT } X = INV(A)$$

Here, **X** is set equal to the inverse of **A**, or in mathematical parlance, $X = A^{-1}$.

DETERMINANT OF A MATRIX

While carrying out each INV(A) operation, the computer usually calculates the *determinant* of **A**. The subsequent statement, of the form

$$101 \quad \text{LET } D = DET$$

will, on some computers, set the variable D equal to the determinant of the *most recently inverted* matrix.

■ EXERCISES

*4.22 Read a matrix **C** (dimension 23) and calculate the average of elements 8 through 14.

4.23 A sample of 100 measurements is taken, with readings expressed in inches. Create a matrix **I** (dimension 11). Read each measurement from data, counting the number of them in each 1 inch increment up to 10 inches. Any reading over 10 inches should be counted in I(11). Print the percentage of results in each range. [*Hint:* Use a statement like 500 LET I(M) = I(M) + 1.]

4.24 The present value (P) of an annuity payable annually for n years, drawing interest rate, r, is

$$P = \frac{(1 + r)^n - 1}{r(1 + r)^n}$$

Generate and print a matrix showing the present value for n = 1, 2, ..., 20 at interest rates of 2, 4, 6, and 8%.

*4.25 A 5 × 4 matrix **H** contains 20 elements. First set X = H(1,1); then search through the matrix and reset X to the smallest number in it. Finally, print out the smallest element, its row, and its column position.

4.26 A company records its costs by an account number according to the following scheme:

Account number	Description
100–199	Salaries
200–299	Office supplies
300–399	Advertising
400–499	Raw materials
500–599	Machinery

Several thousand data entries are given, in the form DATA 253,413.28; the first item is the account number, and the second is the dollar amount of the entry. Generate a cost matrix **C** (dimension 5) by accumulating into **C** all entries in each of the five ranges—i.e., C(1) is the accumulated sum of all Salaries; C(2) the sum of all Office supplies, etc.

4.27 Four employees work on five jobs one day for the number of hours shown in Table 4.10. Each employee is paid the hourly wage shown in Table 4.11. Wages will be represented by the matrix **W**, hours by **H**, and the cost of each job by **J**. What should be the dimensions of each matrix? Give the matrix equations necessary to calculate the

Table 4.10 Hours spent on each job.

Job number	Employee 1	2	3	4
1	3.5	1.2	5.0	6.0
2	0	2.4	0	0
3	3.0	1.0	1.0	1.0
4	1.5	0	2.0	0
5	0	3.4	0	1.0

Table 4.11

Employee	Rate
1	4.12
2	3.08
3	4.88
4	5.04

charges accrued to each job. Give appropriate data and other statements necessary to determine the cost of each job.

*4.28 Three men make sales as shown in Table 4.12. Each is paid a commission as a percentage of his sales as follows: salesman 1, 14%; salesman 2, 8.2%; salesman 3, 11%. Use an accumulator to sum up the total of each man's sales; then determine each man's commission. [*Hint:* Read N and S (number and sales); then use a statement like 100 LET T(N)=T(N)+S.]

Table 4.12

Salesman number	Sales ($)
1	3428.00
3	893.16
2	1204.82
3	1694.43
1	342.08
3	22.14
2	648.24
2	500.00
1	1040.21
3	988.43
1	1204.32
1	144.00
2	3821.42
0	0

4.29 Three matrices are dimensioned X(7,3), R(7), C(3). After **X** is read, the program must calculate **R** and **C**. Each element of **R** is the sum of one of **X**s rows; each element of **C** is the sum of one of **X**s columns.

*4.30 There are 100 elements of data. Read each, placing positive (or zero) numbers sequentially into matrix **P** and negative numbers sequentially into **N**.

4.31 A graph is constructed of several straight lines, as shown in Figure 4.10. The coordinates of the end point of each line segment are stored in a two-column matrix **M**. Ask the user for a value of any X (say x_1), interpolate the graph, and print out the corresponding value, y_1.

4.32 Twenty-five (N) values of **X** are stored in a matrix. Calculate their average and standard deviation, where

$$STD = \sqrt{\frac{\Sigma X^2 - (\Sigma X)^2/N}{N - 1}}$$

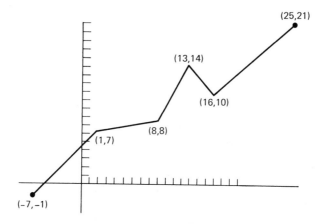

Figure 4.10

Then rescan the matrix, printing out each value which falls more than one standard deviation (either above or below) from the average.

4.33 A 4×4 matrix **D** is a diagonal matrix; i.e., most terms are zero; only those on the diagonal are nonzero. The matrix is shown in Figure 4.11. The program has only the following data statement: 5000 DATA 30,16, $-3,4$. Write the program to first set all elements of **M** equal to zero and then read the diagonal elements from DATA.

4.34 A 4×4 matrix **S** is triangular; i.e., as shown in Figure 4.12. Set all elements equal to zero and then read only the upper triangular elements from the following statement: 5000 DATA 6,3,0,4,2,1,1,8,0, -1.

4.35 Any two dates are given in the form 9,10,70, meaning September 10, 1970. Write a program which determines the number of days between them. Presume the earliest one is given first; ignore the extra day in leap years. [*Hint:* Create a 12-element matrix, **M** which contains the number of days of each month.]

*4.36 The Widget-Gidget Mfg. Co. has five products and can schedule its weekly production in any of four ways, each resulting in the production quantity shown in the body of Table 4.13. Three distribution

$$\begin{bmatrix} 30 & 0 & 0 & 0 \\ 0 & 16 & 0 & 0 \\ 0 & 0 & -3 & 0 \\ 0 & 0 & 0 & 4 \end{bmatrix}$$

Figure 4.11

$$\begin{bmatrix} 6 & 3 & 0 & 4 \\ 0 & 2 & 1 & 1 \\ 0 & 0 & 8 & 0 \\ 0 & 0 & 0 & -1 \end{bmatrix}$$

Figure 4.12

methods are available for shipping production to market. The cost per unit of each method is shown in Table 4.14. Let **P** be the production matrix and **D** be the distribution matrix. Create a new matrix **C** by multiplying **P** and **D** together. Then each element of **C** is the cost of a week's production using all combinations of production and distribution methods. Search through **C** to find the lowest cost combination. Print the number of the production and distribution methods producing the lowest cost, the amount of the lowest cost, and the entire **C** matrix. [Be sure you understand the significance of the answer in, say, $C(1,1)$—i.e., it is the total cost of using production method 1 with distribution method 1, or $C(1,1) = 100*5 + 100*5 + 100*5 + 100*5 + 100*5$.]

Table 4.13

Production method	Product				
	1	2	3	4	5
1	100	100	100	100	100
2	50	50	200	75	125
3	150	150	75	75	50
4	75	125	75	125	100

Table 4.14

Product	Distribution method		
	1	2	3
1	$5	$3	$7
2	5	3	7
3	5	7	7
4	5	7	3
5	5	7	1

4.37 The data in Table 4.15 is broken into two groups. The first is a series of entries for each of several (no more than 100) items in inventory. The data represents the inventory number and on-hand quantity of each item. The last entry is a (-1), indicating the end of that data. Read the first group of data into a subscripted variable—DIM $Q(100,2)$. The second group of data consists of several hundred lines recording additions or withdrawals to each item. These are arranged in random order. There may be several transactions, or none, against each item. Code 1 indicates an addition; code 2 indicates a withdrawal. The end of this data is signified by the presence of a (-2). Read the second group; for each entry, find the corresponding entry in **Q**; update and print out the new inventory record. If no corresponding record is found in **Q**, print an error message.

4.38 A company operates three department stores, designated A, B, and C. Correspondingly, variables A, B, and C are all dimensioned 12-down, 4-across. Elements in the matrices record the sales volume for each store. Rows represent January, February, . . . , December. Columns 1–4 represent sporting goods, housewares, toys, and

Table 4.15

Item number	Balance on hand	Additions or withdrawals
37204	3800	—
61311	1624	—
28409	10916	—
4112	8244	—
8116	16342	—
.	.	.
.	.	.
.	.	.
−1	0	—
3162	412	1
61311	204	2
8116	2416	1
61311	429	1
.	.	.
.	.	.
.	.	.
−2	0	0

notions. Read the matrices from DATA. If store B does not have a toys department, how should that fact be reflected in the data? For each store, calculate (a) the total sales each month; (b) the yearly sales in each department; (c) the yearly commission each store manager receives if he is paid by the following schedule: sporting goods, 8%; housewares, 5.8% toys, 11%; notions, 6.2%; and (d) the annual sales for the whole store. For the chain of three stores, calculate (a), (b), and (d) above.

4.39 A test is performed on ten gadgets. The probability that any individual gadget will pass the test is 0.94. The probability that exactly n of them pass is determined by the binomial probability law

$$P_n = \frac{10!}{n!(10 - n)!} (0.94)^n (0.06)^{1-n}$$

where $n! = n*(n - 1)*(n - 2)*(n - 3) \cdots (1)$; $0! = 1$. If P and C are singly subscripted variables, calculate P(n) for $n = 0, \ldots, 10$. Also, calculate C(n), the cumulative probability that *n or more* pass the test [e.g., $C(8) = P(8) + P(9) + P(10)$]. Also, print out the most likely number to pass (i.e., the number with the maximum probability).

4.40 Data is gathered on 25 automobiles: D(I) is the number of miles the *i*th car is driven and G(I) is the number of gallons of fuel the *i*th car consumes. Read D and G from DATA and calculate M(I), the mileage per gallon achieved by each car. Determine the highest and lowest mileage in the test. Finally, print out I, M(I), D(I), and G(I) for every car whose mileage is not in the upper two-thirds of the mileage range.

4.41 Compute the *determinant* of the matrix in Figure 4.13.

$$\begin{bmatrix} 6 & 3 & 1 & 1 \\ -2 & 4 & 0 & 3 \\ 1 & 2 & 4 & 8 \\ 5 & 9 & 7 & 2 \end{bmatrix}$$

Figure 4.13

4.42 Write a program to add three binary numbers of six digits. Use the program to add 101100, 010010, 111000. [*Hint:* Place one digit of each number into a separate element in a matrix.]

4.43 In certain engineering problems, matrix equations of the form

$$V = E*T*P$$

occur. State the dimensions of $\mathbf{V}$ if $\mathbf{E}$, $\mathbf{T}$, and $\mathbf{P}$ are as shown below. Write a program to compute $\mathbf{V}$.

$$\mathbf{E} = \begin{bmatrix} 1.0 & 0.93 & 0.75 & 0 \end{bmatrix}$$

$$\mathbf{T} = \begin{bmatrix} 0.93 & 0.05 & 0.02 & 0.0 \\ 0.87 & 0.06 & 0.06 & 0.01 \\ 0.51 & 0.07 & 0.33 & 0.09 \\ 0.43 & 0.10 & 0.28 & 0.19 \end{bmatrix}$$

$$\mathbf{P} = \begin{bmatrix} 0.82 \\ 0.10 \\ 0.04 \\ 0.04 \end{bmatrix}$$

4.44 A square matrix is said to be "stochastic" if (a) each element is non-negative and (b) the sum of every row is equal to one. Write a program which reads a matrix, determines if it is stochastic, and, if not, prints out an error message and terminates the run.

4.45 Given two matrices, DIM A(3),B(4), compute the product of all combinations of $\mathbf{A}$ and $\mathbf{B}$ elements. Matrix $\mathbf{C}$ is dimensioned DIM C(3,4) and c_{ij} should be set equal to $a_i \ast b_j$.

4.46 The probability that an equipment will successfully survive operation for t hours can be characterized by the "underlying failure rate" λ of each of its components, and the extent of redundancy (i.e., back-up units) provided. Suppose that three degrees of redundancy can be envisioned for any hardware and that the following reliability expressions can be used for each:

Redundancy of ith component (units)	Reliability of ith components, R_i
None	$e^{-\lambda_i t}$
1	$2e^{-\lambda_i t} - e^{-2\lambda_i t}$
2	$1 - (1 - e^{-\lambda_i t})^3$

If there are n components, the reliability of the entire equipment is $R_e = \Pi_{i=1}^{n} R_i$. Draw a flowchart and write a program which calculates R_e at 1, 2, 3, 4 years (1 year = 8760 hours) for a system with the following components:

i	Name	Redundancy (units)	λ_i
1	Transmitter	1	3025×10^{-9}
2	Receiver	2	6192×10^{-9}
3	Baseband	1	2104×10^{-9}
4	Decoder	2	9982×10^{-9}
5	Power supply	None	1200×10^{-9}

[*Hint:* Use subscripted variables for λ and for a code to indicate the type of redundancy of the *i*th element.]

4.47 The volume expansivities (β) of several liquids are given in Table 4.16. If the initial volume of a liquid is V_0 at temperature T_0, its volume at T_1 is $V_1 = V_0[1 + \beta(T_1 - T_0)]$. Let L = 1, 2, or 3 represent alcohol, mercury, and water, respectively. Let P = 1 or 2 stand for temperatures given in °C or °F, respectively. Store the expansivities in **E**. An engineer puts data into the program to give the computer V_0, T_0, T_1, M, and P. Read that data; compute and print V_1.

Table 4.16 Volume expansivities of liquids.

Liquid	Per °C	Per °F
Alcohol	0.0011	0.00061
Mercury	0.00018	0.0001
Water	0.00037	0.0002

4.48 A matrix **T** is dimensioned T(4,2) and contains two complex numbers, as shown in the table. They are

$$T(1,1) + T(1,2)i = 3 + (-4)i$$
$$T(2,1) + T(2,2)i = -1 + 10i$$

Matrix T

	Real part 1	Imaginary part 2	
1	3	−4	First number
2	−1	10	Second number
3			Sum
4			Product

Calculate the elements for the third row of the matrix as the sum of the first two numbers; for the fourth row, as the product of the first two numbers. [*Hint:* (a + bi) · (c + di) = (ac − bd) + (ad + bc)i.]

4.11   RANDOM NUMBERS

Random numbers are an interesting phenomenon in computing. They are used in simulations of economic, social, and physical behavior, random sampling for auditing and quality control, and interactive "games."

A set of numbers with values ranging between 0 and 1 are available from the computer. They are arranged in a "random" order. The first 200 numbers available on one computer are shown in Table 4.17. They were generated with the following program:*

```
100 FØR I=1 TØ 200
200 LET N=RND(0)
300 PRINT N,
400 IF I/25=INT(I/25) THEN 700
500 IF I/5=INT(I/5) THEN 800
600 GØ TØ 900
700 PRINT
800 PRINT
900 NEXT I
1000 END
RUN
```

The RND(0) function always results in the computer selecting the random number which follows the last selected number; e.g., if N = RND(0) were executed eleven times, and then X = RND(0) were executed, N and X would equal 0.25318545 and 0.20576267, respectively (circled in Table 4.17).

Obviously, the random number table always produces the same sequence of numbers if it is always entered at the beginning. This could nullify the

*Or, avoiding most of the statements designed to print out in five neat columns, this simplified example is the same program:

```
100 FØR I=1 TØ 200
200 LET N=RND(0)
300 PRINT N
400 NEXT I
500 END
RUN

.50279307
.23116435
.38984173
    ⋮
```

Table 4.17 Two hundred "random numbers," generated with a RND(0) function.

RUN

.50279307	.23116435	.38984173	.25741470	.42237083
.91108183	.13568749	.02410334	.32289626	.05256094
.25318545	.20576267	.00935213	.22532681	.14743546
.73653103	.66354960	.59602693	.58738401	.57823599
.99067896	.87711697	.99527006	.22435427	.10833827
.55759445	.48567285	.73031120	.22644092	.62909714
.93196393	.39245893	.43630391	.45198100	.44298881
.34232892	.77974299	.70109395	.92239144	.47832423
.76571804	.87297490	.05135489	.48430209	.44659270
.60464623	.52277128	.66304281	.01240422	.76320365
.01558006	.68776742	.27692536	.39318860	.71655767
.24657227	.53967719	.49408699	.02457598	.79997569
.92832365	.01652031	.62590926	.96977477	.55142763
.21433964	.81248977	.03500262	.38328625	.77163331
.35827187	.60149232	.66675283	.60627239	.60444869
.90548890	.65771085	.34989538	.42494848	.96629131
.66573717	.43231966	.00129430	.04455486	.23409106
.53581801	.43418328	.82504955	.28435839	.62153237
.29197566	.42543522	.48733093	.91182638	.46250740
.33810618	.58362392	.82790390	.20420962	.15603499
.61007849	.49857701	.05590692	.70934810	.71672050
.75544697	.77581645	.43071128	.97512188	.26124769
.40031818	.99644066	.88259472	.11338366	.32454172
.19458812	.08879080	.47166520	.95620884	.15792148
.50536111	.25619904	.62331262	.85533311	.92068367
.14146439	.07689231	.28873150	.28741232	.16499893
.62244895	.15635669	.61553610	.55373149	.41384818
.27781737	.18082870	.09066824	.33863557	.23802891
.84159089	.97620529	.64679683	.24368432	.51477282
.66779032	.84839787	.24802471	.07857978	.56226139
.06983868	.24614943	.21831494	.23523857	.12178960
.59310021	.44140773	.40146748	.58800023	.50384214
.50942518	.95648016	.00579931	.12282446	.82703007
.47356647	.89768509	.27080004	.25149549	.92478040
.94381851	.43792943	.53179575	.86465805	.06107558
.86149042	.16221632	.92686027	.44334496	.45544746
.27578011	.81429511	.67659118	.35114866	.34135334
.73096003	.25412001	.12639564	.98690194	.07388750
.89874688	.58892144	.38275187	.10158389	.45006206
.44637828	.93446475	.20738725	.08618669	.33375422

use of the table in certain cases because the intention is usually to produce a "random," different, set of numbers each time the program is run. For such purposes, the statement $X = RND(-1)$ is also provided. It causes the computer to begin selecting random numbers from a "random place" in the table. To clarify, Programs 4.19a and b have each been executed on two

Program

```
100 FØR I=1 TØ 5          50 LET N=RND(-1)
200 LET N=RND(0)         100 FØR I=1 TØ 5
300 PRINT N              200 LET N=RND(0)
400 NEXT I               300 PRINT N
500 END                  400 NEXT I
                         500 END
```

Printout from run on first day

```
.50279307                .44334496
.23116435                .45544746
.38984173                .27578011
.25741470                .81429511
.42237083                .67659118
```

Printout from run on second day

```
.50279307                .32894482
.23116435                .95434358
.38984173                .32894901
.25741470                .96738211
.42237083                .74384969
```

(a)   **(b)**

Program 4.19 (a) Two separate executions of a program which generates five random numbers. Note that the printouts are the same, and contain the first five numbers in Table 4.17. (b) Addition of line 50 results in a unique series of numbers on each run.

different days, and all printouts are shown. The first program has no RND(-1) statement, and it always produces the same five numbers from the beginning of Table 4.17. The second program is exactly the same as the first, except that line 50 has been added to begin at a random place in the table on each run. Observe then, in (b), two different sets of results are produced. The first printout from Program 4.20b happens to be the series of numbers underlined in Table 4.17; the second printout is from some unknown place in the computer's random number sequence.

It is often necessary to "draw" random numbers with values in ranges other than 0–1. Suppose one desires to draw a number between 0 and 10. The available range of random numbers may be modified with a statement like

$$100 \quad \text{LET } N = 10*\text{RND}(0)$$

To derive whole numbers from 1 to 100, the statement

$$100 \quad \text{LET } N = \text{INT}((100)*\text{RND}(0)+1)$$

can be used. In general, the statement

$$100 \quad \text{LET } N = INT((M2 - M1 + 1) * RND(0) + M1)$$

can be used to select integer random numbers between M1 and M2 inclusively. Program 4.20 presents a program using the latter statement, and has the effect of transforming the first nine entries in the random number table to new numbers in the range 34–116 (i.e., the original number $RND(0) = 0.50279307$ becomes $N = 75$).

The randomness of numbers resulting from the use of $RND(-1)$ can sometimes be troublesome when trying to debug a program, for it continuously produces markedly different answers each time the program is executed. To avoid this problem, it is convenient to first write the program with no $RND(-1)$ statement so that it produces the same series of random numbers during debugging runs, and then to add the statement afterward for randomness in the production runs of the program.

```
100 PRINT "WHAT IS THE LØWER LIMIT ØF THE RANGE";
200 INPUT M1
300 PRINT "WHAT IS THE UPPER LIMIT ØF THE RANGE";
400 INPUT M2
500 PRINT "HØW MANY NUMBERS DØ YØU WANT";
600 INPUT N

700 FØR I=1 TØ N
800 PRINT INT((M2-M1+1)*RND(0)+M1)
900 NEXT I
1000 END
  RUN

WHAT IS THE LØWER LIMIT ØF THE RANGE   ? 34
WHAT IS THE UPPER LIMIT ØF THE RANGE   ? 116
HØW MANY NUMBERS DØ YØU WANT  ? 9
 75
 53
 66
 55
 69
 109
 45
 36
 60
```

Program 4.20 Program for generating random numbers from 34 to 116.

Example 4.14   An Auditor's Sample

An auditor wishes to "spot check" 37 documents out of a group of 1000, numbered consecutively from 1 to 1000. Using the random number generator, write a program which will select 37 of them at random, never selecting the same document twice.

DISCUSSION

Using the random numbers techniques described above, the initial problem of drawing 37 random document numbers is almost a trivial one, as shown in Program 4.21. But there is a complication, for no provision has been

```
50 LET N=RND(-1)
100 PRINT "USE THESE DØCUMENTS"
200 FØR I=1 TØ 37
300 LET N=INT(1000*RND(0)+1)
400 PRINT N
500 NEXT I
600 END
  RUN

USE THESE DØCUMENTS
 454
 298
 615
 370
 786
 236
 977
 737
 155
 117
 215
 783
 739
 573
 592
 597
 562
 602
 146
 118
 138
 724
 328
 924
 333
 874
 478
 35
 208
 291
 291
 935
 353
 536
 199
 322
 4
```

Program 4.21   Random sampling, susceptible to duplication.

made to prevent the same number from being drawn twice, as can be seen from the printout. (The reader should discover for himself why it is possible for the computer to produce the same document number more than once.) [*Hint:* Consider the value of N when RND(0) = 0.304182 or 0.304981.]

The problem is solved by devising a technique by which the computer can "remember" those numbers it previously drew, and can ignore their second drawing. The one chosen in Program 4.22 is to establish a variable of DIM D(1000) and initialize all its elements to zero. The elements of **D** each represent one of the 1000 documents. If a number N is drawn, and D(N) = 0, the number has not previously been drawn; then line 400 will print N and line 410 will change D(N) from 0 to 1. Now when the same number is drawn again, line 310 will return the computer to line 300, selecting a different value of N, rather than proceeding with printing out a duplicate number.

Example 4.15 Heads or Tails

Using the random number feature, write a program which simulates the flip of a coin ten times and keeps count of the number of heads and tails obtained.

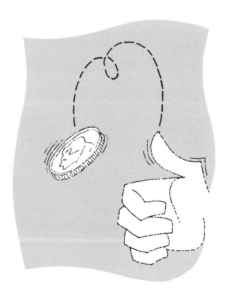

DISCUSSION

A coin should "come up" heads one-half of all the times it is flipped, and should do it "randomly" (i.e., with no discernible pattern or outside influence). The RND function produces a random number which is uniformly distributed from 0 to 1.0. Therefore, exactly half of all random numbers will be in the range 0–0.5 and could be regarded as representing HEADS. Also, the other half will be in the range 0.5–1 and could be regarded as representing TAILS.

```
50 LET N=RND(-1)
60 DIM D(1000)
70 MAT D=ZER
100 PRINT "USE THESE DØCUMENTS"
200 FØR I=1 TØ 37
300 LET N=INT(1000*RND(0)+1)
320 IF D(N)<>0 THEN 300
400 PRINT N
410 LET D(N)=1
500 NEXT I
600 END
RUN

USE THESE DØCUMENTS
 903
 163
 953
 363
  21
 298
 120
 372
 291
 123
 923
 148
 996
 916
 374
 876
 975
 740
  69
 433
 190
 187
 254
 381
 999
 337
 512
 283
 770
 562
 104
  78
 177
  63
 743
 333
 911
```

Program 4.22 Avoiding sample duplication with matrices.

```
50 LET F=RND(-1)

100 LET T=0
200 LET H=0

300 FØR I=1 TØ 10
400 LET F=RND(0)
500 IF F>.5 THEN 900

600 PRINT F,"HEADS"
700 LET H=H+1
800 GØ TØ 1100

900 PRINT F,"TAILS"
1000 LET T=T+1

1100 NEXT I
1200 PRINT
1300 PRINT H;"HEADS AND ";T;" TAILS"
1400 END
```

Program 4.23   Program for simultating the flip
of a coin.

With that in mind, review Program 4.23. Ten random numbers are drawn
(by virtue of the I loop) and assigned to F. Each of them is checked to determine if it is greater than 0.5 (line 500) and the computer is routed to either
the HEADS or the TAILS printout, as appropriate. Program 4.23 also
causes the computer to print out the value of F on each flip so that the printout in Figure 4.14 can be used by the student to correlate the drawn number
with the answers produced.

Using only ten samplings of random flips, the computer may not produce
exactly a 50–50 split of heads and tails, just as such a split would not be
guaranteed if the flips were performed by hand with a real coin. As in real
life, the more flips that are made, the more accurate are the results. The

```
RUN

.99811984        TAILS
.13004939        HEADS
.40493816        HEADS
.43383006        HEADS
.72124424        TAILS
.89220363        TAILS
.14113978        HEADS
6.2493976E-02    HEADS
.29384974        HEADS
.28197484        HEADS

7    HEADS AND    3    TAILS
```

Figure 4.14   Printout of the flipped coin simulation in Program 4.23.

program might have been run for 100, 500, 1000, or 10,000 flips by changing the upper limit of the loop (although then the printout on each flip would probably have been eliminated to conserve printout time).

■ EXERCISES

4.49   Sixteen refrigerators have been tested and it is desired to review, on a spot check basis, the historical background of their manufacture, test, etc. Write a program which randomly identifies three units for detailed study.

4.50   Two urns contain red and white balls, as follows:

Urn 1	64 red,	36 white
Urn 2	50 red,	50 white

Write a program which simulates drawing one ball from each urn and prints if each is red or white. Repeat for 100 experiments. Assume that the balls are returned to the urns so that each new experiment has the same number of balls. Have the computer count the number of times two red, two white, or one of each color are drawn. For the first 15 experiments, print the random number drawn so that you can be sure the program is operating properly. According to exact probability theory you should get 32% red–red, 18% white–white, and 50% red–white draws. How close did the computer come? Run the program again for 5000 experiments, eliminating the PRINT statement for each one. How much closer to the exact results did the computer come this time?

*4.51   Freshly manufactured television tubes are placed into packing boxes in three layers, each layer ten tubes by ten tubes. The rows are labeled 1,...,10; columns are labeled 1,...,10; and layers are numbered 1,2,3.

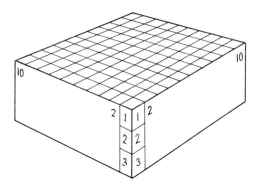

There are twenty such boxes. For quality control purposes, six tubes must be tested from each box. Write a random sampling program which will specify the row, column, and layer from which each tube should be taken. Each box should be independently sampled. Use care that, in one box, the same tube is not drawn twice.

4.52 One hundred couples go on a picnic. Forty percent of the girls bring chicken, 30% bring ham, 20% bring hamburgers, and 10% bring peanut butter. Unknown to them, each boy has a favorite food. Sixty percent favor hamburger, 20% favor peanut butter, 10% favor chicken, 8% favor ham, and 2% favor roast beef. Write a simulation program which prints out the favorite food of each boy and the food his partner brings, and counts the number of couples who are properly matched.

5 ADVANCED EXAMPLES

This chapter presents a number of important examples which are designed to explore the fullest capabilities of the time-share computer and BASIC. The reader is invited to study each program and look for ways to apply the techniques to his own problems.

Example 5.1 Moving Averages

The employment level of the Widget-Gidget Mfg. Co. has fluctuated as follows:

	J	F	M	A	M	J	J	A	S	O	N	D
1968	83	84	79	86	88	92	90	93	90	89	88	89
1969	92	93	91	90	93	95	94	94	94	95	96	95
1970	94	96	98	96	95	98	99	100	100	101	99	100

Beginning with the period January–December 1968, write a program to calculate every twelve-month moving average, i.e.,

■ First average is from January 1968 to December 1968.
■ Second average is from February 1968 to January 1969.
■ Third average is from March 1969 to February 1969.

.
.
.

■ Last (twenty-fifth) average is from January 1970 to December 1970.

The computer should skip a line every fifth printout.

DISCUSSION

In Program 5.1 the matrix **M** contains, as its 36 elements, all the data in the above table (line 200). There are 25 twelve-month periods and the I loop (lines 300–900) is used to determine a single moving average for each one. Within each I loop, T is first set equal to zero; then the J loop is executed, accumulating twelve months of data; i.e., $T = T + M(J)$ for $J = I$ to $I + 11$. The particular twelve numbers represented by $M(J)$ depends, of course on the value of I. When $I = 1$, $T = M(1) + M(2) + M(3) + \cdots + M(12)$; when $I = 2$, $T = M(2) + M(3) + M(4) + \cdots + M(13)$; etc.; thereby "moving" the average along the data.

Lines 850–860 accomplish the required task of printing a blank line. When $I = 1,2,3,4,6,7,\ldots I/5$ is unequal to the integer of $I/5$ and the computer bypasses line 860. Only on $I = 5,10,\ldots$ will the computer execute line 860 and print a blank line.

```
100 DIM M(36)
200 MAT READ M

299 REMARK--THERE ARE 25 PERIØDS ØF 12 MØS. EACH
300 FØR I=1 TØ 25
400 LET T=0

498 REMARK--WHEN I=1, DØ 12 MØNTHS BEGINNING WITH FIRST MØNTH
499 REMARK--WHEN I=2, DØ 12 MØNTHS BEGINNING WITH SECØND MØNTH, ETC.
500 FØR J=I TØ I+11
600 LET T=T+M(J)
700 NEXT J

800 PRINT "FØR PERIØD NØ.";I,"AVERAGE =";T/12
850 IF I/5<>INT(I/5) THEN 900
860 PRINT
900 NEXT I

1000 DATA 83,84,79,86,88,92,90,93,90,89,88,89
1100 DATA 92,93,91,90,93,95,94,94,94,95,96,95
1200 DATA 94,96,98,96,95,98,99,100,100,101,99,100
1300 END
RUN

FØR PERIØD NØ.       1          AVERAGE =    87.583333
FØR PERIØD NØ.       2          AVERAGE =    88.333333
FØR PERIØD NØ.       3          AVERAGE =    89.083333
FØR PERIØD NØ.       4          AVERAGE =    90.083333
FØR PERIØD NØ.       5          AVERAGE =    90.416667

FØR PERIØD NØ.       6          AVERAGE =    90.833333
FØR PERIØD NØ.       7          AVERAGE =    91.083333
FØR PERIØD NØ.       8          AVERAGE =    91.416667
FØR PERIØD NØ.       9          AVERAGE =    91.5
```

Program 5.1 Calculating moving averages.

Example 5.2   Arranging Data in Order

A test resulted in the following 16 scores: 63,88,58,73,69,88,45,100,93, 77,76,48,79,82,99,82. Write a program which will arrange these scores in descending order, i.e., 100,99,...,45.

DISCUSSION
In Program 5.2 the data is placed in lines 1900–2000; line 1800 is provided to inform the program that there are 16 such scores. Lines 100–300 dimension and read the variable **S**. At this point, $S(1) = 63$, $S(2) = 88$, $S(3) = 58, \ldots, S(16) = 82$.

```
100  READ N
200  DIM S(N)
300  MAT READ S

400  FØR I=1 TØ N-1
500  FØR J=I+1 TØ N
600  IF S(I)>S(J) THEN 1000
700  LET X=S(I)
800  LET S(I)=S(J)
900  LET S(J)=X
1000 NEXT J
1100 NEXT I

1200 PRINT N;"DATA, IN ØRDER, ARE:"
1300 PRINT
1400 FØR I=1 TØ N
1500 PRINT S(I)
1600 NEXT I

1800 DATA 16
1900 DATA 63,88,58,73,69,88,45,100
2000 DATA 93,77,76,48,79,82,99,82
2100 END
  RUN

16    DATA, IN ØRDER, ARE:

100
99
93
88
88
82
82
79
77
76
73
69
63
58
48
45
```

Program 5.2 Arranging data in order.

The key to the program is line 600, which is governed by the I and J loops of lines 400 and 500. The intention of this segment is to sort through the list of data comparing the first item to the second, third, fourth, . . . , sixteenth, ascertaining if any of the numbers is greater than the first; if so, lines 700–900 effect interchanging the position of the first and the largest numbers in the matrix, always resulting in the larger of the two numbers being placed (or retained) in the first location.

Examine, now, the behavior of line 600 during the J loop: When $I = 1$ and $J = I + 1 = 2$, S(1) and S(2) are compared. Since S(1) is not greater than S(2), branching to line 1000 does not occur. Instead, lines 700–900 are executed, resulting in the series of manipulations

$$X = S(1) = 63$$
$$S(1) = S(2) = 88$$
$$S(2) = X = 63$$

or the exchange of S(1) and S(2), putting the larger of the numbers into S(1). The NEXT J statement iterates the loop, with line 600 next comparing S(1) to S(3), or 88 to 58. Now, however, S(I) *is* greater than S(J), and statements 700–900 are bypassed, leaving $S(1) = 88$. The process is repeated for the remaining scores, always comparing a new number to the first one. No exchange will be made unless a larger number greater than the first one is found. Eventually, then, the largest of all the data will be moved into S(1).

After $J = 16$, the NEXT I statement is incurred, setting $I = 2$. Again the J loop is iterated, this time with $J = 3,4,...,16$. Careful examination shows that the second largest datum is eventually placed in S(2). Continuing through all the I iterations, it can be seen that, in the end, all the data are aligned in descending order.

Example 5.3   Survey Analysis

A survey is made of 5000 high school students. The survey form, filled out in a typical fashion, is shown in Figure 5.1. For computer purposes, entries on each line are numbered 1,2,... from the left. If a student does not answer a particular question, a zero is used for that answer. One data line is entered for each questionnaire, as shown in Program 5.3. Line 400, for example, corresponds to Figure 5.1, where the student answered "3" to question 1, "4" to question 2, etc. The computer should organize and summarize the data into a table as shown in Figure 5.2.

DISCUSSION

The main part of the program is in lines 300–1000; **Q** is dimensioned "4-down, 0:5-across" and initialized to zero. Rows 1–4 each represent one

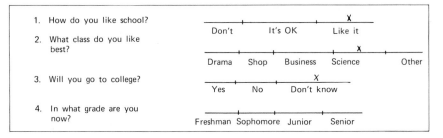

Figure 5.1 Student's questionnaire.

```
100 DIM Q(4,0:5)
200 MAT Q=ZER

298 REM--CHANGE NEXT LINE TO N1=5000 FOR
299 REM--FULL SURVEY OF ALL STUDENTS
300 LET N1=3
400 FOR N=1 TO N1
500 READ A1,A2,A3,A4
600 LET Q(1,A1)=Q(1,A1)+1
700 LET Q(2,A2)=Q(2,A2)+1
800 LET Q(3,A3)=Q(3,A3)+1
900 LET Q(4,A4)=Q(4,A4)+1
1000 NEXT N

1100 PRINT " ","NUMBER","PERCENT"
1200 PRINT
1300 PRINT
1400 PRINT "1.  HOW DO YOU LIKE SCHOOL?"
1500 PRINT
1600 PRINT "  DON'T",Q(1,1),Q(1,1)*100/N1
1700 PRINT "  IT'S OK",Q(1,2),Q(1,2)*100/N1
1800 PRINT "  LIKE IT",Q(1,3),Q(1,3)*100/N1
1900 PRINT "  NO ANSWER",Q(1,0),Q(1,0)*100/N1
2000 PRINT
2100 PRINT "2.  WHAT CLASS DO YOU LIKE BEST?"
2200 PRINT
2300 PRINT "  DRAMA",Q(2,1),Q(2,1)*100/N1
2400 PRINT "  SHOP",Q(2,2),Q(2,2)*100/N1
2500 REM
2700 REM            *
2800 REM       CONTINUE QUESTIONS AND
2900 REM       ANSWERS IN THIS MANNER
3000 REM

4000 DATA 3,4,3,0
4100 DATA 3,1,1,4
4200 DATA 2,4,2,1
4300 REM
4500 REM            *
4600 REM       CONTINUE DATA IN THIS MANNER
4700 REM            *
9999 END
```

Program 5.3 Survey analysis.

```
RUN

                    NUMBER              PERCENT


   1.  HØW DØ YØU LIKE SCHØØL?

       DØN'T            0                   0
       IT'S ØK          1                  33.333333
       LIKE IT          2                  66.666667
       NØ ANSWER        0                   0

   2.  WHAT CLASS DØ YØU LIKE BEST?

       DRAMA            1                  33.333333
       SHØP             0                   0
                        .
                        .
                        .
```

Figure 5.2 Printout of student's questionnaire problem.

question. There are a sufficient number of columns for the maximum number of answers (in this case six, including 0 for a nonanswer). All 5000 responses are processed by virtue of the N loop; A1, A2, A3, and A4 are read for each of the student's responses. On the first iteration, A1 = 3, A2 = 4, A3 = 3, and A4 = 0. Thus, when N = 1, lines 500–900 are, in effect, the accumulator statements

$$
\begin{array}{ll}
600 & \text{LET } Q(1,3) = Q(1,3) + 1 \\
700 & \text{LET } Q(2,4) = Q(2,4) + 1 \\
800 & \text{LET } Q(3,3) = Q(3,3) + 1 \\
900 & \text{LET } Q(4,0) = Q(4,0) + 1
\end{array}
$$

After all data lines are processed, the **Q** matrix elements represent the total number of all responses in each row and column. For illustration, Figure 5.3 shows **Q** after N = 2. The printout in lines 1100–3999 is obvious.

$$
\begin{array}{c}
\text{Answers} \\
\begin{array}{cccccc}
0 & 1 & 2 & 3 & 4 & 5
\end{array}
\end{array}
$$

$$
\text{Questions}\begin{array}{c}1\\2\\3\\4\end{array}
\begin{bmatrix}
0 & 0 & 0 & 2 & 0 & 0 \\
0 & 1 & 0 & 0 & 1 & 0 \\
0 & 1 & 0 & 1 & 0 & 0 \\
1 & 0 & 0 & 0 & 1 & 0
\end{bmatrix}
$$

Figure 5.3 The value of **Q** after lines 600–900 are executed twice.

Example 5.4   Distribution of Sales Volume

Except for the last entry, the DATA in Program 5.4 represents the annual sales that Widget-Gidget Mfg. Co. made to each of its customers. Write a program which reads this data and determines

■ the number of transactions which had a value in the range $0–100,000, $100,000–200,000, . . . , $900,000–1,000,000;
■ the total value of all sales in each range;
■ the percentage of sales and transactions in each range.

DISCUSSION
A 10×2 S matrix is defined in line 100. Each row represents the upper limit of a $100,000 increment in sales (i.e., row 1 represents $0–100,000, row 2 represents $100,000–$200,000, etc.) The first column is used to accumulate the sales volume in each increment, and the second column is used to count the number of entries in that increment. Each sale (S1) can be related to one of the rows of S by the expression $INT(S1/1E5)+1$. For example, $231,164.33 corresponds to the third row (i.e., $200,000–$300,000). The above expression thus reduces to

$$INT(231164.33/100000)+1=3$$

Then for this example, $S(INT(S1/1E5)+1,1)=S(3,1)$, and line 800 is an accumulator which sums all data entries in each range; that is, when $200,000 \leqslant S1 \leqslant 300,000$, line 800 means $S(3,1)=S(3,1)+S1$ etc. It should be obvious that the same principles result in line 900 counting the number of entries in each row.

The data entry 0 (line 9998) is used to indicate the end of the data. After reading each S1, a check is made (line 500) to determine if it is the zero, and if so, the program is routed to the printout. The remainder of the program is straightforward.

Example 5.5   Simultaneous Equations

Using matrix algebra, write a program to solve the following for X_1, X_2, and X_3 :

$$3X_1 + 2X_2 + 1X_3 = 6$$
$$2X_1 - 1X_2 - 1X_3 = -9$$
$$-2X_1 + 0.5X_2 + 2X_3 = 13$$

```
100  DIM S(10,2)
101  MAT S=ZER
148  REMARK-T1=TØTAL SALES,T2=SUM ØF SALES PERCENTAGES,N1=#TRANSAC-
149  REMARK   TIØNS,N2=TØTAL % ØF TRANSACTIØNS FRØM PRINTØUT LØØP.

150  LET T1=0
151  LET T2=0
152  LET N1=0
153  LET N2=0
199  REMARK--N=#TRANSACTIØNS,T=TØTAL SALES
200  LET N=0
300  LET T=0

400  READ S1
500  IF S1=0 THEN 1100
600  LET T=T+S1
700  LET N=N+1
800  LET S(INT(S1/1E5)+1,1)=S(INT(S1/1E5)+1,1)+S1
900  LET S(INT(S1/1E5)+1,2)=S(INT(S1/1E5)+1,2)+1
1000 GØ TØ 400

1100 PRINT "TØ","SALES","%SALES","#TRANSACT","%TRANSACT"
1200 FØR I=1 TØ 10
1300 PRINT I*1E5,S(I,1),S(I,1)*100/T,S(I,2),S(I,2)*100/N
1303 LET N1=N1+S(I,2)
1304 LET N2=N2+S(I,2)*100/N
1400 NEXT I

1500 LET T2=T2+S(I,1)*100/T
2000 PRINT " ","==========","==========","===","=========="
2100 PRINT " ",T1,T2,N1,N2

5000 DATA 928323.60,218314.92,16502.36,338106.25
5100 DATA 763203.70,966291.36,287412.31,333754.25
5200 DATA 231164.33,204209.61,277817.41,422370.89
5300 DATA 657710.83,905488.96,135687.50,478324.27
5400 DATA 24576.07,730960.02,462507.43,52560.92
5500 DATA 214339.68,156035.06,432319.70,1294.30
5600 DATA 976205.26,502793.12,290693.71,736531.06
5700 DATA 535818.04,246149.42,956208.81
9998 DATA 0
9999 END
 RUN
```

TØ	SALES	%SALES	#TRANSACT	%TRANSACT
100000	94933.65	.70406361	4	12.903226
200000	291722.56	2.1635241	2	6.4516129
300000	1970101.4	14.611012	8	25.806452
400000	671860.5	4.9827698	2	6.4516129
500000	1795522.3	13.316268	4	12.903226
600000	1038611.2	7.7027305	2	6.4516129
700000	657710.83	4.8778306	1	3.2258065
800000	2230694.8	16.54367	3	9.6774194
900000	0	0	0	0
1000000	4732518	35.098131	5	16.129032
	==========	==========	===	==========
	0	35.098131	31	100

Program 5.4 Analysis of sales volume.

DISCUSSION

Recalling the discussions on matrix algebra, the above equations could be written

$$\begin{bmatrix} 3 & 2 & 1 \\ 2 & -1 & -1 \\ -2 & 0.5 & 2 \end{bmatrix} * \begin{bmatrix} X_1 \\ X_2 \\ X_3 \end{bmatrix} = \begin{bmatrix} 6 \\ -9 \\ 13 \end{bmatrix}$$

or $\mathbf{M} * \mathbf{X} = \mathbf{B}$, where

$$\mathbf{M} = \begin{bmatrix} 3 & 2 & 1 \\ 2 & -1 & -1 \\ -2 & 0.5 & 2 \end{bmatrix} \quad \mathbf{X} = \begin{bmatrix} X_1 \\ X_2 \\ X_3 \end{bmatrix} \quad \mathbf{B} = \begin{bmatrix} 6 \\ -9 \\ 13 \end{bmatrix}$$

As with an ordinary algebraic statement, $\mathbf{X}$ can be found by

$$\mathbf{X} = \frac{\mathbf{B}}{\mathbf{M}} = \mathbf{M}^{-1} * \mathbf{B} = \mathrm{INV}(\mathbf{M}) * \mathbf{B}\dagger$$

Program 5.5 is a direct implementation of this equation.

```
100 DIM M(3,3),X(3,1),B(3,1),I(3,3)
200 MAT READ M,B
300 MAT I=INV(M)
400 MAT X=I*B

500 FØR I=1 TØ 3
600 PRINT "X";I;"=";X(I,1)
700 NEXT I
800 DATA 3,2,1,2,-1,-1,-2,.5,2
900 DATA 6,-9,13
1000 END
RUN

X 1    =-1
X 2    = 2
X 3    = 5
```

Program 5.5 Solving simultaneous equations with matrix algebra.

Example 5.6   A Puzzling Problem Using Simultaneous Equations

Use the program in Example 5.5 to find the ages of Nancy, Alfie, and Reggie if the following facts are established:

†Actually, the expression $\mathbf{B}/\mathbf{M}$ (i.e., division by a matrix) is not defined mathematically, but the distinction is not important here. Suffice it to say that, rather than dividing by $\mathbf{M}$, we shall simply multiply by the inverse of $\mathbf{M}$ (i.e., $\mathbf{M}^{-1}$).

■ Reggie and Alfie together are twice as old as Nancy.
■ Two years from now, Nancy will be a year older than Alfie is today.
■ One year ago, Reggie was half as old as Alfie will be two years from now.

DISCUSSION

If the ages of Nancy, Alfie, and Reggie are a_1, a_2, and a_3, respectively, the above statements may be expressed mathematically as three simultaneous equations in three unknowns:

$$a_2 + a_3 = 2a_1$$
$$a_1 + 2 = a_2 + 1$$
$$2(a_3 - 1) = a_2 + 2$$

This set of equations may be reorganized as

$$-2a_1 + 1a_2 + 1a_3 = 0$$
$$1a_1 - 1a_2 + 0a_3 = -1$$
$$0a_1 - 1a_2 + 2a_3 = 4$$

Or, as a matrix equation

$$\begin{bmatrix} -2 & 1 & 1 \\ 1 & -1 & 0 \\ 0 & -1 & 2 \end{bmatrix} * \begin{bmatrix} a_1 \\ a_2 \\ a_3 \end{bmatrix} = \begin{bmatrix} 0 \\ -1 \\ 4 \end{bmatrix}$$

The equations are now expressed in the same form as those of Example 5.5, and the matrices can replace the data in Program 5.5, solving the problem.

Example 5.7 Coin and Die Game

In a manner similar to that in Example 4.15, conduct ten thousand simulations of a "game" where a coin is flipped and a die is tossed. From them, determine the probability that a "HEADS" and a "FIVE" result from a pair of tosses.

DISCUSSION

A flowchart is given in Figure 5.4. Program 5.6 conducts 10,000 experimental tosses by virtue of the I loop. On each one, two random numbers are drawn— one to represent the coin toss (line 400) and another to represent the die roll (line 500). Since the probability of the coin coming up heads is 1/2 and the probability of a die coming up 1, 2, 3, 4, 5, or 6 is 1/6 each, Table 5.1 can be constructed to relate random numbers to possible outcomes of the tosses; i.e., as in Example 4.15, any random number between 0 and 0.5 will be regarded as HEADS. Any number between 4/6 and 5/6 will be regarded as a FIVE on the die.

A counter is installed in line 900. Its purpose is to keep track of the number of experiments in which a "successful" result is attained. The computer is routed away from that counter if the random number of the die is less than 4/6 or greater than 5/6, or if the number of the coin is greater than 0.5; this is accomplished by lines 600–800.

Examples 4.15 and 5.7 are two of a class of problems known as *Monte Carlo simulations*. Such simulations are valuable in a wide range of business and engineering problems which involve a number of uncertainties about the course of future events. Examples 5.8 and 5.9 further illustrate the principles of Monte Carlo simulations.

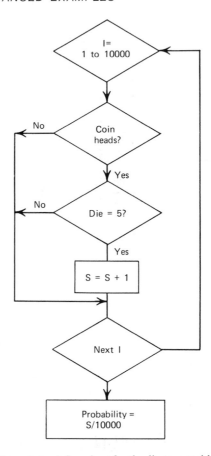

Figure 5.4 A flowchart for the die-toss problem.

Example 5.8 Monte Carlo Simulation of a Business Decision

Draw a flowchart and write the program to analyze the following business problem and to assist the company's managers in making their decision. The Widget-Gidget Mfg. Co. is contemplating going into a new product line, "Zonks." The company wishes to go into the enterprise only if it has an 80% chance of achieving a 60% return on its initial investment within five years. They have undertaken preliminary market research and come up with the following facts:

■   At the moment, there is no competition in the field, but there are two potential competitors. The probability that Ajax Mfg. will go into the business is 50%; that World-Wide Sales will do so is 30%.

```
 100 LET S=0
 200 LET R=RND(-1)
 300 FOR I=1 TO 10000

 400 LET C=RND(0)
 500 LET D=RND(0)

 600 IF C>.5 THEN 1000
 700 IF D<4/6 THEN 1000
 800 IF D>5/6 THEN 1000
 900 LET S=S+1

1000 NEXT I
1100 PRINT "PROBABILITY OF "
1200 PRINT "WINNING IS";S/10000
1300 PRINT "LOSING IS";(10000-S)/10000
1400 END
RUN

PROBABILITY OF
WINNING IS    8.71E-02
LOSING IS     .9129
```

Program 5.6 Simulation of a coin toss and a die roll.

Table 5.1 Translating any given random number with value $0 \to 1.0$ into an equivalent flip of a coin or toss of a die.

Coin or die?	Outcome	Probability	Applicable range of random numbers
Coin	Heads	1/2	$0.0000000 \to 0.5000000$
Coin	Tails	1/2	$0.5000001 \to 1.000000$
Die	1	1/6	$0.0000000 \to 0.1666666$
Die	2	1/6	$0.1666667 \to 0.3333333$
Die	3	1/6	$0.3333334 \to 0.5000000$
Die	4	1/6	$0.5000001 \to 0.6666666$
Die	5	1/6	$0.6666667 \to 0.8333333$
Die	6	1/6	$0.8333334 \to 1.0000000$

■   If either competitor goes into the business, they will not be able to do so immediately. The length of time their entry will take depends on the amount of money each wishes to invest in the venture. Table 5.2 shows the probability that each will be marketing the product within specified months after Widget-Gidget is, provided they go into the business at all.

■   The eventual sales volume of Zonks is not known, and it is naturally somewhat dependent on the number of competitors in the field. Table 5.3 shows the probability that various levels of sales will be achieved.

■   The company will make a profit of $0.19 per Zonk on the first 250,000 sold, and $0.295 on each unit over 250,000. An initial investment of $35,000 is required.

DISCUSSION

Program 5.7, flowcharted in Figure 5.5, conducts 5000 simulations of possible developments of the future competitive scene. During each one, random numbers are drawn (lines 500, 600) to establish whether or not each competitor enters the market. Other numbers are used to establish how long they take to enter, and the monthly sales volume of Widget-Gidget during the periods when there is 0, 1, or 2 competitors. From this point, let us concentrate on one actual scenario that developed when the author ran the program. The sequence of random numbers that were drawn on the thirteenth, fourteenth, and fifteenth simulations are given in Table 5.4. Picking up with the thirteenth simulation, the variables A and W are assigned the values A = 0.6328110, W = 0.2316923. Since A > 0.50, Atlas does not go into business, and lines 701–1300 are bypassed. Since W is less than 0.30, World-Wide does enter the market, and lines 1401–2000 are executed. In line 1500, C is set equal to one, meaning there is one competitor. (If Atlas had entered, C would have been set equal to one in line 800, and to two in line 1500.)

Table 5.2 Probability distribution of time necessary for two competitors to enter the market.

Time (months)	Ajax (%)	World-Wide (%)
6	50	20
12	75	60
18	100	80
24		100

Table 5.3 Distribution of sales probabilities

Monthly sales volume, less than or equal to (units)	Probability that volume is not exceeded (%)		
	No competitor	One competitor	Two competitors
1,000	0	0	0
2,000	0	4	7
3,000	5	11	15
4,000	13	20	40
5,000	25	35	60
6,000	50	62	85
7,000	70	85	95
8,000	85	95	100
9,000	95	100	100
10,000	100	100	100

Lines 1600–2000 simulate the time it takes World-Wide to actually become a competitor. From Table 5.4, X is set to 0.7781239 in line 1600. Lines 1700–1900 search through W, the second column of Table 5.2, determining the number of months required of World-Wide Sales. Since X = 0.7781239, it takes 18 months (assigned to the variable M1). Therefore, during the first 18 months, Widget-Gidget has the market to itself. During the remaining three and a half years, the market is shared with World-Wide.

Since C = 1, the computer is directed from line 2200 to line 3000, where Widget-Gidget's sales during those two periods are simulated. From Table 5.4, S1 = 0.9410036, and lines 3100–3300 establish the sales volume during the period when there is no competitor by scanning the second column of Table 5.3. Line 3400 calculates the total items sold during the eighteen-month period. The process of establishing the number of items sold is repeated in lines 3500–3900 for the period when there is one competitor. The total number of sales is equal to the number in the first 18 months, plus the number in the remaining 42 months (line 3900). On the thirteenth simulation, S1 = 0.9410036 in line 3000, and S1 = 0.6204169 in line 3500. Therefore, the company sells 9000/month for 18 months, and 7000/month afterward, or 456,000 items in all.

The computer is instructed to proceed from line 4000 to line 5600, where it begins to determine the profit from 456,000 sales. Since the sales exceed 250,000, line 5900 is used to determine the profit, which turns out to be $97,970. Since this profit exceeds the initial investment plus 60%, the computer is directed to go from line 6000 to line 6100, where the counter Y

```
50 DIM A(3,2),W(4,2),S(10,0:2)
100 MAT READ A,W,S
110 LET Y=0
200 LET R=RND(-1)

299 LET N9=5000
300 FOR I=1 TO N9
400 LET C=0
410 LET M1=60
420 LET M2=60
500 LET A=RND(0)
600 LET W=RND(0)

700 IF A>.50 THEN 1400
701 REM--HOW LONG DOES ATLAS TAKE
702 REM--TO GET INTO MARKET?
800 LET C=C+1
900 LET X=RND(0)
1000 FOR J=1 TO 3
1100 IF X<A(J,2) THEN 1300
1200 NEXT J
1300 LET M1=A(J,1)

1400 IF W>.30 THEN 2010
1401 REM--HOW LONG DOES W-WIDE TAKE
1402 REM--TO GET INTO MARKET?
1500 LET C=C+1
1600 LET X=RND(0)
1700 FOR J=1 TO 4
1800 IF X<W(J,2) THEN 2000
1900 NEXT J
2000 LET M2=W(J,1)

2009 REM--LOWEST IN M1, HIGHEST IN M2
2010 IF M1<M2 THEN 2100
2020 LET X=M1
2030 LET M1=M2
2040 LET M2=M1

2100 IF C=0 THEN 2400
2200 IF C=1 THEN 3000
2300 IF C=2 THEN 4100

2398 REM--MONTHLY SALES
2399 REM--WHEN NO COMPETITORS
2400 LET S1=RND(0)
2500 FOR J=1 TO 10
2600 IF S1<S(J,0) THEN 2800
2700 NEXT J
2800 LET S=(J-1)*1000*60
2900 GO TO 5600

2998 REM--MONTHLY SALES WHEN
2999 REM--ZERO AND ONE COMPETITOR
3000 LET S1=RND(0)
3100 FOR J=1 TO 10
3200 IF S1<S(J,0) THEN 3400
3300 NEXT J
3400 LET S=(J-1)*1000*(M1)

3500 LET S1=RND(0)
3600 FOR J=1 TO 10
3700 IF S1<S(J,1) THEN 3900
3800 NEXT J
3900 LET S=S+(J-1)*1000*(60-M1)
4000 GO TO 5600
```

Program 5.7 Monte Carlo program for Example 5.8.

```
4097 REM--MONTHLY SALES WHEN
4098 REM--ZERO, ONE AND TWO
4099 REM--COMPETITORS
4100 LET S1=RND(0)
4200 FOR J=1 TO 10
4300 IF S1<S(J,0) THEN 4500
4400 NEXT J
4500 LET S=(J-1)*1000*(M1)

4600 LET S1=RND(0)
4700 FOR J=1 TO 10
4800 IF S1<S(J,1) THEN 5000
4900 NEXT J
5000 LET S=S+(J-1)*1000*(M2-M1)

5100 LET S1=RND(0)
5200 FOR J=1 TO 10
5300 IF S1<S(J,2) THEN 5500
5400 NEXT J
5500 LET S=S+(J-1)*1000*(60-M2)

5599 REM--DETERMINE PROFIT
5600 IF S>250000 THEN 5900
5700 LET P=.19*S
5800 GO TO 6000
5900 LET P=.19*250000+.295*(S-250000)

5999 REM--SUCCESSFUL SCENARIO?
6000 IF P<35000+.60*35000 THEN 6200
6100 LET Y=Y+1
6200 NEXT I

6300 PRINT "THE PROBABILITY OF ACHEIVING 60% PROFIT"
6400 PRINT "IN FIVE YEARS IS";(Y/N9)
6500 IF (Y/N9)>.80 THEN 6800
6600 PRINT "DON'T GO INTO THE BUSINESS"
6700 STOP
6800 PRINT "GO AHEAD INTO THE BUSINESS"
6900 STOP

6999 REM--AJAX'S ENTRY TIME DISTRIBUTION
7000 DATA  6, .50
7001 DATA 12, .75
7002 DATA 18,1.00

7010 REM--WORLD-WIDE'S ENTRY TIME DISTRIBUTION
7011 DATA  6, .20
7012 DATA 12, .60
7013 DATA 18, .80
7014 DATA 24,1.00

7020 REM--SALES DISTRIBUTION
7021 DATA    0,    0,    0
7022 DATA    0, .04, .07
7023 DATA  .05, .11, .15
7024 DATA  .13, .20, .40
7025 DATA  .25, .35, .60
7026 DATA  .50, .62, .85
7027 DATA  .70, .85, .95
7028 DATA  .85, .95,1.00
7029 DATA  .95,1.00,1.00
7030 DATA 1.00,1.00,1.00
7031 END
RUN

THE PROBABILITY OF ACHEIVING 60% PROFIT
IN FIVE YEARS IS   .658
DON'T GO INTO THE BUSINESS
```

Program 5.7 *(continued)*

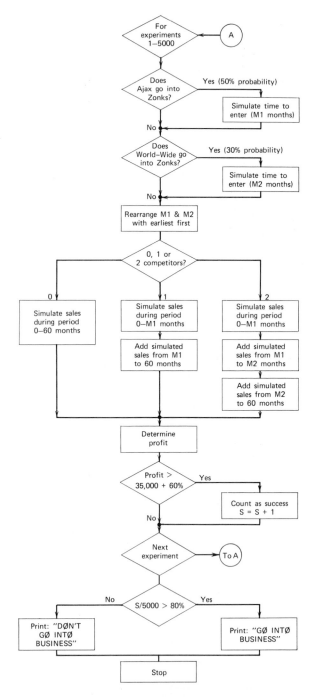

Figure 5.5 Flowchart representing the simulation of the business problem in Example 5.8.

Table 5.4 Random numbers generated on three simulations of the Widget-Gidget problem.

Thirteenth simulation	Fourteenth simulation	Fifteenth simulation
0.6328110	0.0314065	0.6211480
0.2316923	0.2138124	0.7314289
0.7781239	0.4098164	0.8492166
0.9410036	0.8191624	
0.6204169	0.1430411	
	0.9643218	
	0.7921483	

(for YES, the simulation is a success) is incremented. The simulation is repeated in this manner, 5000 times. At the end of all the simulations, the probability that a decision to go into the business will result in 60% profit is Y/5000. This number is used in lines 6300–6800 to advise whether or not to commit to the project. The actual run shows that the manager should not go into the market under the stated conditions.

The student should work through the fourteenth and fifteenth simulations in a similar manner to see what other conditions might develop.

Example 5.9 Mouse in a Maze, or a Random Walk

A mouse is put in a maze at the place labeled "Start" in Figure 5.6a and he walks until he arrives at "Cheese." From any intersection except those on

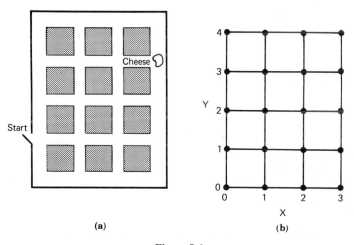

(a)

(b)

Figure 5.6

the border, he can move one space north, south, east, or west with equal probability. He cannot leave the borders of the maze. Simulate ten trips through the maze, printing the position of the mouse after each move.

DISCUSSION

The intersections of corridors can be imagined as the points on an X,Y plane, shown in Figure 5.6b. The mouse starts at $(X, Y) = (0, 1)$. At each move, he can progress ± 1 in either the X or the Y direction.

In Program 5.8, ten trips are simulated by virtue of the FØR/NEXT loop, lines 100–3400. After N moves, the mouse's position is designated by X and Y. He begins at $X = 0$, $Y = 1$ when $N = 0$ (lines 110–300).

```
 99 LET R=RND(-1)
100 FOR I=1 TO 10
110 LET N=0
200 LET X=0
300 LET Y=1
400 LET X1=0
500 LET Y1=0

600 LET R=RND(0)
700 REM-IF R IS LESS THAN .25, MOVE NORTH
800 IF R<.25 THEN 1500
900 REM-IF R IS BETWEEN .25 AND .50, MOVE EAST
1000 IF R<.50 THEN 1700
1100 REM-IF R IS BETWEEN .50 AND .75, MOVE SOUTH
1200 IF R<.75 THEN 1900
1300 REM-IF R IS BETWEEN .75 AND 1, MOVE WEST
1400 IF R<1.00 THEN 2100

1500 LET Y1=1
1600 GO TO 2200
1700 LET X1=1
1800 GO TO 2200
1900 LET Y1=-1
2000 GO TO 2200
2100 LET X1=-1

2200 IF X+X1<0 THEN 400
2300 IF X+X1>3 THEN 400
2400 IF Y+Y1<0 THEN 400
2500 IF Y+Y1>4 THEN 400

2600 LET N=N+1
2700 LET X=X+X1
2800 LET Y=Y+Y1
2900 PRINT "ON MOVE #";N,"THE MOUSE IS AT";X;Y

3000 IF X<>3 THEN 400
3100 IF Y<>3 THEN 400
3200 PRINT "THE MOUSE MADE IT TO THE CHEESE IN ";N;"MOVES."
3300 PRINT
3400 NEXT I
3500 END
```

Program 5.8 Monte Carlo simulation of the mouse problem.

Table 5.5 Output to Program 5.8

```
    RUN
ON MOVE #   1 THE MOUSE IS AT   1   1
ON MOVE #   2 THE MOUSE IS AT   0   1
ON MOVE #   3 THE MOUSE IS AT   0   0
ON MOVE #   4 THE MOUSE IS AT   1   0
ON MOVE #   5 THE MOUSE IS AT   2   0
ON MOVE #   6 THE MOUSE IS AT   3   0
ON MOVE #   7 THE MOUSE IS AT   3   1
ON MOVE #   8 THE MOUSE IS AT   3   2
ON MOVE #   9 THE MOUSE IS AT   3   3
THE MOUSE MADE IT TO THE CHEESE IN    9   MOVES.
```

A random number is drawn (line 600), and from it, the direction the mouse moves (i.e., in the direction $X_1 = +1$, $X_1 = -1$, $Y_1 = +1$, or $Y_1 = -1$) is deduced (lines 700–2100). Each of the four moves is equally likely with a probability 0.25, except when the mouse is on the border.

If the selected move puts the mouse outside the maze, it is abandoned and a new one is determined (lines 2200–2500). If the prospective move does not put him outside the maze, lines 2600–3100 are executed, counting the move, changing his position by X1 and Y1, and printing his new position. Finally, if the mouse is not then at the cheese (i.e., $X \neq 3$ or $Y \neq 3$), another move is simulated (lines 3000–3100) until it arrives there. When it does arrive, lines 3200–3400 are executed, terminating the simulation of one trip and initiating another. The printout from one simulated trip in this program is given in Table 5.5.

If one were to delete the printout on each move and run the program for 1000 simulations, some startling new information would be derived. First, no trips take less than five moves; a quick analysis of the construction of the maze reveals that this is inevitable. Second, one would probably have been surprised to find that, when the author ran the program, seven of the thousand trips took over 200 moves (one took 251). Finally, most surprisingly, *not a single trip* was completed in an even number of moves. If one studies the mechanics of the mouse's movements, he will see that arrival in an even number of moves is indeed impossible.

Example 5.10   Production Sampling Plans— Acceptable Quality Level

Table 5.6, adapted from MIL-STD-105D, is used to determine rules for quality control sampled testing of production units. For a given production lot, the indicated sample is tested. For a selected acceptable quality level

Table 5.6 Sampling plan.

Production		Sample size	AQL				
From	To		1.5	2.5	4.0	6.5	10
0	150	Table not valid					
151	280	13	1	2	2	3	4
281	500	20	2	2	3	4	6
501	1,200	32	2	3	4	6	8
1,201	3,200	50	3	4	6	8	11
3,201	10,000	80	4	6	8	11	15
10,001	35,000	125	6	8	11	15	22
35,001	150,000	200	8	11	15	22	22
150,001	500,000	315	11	15	22	22	22
500,001	1,000,000	500	15	22	22	22	22

(AQL), the body of the table specifies the maximum number of defective units which may be tolerated in the sample. If there are more defectives, the lot is "rejectable"; if not, it is "acceptable." To demonstrate the principles of a program segment which executes a "table look up," write a program which asks the user how large a lot is, and the AQL to which it is to be tested. Print the required sample size and maximum number of defective units.

DISCUSSION

In Program 5.9 the data pertinent to the problem is included in lines 3200–4300. Three variables are dimensioned and read; U represents the upper limit of each lot, S represents sampling sizes, and N is the body of the table. In response to line 400, the user must type in the particular details of his lot. Lines 500–1600 prevent the user from entering invalid conditions. Lines 900–1300 route the computer to lines 1700, 1900, 2100, 2300, or 2500, setting a value for J which will later be used (line 3100) as the number of the column in N to be utilized. Lines 2600–2800 establish the value of I, the other index of N. It works this way: U1 and U(1) are compared (i.e., U1 versus 280); if U1 is the lesser, the computer is diverted to line 3000 with I remaining at one; if not, the loop is repeated, comparing U1 to U(2), U1 to U(3), etc., until the appropriate value of I is set. Once I and J are established to identify the row and column appropriate to U1 and A1, the sample size element in the S matrix and the number of defectives in the N matrix can be printed (lines 3000–3100).

```
100 DIM U(9,1),S(9,1),N(9,5)
200 MAT READ U,S,N

300 PRINT "HOW MANY UNITS, AND WHAT AQL";
400 INPUT U1,A1
500 IF U1>150 THEN 900
600 PRINT "ERROR...MY TABLE CAN'T BE USED FOR LESS THAN"
700 PRINT "150 UNITS."
800 STOP

900 IF A1=1.5 THEN 1700
1000 IF A1=2.5 THEN 1900
1100 IF A1=4.0 THEN 2100
1200 IF A1=6.5 THEN 2300
1300 IF A1=10 THEN 2500
1400 PRINT "ERROR...MY TABLE CAN ONLY BE USED FOR"
1500 PRINT "AQL'S OF 1.5, 2.5, 4.0, 6.5 AND 10%"
1600 STOP

1700 LET J=1
1800 GO TO 2600
1900 LET J=2
2000 GO TO 2600
2100 LET J=3
2200 GO TO 2600
2300 LET J=4
2400 GO TO 2600
2500 LET J=5

2600 FOR I=1 TO 9
2700 IF U1<U(I,1) THEN 3000
2800 NEXT I
3000 PRINT "SAMPLE SIZE SHOULD BE";S(I,1);"UNITS"
3100 PRINT "ACCEPT UP TO ";N(I,J);"DEFECTS"

3199 REM--NUMBER OF UNITS
3200 DATA 280,500,1200,3200,10000,35000,150000,500000,1000000
3299 REM--SAMPLE SIZE
3300 DATA 13,20,32,50,80,125,200,315,500
3499 REM--ACCEPT/REJECT QUANTITIES
3500 DATA 1,2,2,3,4
3600 DATA 2,2,3,4,6
3700 DATA 2,3,4,6,8
3800 DATA 3,4,6,8,11
3900 DATA 4,6,8,11,15
4000 DATA 6,8,11,15,22
4100 DATA 8,11,15,22,22
4200 DATA 11,15,22,22,22
4300 DATA 15,22,22,22,22
4400 END

 RUN
HOW MANY UNITS, AND WHAT AQL   ? 1635,4.0
SAMPLE SIZE SHOULD BE    50    UNITS
ACCEPT UP TO    6     DEFECTS
```

Problem 5.9 Acceptable quality level program.

Example 5.11   Simultaneous Differential Equations

Construct the program necessary to solve the four simultaneous differential equations below for $P_1(t)$, $P_2(t)$, $P_3(t)$, and $P_4(t)$ at time $t = T$.

$$P'_1(t) = a_{11}P_1(t) + a_{12}P_2(t) + a_{13}P_3(t) + a_{14}P_4(t)$$
$$P'_2(t) = a_{21}P_1(t) + a_{22}P_2(t) + a_{23}P_3(t) + a_{24}P_4(t)$$
$$P'_3(t) = a_{31}P_1(t) + a_{32}P_2(t) + a_{33}P_3(t) + a_{34}P_4(t)$$
$$P'_4(t) = a_{41}P_1(t) + a_{42}P_2(t) + a_{43}P_3(t) + a_{44}P_4(t)$$

At $t = 0$, the initial conditions of the equations are $P_1(0)$, $P_2(0)$, $P_3(0)$, and $P_4(0)$.

This type of equation occurs quite frequently in physics, engineering, and mathematics. This program was originally created to solve a *Markov chain* problem.

DISCUSSION

The above equations can be rewritten in matrix form as follows:

$$\mathbf{P}' = \mathbf{M} \cdot \mathbf{P} \qquad \mathbf{P}_0 = \mathbf{P}(0)$$

where

$$\mathbf{P}' = \begin{bmatrix} P'_1(t) \\ P'_2(t) \\ P'_3(t) \\ P'_4(t) \end{bmatrix} \qquad \mathbf{P} = \begin{bmatrix} P_1(t) \\ P_2(t) \\ P_3(t) \\ P_4(t) \end{bmatrix} \qquad \mathbf{P}_0 = \begin{bmatrix} P_1(0) \\ P_2(0) \\ P_3(0) \\ P_4(0) \end{bmatrix}$$

$$\mathbf{M} = \begin{bmatrix} a_{11} & a_{12} & a_{13} & a_{14} \\ a_{21} & a_{22} & a_{23} & a_{24} \\ a_{31} & a_{32} & a_{33} & a_{34} \\ a_{41} & a_{42} & a_{43} & a_{44} \end{bmatrix}$$

The above matrix equation has the solution

$$\mathbf{P} = e^{\mathbf{M}t}\mathbf{P}_0$$

Raising e to a matrix power might present some conceptual difficulties until one realizes that e^{xt} can be expanded

$$e^{xt} = \frac{x^0 t^0}{0!} + \frac{x^1 t^1}{1!} + \frac{x^2 t^2}{2!} + \frac{x^3 t^3}{3!} + \cdots$$

In a similar manner, the matrix equation can be expanded:

$$\mathbf{P} = e^{\mathbf{M}t}\mathbf{P}_0 = \left[\frac{\mathbf{M}^0 t^0}{0!} + \frac{\mathbf{M}^1 t^1}{1!} + \frac{\mathbf{M}^2 t^2}{2!} + \frac{\mathbf{M}^3 t^3}{3!} + \cdots\right]\mathbf{P}_0$$

where $\mathbf{M}^0$ = identity matrix. Observe that each term of the expansion can be related to the preceding term by

$$(i + 1)\text{th term} = \left(\frac{\mathbf{M}t}{i}\right) * (i\text{th term}) \qquad i > 1$$

At this point, the complete program is left to the reader. [*Hint:* Sum only the first 20 terms of the infinite series.]

■ EXERCISES

5.1 Rewrite Program 5.2 so that the numbers are put in reverse order— i.e., smallest one first.

5.2 Rewrite Program 5.2 so that, in addition to printing out the numbers in order, their original position in the table is also printed—e.g., the first part of the printout should look like

16 DATA, IN ∅RDER, AND THEIR ∅RIGINAL
P∅SITI∅NS, ARE:
100 8
99 15
93 9
.
.
.

[*Hint:* Before rearranging the numbers, create a subscripted variable, **P**, whose elements have values P(1) = 1, P(2) = 2, P(3) = 3, . . . , P(16) = 16, representing the initial position of each number. Then, whenever the values in **S** are interchanged, simultaneously interchange the values in **P**.]

*5.3 The *drunkard's walk* problem is a classic in statistics. Embellished a bit, it goes like this: Over an eight block line, a drunk's home is at block number eight; a pub is at block one. The drunk starts at block n, 1 < n < 8, and wanders at random, one block at a time, either toward or away from home. At any intersection, he moves toward the pub with probability 2/3, toward home with probability 1/3. Having gotten either home or to the pub, he remains there. Simulate a thousand trips where he starts at block two, another thousand where he starts at block three, and so forth up to block seven. For each starting point, determine (a) the probability that he ends up in the pub, (b) the probability that he ends up at home, and (c) the average number of blocks he walks.

5.4 A company must ship 10 items a day for 30 consecutive days. It can never ship more. It produces 12 items per day, each with a 20% probability of requiring repair before shipping. If repair is required, the actual time of repair follows this probability schedule:

Time to repair (days)	Probability
1	0.40
2	0.30
3	0.25
4	0.05

Once repaired, the failed item can be held in inventory until needed to replace other failed items. For each unit less than 10 shipped on any day, the company suffers a $1000 incentive penalty. Conduct 1000 30-day Monte Carlo simulations and determine

■ the expected (i.e., average) incentive loss;
■ the 90 percentile loss (i.e., the amount which will not be exceeded more than 90% of the time);
■ the average number of unshipped units on hand at the end of the 30th day;
■ the average loss for each of the 30 days.

In which period is the largest average loss? Why? What parameter(s) in the problem lead to that fact? How could these losses be reduced?

5.5 Four hundred amplifier circuits are tested and their amplification factors (μ) are recorded in DATA statements. The measurements range approximately from 1.0 to 3.0. Read the data and print a histogram with 0.1 increments of μ, similar to that shown in Table 5.7.

5.6 In *game theory*, a matrix is said to have a *saddle point* if one of its elements is both (a) the smallest value in its row and (b) the largest value in its column. Read an M × N matrix and determine if it has a saddle point. If so, print out the value and indices of the point.

5.7 A 6 × 6 matrix **M**, shown in Figure 5.7a, is to be divided into four submatrices, **I**, **Q**, **Ø**, and **R**, (Fig. 5.7b).

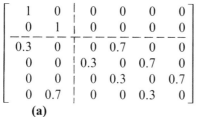

$$
\begin{bmatrix}
1 & 0 & 0 & 0 & 0 & 0 \\
0 & 1 & 0 & 0 & 0 & 0 \\
0.3 & 0 & 0 & 0.7 & 0 & 0 \\
0 & 0 & 0.3 & 0 & 0.7 & 0 \\
0 & 0 & 0 & 0.3 & 0 & 0.7 \\
0 & 0.7 & 0 & 0 & 0.3 & 0
\end{bmatrix}
\qquad
\begin{bmatrix}
I & \emptyset \\
R & Q
\end{bmatrix}
$$

(a)   (b)

Figure 5.7

*5.8   A machine is composed of two nonrepairable units, Figure 5.8, which must both operate successfully if the machine is to operate. The units are said to be *in series-reliability*. The probability that unit 1 is still unfailed at time t (hours) is $P_1 = e^{-10000 \times 10^{-9}t}$; that unit 2 is still unfailed is $P_2 = e^{-16000 \times 10^{-9}t}$. Some of the physical properties of unit 2 prevent its usefulness after 2 years (17,520 hours). Perform a Monte Carlo simulation to determine the average operating life (or mean-time-before-failure) of the machine. [*Hint:* If $P = e^{-\lambda t}$, then $t = -\ln(P)/\lambda$. For each of 10,000 simulations, draw random numbers between zero and one (since all probability numbers are in that range). Substitute one of them for P_1, the other for P_2, solving for simulated failure times of units 1 and 2. The failure time of the machine is the minimum of these times, or 2 years, whichever comes first.]

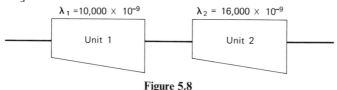

$\lambda_1 = 10{,}000 \times 10^{-9}$ Unit 1 $\lambda_2 = 16{,}000 \times 10^{-9}$ Unit 2

Figure 5.8

Table 5.7

μ	Number of readings
1.0	XXXX
1.1	XXX
1.2	XXXXX
1.3	XXX
1.4	XXXXXXXXXXX
.	
.	
.	
2.8	XXXXX
2.9	XXX
3.0	X

5.9   Figure 5.9 represents four "viewing stations" located at coordinates $(X_1Y_1) = (10,3)$, $(X_2Y_2) = (-1.5,7)$, $(X_3Y_3) = (-10,15)$, and $(X_4Y_4) = (-12,-12)$. A target object is located somewhere in a circle centered at the origin, with radius $r = 6$. The angle θ is uniformly distributed over $\theta = 0$ to 360°, but r is distributed according to

$$P[r = 0] = 0.001 \qquad P[r = 4] = 0.09$$
$$P[r = 1] = 0.019 \qquad P[r = 5] = 0.43$$
$$P[r = 2] = 0.04 \qquad P[r = 6] = 0.36$$
$$P[r = 3] = 0.06$$

where $P[r]$ means the probability of radius r. The viewing station looking toward the origin can "see" $\pm 15°$ on either side of itself. Perform 1000 Monte Carlo simulations, choosing an r, θ on each one, and determine the probability that each station and all combinations of two or more stations can "see" the object. [*Hint:* After determining r, θ, convert the position of the object to x,y coordinates (x_0y_0). It is viewable by the ith station if the angle between their line of sight and the origin is less than $\pm 15°$—that is, if

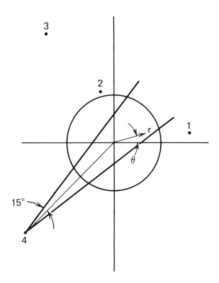

Figure 5.9

$$\frac{x_0(-x_i) + y_0(-y_i)}{\sqrt{x_0^2 + y_0^2}\sqrt{x_i^2 + y_i^2}} \geqslant \cos 15°$$

In a piecemeal fashion, construct a binary number such as 0100, which means (from the left) that it is not visible to station 1, is visible to station 2, etc. Convert the binary number to a decimal number which represents a position in an array where a count of the occurrence of each combination is kept. [That is, the number 0101 converts to $0·8 + 1·4 + 0·2 + 1·1 = 5$. Therefore, LET $Z(5) = Z(5) + 1$.]

5.10 A group of twenty expense accounts, similar to the form shown in Table 5.8 are entered as data. Read the body of each one as the matrix I, the purported column totals as C, the row totals as R, and the other quantities shown. First determine if all calculations are correct. If not, print an appropriate error message. If so, accumulate the totals in each expense category and the amount of money owed the company.

Table 5.8 Typical expense account.

	M	T	W	T	F	Total
Travel	132.50	0	0	132.50	0	265.00
Hotel	19.30	19.30	19.30	19.30	21.50	98.70
Food	11.05	10.45	13.14	12.50	9.50	56.64
Valet	0.00	0.00	3.00	0.00	0.00	3.00
Entertainment	0.00	0.00	25.00	0.00	0.00	25.00
Miscellaneous	2.50	1.50	1.75	3.00	2.25	11.00
Total	165.35	31.25	62.19	167.30	33.25	459.34
					Advance	500.00
					Expenses	459.34
					Owed	40.66

5.11 Write a general program to calculate the function

$$f(x) = a_0 x^n + a_1 x^{n-1} + a_2 x^{n-2} + \cdots + a_{n-1} x + a_n$$

the first derivative

$$f'(x) = n a_0 x^{n-1} + (n-1) a_1 x^{n-2} + (n-2) a_2 x^{n-3} + \cdots + a_{n-1}$$

and the second derivative

$$f''(x) = n(n - 1)a_0x^{n-2} + (n - 1)(n - 2)a_1x^{n-3}$$
$$+ (n - 2)(n - 3)a_2x^{n-4} + \cdots$$

Use it to calculate $d = d_0 + v_1t - (1/2)gt^2$, $v = d(d)/dt$, $a = d(v)/dt = d^2(d)/dt$, where $g = 32.174$, $d_0 = 410$, $v_1 = 310.8$, $t = 0$–200 sec in steps of 10 sec.

5.12 Five products, P_1, P_2, P_3, P_4, and P_5, are manufactured each month; the quantity and total production costs each month are

| | Quantity | | | | | |
Month	P_1	P_2	P_3	P_4	P_5	Total cost ($)
May	100	300	200	500	1,000	14,800
June	150	400	200	700	900	15,600
July	200	300	300	600	1,100	16,800
August	100	400	150	700	1,000	16,450
September	100	500	250	600	1,500	21,150

Find the average cost for each product line. [*Hint:* First write five simultaneous equations in five unknowns, $c_1, \ldots, c_5$, of the form $100c_1 + 300c_2 + 200c_3 + 500c_4 + 1000c_5 = 14,800$.]

5.13 The expression $\binom{m}{n}$ means $m!/n!(m - n!)$, where $m!$ represents $m*(m - 1)*(m - 2)*\cdots*1$. For example,

$$\binom{6}{2} = \frac{6*5*4*3*2*1}{(2*1)(4*3*2*1)}$$

Create an array $F(0:20)$, with each element containing the factorial of its subscript:

$$F(0) = 1$$
$$F(1) = 1$$
$$F(2) = 1*2$$
$$F(3) = 1*2*3$$
.
.
.
$$F(20) = 1*2*3*\ldots*20$$

Use the array to determine $\binom{20}{i}$, $i = 0$–20.

5.14 Tables 5.9 and 5.10 are entered as data. Dimension two variables **P** (for Table 5.9) and **S** (for Table 5.10) plus any others needed. (a) Read both tables; put Table 5.10 into product number ascending order. (b) Write out, *by hand*, how the second column of Table 5.10 will look after it has been reorganized. (c) For each product number, scan through **P** and accumulate the quantity of items in **S**; multiply the quantity by the price; print out the total sales dollar and new year-to-date for each product; if a particular product does not appear in **S**, assume no sales; if a product number appears in **S** but not in **P**, print an error message. (d) As **S** is processed, accumulate the total sales for each district and salesman. [*Hint*: Use district and salesmen numbers as subscripts for other variables.]

Table 5.9 Cost data.

Product number	Unit price	Year-to-date sales
00961	43.60	1,264.40
10229	1.87	523.60
10437	87.50	1,487.50
10558	90.00	720.00
12911	2.25	519.75
13061	48.75	2,047.50
17850	21.80	1,068.20
27128	8.37	878.85
36615	52.00	624.00
36618	40.00	320.00
36619	47.00	705.00
47128	105.00	0.00
48198	1.45	68.15
48614	0.87	381.06
49006	127.50	637.50
53828	75.25	1,806.00
56030	1.45	3,306.00
60189	1.93	1,592.25
62379	15.39	446.31
77083	29.40	323.40
84326	43.10	1,163.70
87125	26.60	347.80
92379	59.90	239.60
94864	160.00	160.00
98814	5.39	598.29

Table 5.10   Sales data.

Product number	Quantity	Salesman	District
56030	15	36	3
12911	10	52	1
92379	2	18	2
47128	1	41	1
56030	12	39	3
56030	50	18	2
36615	3	32	2
62379	1	18	2
12911	25	69	1
62379	5	69	1
48198	6	50	3

*5.15   Given two equations of the form

$$x^5 - 3x^4 + 6x^3 + 12x^2 + x - 10 = 0$$
$$-65x^4 - 2x^3 + 9x^2 - 4x + 2 = 0$$

write a program to determine the coefficients of each term of the product of the two equations. That is, the product is an equation of the form $a_1x^9 + a_2x^8 + a_3x^7 + \cdots + a_9x^0 = 0$. [*Hint:* Use one subscripted variable for the coefficients of each of the above equations, and another for the coefficients of the product. What elements of the first two equations contribute to the value of a_2, the coefficient of x^8?]

6 ADVANCED BASIC FEATURES

```
100    PRINT "DØ YØU UNDERSTAND THIS MATERIAL SØ FAR";
200    INPUT A$
300    IF A$ = "YES" THEN 600
400    PRINT "THEN GØ BACK FØR A REVIEW."
500    STØP
600    PRINT "GØØD. THEN PRØCEED."
700    END
```

The previous chapters were primarily concerned with the format and applications of programming statements which are available in the "conventional" BASIC versions offered by most time-sharing services. We shall now investigate some very useful features offered in many "advanced" BASIC packages. The student is here reminded of the words in the preface of this book—that each company provides a unique combination of advanced features, and that the implementation of common features may vary. This book cannot cover all the various rules and details associated with each version currently available to the public. The treatment given in the following chapters is, nonetheless, quite comprehensive. It teaches vital principles which are universally applicable. When the student has mastered this material, he will be able to adjust easily to new rules imposed by the particular computer he is using. The reader therefore is advised to become very familiar with the material presented in the remaining chapters and to consult reference material available from his supplying company if specific problems with implementation should arise.

6.1 "STRING" VARIABLES

Until now this book has considered only variables which may assume numeric values. But with the advanced BASIC languages special variables are available which may assume any sequence of alphabetic or numeric characters; these are referred to as string variables (sometimes, "alphanumeric" variables). For example, the following is a valid advanced BASIC string statement:

100 LET A$ = "23446 ANZA, APT. C"

The implementation of this feature takes on distinctly differing characteristics with each time-sharing company. Two representative versions are discussed below.

STRING FUNDAMENTALS

Certain general characteristics of strings should be discussed before approaching specific implementations. The computer is informed that a variable will contain strings of characters by combining a $ sign with the letter representing the variable. Typical string names are A$, B$, C$, . . . , Z$, A$(1), A$(12), Z$(11). Some systems permit the use of such names as A1$, B1, B(2) (i.e., without the $ sign), and C$(3,4). The following are examples of invalid string names: $, X, BY, 3A$, A$3. As inferred by

```
100 DIM N$(8)
200 MAT READ N$
300 LET P$="THAT'S A VERY NICE NAME."
400 LET R$="SORRY, I'VE NEVER HEARD OF IT."

500 PRINT "WHAT IS YOUR NAME";
600 INPUT Y$

700 IF Y$="THAT'S ALL" THEN 2000
800 FOR I=1 TO 8
900 IF Y$=N$(I) THEN 1300
1000 NEXT I

1100 PRINT R$
1200 GO TO 500
1300 PRINT P$
1400 PRINT "NEXT KID..."
1600 GO TO 500

2000 PRINT "OKAY, SEE YOU KIDS TOMORROW..."
2100 PRINT "GOODBYE!"

2200 DATA "SAM","JOE","JANE","HARRY"
2300 DATA "HENRY","NANCY","PETE","ELOISE"
2400 END
```

Program 6.1 Using alpha-numeric "strings."

```
WHAT IS YOUR NAME      ? "NANCY"
THAT'S A VERY NICE NAME.
NEXT KID...
WHAT IS YOUR NAME      ? "ALPHONSO"
SORRY, I'VE NEVER HEARD OF IT.
WHAT IS YOUR NAME      ? "PETER"
SORRY, I'VE NEVER HEARD OF IT.
WHAT IS YOUR NAME      ? "THAT'S ALL"
OKAY, SEE YOU KIDS TOMORROW...
GOODBYE!
```

Figure 6.1 Printout from Program 6.1.

these remarks, a string variable name may be dimensioned as an array and used in much the same manner as a numeric array. Use of A$ or B$(I) does not prevent using A or B(I) as distinct numeric variables.

Program 6.1 and Figure 6.1 illustrate many of the fundamental conventions applied to string variables. While they may seem like a bit of entertaining nonsense, they introduce either directly or indirectly, the following rules for using strings:

■ Strings may be used in LET, READ, DATA, INPUT, MAT INPUT, and PRINT statements. Line 200, in Program 6.1, causes the computer to sequentially retrieve values of N$(1),N$(2), . . . from the DATA statements. Line 300 assigns a specific value to P$ (which is equivalent to the numeric assignment statement LET X = -4.134).

■ String variables may be used in IF/THEN statements, as shown in lines 700 and 900. All six relational operators (=, >, <, > =, < =, and < >) are permissible. Examples of valid IF/THEN statements are

```
100    IF  A$ = B$  THEN  1000
200    IF  A$ < > "JULY"  THEN  2000
300    IF  "JUNE" < = "JULY"  THEN  3000
400    IF  A$ > "ØNE"  THEN  4000
500    IF  "!#$" = "!&A"  THEN  5000
600    IF  "!#$" = B$  THEN  6000
```

■ The phrase "JUNE" < = "JULY" is interpreted in a "dictionary" sense: Each character in the first word is sequentially compared to the corresponding character in the second word until one character is found to be different (e.g., the N in JUNE does not "equal" the L in JULY). The character which is earliest in the alphabet (and the string containing it) is then taken as the least, or lowest, of the two. In the above example, at line 300, JULY is less than JUNE, and the transfer to line 3000 will not be executed. Actually, the computer assigns each letter an equivalent numeric code and the coded values are compared (in lieu of the character the code represents). All nonalphabetic characters in a string are also assigned a coded value, and thus each character can be ranked relative to all others. The ranking of all generally used characters is given in Table 6.1. From it, the computer concludes that, for example, "JUNE!" is greater than "JUN.!" because "E" is ranked higher than ".". However, "JUNE!" is less than "JUNE*" because "!" is ranked lower than "*".

■ Note that all strings are enclosed in quotation marks. Most advanced BASIC languages can tolerate deviations from this convention in some instances. The rules are generally a bit complicated, and highly dependent on the system being used. However, it is always safe to use quotation marks when in doubt, and for simplicity this book will generally employ them liberally. To give the reader an appreciation of the rules, the following generalities can be made:

(1) Quotations are always required in the statements

IF A$ = "ABC" THEN 1000

and

LET A$ = "ABC"

Table 6.1 BASIC code.*

Characters	BASIC code Number	Characters	BASIC code Number
(blank)	32	@	64
!	33	A	65
"	34	B	66
#	35	C	67
$	36	D	68
%	37	E	69
&	38	F	70
'	39	G	71
(	40	H	72
)	41	I	73
*	42	J	74
+	43	K	75
,	44	L	76
−	45	M	77
.	46	N	78
/	47	Ø	79
0	48	P	80
1	49	Q	81
2	50	R	82
3	51	S	83
4	52	T	84
5	53	U	85
6	54	V	86
7	55	W	87
8	56	X	88
9	57	Y	89
:	58	Z	90
;	59	[	91
<	60	\	92
=	61	]	93
>	62	↑	94
?	63		

*Some computers use a different series of numbers for each letter. Check the computer manuals.

but never in

    IF A$ = B$ THEN 1000
    LET A$ = B$

(2) In INPUT and DATA statements, quotations are required if any of the following are true:

the string contains a comma;
the string begins with a numeric character;
the string begins with one or more blank spaces.

■ Although a person can readily adapt to small anomolies in string composition—e.g., he can interpret "ANZA AVE." as "ANZA AVENUE" and he can mentally correct minor misspellings—the computer cannot. Equality of two strings is established only when they are exactly alike, character for character. Notice that, in Program 6.1 and Figure 6.1 the name PETER, given by one of the children, is not the same as PETE in the data, although to a person they probably would be assumed so.

■ A string may exclusively contain numerals, as in $X = $"125". Now, A$ is not equal to the number one-hundred twenty-five. Instead, it is a string composed of "one," "two," and "five" characters. Therefore, one cannot presume that "125" + "125" = 250.

■ The string variable cannot be used in arithmetic operations such as $B\$ = 3*A\$$, $B\$ = A\$/2.34$, and $X = $"STRING"-"XYZ".

Example 6.1 *Putting Strings in Alphabetical Order*

Write a program which puts the names in Program 6.1 into alphabetical order.

DISCUSSION
Example 5.2 was designed to put numeric values into ascending order. It relied on recognizing whether or not one number was larger than another. The same principle can be applied to this problem, as shown in Program 6.2.

MISCELLANEOUS STRING FUNCTIONS

Some miscellaneous string functions should also be mentioned here.

ASC(Character)
The function ASC(Character) converts an alpha-numeric character to its equivalent BASIC code, as in the statement

```
50      LET  X$ = "@"
100     LET  X = ASC(M)
200     LET  Y = ASC($)
300     LET  Z1 = ASC(X$)
```

results in X = 77, Y = 36, and Z1 = 64 (see Table 6.1).

```
100 DIM A$(8)
200 MAT READ A$

300 FØR I=1 TØ 7
400 FØR J=I+1 TØ 8
500 IF A$(I)<A$(J) THEN 900
600 LET X$=A$(J)
700 LET A$(J)=A$(I)
800 LET A$(I)=X$
900 NEXT J
1000 NEXT I

1100 PRINT "NAMES, IN ALPHABETICAL ØRDER"
1200 PRINT
1300 FØR I=1 TØ 8
1400 PRINT A$(I)
1500 NEXT I

1600 DATA "SAM","JØE","JANE","HARRY"
1700 DATA "HENRY","NANCY","PETE","ELØISE"
1800 END
RUN

NAMES, IN ALPHABETICAL ØRDER ·

ELØISE
HARRY
HENRY
JANE
JØE
NANCY
PETE
SAM
```

Program 6.2 Putting strings in alphabetical order.

CHAR(Numeric)

The function CHAR(numeric), used in the statement

$$
\begin{array}{ll}
50 & \text{LET } N = 64 \\
100 & \text{LET } X\$ = CHAR(77) \\
200 & \text{LET } Y\$ = CHAR(30+6) \\
300 & \text{LET } Y\$ = CHAR(N)
\end{array}
$$

results in X$ = "M", Y$ = "$", Z$ = "@" (see Table 6.1).

STR(Numeric)

The function STR(numeric), used in the statement

$$
\begin{array}{ll}
100 & \text{LET } A = 12.3 \\
200 & \text{LET } X\$ = STR(10) \\
300 & \text{LET } Y\$ = STR(A)
\end{array}
$$

results in X$ = "10", Y$ = "12.3".

VAL(String)

The function VAL(string), used in the statement

$$100 \quad \text{LET } A\$ = \text{``} -100.3\text{''}$$
$$200 \quad \text{LET } X = VAL(A\$)$$

results in changing the string "-100.3" to the variable $X = -100.3$.

LENGTH Statement

The string function $X = LEN(A\$)$ sets X equal to the number of characters in the string A\$. For example, $X = LEN(\text{``THIS''}) = 4$.

The Null String

It is sometimes convenient to construct a string with no characters of any sort contained therein. This is called a "null" string, and it is created with the statement

$$100 \quad \text{LET } Z\$ = \text{`` ''}$$

with no spaces between the quotation marks.

ADVANCED STRINGS—ONE POPULAR METHOD

It often occurs that, having assigned a string to a variable, say X\$ = "THIS", one wishes to manipulate the individual characters of the string in some way, perhaps to combine X\$ = "THIS" and Y\$ = "STRING", into Z\$ = "THIS STRING" or to extract certain characters from the string (e.g., "FEB" from X\$ = "FEBRUARY"). The CHANGE statement is designed for this kind of a problem.

CHANGE Statement

If A\$ is a string and a numeric variable **Z** has been dimensioned, as in DIM Z(O:LEN(A\$)),* then **Z** will be dimensioned with subscripts 0,1,2,..., LEN(A\$). The subsequent statement 1000 in the program

$$100 \quad \text{LET } X\$ = \text{``FEBRUARY''}$$
$$200 \quad \text{DIM } Z(LEN(A\$))$$

$$1000 \quad \text{CHANGE } X\$ \text{ T}\emptyset \text{ Z}$$

---

*Or, DIM Z(LEN(A\$)) if the DIM statement automatically reserves space for Z(0); see Section 4.8.

results in the manipulation of X$ in such a way that the BASIC code* for each character in X$ is assigned to one of the Z(I)s. In the example, the BASIC code 70 (for F) is assigned to Z(1), the BASIC code 69 (for E) is assigned to Z(2), etc. The element Z(0) is assigned the value LEN(X$). After execution of the above statements **Z** has the values

$$
\begin{array}{llll}
Z(0) = & 8 & \text{for} & LEN(X\$) \\
Z(1) = & 70 & \text{for} & F \\
Z(2) = & 69 & \text{for} & E \\
Z(3) = & 66 & \text{for} & B \\
Z(4) = & 82 & \text{for} & R \\
Z(5) = & 85 & \text{for} & U \\
Z(6) = & 65 & \text{for} & A \\
Z(7) = & 82 & \text{for} & R \\
Z(8) = & 89 & \text{for} & Y
\end{array}
$$

Thus each letter in the string is isolated from the others and each character can be individually utilized by manipulating the elements of Z(I).

There is a corollary statement,

$$2000 \quad \text{CHANGE Z TØ X\$}$$

whose function is to reconstruct a string X$ from the matrix **Z**. [*Note:* The matrix must obviously have the correct value, representing the length of the string, in Z(0) before attempting to "change" it back to a string.]

Example 6.2 Analyzing Strings

Read strings out of the data in Program 6.3 and print out (a) the first three letters, and (b) every other (i.e., first, third, fifth, . . .) letter of the string.

DISCUSSION

Carefully study Program 6.3 and then make the following observations:

■ One of the strings, X$, is read and changed to the **Z** matrix.

■ The variable **B** is dimensioned (0:3) and, by virtue of lines 700–900, B(1)=Z(1), B(2)=Z(2), and B(3)=Z(3). The reverse change in line 1400 converts B to Y$="FEB". Note that B(0) is set equal to the eventual length of Y$.

■ Study the way in which the values of C and Z$ are created in lines 1000–1400.

*See Table 6.1.

```
100 READ N
200 FØR I=1 TØ N
300 READ X$
400 DIM Z(Ø:LEN(X$)),B(Ø:3),C(Ø:INT(LEN(X$)/2))
500 CHANGE X$ TØ Z

600 LET B(O)=3
700 FØR J=1 TØ 3
800 LET B(J)=Z(J)
900 NEXT J

1000 LET C(O)=INT(Z(O)/2)
1100 FØR J=1 TØ Z(O) STEP 2
1200 LET C(J)=Z(J)
1300 NEXT J

1400 CHANGE B TØ Y$
1500 CHANGE C TØ Z$

1600 PRINT "THE WØRD IS ";X$
1700 PRINT "THE FIRST THREE LETTERS ARE ";Y$
1800 PRINT "EVERY ØTHER LETTER IS ";Z$
1900 PRINT
2000 NEXT I

2100 DATA 2,"FEBRUARY","TIME-SHARED CØMPUTERS"
2200 END
RUN

THE WØRD IS FEBRUARY
THE FIRST THREE LETTERS ARE FEB
EVERY ØTHER LETTER IS FBUR

THE WØRD IS TIME-SHARED CØMPUTERS
THE FIRST THREE LETTERS ARE TIM
EVERY ØTHER LETTER IS TM-HRDCMUES
```

Program 6.3 Analyzing strings.

Example 6.3 Combining Strings

Another application of string manipulation techniques is to combine two or more strings into one. Program 6.4 shows how two strings, A$ = "THIS" and B$ = "STRING", may be combined into C$ = "THIS STRING". C has been dimensioned large enough to contain A$, B$, and the space between them. In lines 800–1000, four elements of C are set equal to the BASIC codes for "T", "H", "I", and "S". The fifth element, C(5), is set equal to the BASIC code for "space" in line 1100. Finally, the last six C(I)s—C(6) . . . C(11)—are set equal to the BASIC codes for "S", "T", "R", "I", "N", and "G" in lines 1200–1400. The reverse CHANGE statement in line 1500 then accomplishes the creation of the phrase THIS STRING.

Example 6.4 Information Retrieval

Let us now turn attention to an extensive example which has wide applicability in business, inventory control, sales analysis, and certain engineering problems. It also illustrates in one program many of the string attributes studied so far, and it deserves a detailed review.

The Widget-Gidget Mfg. Co. wishes to store, in the computer, paired data entries on many hundreds of inventoried or ordered parts, each entry being of the form

10000   DATA "WQØAC",37000

The data word "WQØAC" gives a complete description of the particular item being entered, as defined by Table 6.2. For example, the first character in the word always represents the name of the part—if it is "W", the entry pertains to "Widgets"; if it is "G"; the entry pertains to "Gidgets"; etc. Similar interpretations are put on the second, third, fourth, and fifth characters.

If the second character is "$", the numeric data (e.g., 37000, above) represents the value, in dollars, of the entered item. If it is a "Q", the numeric data represents the quantity of items. Now review carefully the representative data given in Program 6.5 and understand the meaning of each character.

The intent of the program is this: Typically a salesman, say Collins, will

```
100 LET A$="THIS"
200 LET B$="STRING"
300 DIM A(0:LEN(A$)),B(0:LEN(B$))

400 CHANGE A$ TO A
500 CHANGE B$ TO B
600 DIM C(0:A(0)+B(0)+1)

700 LET C(0)=A(0)+B(0)+1
800 FOR I=1 TO A(0)
900 LET C(I)=A(I)
1000 NEXT I

1100 LET C(A(0)+1)=32
1200 FOR I=1 TO B(0)
1300 LET C(A(0)+1+I)=B(I)
1400 NEXT I

1500 CHANGE C TO C$
1600 PRINT C$

1700 END
RUN

THIS STRING
```

Program 6.4   Combining strings.

Table 6.2 Character representation for information retrieval program, Example 6.4.

		Character		
First (item)	Second (type of entry)	Third (item status)	Fourth (supplier or customer)	Fifth (salesman)
W = Widgets	$ = Cost/Value	Ø = On order	A = Atlas Mfg.	C = Collins
G = Gidgets	Q = Quantity	R = Ready to	B = Barnes Co.	H = Hughes
T = Things		use	D = Delta Sales	J = Jones
S = Stuff		I = In inspection	E = Engr. Assoc.	K = King
		F = Finished	M = Miscellaneous	L = Larson
		U = Unordered	N = None	
		inventory		

tell the computer that he is interested in retrieving all data on his account with Atlas Mfg. The computer must then search through the data to find those entries with "A" as the fourth digit (for Atlas) and "C" as the fifth digit (for Collins). The way Collins will instruct the computer is by giving it a five-character word of the form "***AC". The asterisks will be used to indicate that Collins is interested in retrieving all codes in the first, second, and third digits. Similarly, at some later time the Manufacturing Supervisor may ask the computer for all entries under the code "G**U*".

DISCUSSION

Having thus defined the problem, the programming logic becomes obvious. The program must ask the salesman to specify the coded word of interest. Then after reading each data, it must check to see if each character in the data word conforms to the salesman's description. If so, it must print out the unabbreviated description of the entry and the associated numerical data. If the word does not conform, the computer should repeat the process with a new data entry.

In Program 6.5 the variables C$ and Y$ are the salesman's description and the data entry, respectively. The variables C$ and Y$ are changed to C and Y, respectively (lines 600 and 1100). The variable J in lines 1200, 1600, and 1800 represent the number of mismatched characters in the two words. If any are found (i.e., if $J > 0$ at line 1800), the words are presumed to be uninteresting, the printout in lines 1900–2400 is avoided, and a new data word is examined by returning the computer from line 1800 to line 800.

Let us study the effect of lines 1300–1700 more closely. The I loop is executed once for each character in C$ and Y$. Line 1600 is a counter which is bypassed if the ith character is an asterisk (line 1400) or if it is equal to the corresponding character of Y$. So, when line 1800 is executed, if $J = 0$, the computer proceeds to line 1900, where it prints out the verbal description of each matching data entry and the value of H.

Observe the form of the print statement in line 1900. Note that Y(1) is the numeric BASIC code for the first character in the data word. If Y(1) is 87 (representing a "W"), $X\$(Y(1)) = X\$(87) = $ "WIDGETS" (see lines

```
100 DIM C(0:5),Y(0:5),X$(94)
200 LET X$(87)="WIDGETS "
210 LET X$(71)="GIDGETS "
220 LET X$(84)="THINGS "
230 LET X$(83)="STUFF "
240 LET X$(36)="CØST/VALUE "
250 LET X$(81)="QUANTITY "
260 LET X$(79)="ØN-ØRDER "
270 LET X$(82)="READY-TØ-USE "
280 LET X$(73)="IN INSPECTIØN "
290 LET X$(70)="FINISHED "
300 LET X$(85)="UNØRDERED INVENTØRY "
310 LET X$(65)="ATLAS MFG. "
320 LET X$(66)="BARNES "
330 LET X$(68)="DELTA MFG. "
340 LET X$(69)="ENGR. ASSØC. "
350 LET X$(77)="MISCELLANEØUS "
360 LET X$(78)="NØNE "
370 LET X$(67)="CØLLINS "
380 LET X$(72)="HUGHES "
390 LET X$(74)="JØNES "
400 LET X$(75)="KING "
410 LET X$(76)="LARSØN "
420 LET Q1=0
430 LET V1=0

500 PRINT "GIVE THE CØDE FØR THE ENTRIES THAT INTEREST YØU":
600 INPUT C$
700 CHANGE C$ TØ C

800 READ Y$
900 IF Y$="END" THEN 2500
1000 READ H
1100 CHANGE Y$ TØ Y

1200 LET J=0
1300 FØR I=1 TØ 5
1400 IF C(I)=41 THEN 1700
1500 IF C(I)=Y(I) THEN 1700
1600 LET J=J+1
1700 NEXT I

1800 IF J>0 THEN 800

1900 PRINT X$(Y(1));X$(Y(2));X$(Y(3));X$(Y(4));X$(Y(5));H
2000 IF Y(2)=36 THEN 2300
2100 LET Q1=Q1+H
2200 GØ TØ 800
2300 LET V1=V1+H
2400 GØ TØ 800
```

Program 6.5   Information retrieval. (*Continued on next page.*)

```
2500 PRINT
2600 PRINT
2700 PRINT "TØTAL VALUE =";V1
2800 PRINT "TØTAL QUANTITY =";Q1

10000 DATA "WQOAC", 37000
10100 DATA "GQØBH", 143000
10200 DATA "G$FMC", 39123.87
10300 DATA "S$INK", 877.26
10400 DATA "WQUNL", 88000
10500 DATA "SQFAH", 6610
10600 DATA "T$RNC", 2384.16
10700 DATA "T$FAC", 1438.29
10800 DATA "GQRAC", 10000
10900 DATA "END"
11000 END

RUN

GIVE THE CØDE FØR THE ENTRIES THAT INTEREST YØU? "***AC"
WIDGETS QUANTITY ØN-ØRDER ATLAS MFG. CØLLINS 37000
THINGS CØST/VALUE FINISHED ATLAS MFG. CØLLINS 1438.29
GIDGETS QUANTITY READY-TØ-USE ATLAS MFG. CØLLINS 10000


TØTAL VALUE 1438.29
TØTAL QUANTITY 47000
```

Program 6.5 *(continued)*

200–410) and the entries of Table 6.2 are printed in lieu of the abbreviated characters which represent the words. Finally, if $Y(2)$ represents a $ sign, the computer is diverted to line 2300, where the value of all entries is accumulated for printing at the end of the completed data search. The computer continues to line 2100 if the second character of Y$ is a "Q", accumulating "Quantity" for later printout.

ADVANCED STRINGS—ANOTHER POPULAR METHOD

Another method of string manipulations, available on some systems, will now be investigated. Examples 6.2, 6.3, and 6.4 will be reprogrammed, disregarding the CHANGE statement entirely.

String Concatenation

Two strings may be combined into a single string by the act of "concatenation" with instructions given in lines 300 and 500 below:

```
100 LET A$="TIME"
200 LET B$="CØMPUTING"
300 LET C$=A$+"-SHARING "+B$
400 PRINT C$
500 LET D$=B$+"-SHARING "+A$
600 PRINT D$
700 END
   RUN

TIME-SHARING CØMPUTING
CØMPUTING-SHARING TIME
```

The " + " sign instructs the computer to combine the strings, end-to-end. As many strings can be concatenated in one statement as desired. Concatenation cannot be performed with a string and a variable, as in LET A$ = A$ + 300.

LEFT and RIGHT Functions

The function LEFT(A$,I) and RIGHT(A$,I), where I = 1, 2, 3, . . . can be used to extract certain "substrings" of characters from the body of A$. Consider the program

```
100 LET A$="STRING"
200 FØR I=1 TØ 6
300 LET B$=LEFT(A$,I)
310 LET C$=RIGHT(A$,I)
400 PRINT I;"B$=";B$, "C$=";C$
500 NEXT I
600 END
```

The printout from this simple example is

```
RUN

1    B$=S        C$=G
2    B$=ST       C$=NG
3    B$=STR      C$=ING
4    B$=STRI     C$=RING
5    B$=STRIN C$=TRING
6    B$=STRINGC$=STRING
```

The meaning of B$ = LEFT(A$,3), then, is "set B$ equal to the left three characters of A$"; C$ = RIGHT(A$,4) means "set B$ equal to the right four characters of A$." With this in mind, what is the meaning of the fabricated statement below?

```
100    LET A$ = "STRING"
200    LET B$ = RIGHT(LEFT(A$,3),1)
```

Beginning inside the parentheses, the function LEFT(A$,3) extracts "STR"; then working outward on the resulting string, RIGHT("STR",1) results in B$ = "R". Thus, B$ has been set equal to the third character, "R", in A$. Incorporating a statement of that form into the above program,

```
100 LET A$="STRING"
200 FØR I=1 TØ 6
300 LET B$=LEFT(A$,I)
310 LET C$=RIGHT(A$,I)
320 LET D$=RIGHT(LEFT(A$,I),1)
400 PRINT IJ"B$=";B$, "C$=";C$, "D$=";D$
500 NEXT I
600 END
```

results in the modified printout

```
RUN

1     B$=S        C$=G          D$=S
2     B$=ST       C$=NG         D$=T
3     B$=STR      C$=ING        D$=R
4     B$=STRI     C$=RING       D$=I
5     B$=STRIN    C$=TRING      D$=N
6     B$=STRING   C$=STRING     D$=G
```

This method is used to extract one (or more) character from the interior of a string.

INDEX Function

The INDEX function is used to deduce whether or not one string contains another, and it is written

```
100 LET X$="ANNUAL SNØWFALL."
200 LET Y$="SNØW"
300 LET P=INDEX(X$,Y$)
400 PRINT "P= "JP
500 END
    RUN

P=     8
```

That is, if Y$ is contained anywhere in X$, then P is set equal to the character position (counting from the left) at which Y$ begins. If Y$ does not contain X$ at all, P is set equal to zero in line 300. This is most useful in a program which uses "key word" principles to search data files, as illustrated by the program,

```
100 PRINT "WHAT WØRD (ØR LETTERS) DØ YØU WANT";
101 INPUT X$
200 FØR I=1 TØ 5
210 READ Y$
300 IF INDEX(Y$,X$)=0 THEN 500
400 PRINT Y$
500 NEXT I
600 DATA "YES","NØ","ØK","MAYBE","I DØN'T KNØW"
700 END
RUN

WHAT WØRD (ØR LETTERS) DØ YØU WANT  ?  "E"
YES
MAYBE
```

Each data is read; if it does not contain X$(="E"), then INDEX(Y$,X$) is equal to 0, and line 400 is bypassed.

With concatenation, LEFT, RIGHT, and ASC functions, Examples 6.2–6.4 can now be reprogrammed. The remarks below are confined to explaining the differences from the preceding solutions.

Example 6.5   Analyzing Strings

Reprogramming Example 6.2 in Program 6.6, Y$ is set equal to the LEFT three characters (e.g., FEB) of X$ by virtue of line 400. The string Z$ is first initialized to the null string in line 500, and successive concatenation is performed on Z$ in line 700, adding together every other character in X$.

Example 6.6   Combining Strings

Reprogramming Example 6.3 in Program 6.7, note that the string " " (one space in quotes) is concatenated between A$ and B$.

Example 6.7   Retrieving Information

Reprogramming Example 6.4, the variables C$ and Y$ are never changed in Program 6.8; equality checks in lines 1200 and 1800 are made immediately in terms of the actual characters in the coded words, rather than in terms of their BASIC codes. However, the individual characters in Y$ are converted to BASIC codes in line 1700 with a programmer-defined function which extracts an individual character, converts it to a BASIC code number with ASC, and uses that code for the index of X$. Therefore, line 1700 of Program 6.8 is equivalent to line 1800 in Program 6.5.

```
100 READ N
200 FØR I=1 TØ N
300 READ X$
400 LET Y$=LEFT(X$,3)

500 LET Z$=""
600 FØR J=1 TØ LENGTH(X$) STEP 2
700 LET Z$=Z$+RIGHT(LEFT(X$,J),1)
800 NEXT J

900 PRINT "THE WØRD IS ";X$
1000 PRINT "THE FIRST THREE LETTERS ARE ";Y$
1100 PRINT "EVERY ØTHER LETTER IS ";Z$
1200 PRINT
1300 NEXT I

1400 DATA 2,"FEBRUARY","TIME-SHARED CØMPUTERS"
1500 END
RUN

THE WØRD IS     FEBRUARY
THE FIRST THREE LETTERS ARE    FEB
EVERY ØTHER LETTER IS    FBUR

THE WØRD IS     TIME-SHARED CØMPUTERS
THE FIRST THREE LETTERS ARE    TIM
EVERY ØTHER LETTER IS    TM-HRDCMUES
```

Program 6.6   Analyzing strings.

```
100 LET A$="THIS"
200 LET B$="STRING"
300 LET C$=A$+" "+B$
400 PRINT C$
500 END
 RUN

THIS STRING
```

Program 6.7   Combining strings.

■ EXERCISES

*6.1   The Payroll Journal Program has heretofore either avoided using employee's names or has been very cumbersomely written to include them. With the introduction of string variables, however, they can quite easily be included. Write a program to read Table 6.3, and print out the employee's name, number, gross pay, tax, and net pay. Use the word "END" in the place of the employee's name to indicate expiration of data.

```
50 DEF FNA(I)=X$(ASC(RIGHT(LEFT(Y$,I),1)))
100 DIM C(5),Y(5),X$(94)
200 LET X$(87)="WIDGETS ",X$(71)="GIDGETS ",X$(84)="THINGS ",
    X$(83)="STUFF ",X$(36)="CØST/VALUE ",X$(81)="QUANTITY ",
    X$(79)="ØN ØRDER ",X$(82)="READY-TØ-USE ",X$(73)="IN INSPECTIØN "
300 LET X$(70)="FINISHED, READY TØ SHIP ",X$(85)="UNØRDERED INVENTØRY ",
    X$(65)="ATLAS MFG. ",X$(66)="BARNES ",X$(68)="DELTA SALES ",
    X$(69)="ENGR. ASSØC. ",X$(77)="MISCELLANEØUS ",X$(78)="NØNE "
400 LET X$(67)="CØLLINS ",X$(72)="HUGHES ",X$(74)="JØNES ",
    X$(75)="KING ",X$(76)="LARSØN ",Q1=0,V1=0
401 LET X$(86)="VALUE "

500 PRINT "GIVE THE CØDES FØR THE ENTRIES THAT INTEREST YØU";
600 INPUT C$
700 READ Y$
800 IF Y$="END" THEN 2300
900 READ H

1000 LET J=0
1100 FØR I=1 TØ 5
1200 IF RIGHT(LEFT(C$,I),1)="*" THEN 1500
1300 IF RIGHT(LEFT(C$,I),1)=RIGHT(LEFT(Y$,I),1) THEN 1500
1400 LET J=J+1
1500 NEXT I
1600 IF J>0 THEN 700

1700 PRINT FNA(1);FNA(2);FNA(3);FNA(4);FNA(5);H
1800 IF RIGHT(LEFT(Y$,2),1)="$" THEN 2100
1900 LET Q1=Q1+H
2000 GØ TØ 700
2100 LET V1=V1+H
2200 GØ TØ 700

2300 PRINT
2400 PRINT
2500 PRINT "TØTAL VALUE = ";V1
2600 PRINT "TØTAL QUANTITY =";Q1

10000 DATA "WQØAC",37000
10100 DATA "GQØBH",143000
10200 DATA "G$FMC",39123.87
10300 DATA "S$INK",877.26
10400 DATA "WQUNL",88000
10500 DATA "SQFAH",6610
10600 DATA "T$RNC",2384.15
10700 DATA "T$RAC",1438.29
10800 DATA "GQRAC",10000
10900 DATA "END"
11000 END
 RUN

GIVE THE CØDES FØR THE ENTRIES THAT INTEREST YØU   ? "***AC"
WIDGETS QUANTITY ØN-ØRDER ATLAS MFG. CØLLINS   37000
THINGS VALUE READY-TØ-USE ATLAS MFG. CØLLINS   1438.29
GIDGETS QUANTITY READY-TØ-USE ATLAS MFG. CØLLINS   10000


TØTAL VALUE =      1438.29
TØTAL QUANTITY =   47000
```

Program 6.8 Solution to Example 6.7.

Table 6.3

Employee	Number	Hours worked	Hourly rate	Tax rate
Adams, Jim	40312	40	3.32	0.103
Smith, Sam	08140	42	5.25	0.172
Barnett, Mike	31402	38	4.28	0.145
Barnett, Deborah	12440	40	2.13	0.085
Roberts, Cliff	21443	40	6.28	0.18
Jones, Alvin	41102	41.5	5.03	0.163

6.2   Suppose a company maintains a job-related dossier on every employee. Each person's record contains the following data:

Record	Examples of possible entries
Name	Kimberley Ann Shea
Degree	BS, MS, MA, PhD, None
Major	Electronics, Physics, Business, Math, Philosophy
Sex	M, F
Marital status	S, M, D, W

For some reason, the management wishes to retrieve from the file the names of all employees who are single and have an MS degree in Electronics. (a) Write a program which will print out the appropriate names. (b) So the program can be used again another day, include a segment which asks the manager what data he wishes to key upon each time the program runs.

6.3   Compute the volume of the objects described below:

Object	A	B	C
Brick	5	6	3
Brick	5	3	8
Cylinder	10	6	0
Cone	1	1	0
Cylinder	3	2	0
Sphere	6	0	0
Sphere	6	0	0
Brick	6	1	1

Put the name of the object, along with its dimensions, in the DATA statements. Use the name to route the computer to one of the following equations:

Brick	$V = A*B*C$
Cone	$V = \frac{1}{3}\pi A^2 B$
Sphere	$V = \frac{4}{3}\pi A^3$
Cylinder	$V = \pi A^2 B$

*6.4   Write a program segment which asks the operator if he wishes to "execute part 1 of the program," and allows him to answer "yes" or "no." When the operator answers "no," the computer should bypass part 1, going directly to line 5000.

6.5   Improve the segment in Exercise 6.4 so that if the programmer erroneously or ambiguously answers something besides "yes" or "no," the program will print out a message informing him to use only the words "yes" or "no," and ask its first question again.

6.6   Improve the segment of Exercise 6.5 so that the operator need not spell "yes" or "no" correctly, but only has to get the first letter, "y" or "n" correct. Example: A usable answer is "Yes I would."

6.7   Rewrite Example 6.1 so that the strings are put in *reverse* alphabetical order.

6.8   Rewrite either Example 6.2 or 6.5 so that Z$ is set equal to the first and last letters of the data word.

6.9   Five candidates—Jones, Smith, Adams, Green, and Doe—are vying for two public offices. They are placed on the ballot in alphabetical order and are thus identified as candidates number 1, 2, 3, 4, and 5 as they appear. The following data statements are given, representing hundreds of ballots:

5000 DATA "JØNES","SMITH","ADAMS","GREEN","DØE"
5100 DATA 3,1,5,3,2,4,1,5,4,1,3,2,1,1,1,2,4,3,...

Obviously, a "3" is a vote for the third person on the ballot. Read the candidate's names into a matrix and arrange them in alphabetical order. Count votes for each person; print out their names and total tallies in order of their placement in the race. Print the word "WINS" beside the highest two candidates.

6.10   Suppose that Table 6.2 was much more complex and it was desired to represent "Widgets" by the abbreviation "W1," watches by "W2," "on-order" by "!," etc. Furthermore, suppose that we do not wish to require the operator to know the proper abbreviations for these entries. Write a program which will (a) ask the operator to give the unabbreviated entry name for the inventoried item (all five columns at once); (b) printout for the proper abbreviation.

6.11   Using string functions, generate all binary numbers between 0000 and 1111. Check each number to see if it has at least two adjacent zeros, and print it out if it does. Store all 16 binary numbers in an array with elements Z$(0) through Z$(15). The subscript of Z$ in which each binary number is to be saved must be calculated as the decimal (base 10) equivalent of the binary number.

6.12   A list and description of documents is maintained in data statements, for example:

Number	Title	Author	Key word abstract
TA286.1	Annual Snowfall at Mt. Baldy	H. T. Zizler	"Snow, Precipitation, Mt. Baldy, Weather, Winter,"
LØ486A	Annual Rainfall at Melbourne	E. N. Smith	"Rain, Precipitation, Melbourne, Weather, Australia"
MA419	Effect of Society on the Individual	S. T. Jones	"Humanity, Society, Philosophy, People"

Write a program to inquire of the user for one or more key words. Read the data for each document and print its name, number, and author if any key word appears in either the title or the key word abstract.

*6.13   The effect of a meteoroid impacting a box on a spacecraft depends, among other things, upon the material of the housing of the box. Imagine a program with several sets of equations applicable to boxes made of steel, aluminum, honeycomb, stainless steel, and titanium. Write a program segment which reads material from DATA and routes the computer to an appropriate line number for calculations.

*6.14   A company's sales records for the thirty-year period 1941–1970 is given in Table 6.4. Write a program to read that data and plot it. In particular, imagine a piece of graph paper which is composed of blank squares, 32 down (numbered −1 through 30), and 52 across (numbered −1 through 50). The −1 row and column is used to label the axis of the grid; the 0 row and column are where the grid is printed; and the remainder is the body of the graph. Now, use a matrix, **G$**, dimensioned the size of the graph and whose elements are *strings*, each representing one square on the graph. Begin by setting each element to a single blank space. Then, selectively change some of the spaces to hold the grid markings and labels. Then, after reading each

Table 6.4 Company sales.

Year	Sales ($)	Year	Sales ($)
1941	3,000,000	1956	18,000,000
1942	5,000,000	1957	17,000,000
1943	7,000,000	1958	19,000,000
1944	10,000,000	1959	21,000,000
1945	11,000,000	1960	23,000,000
1946	9,000,000	1961	25,000,000
1947	13,000,000	1962	24,000,000
1948	12,000,000	1963	29,000,000
1949	10,000,000	1964	29,000,000
1950	15,000,000	1965	28,000,000
1951	20,000,000	1966	32,000,000
1952	18,000,000	1967	30,000,000
1953	19,000,000	1968	29,000,000
1954	20,000,000	1969	27,000,000
1955	18,000,000	1970	29,000,000

data, change corresponding squares in the graph (i.e., elements in the matrix) to an "*." Finish by printing the matrix **G$**, with a result similar to Figure 6.2. [*Note:* If the reader uses a computer which does not permit zero or negative dimensions, he will have to make slight adjustments in the composition of the matrix.]

6.15 The "linear expansivity" of various materials is given in Table 6.5. Put the material names in **N$** and the expansivity coefficients in the two-column matrix **E**. If a bar of material, linear expansivity = α, is of length L_0 at temperature T_0, its length at T_1 is $L_1 = L_0[1 + \alpha(T_1 - T_0)]$. Program the computer to assist an engineer by calculating the new length of a rod as its environmental temperature changes. Make it a general program so that it can be reused many times. The computer must ask the following questions (with typical user responses underlined):

WHAT MATERIAL? "COPPER"

IT'S INITIAL LENGTH? 31.5

IT'S INITIAL TEMPERATURE? "78F"

IT'S FINAL TEMPERATURE? "113F"

The nomenclature 78F means $78°F$; on the other hand, 78C means $78°C$. Prevent erroneous or unrecognizable material from being

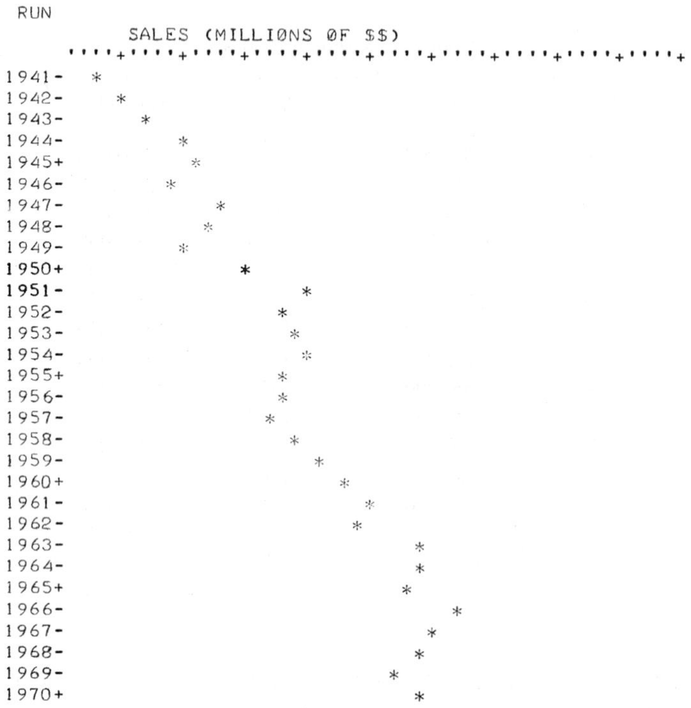

```
RUN
                SALES (MILLIØNS ØF $$)
      ' ' ' ' +' ' ' ' +' ' ' ' +' ' ' ' +' ' ' ' +' ' ' ' +' ' ' ' +' ' ' ' +' ' ' ' +' ' ' ' +
1941 -     *
1942 -      *
1943 -        *
1944 -           *
1945+           *
1946 -         *
1947 -            *
1948 -           *
1949 -         *
1950+              *
1951 -                *
1952 -              *
1953 -               *
1954 -               *
1955+             *
1956 -             *
1957 -             *
1958 -              *
1959 -                *
1960+                 *
1961 -                 *
1962 -                *
1963 -                   *
1964 -                   *
1965+                  *
1966 -                     *
1967 -                    *
1968 -                   *
1969 -                 *
1970+                   *
```

Figure 6.2 Graph required by Exercise 6.14.

Table 6.5

Material	α (per °C)	α (per °F)
Aluminum	0.000022	0.000012
Brass	0.000019	0.000011
Copper	0.000017	0.0000094
Glass	0.0000095	0.0000053
Iron	0.000012	0.0000067
Oak	0.000005	0.000003
Platinum	0.0000089	0.0000049
Quartz	0.00000059	0.00000033
Steel	0.000011	0.0000061
Tungsten	0.0000043	0.0000024

entered. [*Hint:* Find the vertical index of **E** by searching through **N$** until the name of the material is found. Its index can then be used to enter the appropriate row in **E**. Select the horizontal index by extracting "F" or "C" from the end of the temperature strings. Use the numeric portion of 78F and 113C for T_0 and T_1.]

6.16 Discuss other applications for which you might use string variables, and expand on those illustrated in the exercises above.

6.17 As pointed out in Chapter 4, some of your most profitable learning experiences come from defining unorthodox problems and writing programs to solve them. This exercise is a good example of the principle. The intricacy of the program is a lesson in patience, ingenuity, logic, and attention to detail, as well as the disection and recomposition of string variables. *Problem:* The 25 × 25 table in Figure 6.3 (see the following page) contains the names of all fifty states. The 25 × 25 table in Figure 6.3 contains the names of all fifty states. The names may be spelled forward, backward, top-to-bottom, bottom-to-top, or on any right-to-left or left-to-right diagonal. The task is twofold: (a) to print out the name of each state along with the beginning and ending coordinates of each one; and (b) print out a new matrix containing only the letters of the original matrix which are used in at least one name. [*Hint:* Create a 25 × 25 matrix with each element containing one letter of Figure 6.3. Create another 25 × 25 matrix with each element containing a single blank space. Search each line of Figure 6.3 looking for state names. As one is found, move the appropriate letters from the first matrix into corresponding elements in the blank matrix. Search Figure 6.3 in a methodical manner—first every horizontal line; then every horizontal line reversed; then every vertical line from top-to-bottom, etc. Put the names of all 50 states into a **DIM S$(50)** matrix for ease in typing and subsequent manipulation.]

6.2 LET STATEMENT VARIATIONS

Some program memory space, typing, and execution time can be saved if the reader's computer system permits dispensing with the word "LET" from the statement. In such cases, 100 LET X=5 and 100 X=3 are equivalent.

Some systems permit several variables to be given values in one statement, as in

$$100 \quad \text{LET} \ \text{X,Y,Z}=0$$

```
TUC ITCENNØCABKYESREJWENXE
NEWMEXICØØDARØLØCVWEIRWLZ
NLUIXTHGDAWUAGVINGSGSYAYL
KØIXAINAVLYSNNEPETTWCJSXJ
KCUDSBEESSENNETPVAMDØJHØA
ZNQQIØNFTHAWAIIIERLØNQIAY
SXAWDNALSIEDØHRSRXYKSHNNK
NØCALIFØRNIAHGBSMKMFIZGAC
NØUGWØQRMYRIIEWIØRABNZTTU
EMRTKANIIASNØØØSNØWWWFØNT
WASTHQNDXVIAFRISTYUESUNØN
HKMTHCCASAVNXGSIØWAWCAAME
AMQØTDAØIØFKEIQMSEVQFXSAK
MAJHHEARQDMIAAIEMNSHADJRN
PDNYBASKØNNPATØKADHTUØSKE
SCKACBLUØLVIGCECDJJKWNGAB
HYNGINØKHTILLINØISCBAJPNR
IKKDJSVPØCANTLFDWNØGERØSA
RQASUTUAKSALABAMAAIDFYJAS
EHVJTYHØVIXSHAMYGHYRPKJSK
ØECLAYSDLJYESAWHCGNIMØYWA
NØRTHCARØLINAAWILØUISIANA
HIYUYMATØSENNIMISSØURIMUA
LPTVØRIVYAINIGIRIVHGWKXLT
WANØZIRAERAWALEDBDNALYRAM
```

Figure 6.3 Matrix of state names for Exercise 6.17.

or,

$$100 \quad X,Y,Z=0$$

or

$$100 \quad X=3,Y=-1,Z=10$$

6.3 LINE CONTINUATION

Sophisticated programs sometimes contain very long program statements—so long, in fact, that they cannot be fitted on a single teletype line. Many computers permit a continuation of a statement over to a second line. To accomplish line continuation, a line feed rather than a carriage return, is typed at the end of the line.

6.4 ADVANCED IF/THEN STATEMENTS

Earlier chapters investigated the properties and applications of IF/THEN statements. There are a number of very powerful variations.

MULTIPLE TRANSFER CRITERIA

It might be desirable to execute a program branch if any one of several criteria are met, say if $X = 0$ or $Y = 0$ in

```
100     READ X,Y
200     IF X=0 THEN 1000
300     IF Y=0 THEN 1000
```

The program can often be simplified with a variation of the IF/THEN statement which permits multiple transfer criteria, as in

```
100     READ X,Y
200     IF X=0 ØR Y=0 THEN 1000
```

The computer is no longer bound to a single criteria for transferring; in this case it will transfer if either $X = 0$ or $Y = 0$. Similarly, two or more criteria which must be satisfied simultaneously before transfer can occur may be stipulated thus:

```
100     READ X,Y
200     IF X=0 AND Y=0 THEN 1000
```

Now both X and Y must be equal to zero before transfer will occur.

In any statement in which both ØR and AND terms exist, the AND has priority and is associated only with those conditions immediately adjacent to it unless parentheses usurp this rule. To illustrate,

```
200     IF X=0 ØR X=1 AND Y<0 THEN 1000
```

means that transfer should occur if $X = 0$ or, if not, then it should occur if both $X = 1$ and $Y < 0$. Parentheses may be used to specify any other desired sequence of making the decision.

```
200     IF(X=0 ØR X=1) AND Y<0 THEN 1000
```

transfer will take place if Y is negative and, simultaneously, X equals either zero or one.

Example 6.8   An Unhealthy Problem

Certain benefits are potentially accruable to a recipient if he is under 18 years of age, 60 years or over, or disabled for more than 30 days. Write a program which reads age and health data on one person and prints out whether he is eligible or ineligible for benefits.

DISCUSSION

By rather cumbersome means, Program 6.9a uses the simple IF/THEN statement discussed in previous chapters to accomplish the specified task. By contrast, Program 6.9b accomplishes the same objective with a single IF/THEN statement which imposes all the stated criteria before branching to line 500 can take place.

In this case, the parentheses in line 200 are superfluous, for the proper program logic would have been developed without them, but they are an aid to the programmer, as it is easy to become confused when a number of ØRs and ANDs are employed.

```
100 READ A,H$,T
200 IF A<18 THEN 800
300 IF A>=60 THEN 800
400 IF H$="DISABLED" THEN 700
500 PRINT "NØT ELIGIBLE"
600 STØP
700 IF T<=30 THEN 500
800 PRINT "ELIGIBLE"
900 STØP
1000 DATA 43,"DISABLED",29
1100 END
RUN

NØT ELIGIBLE
```

(a)

```
100 READ A,H$,T
200 IF A<18 ØR A>=60 ØR (H$="DISABLED" AND T>30) THEN 500
300 PRINT "NØT ELIGIBLE"
400 STØP
500 PRINT "ELIGIBLE"
600 DATA 43,"DISABLED",29
700 END
 RUN

NØT ELIGIBLE
```

(b)

Program 6.9   (a) Using conventional IF/THEN statements in Example 6.8. (b) Using multiple-criteria IF/THEN statements in Example 6.8.

IF/THEN/ELSE STATEMENT

The statements

63 IF X < = 0 THEN 903
64 PRINT

infer that the computer should proceed to line 64 and PRINT if X is positive. A new instruction, of the form

63 IF X < = 0 THEN 903 ELSE 412

instructs the computer to go to line 903 if X is zero or negative, or else to go to line 412 if X is positive. (Line 64 is skipped in either case.) This is a very important feature for the discussion which follows.

IF/THEN (ANY STATEMENT)

Observe that the second form of statement 63 above could be imagined as equivalent to

63 IF X < = 0 THEN GØ TØ 903 ELSE GØ TØ 412

In fact, some computer systems permit writing the statement in the latter manner. This is not too important in itself until one realizes that the underscored parts are, literally, BASIC statements of their own entity—that is, 49 GØ TØ 903 is a perfectly legitimate statement. Expanding the principle, other statements may be used in place of the GØ TØ statement, as in

100 IF X = Y THEN GØ SUB 1000

100 IF X < 0 THEN GØ SUB 1000 ELSE PRINT X

100 IF T − 2 = X + 1 THEN READ G

100 IF L/2 = INT(L/2) THEN PRINT ELSE LET X = 9

Example 6.9 The Unhealthy Problem—Another Way

Rewrite Example 6.8 to exploit IF/THEN/ELSE and IF/THEN (any statement).

DISCUSSION

Program 6.10 satisfies the problem with an impressive simplification over Program 6.9a.

```
100 READ A,H$,T
200 IF A<18 ØR A>=60 ØR (H$="DISABLED" AND T>30)⊃
       THEN PRINT "ELIGIBLE" ELSE PRINT "NØT ELIGIBLE"
300 DATA 43,"DISABLED",29
400 END
RUN

NØT ELIGIBLE
```

Program 6.10 Using IF/THEN/ELSE in Examples 6.8 and 6.9.

6.5 "COMPUTED GØ TØ" OR "COMPUTED GØ SUB" STATEMENT

The series of IF/THEN statements

$$100 \quad \text{IF } X=1 \text{ THEN } 1000$$
$$200 \quad \text{IF } X=2 \text{ THEN } 2000$$
$$300 \quad \text{IF } X=3 \text{ THEN } 3000$$

$$\cdot$$
$$\cdot$$
$$\cdot$$

$$900 \quad \text{IF } X=9 \text{ THEN } 9000$$

can be conveniently shortened with the statement

100   ØN X GØ TØ 1000,2000,3000,4000,5000,6000,7000,8000,9000

which is called a "computed GØ TØ" statement. Its implied meaning to the computer is

if $X=1$, then go to the first line number in the list (i.e., 1000)
if $X=2$, then go to the second line number in the list (i.e., 2000)
if $X=3$, then go to the third line number in the list (i.e., 3000)
etc.

Any mathematical expression may replace X; the line numbers in the list may be in any order, i.e.,

300   ØN A+B−1 GØ TØ 105,300,1000,610,1000,900

In this example, the computer transfers to line 1000 whenever the term $(A+B-1)$ is equal to either 3 or 5. Two rules must be followed when using the computed GØ TØ statement:

■   The variable X, or the expression replacing it, cannot take on values less than 1, nor more than the number of lines in the list.

■   If X cannot take on all values, say from 1 to 10 *except* X = 5, a phony line number must be inserted in the missing location in the list, even though it will never be used. In this case, if the fifth number were omitted, the computer would be forced to interpret the intended sixth line number as the fifth, the seventh as the sixth, and so on.

An analogous statement, the "computed GØ SUB" may also be available:

510   ØN X GØ SUB 105,300,1000,610,1000,900

The rules for applying this statement are identical to those governing the "computed GØ TØ ...". Recognize that, if this statement is used, lines 105, 300, etc., will be regarded as the beginning of *subroutines*, each of which requires a RETURN statement. Also, regardless of which subroutine is selected by the ØN X statement, the computer will return to line 511 when it reaches the RETURN statement.

Example 6.10   A Lot of Subroutines

Write the segments of a program which GØ SUB from line 500 as follows:

if $0 \leqslant X < 100$, GØ SUB to 1000
if $100 \leqslant X < 200$, GØ SUB to 2000
if $200 \leqslant X < 500$, GØ SUB to 3000
if $500 \leqslant X < 600$, GØ SUB to 4000

DISCUSSION
The computed GØ SUB statement can be used only when the value of its variable takes on values from the series of numbers 1,2,3,... .
 In Program 6.11, the expression $INT(X/100)+1$ converts X into the appropriate increments for use in line 500 (i.e., if $X = 312.2$, $INT(X/100) + 1 = 4$ and the computer is diverted to the fourth line in the list, line 3000, as required). Since the computer should go to line 3000 when $200 \leqslant X < 500$ (i.e., $INT(X/100) + 1 = 3,4,5$), that line number is entered several times in Program 6.11. Observe that each subroutine has its own RETURN statement, and that the computer always returns to line 501 after executing the subroutine.

6.6   AESTHETIC PRINTOUT CONTROL

Chapter 2 investigated controlling printout format by selective punctuation in the PRINT statement, using commas, colons, and semicolons. However, that technique is not entirely effective, as the appearance of the output is still largely dependent upon the number of digits generated by

```
                .
                .
                .
500 ON INT(X/100)+1 GO SUB 1000,2000,3000,3000,3000,400C
501 REM-ALWAYS RETURNS TO THIS POINT
                .
                .
                .
1000 REM-BEGIN SUBROUTINE #1
                .
                .
                .
1999 RETURN

2000 REM-BEGIN SUBROUTINE #2
                .
                .
2999 RETURN

3000 REM-BEGIN SUBROUTINE #3
                .
                .
3999 RETURN

4000 REM-BEGIN SUBROUTINE #4
                .
                .
4999 RETURN
```

Program 6.11 Illustrating computed GO SUB statement as described in Example 6.10.

the computer, unaligned decimal points, and irregular column alignment. In short, aesthetically unpleasing formats are usually generated.

Advanced BASIC statements similar to those given in this section are quite valuable when the output should be neat and pleasing for presentation to other persons, inclusion in formal reports, etc.

TAB FUNCTION

The distance across the printing area on a standard teletype paper is divided into 72 spaces, usually numbered from 0 to 71. The TAB function is used to space the printer across the page to an exact specified location before printing. The TAB function is used as part of the PRINT statement in the following manner:

```
100 FOR I=-1.5 TO 3.5 STEP .5
200 PRINT TAB(9):"I=":TAB(14):I:TAB(25):"I2=":TAB(30):I↑2
300 NEXT I
400 END
```

In this case the printer is moved to position number 9 on the page before printing "I=", as illustrated in Figure 6.4. Likewise, it is moved to position number 30 before printing I^2. Observe that the first space after tabbing is consumed by the sign of I and I^2. If the number being printed is negative, a ($-$) is printed; if it is positive, a blank space is printed.

The TAB printing described is exactly like setting tabular stops on a standard typewriter and then using the tab key to automatically space to each of them.

I=	-1.5	I2=	2.25
I=	-1	I2=	1
I=	-0.5	I2=	.25
I=	0	I2=	0
I=	0.5	I2=	.25
I=	1	I2=	1
I=	1.5	I2=	2.25
I=	2	I2=	4
I=	2.5	I2=	6.25
I=	3	I2=	9
I=	3.5	I2=	12.5

Position   1   2   3   4

01234567890123456789012345678901234567890123456789012345 . . . .

Figure 6.4 Illustrating position numbering across the teletype page, and location of output using the TAB function.

IMAGE PRINTING (OR, PRINT USING)

Image printing permits exact customizing of a printout at the programmer's discretion. One first constructs a prototype image of his desired line of printout, something like this:

$$I = \#\#.\# \quad I2 = \#\#\#.\#\#$$

Now the computer will be instructed to place the value of appropriate variables into the positions (temporarily) reserved by #s. Typically, two steps are undertaken. First, the image of the line is defined for the computer, with a statement of one of the forms,*

      50   :I = ##.# I2 = ###.##

or

      51   LET Q = "I = %%.% I2 = %%%.%%"

---

*Again, the reader must contend with nonuniformity among various computers.

Second, at those PRINT statements in the program where image printing is desired, the statement is changed to one of these:

200   PRINT USING 50,I,I↑2

or

201   PRINT IN IMAGE Q:I,I↑2

The defined image line is printed verbatim, with the specified values of the variable inserted into the location of the # (or %) signs. In the above case, the value of I goes into the field defined by ##.#; I^2 goes into the one defined by ###.##. The interesting property of image printing is that the numeric values are centered around the decimal point of the image, filling all locations to the right of the decimal, as shown in Example 6.11.

Example 6.11   Using Image Printing

Programs 6.12 and 6.13 incorporate image printing into the program above which calculates I^2 for I = −1.5 to 2.5 in steps 0.5. Program 6.12 utilizes the statements exemplified by lines 50 and 200 above. Its output is shown in Figure 6.5. Program 6.13 utilizes lines 51 and 201 above. Its output is shown in Figure 6.6. Notice that the outputs are identical. Study them and observe that

■   the decimal points are properly aligned;
■   all the digits to the right of the decimal point are filled, with zeroes if necessary;
■   the change in output is effected by a minor alteration of the print statement.

```
50 :I=##.#   I2=###.##
100 FØR I=-1.5 TØ 3.5 STEP .5
200 PRINT USING 50,I,I↑2
300 NEXT I
400 END
```

Program 6.12   Using image printing to customize the printout (one method).

```
50 LET Q="I=%%.%   I2=%%%.%%"
100 FØR I=-1.5 TØ 3.5 STEP .5
200 PRINT IN IMAGE Q:I,I↑2
300 NEXT I
400 END
```

Program 6.13   Using image printing to customize the printout (another method).

```
I=-1.5   I2=   2.25
I=-1.0   I2=   1.00
I=-0.5   I2=   0.25
I= 0.0   I2=   0.00
I= 0.5   I2=   0.25
I= 1.0   I2=   1.00
I= 1.5   I2=   2.25
I= 2.0   I2=   4.00
I= 2.5   I2=   6.25
I= 3.0   I2=   9.00
I= 3.5   I2=  12.25
```

Figure 6.5   Printout from Program 6.12.

```
RUN

I=-1.5   I2=   2.25
I=-1.0   I2=   1.00
I= -.5   I2=    .25
I=  .0   I2=    .00
I=  .5   I2=    .25
I= 1.0   I2=   1.00
I= 1.5   I2=   2.25
I= 2.0   I2=   4.00
I= 2.5   I2=   6.25
I= 3.0   I2=   9.00
I= 3.5   I2=  12.25
```

Figure 6.6   Printout from Program 6.13.

Several other points, not obvious from the subject printouts, deserve mentioning:

■   If the number being placed in the # field contains more than the specified number of decimal places, it is rounded off to fit (e.g., 4.29 prints as 4.3 in the image #.#).

■   There must be sufficient #s to the left of the decimal point to hold the largest anticipated number (e.g., the computer obviously cannot fit 256.23 into ##.##).

■   If the number may be negative, a # symbol must be provided for the minus sign (e.g., the smallest field in which the number −1234 may be placed is #####). On some systems, a # symbol may also be required for the + sign associated with a positive number.

OTHER CHARACTERS IN IMAGE SPECIFICATIONS

Just as special symbols # or % are used to indicate the positions of the digits of a numeric variable in the printout, most computers recognize various symbols for other kinds of printouts as well. For example, to print a string variable, the computer may require that the position be identified in the image definition by the sequence of characters 'LLLLLL, as in

```
50 :UNIT-PRICE ØF 'LLLLLL IS ###.##
60 LET X$="BØLT"
70 LET P=3.8
80 PRINT USING 50,X$,P
90 END
RUN

UNIT-PRICE ØF BØLT    IS    3.80
```

Here, the apostrophe indicates that the Ls are not to be printed, but instead mark the location of the string in the printout. String variables are printed beginning at the left of the field. If the string is shorter than the specified field (i.e., in the above example, BØLT is shorter than the field indicated by seven Ls, including the apostrophe), the remainder of the field is left blank. On the other hand, if the string is longer than the field, the string will be cut off (i.e., *truncated*) when the field is filled.

These principles are illustrated in Program 6.14 and Figure 6.7.

If the # or % symbols in the previous examples are replaced by a $ sign, the computer will print a "floating" $ sign immediately to the left of the numeric value, in such a way that there will be no space between the $ sign and the number. This prevents tampering with the printout and is particularly useful for writing checks or billings. This feature is also illustrated in Program 6.14 and Figure 6.7.

Finally, a special field is usually required if the printout is to be presented in E notation. The field specification might take a form similar to $\#.\#\#\#\uparrow\uparrow\uparrow\uparrow$, in which case the number 123400000 would be printed as $1.234E+08$. The characters $E+08$ are printed in the positions indicated by $\uparrow$.

ITEM	QUANTITY	UNIT PRICE	TOTAL COST	DISCOUNT
----------	----------	----------	----------	----------
NUT	37	$0.03-EA.	$1.11	$0.02
BØLT	37	$0.07-EA.	$2.59	$0.05
WASHER	74	$0.02-EA.	$1.48	$0.03
HANDLE	36	$2.56-EA.	$92.16	$1.84
WEDGE	12	$0.63-EA.	$7.56	$0.15
----------	----------	----------	----------	----------
SUMMARY	196		$104.90	$2.09

Figure 6.7 Printout from Program 6.14.

```
100  READ A$,B$,C$,D$,E$
200  PRINT USING 1500,A$,B$,C$,D$,E$
300  LET F$="----------"
400  PRINT USING 1500,F$,F$,F$,F$,F$
500  PRINT

510  LET Q1,T1,D1=0
600  READ A$,Q,P
700  IF A$="END" THEN 1300
800  LET T=Q*P
900  LET D=T*.02
1000 PRINT USING 1600,A$,Q,P,T,D
1100 LET Q1=Q1+Q,T1=T1+T,D1=D1+D
1200 GØ TØ 600

1300 PRINT USING 1500,F$,F$,"   ",F$,F$
1400 PRINT USING 1700,"SUMMARY",Q1,T1,D1

1500 :'LLLLLLLLLL    'LLLLLLLLL    'LLLLLLLLL    'LLLLLLLLL    'LLLLLLLLL
1600 :'LLLLLLLLLL    #########    $$$.##-EA.    $$$$$$$.##    $$$$$$$.##
1700 :'LLLLLLLLLL    #########                  $$$$$$$.##    $$$$$$$.##

1800 DATA "ITEM","QUANTITY","UNIT PRICE","TØTAL CØST","DISCØUNT"
1900 DATA "NUT",37,.03
2000 DATA "BØLT",37,.07
2100 DATA "WASHER",74,.02
2200 DATA "HANDLE",36,2.56
2300 DATA "WEDGE",12,.63
2400 END
```

Program 6.14   Several PRINT USING statements.

6.7   DOUBLE PRECISION VARIABLES

As stated in Chapter 2, the computer normally maintains 8 digits of accuracy for a numeric value. To increase capacity the variables may, on some computers, be declared as double precision—i.e., accuracy up to 16 digits. This is accomplished with a statement akin to

$$10 \quad \text{DØUBLE A,B,C}$$

Increased accuracy then results, as in the following example:

```
10 DØUBLE C1,C2,C3
20 LET C1=84412614.82
30 LET C2=964801128.43
40 LET C3=C1+C2
50 PRINT "TØTAL IS":C3
60 END
   RUN

TØTAL IS  1049213743.25
```

6.8 CALL STATEMENT

One program, during the course of its execution, can call another program, already existing in the computer's memory, into service, effectively making the second program a huge subroutine of the first. This is accomplished with a statement of the form

100   CALL <u>program name</u>

Programs 6.15a, b, and c, and Figure 6.8 illustrate. Note that, in this example, PGM1 calls both PGM2 and PGM3. The called programs are terminated with a RETURN statement, as in an ordinary subroutine.

```
100 PRINT "THIS PRØGRAM ILLUSTRATES"
101 PRINT "THE CALL FUNCTIØN."
102 PRINT
103 PRINT "THIS IS PRØGRAM NUMBER ØNE."
104 CALL PGM2
105 PRINT "NØW BACK IN PGM1."
106 CALL PGM3
107 PRINT "NØW BACK IN PGM1."
```

(a)

```
100 PRINT "THIS IS PRØGRAM NUMBER TWØ."
101 RETURN
```

(b)

```
100 PRINT "THIS IS PRØGRAM NUMBER THREE."
101 RETURN
```

(c)

Program 6.15 Three separate programs, two of which will be called as subroutines to the first: (a) PGM1; (b) PGM2; (c) PGM3. Coordinate with Figure 6.8.

6.9 "LOGICAL" VARIABLES

Consider the statement "JANE LIKES JØHN." That statement may be true, or it may be false, depending upon whether or not Jane *does*, in fact, like John. Suppose we let the variable Q have a value which is dependent upon the truth or falsity of the statement. That is, if Jane does like John, then the value of Q will be "TRUE"; but if Jane does not like John, then the value of Q will be "FALSE." In a case where Q takes on a sense of true-

```
ØLD
ØLD PRØGRAM NAME--PGM1

READY.

RUN

THIS PRØGRAM ILLUSTRATES
THE CALL FUNCTIØN.

THIS IS PRØGRAM NUMBER ØNE.
THIS IS PRØGRAM NUMBER TWØ.
NØW BACK IN PGM1.
THIS IS PRØGRAM NUMBER THREE.
NØW BACK IN PGM1.
```

Figure 6.8 Results from executing Programs and 6.15a–c with CALL statements. After PGM2 and PGM3 are each executed, the computer returns to PGM1.

ness or falseness, rather than a numeric value,* the variable is called a *logical* variable.

Unfortunately, the computer does not understand sentences, ideas, or abstractions like "JANE LIKES JØHN." It only understands numbers, so we must somehow communicate the thought via numbers. To permit this, the computer establishes a certain set of conventions, namely: If a variable has a value of zero, that fact corresponds to a "FALSE" sense for the logical variable. If its value is nonzero (i.e., either positive or negative), the logical variable is "TRUE." Study Program 6.16 for an example. First, the computer is instructed that the variable Q is logical (line 100), meaning that it will adopt values of "TRUE" or "FALSE." Now if the user types a nonzero value in response to line 400, Q will be "TRUE." If he types zero, Q will be "FALSE." Next, line 500 is interpreted like this: "*If Q is true, then go to line 800.*" Now study the three runs in Program 6.16 and co-ordinate them with lines 400–800 in the program. Recognize that on the first and third runs, the response to the question was, effectively, "TRUE," and the computer branched to line 800; on the second run, the response was false, and the computer proceeded from line 500 to line 600.

Multiple conditions can be specified with logical variables, as in the following examples where AND and ØR are called *logical operators:*

50	IF Q AND S THEN 100
50	IF Q ØR S THEN 100

The first statement causes transfer only if both Q and S are TRUE. The second causes transfer if at least one of them is TRUE. There are other

---

*Actually, inside the computer, the variable takes on a binary value: 0 if Q is false, and 1 if Q is true. But this need not concern us for this discussion.

```
100 LØGICAL Q
200 PRINT "I HAVE BEEN TØLD THAT JANE LIKES JØHN."
300 PRINT "IS THAT TRUE";
400 INPUT Q

500 IF Q THEN 800
600 PRINT "GEE, THAT'S TØØ BAD."
700 STØP
800 PRINT "THAT'S NICE.  PEØPLE SHØULD LIKE EACH ØTHER."
900 END
    RUN
I HAVE BEEN TØLD THAT JANE LIKES JØHN.
IS THAT TRUE    ? 1
THAT'S NICE.  PEØPLE SHØULD LIKE EACH ØTHER.

    RUN
I HAVE BEEN TØLD THAT JANE LIKES JØHN.
IS THAT TRUE    ? 0
GEE, THAT'S TØØ BAD.

    RUN
I HAVE BEEN TØLD THAT JANE LIKES JØHN.
IS THAT TRUE    ? -3
THAT'S NICE.  PEØPLE SHØULD LIKE EACH ØTHER.
```

Program 6.16 Application of logical variables, showing three runs, two with a "TRUE" response to the question posed by the computer, and one with a "FALSE" response.

logical operators, shown in Table 6.6. With these operators, logic problems like the example below are solvable with the computer.*

Example 6.12   Should I Take the Course?

Consider the following premises:

(1) If this is a good course, then it is worth taking.
(2) Either the grading is lenient, or the course is not worth taking.
(3) But the grading is not lenient.

Under these conditions, is it valid to conclude that

(4) "THIS IS NØT A GØØD CØURSE"?

Program the computer to decide this question.

---

*The interested student who is unfamiliar with logic might like to read J. Kemeny, J. Snell, and G. Thompson, *Introduction to Finite Mathematics*, Englewood Cliffs, N.J.: Prentice-Hall, Inc.

Table 6.6 Logical operators, their TRUE/FALSE interpretation, and their order of execution priority.*

Priority	Operator	A B	T T	T F	F T	F F
2	AND	A AND B	T	F	F	F
3	ØR	A ØR B	T	T	T	F
5	EQUIVALENCE	A EQV B	T	F	F	T
4	IMPLICATIØN	A IMP B	T	F	T	T
1	NØT	NØT A	If A is TRUE, then NØT is FALSE If A is FALSE, then NØT A is TRUE			

*T = TRUE; F = FALSE.

DISCUSSION

Instead of letting Q be equivalent to the statement "JANE LIKES JØHN," let it, and other variables represent the statements

P represents "THIS IS A GØØD CØURSE"
Q represents "IT IS WØRTH TAKING"
R represents "GRADING IS LENIENT"

The above four statements can then be written as follows:

Statement	Symbolic translation	Logic translation
1	IF P THEN Q	P IMPLIES Q
2	EITHER R ØR (THE ØPPØSITE ØF Q)	R ØR (NØT Q)
3	THE ØPPØSITE ØF R	(NØT R)
4	IS THE ØPPØSITE ØF P TRUE?	DØ 1 AND 2 AND 3 IMPLY (NØT P)?

The key statement here is the logic translation of 4. Without proof, let us say that the argument* is valid if and only if, the following logical statement, derived from 4 is true for all combinations of TRUE and FALSE P, Q, and R:

*The "argument" is the entire progression of thought from premises to conclusion. An argument is *valid* (or not valid) in the sense that it does (or does not) *follow logically* from the premises.

[(P IMPLIES Q) AND (R ∅R (N∅T Q)) AND (N∅TR)] IMPLIES (N∅T P)

This fact can be translated into the computer statement

IF ((P IMP Q) AND (R ∅R (N∅T Q)) AND (N∅T R)) IMP (N∅T P) THEN
 go to a line where TRUE is printed; otherwise, go to a line where FALSE is printed

Program 6.17 implements this last equation in line 1700. At this point, reflect for a moment on how verbal statements defining the problem were translated by a very methodical procedure, eventually into line 1700. The same process can be duplicated, almost by rote, to work similar exercises at the end of this chapter.

But the program to solve this problem is not yet fully described, for some mechanism must be provided to exercise line 1700 for all possible TRUE/FALSE combinations of P, Q, and R. The I, J, and K loops in Program 6.17 accomplish this, although how they do it needs some discussion. It is readily apparent that the loops create all eight combinations of (-1) and (0) values

```
  50 L∅GICAL P,Q,R
 100 REM--P REPRESENTS "THIS IS A G∅∅D C∅URSE"
 200 REM--Q REPRESENTS "IT IS W∅RTH TAKING"
 300 REM--R REPRESENTS "GRADING IS LENIENT"
 400 REM
 500 REM--DETERMINE IF IT IS VALID T∅ C∅NCLUDE FR∅M THE GIVEN
 600 REM--PREMISES THAT "THIS IS N∅T A G∅∅D C∅URSE" (I.E.,
 700 REM--IF (N∅T Q) CAN BE DEDUCED )
1100 F∅R I=-1 T∅ 0
1200 F∅R J=-1 T∅ 0
1300 F∅R K=-1 T∅ 0
1400 LET P=I
1500 LET Q=J
1600 LET R=K
1700 IF ((P IMP Q) AND (R ∅R (N∅T Q)) AND (N∅T R)) IMP (N∅T P)
     THEN 2000
1800 PRINT "FALSE"
1900 G∅ T∅ 2100
2000 PRINT "TRUE"
2100 NEXT K
2200 NEXT J
2300 NEXT I
2400 END
 RUN

TRUE
TRUE
TRUE
TRUE
TRUE
TRUE
TRUE
TRUE
```

Program 6.17 Solution to Example 6.12, using logical variables.

of I, J, K. The values of I, J, and K on each iteration of the inside loop are given in Table 6.7. But now study the effect of lines 1400–1600, which assign new values to P, Q, and R on each iteration. When (I = −1), P, being a logical variable (see line 50), is set equal to "TRUE," for I is nonzero. On the other hand, whenever I = 0, P = "FALSE." The same argument can be made for the values of Q and R. Table 6.7 shows that, depending on I, J, and K, all combinations of TRUE/FALSE are treated by line 1700.

As can be seen from the printout, the program produces all "TRUE" answers for each execution of line 1700, the condition required to state that conclusion 4 is valid.* However, had one or more of the iterations produced a "FALSE," the conclusion would have been invalid. This leads to a natural improvement in the program so that the computer keeps track of whether or not any FALSE answers were produced, and prints out a message accepting or rejecting the validity of the arguments. In Program 6.18, a counter— the variable F—is installed to count every time the "FALSE" branch is executed. Then, after all iterations are executed, line 2310 makes a determination of whether or not any FALSE conditions have arisen. If not (i.e., if F is still equal to zero), the computer is sent to line 2350, printing a message accepting the argument. If F = 0, the conclusion is rejected with line 2320. (In this version of the program, the author has arbitrarily decided to drop the TRUE/FALSE printout from each iteration. Obviously it could be retained if desired.)

Table 6.7 Showing the values of I, J, K, P, Q, and R with each iteration of the loops in Program 6.17.

Iteration number	I	J	K	P	Q	R
1	−1	−1	−1	TRUE	TRUE	TRUE
2	−1	−1	0	TRUE	TRUE	FALSE
3	−1	0	−1	TRUE	FALSE	TRUE
4	−1	0	0	TRUE	FALSE	FALSE
5	0	−1	−1	FALSE	TRUE	TRUE
6	0	−1	0	FALSE	TRUE	FALSE
7	0	0	−1	FALSE	FALSE	TRUE
8	0	0	0	FALSE	FALSE	FALSE

*It should be pointed out that these validity tests only determine whether or not the conclusion logically follows from the stated premises. It says nothing of whether or not the conclusion is actually true.

```
50 LØGICAL P,Q,R
100 REM--DELETED TRUE/FALSE PRINTØUT FRØM EACH LØØP,
200 REM--REPLACING IT WITH ØNE DECISIØN AT THE END ØF THE LØØP.
300 LET F=0

1100 FØR I=-1 TØ 0
1200 FØR J=-1 TØ 0
1300 FØR K=-1 TØ 0
1400 LET P=I
1500 LET Q=J
1600 LET R=K
1700 IF ((P IMP Q) AND (R ØR (NØT Q)) AND (NØT R)) IMP (NØT P)
     THEN 2000
1800 LET F=F+1
1900 GØ TØ 2100
2000 REM--DELETED

2100 NEXT K
2200 NEXT J
2300 NEXT I

2310 IF F=0 THEN 2350
2320 PRINT "THE ARGUMENT IS NØT VALID"
2330 STØP
2350 PRINT "IT IS VALID TØ CØNCLUDE THAT 'THIS IS NØT A GØØD CØURSE'!"
2400 END
 RUN

IT IS VALID TØ CØNCLUDE THAT 'THIS IS NØT A GØØD CØURSE'!
```

Program 6.18 The computer determines the validity of the conclusion by counting the number of "TRUE" results attained.

6.10 COMPLEX VARIABLES

Many engineering and mathematical problems involve the application of *complex* numbers, i.e., those containing *real* and *imaginary* parts. Some advanced BASIC languages have special functions which are most useful in these problems. First the computer must be informed that a particular variable will be complex:

100   CØMPLEX A,B,C

whereafter it will recognize that A, B, and C must simultaneously contain two distinct values—a real part and an imaginary one. The program

```
100 CØMPLEX A,B,C
200 LET A=CMPLX(5,4)
300 LET M=-2
400 LET N=0
500 LET B=CMPLX(M↑2+1,N)
600 LET C=A+B
    RUN
```

will set $A = 5 + 4i$, $B = 5 + 0i$, and $C = 10 + 4i$.

Complex variables are treated in a manner quite similar to ordinary ones, except that the computer will always know that each variable will be composed of both parts. When reading data, for example, it will expect that the data will be organized into pairs of real and imaginary parts, and will retrieve both values simultaneously. Similarly, it will print both parts simultaneously.

There are two convenient functions available for manipulation of complex numbers: REAL(C) and IMAG(C). In practice, if $C = 2 + 10i$, then the statement 304 LET X=REAL(C) sets X = 2, i.e., the *real* part of C; 305 LET Y=IMAG(C) sets Y = 10.

Example 6.13   Vector Sum

Calculate the resultant force vector, R, resulting from the application of $v_1, v_2, ..., v_5$, where

$$v_1 = 4 + 2.5i$$
$$v_2 = 4 + 4i$$
$$v_3 = -1.5 + 1.25i$$
$$v_4 = -4 - 3i$$
$$v_5 = 1 - 1i$$

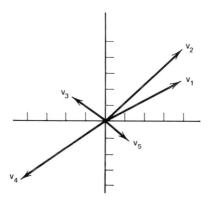

DISCUSSION

Program 6.19 is designed to print out R as the computer progresses through its accumulator loop, so the reader may study the way each variable is composed of two parts. It also illustrates the effect of REAL and IMAG.

```
100 CØMPLEX V, R
200 LET R=CMPLX(0,0)
201 PRINT "INITIAL VECTØR SUM IS"; R

300 FØR I=1 TØ 5
400 READ V
500 LET R=R+V
501 PRINT "INTERMEDIATE SUM IS"; R
600 NEXT I

700 PRINT
800 PRINT "RESULTANT VECTØR IS"; R
900 PRINT "ØR, USING REAL AND IMAG,"
1000 PRINT "RESULTANT VECTØR IS"; REAL(R); " +"; IMAG(R); I

1100 DATA 4, 2.5
1200 DATA 4, 4
1300 DATA -1.5, 1.25
1400 DATA -4, -3
1500 DATA 1, -1
1600 END
 RUN

INITIAL VECTØR SUM IS     0, 0
INTERMEDIATE SUM IS     4, 2.5
INTERMEDIATE SUM IS     8, 6.5
INTERMEDIATE SUM IS     6.5, 7.75
INTERMEDIATE SUM IS     2.5, 4.75
INTERMEDIATE SUM IS     3.5, 5.75

RESULTANT VECTØR IS     3.5, 5.75
ØR, USING REAL AND IMAG,
RESULTANT VECTØR IS     3.5 + 5.75 I
```

Program 6.19 Vector sum.

Example 6.14 Analysis of a Reactive Electronic Circuit

Find the currents I_1, I_2, I_3, and I_L, and the voltages V_1, V_2, V_3, and V_L in the electronic circuit in Figure 6.9.

DISCUSSION
If I_1, I_2, and I_3 are found, the remaining unknowns in the circuit can be determined from

$$I_L = (I_1 - I_2)$$
$$V_1 = I_1 Z_1$$
$$V_2 = I_2 Z_2$$
$$V_3 = (I_1 - I_3)Z_4$$
$$V_L = I_L Z_L$$

An electrical engineer would write the Maxwell matrix equation $\mathbf{MI} = \mathbf{V}$, from which $\mathbf{I} = \mathbf{V}/\mathbf{M}$† $= $ INV $(\mathbf{M})*\mathbf{V}$,

†See footnote to Example 5.5 for a discussion of matrix division.

$$\mathbf{M} = \begin{bmatrix} (8 + 6i) & -(3 + 0i) & -(4 - 6i) \\ -(3 + 0i) & (9.72 + 3.46i) & -(6.12 + 10.16i) \\ -(4 - 6i) & -(6.12 + 10.16i) & (10.12 + 4.16i) \end{bmatrix}$$

$$\mathbf{I} = \begin{bmatrix} I_1 \\ I_2 \\ I_3 \end{bmatrix} \qquad \mathbf{V} = \begin{bmatrix} 0 \\ 0 \\ 100 \end{bmatrix}$$

Any solution which did not employ complex variables would be difficult, but their use in Program 6.20 makes the problem quite simple, particularly since they can be utilized in matrix equations. The problem is essentially solved when I_1, I_2, and I_3 are found in line 400. The remainder of the program is printout. On the computer on which the problem was executed, the variables may be dimensioned while they are being declared complex (line 100). This problem illustrates the extremely useful nature of complex variables.

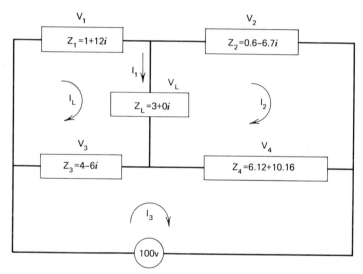

Figure 6. 9

■ EXERCISES

*6.18 The invoice shown in Figure 6.10 is preprinted with the words NAME, ADDRESS, CITY, CUSTØMER NØ., QTY., underlines, etc. Write the image statements required to locate each line of print-out in the proper position. Also, write the PRINT statements necessary to use the image statements and fill in the invoice. The italicized

```
100 CØMPLEX M(3,3),X(3,3),Z(5),I(3,1),V(3,1)
200 MAT READ M,V,Z
300 MAT X=INV(M)
400 MAT I=X*V

500 FØR J=1 TØ 3
600 PRINT "I":J:" = ":I(J,1)
700 NEXT J
800 PRINT "IL =";I(1,1)-I(2,1)

900 PRINT
1000 PRINT "V1 =":I(1,1)*Z(1)
1100 PRINT "V2 =":I(2,1)*Z(2)
1200 PRINT "V3 =":(I(1,1)-I(3,1))*Z(3)
1300 PRINT "V4 =":(-I(2,1)+I(3,1))*Z(4)
1400 PRINT "VL =":(I(1,1)-I(2,1))*Z(5)

1500 DATA 8,6,-3,0,-4,6
1600 DATA -3,0,9.72,3.46,-6.12,-10.16
1700 DATA -4,6,-6.12,10.16,10.12,4.16

1800 DATA 0,0
1801 DATA 0,0
1802 DATA 100,0

1900 DATA 1,12
2000 DATA .6,-6.7
2100 DATA 4,-6
2200 DATA 6.12,10.1
2300 DATA 3,0
2400 END
RUN

I 1 = -4.561359,-2.7591887
I 2 =  4.4438813,-5.0502765
I 3 =  1.3976052,-6.4763008
IL =  -9.0052403, 2.2910878

V1 = 28.548905,-57.495497
V2 =-31.170524,-32.804171
V3 =-1.5331843, 50.622234
V4 =-4.2403642,-39.494657
VL =-27.015721, 6.8732634
```

Program 6.20 Using complex variables in the solution of the electronic circuit of Example 6.14. Note that the matrices **M**, **X**, **V**, **I**, and **Z** all contain complex numbers.

information gives the variable names and spacing allotted for each blank.

6.19 Using the "computed GØ SUB" statement, write a program segment which branches to lines 10000, 20000, 30000, 40000 when Q = 50, 100, 150, 200.

6.20 Using the "computed GØ TØ" statement, write a program segment which branches to lines 100, 110, 120, 130 when X = 1.0, 1.1, 1.2, 1.3.

6.21 Using a "computed GØ TØ" statement, transfer to lines 1000,

NAME	(*N$–50 characters*)		
ADDRESS	(*A$–50 characters*)		
CITY	(*C$–50 characters*)		

CUSTØMER NØ. (*N–10 characters*   SALESMAN: (*S$–30 characters*)

QTY: (*Q*) (5 char)	DESCRIPTION (*D$*) (40 char)	EACH *$$$.##*(E)	PRICE *$$$$.##*(P)

SUBTØTAL			*$$$$$.##(S)*
TAX (5%)			*$$$$$.##(T)*
TØTAL			*$$$$$.##(S-T)*

Figure 6.10 Preprinted invoice, Exercise 6.18.

1500, 300, and 1600 if angle A is between $0°$ and $90°$, $90°$ and $180°$, $180°$ and $270°$, $270°$ and $360°$, respectively.

*6.22 Write (a) symbolic and (b) logical translations of the following problem, and then write a program to test its validity:

(1) If I can be proud of myself, then father praises me. (2) Either I do well in sports or I cannot be proud of myself. (3) If I study hard, then I cannot do well in sports. (4) Therefore, is it true that if my father praises me, then I do not study hard.

6.23 Write a program to determine the validity of each of these arguments:

(a) $P \rightarrow Q$
        $\sim R \rightarrow \sim Q$
        $\overline{\therefore \sim R \rightarrow \sim P}$

(b) $P \leftrightarrow Q$
        $Q \vee R$
        $\dfrac{\sim R}{\therefore \sim P}$

6.24 Write a program to read a complex number, C, and then
(a) create its conjugate as C1;
(b) determine its magnitude and phase angle in degrees.

6.25 Write a program which reads a vector in polar notation and constructs its complex number equivalent.

6.26 Calculate $e^{a + bi}$ for a = 0, 0.1, 0.2, . . . , 1.0, b = 0, 0.2, 0.4, . . . , 2.0.

6.27 Suppose C = a + bi. Write the statements necessary to transfer the computer as follows:
(a) to line 1000 if a + bi is in the first quadrant;
(b) to line 1100 if a + bi is in the second quadrant;
(c) to line 1200 if a + bi is in the third quadrant;
(d) to line 1300 if a + bi is in the fourth quadrant.

7 DATA FILES: INPUT/ØUTPUT

All programs developed so far have either had the applicable data contained within themselves (in DATA statements), or have asked the user to INPUT information from the keyboard. In many practical problems, those procedures may have drawbacks which can be eliminated with the use of data input and output files, whereby data is saved in a separate file in the computer's permanent memory, and not in the program's data statement. The following definitions are adopted for later use in this chapter:

■ "INPUT" file (or, "READ" file)—a permanent memory file containing data which the program is going to read in lieu of its own data statements.

■ "ØUTPUT" file (or, "PRINT" or "WRITE" file)—a permanent memory file which receives the output generated by the program, in lieu of printing on the teletype.

Sections 7.1 and 7.2 give technical instructions for implementing data files. Section 7.3 gives the reader some ideas for their application. The author suggests that the student give a light reading to Section 7.3 before proceeding with 7.1. This will put data files into the proper perspective while studying their implementation. After studying Sections 7.1 and 7.2, the student should review Section 7.3 more thoroughly. Section 7.4 introduces random-access files, which may be used for both input and output. They are a powerful and relatively new innovation in BASIC languages.

Although the author relies mainly on an economic application to illustrate the use of data files, it is used only for simplicity. The student should realize that this material is equally applicable to engineering, mathematics, and other problems. Some of the exercises given at the end of this chapter will illustrate the application of data files to technical problems.

7.1 INPUT (OR READ) FILES

Program 7.1 is a brief version of the familiar Payroll Journal problem. It shows the essential parts of the program, primarily those statements which are designed to get data into (lines 100, 800–805) or out of (line 500) the program. Also important here, lines 200 and 9990 act together to recognize the expiration of data and to terminate processing before an attempt to execute line 100 is made after the data expires.

For now, let us be concerned only with those statements related to getting data into the program. The objective of this discussion is to remove those statements in Program 7.1 which are enclosed in the box and to create a separate file containing only the unshaded portion of the box.* Such a file is created in a manner very similar to the creation of an ordinary program, as shown in Figure 7.1. A paper tape is created and fed into a file in the computer. It is then SAVE'd for future use.†

The data file is given a unique name for later reference; in Figure 7.1 it was given the name WEEK. Now two files exist, as illustrated in Figure 7.2—one is the original program, stripped of its data; the other is the

```
100 READ E,H,R,T
200 IF E=0 THEN 9999
300 LET G=H*R
400 LET N=G-T*G
500 PRINT E,H,G,N
600 GØ TØ 100

800 DATA 40312,40,3.32,.103
801 DATA 08140,42,5.25,.172
802 DATA 31402,38,4.28,.145
803 DATA 12440,40,2.13,.085
804 DATA 21443,40,6.28,.18
805 DATA 41102,41.5,5.03,.163

9990 DATA 0,0,0,0
9999 END
```

Program 7.1 Skeleton version of Payroll Journal Program, showing statements for getting data into, or out of, the program.

*Some computers also require removal of the line numbers.

†The precise way in which this is accomplished is somewhat dependent on the particular computer being used. In general, the procedure is closely related to that for saving any other program. Consult the supplier's manuals.

```
NEW
NEW FILE NAME--WEEK

READY.
TAPE

800  40312,40,3.32,.103
801  08140,42,5.25,.172
802  31402,38,4.28,.145
803  12440,40,2.13,.085
804  21443,40,6.28,.18
805  41102,41.5,5.03,.163

KEY

READY.
SAVE
READY.
```

Figure 7.1   Saving a DATA file named WEEK.

data itself. Since the data is no longer located in the main program, line 100 in Program 7.1 obviously cannot be used, for it would instruct the computer to retrieve values for E,H,R,T from DATA statements which do not exist. What one would like to do is to instruct the computer to

100   READ *from the file named WEEK*
             (instead of DATA statements)
         E,H,R,T

Time-sharing computers are endowed with an abbreviated version of that statement, employing a new statement, FILES:

1   FILES WEEK;RESULTS;XYZ

The FILES statement contains one or more names identifying data files. The computer automatically regards all named files as input files. After this statement is added to the program, all subsequent referrals to the file name are made in terms of the file number, determined by the position of its

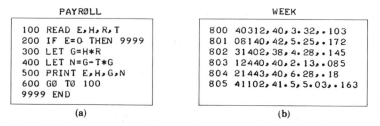

Figure 7.2   Illustrating two files created by removing data from the payroll program and placing it in WEEK.

name in the FILES statement. In the above example, WEEK is file 1, RESULTS is file 2, XYZ is file 3, etc. Line 100 can now be rewritten as 100 READ #1,E,H,R,T, which is interpreted by the computer as was intended by the verbal italicized READ statement above. The necessary changes are shown in Program 7.2. Instead of attempting to READ from DATA, the computer will now read the same information from WEEK.

The implementation of input (or, read) data files is now clear. One simply associates a number with a file name (using FILES) and changes all READ statements to READ #1, READ #2, etc., as appropriate. It is that simple.

At the programmer's discretion some of the data may be placed in one or more data files, and some of it can be retained in the program. At any point in the program where it is desired to retrieve values from DATA, the READ statement is simply not changed.

END-OF-FILE TESTS

Observe that, in Program 7.2, line 200 is useless because the DATA statement which originally signified the expiration of data (i.e., 9990 DATA 0,0,0,0) was not put in the file. It could have been, of course, and all would have been well. But use of such a terminating indicator is awkward, so most computers permit a more convenient, automatic, recognition of exhausted data with another new statement:

$$100 \quad \text{IF END } \#1 \text{ THEN } 9950$$
$$200 \quad \text{IF END } \#6 \text{ THEN } 512$$

Each time the computer incurs this statement it immediately checks the indicated file to determine whether the end of the data has been reached or there still remains some unread data. If there is no more, the computer is diverted to the indicated line number. If there is more, the computer continues to the next line and continues processing. The programmer, then, places such statements at strategic spots in the program which suit his purpose. In Program 7.3, the original line 200 is removed, for it no longer

```
50 FILES WEEK
100 READ #1,E,H,R,T
200 IF E=0 THEN 9999
300 LET G=H*R
400 LET N=G-T*G
500 PRINT E,H,G,N
600 GO TO 100
9999 END
```

Program 7.2 Alteration of the payroll program, utilizing an INPUT data file.

```
50 FILES WEEK
99 IF END#1 THEN 9999
100 READ #1,E,H,R,T
300 LET G=H*R
400 LET N=G-T*G
500 PRINT E,H,G,N
600 GØ TØ 99
9999 END
```

Program 7.3 Using the END # statement to
detect the expiration of the data file.

serves any purpose. Instead, line 99 is inserted and a check is made to determine if any data remains in WEEK *before* attempting to read from it.
Also, line 600 is changed to return the computer to the end-of-file check,
ensuring that a new check is made before each READ.

RESTORING A DATA FILE

It was shown in Chapter 4 that a RESTØRE statement caused the computer to again initiate reading data from the beginning. The corresponding
statement when using data files is

$$1030 \quad \text{RESTØRE } \#4$$

This statement causes the data in, for example, file number four to be
restored. It does not cause the restoration of any other files or the program's
own data statements.

VARIATIONS ON IMPLEMENTING INPUT FILES

The implementation of the details of INPUT data files are not universal.
The reader may encounter slight differences in the format of the above
statements, but if he understands the simple principles espoused in the
preceding discussion, he should have no difficulty at all adjusting to them.
The following points give the reader an idea of the range of variations he is
likely to encounter:

■ The statement 50 FILES WEEK, RESULTS, XYZ might instead be
written

$$50 \quad \text{ØPEN WEEK, INPUT,1}$$
$$51 \quad \text{ØPEN RESULTS, INPUT,2}$$
$$52 \quad \text{ØPEN XYZ, INPUT,3}$$

■ The statement 100 READ #1,E,H,R,T might instead be written
100 INPUT FRØM 1:E,H,R,T.

■ The RESTØRE #1 command may be replaced by the command CLØSE #1, followed by another FILES or ØPEN command.

■ There are usually practical limitations on the number of files which may be named simultaneously.

■ It may be required that FILES be the first statement in the program.

■ A very useful variation is one where the file name may be a string variable. The sequence

  50   PRINT "WHAT DATA FILE SHØULD I USE";
  51   INPUT F$
  52   FILES F$

may then be used to effectively allow the computer to ask which file should be used on each execution of the program. See Section 7.3 for typical applications.

■ In general, statements attempting to read matrices from a data file are written 500 MAT READ #3, A or 500 MAT INPUT FRØM 3: A.

7.2 ØUTPUT (OR PRINT) FILES

Just as the computer can read data from a file in its memory, it can also print (or write) its results on another file. If the principles of Section 7.1 are understood, those of this section need little explanation. Program 7.4 illustrates how one changes Program 7.3 to cause the output to be printed on the file named RESULTS, rather than on the teletype; RESULTS is included in the FILES statement, and the appropriate PRINT statements are changed to WRITE #2,E,H,G,N. However, one additional change must be made. To inform the computer that RESULTS will be used for writing, line 51 is added, SCRATCH #2. This causes the existing data in RESULTS to be *immediately erased* so that new output begins at the first line

```
50 FILES WEEK,RESULTS
60 SCRATCH #2
99 IF END #1 THEN 9999
100 READ #1,E,H,R,T
300 LET C=H*R
400 LET N=G-T*G
500 WRITE #2,E,H,G,N
600 GØ TØ 99
9999 END
```

Program 7.4 Incorporating ØUTPUT data files into the payroll program.

110	40312	40	132.8	119.1216
120	8140	42	220.5	182.574
130	31402	38	162.64	139.0572
140	12440	40	85.2	77.958
150	21443	40	251.2	205.984
160	41102	41.5	208.745	174.71957

Figure 7.3   The contents of RESULTS after execution of Program 7.4. (If the computer requires line numbers in data files, it will insert them automatically when executing the WRITE statement.)

in the file. Figure 7.3 illustrates the contents of RESULTS after execution of Program 7.4.

7.3 APPLICATIONS OF DATA FILES

There are several very valuable applications of data files with which a proficient programmer must be familiar.

TWO OR MORE PROGRAMS SHARE THE SAME DATA

It is quite common to process a particular set of data by two or more different programs. For example, consider the data representing an employee's up-to-date earnings, deductions, etc. That data might be used to (1) calculate and write the employee's year-end tax (W-2) form; (2) incorporate salary payouts into the company's financial statements; and (3) perform analyses of sick pay, overtime, and bonus expenses. It is not practical to have a single program do all three tasks if the first is done annually, the second quarterly, and the last weekly. Therefore, a separate program might well be developed for each task.

Should the data be duplicated in each of the three programs? Or, would it be more reasonable to store only one set of data in an input file and instruct each program to read its data from that file? The latter approach is illustrated by Figure 7.4. Observe that the HISTØRY file is used for input to two programs, W-2 and FINSTA. Note, too, that HISTØRY contains data which is not actually processed in FINSTA (i.e., the employee's name, which is of no interest when summing costs in the financial statement). However, since that data is used in W-2, it must be included in the file. In fact, it is obvious that any input data file which will be shared by two or more programs must contain all the data to be used by either program, even though some data is not common to both.

Although the program FINSTA does not use some of the data in HISTØRY, it must still read it in order to maintain the sequence of read statements in correlation with that of the data, since the program always reads the data in sequential order. This is accomplished by reading N$, in program FINSTA, but simply not processing that variable.

SERVICE PROGRAMS

A "service program" may be thought of as one which, as one of its several purposes, generates output data for use by a second program; that is, to perform a "service" for the latter program.

The genesis of the data in HISTØRY, Figure 7.4, has not yet been discussed. Until now the reader has probably conceptualized its origin as something like this: An operator pours over all the paycheck stubs or other records generated for the last year; then she sorts out that data pertinent to W-2 and FINSTA and generates a paper tape; finally, she runs the paper tape into permanent memory and saves it in HISTØRY.

But better than that, let us visualize some pertinent modification to the Payroll Journal Program so that, in addition to writing the journal on the teletype, it also writes data onto an output file (say, HØLD) for later use by W-2 and FINSTA. The principle is very simple, as illustrated by Figure 7.5. The value of the technique is obvious, for HØLD can be saved in the

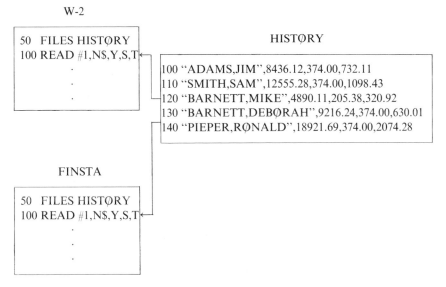

Figure 7.4 Illustrating the flow of data from HISTØRY to either program W-2 or FINSTA. HISTØRY contains each employee's year-to-date records.

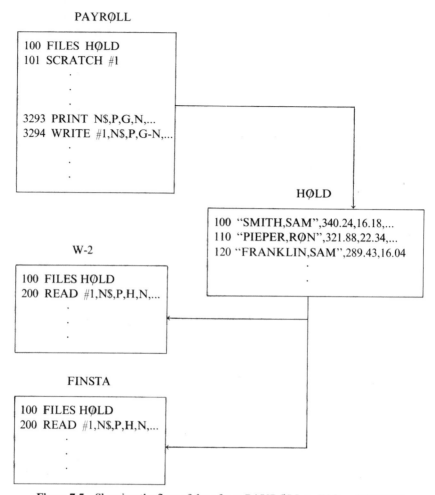

Figure 7.5 Showing the flow of data from PAYRØLL to W-2 and FINSTA.

computer's memory for weeks, always available for later use by another program.

ONE PROGRAM USES SEVERAL DATA FILES

Many programs are written in such a way that they may be used with several sets of similar data. For example, are not the program requirements for the Widget-Gidget Mfg. Co.'s and World-Wide Sales' payroll journals at least quite similar, if not nearly identical? It is only the data for each company that is truly unique. Figure 7.6 illustrates how one program (in this case PAYRØLL) can read data from any of several data files upon the direction of the user. If the user responds WIDGID to line 200 of PAYRØLL, the computer processes Widget-Gidget's data; if he answers AJAX, the computer reads the last file shown in Figure 7.6.

UPDATING DATA

Some very useful programs read existing data which was generated at a previous time, and "update it" in some fashion. For instance, imagine this sequence of events: On the first week of a new calendar year the computer is given data on each employee—hours worked, rate, number of deductions, etc. It proceeds to print journal information on the teletype and also to write historically important information onto the output file named YTD. On the second week, it is again given data on each employee, but this time it creates year-to-date records by accumulating the results of the current week with those generated previously for each employee. If the same procedure is used each week, YTD will, at any time, contain accumulated year-to-date totals. At the end of the year, YTD will obviously contain accumulated data for the full year. Then W-2 and FINSTA can access the year-to-date records in YTD for their own purposes. The flow of data among the files is illustrated in Figure 7.7. By properly employing input and output data files, a tidy technique seems to have developed for updating files from one week to the next; i.e., read old data, read new data, add them together,

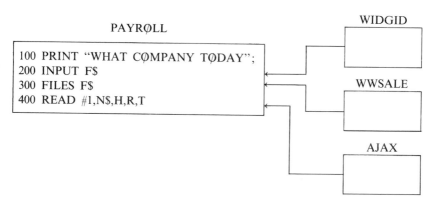

Figure 7.6   Illustrating how one program can accept data from several data files, the particular one being specified by the operator each time the program is run.

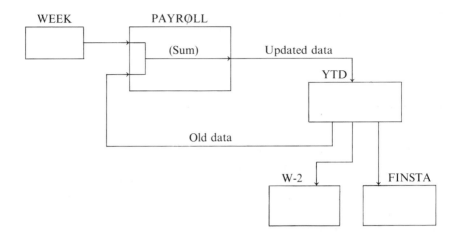

Figure 7.7   Data flow in a complex series of programs and files which involve periodic updating of one of them. Certain problems are inherent in the updating process, which are discussed and solved in the text.

write the sum on YTD for use next week, and then repeat the cycle for each employee. But there is a flaw which must not be overlooked. The data flow in Figure 7.7 requires the computer both to read from, and to write onto, YTD. In order to write on the file, the SCRATCH command must be executed; however, that action causes the existing year-to-date information on the file to be erased before it is all read. The results are disastrous. The historical record which is vital to the procedure is suddenly lost!

Consider this alternative: Create two year-to-date files, named YTD1 and YTD2. On the first week of the year the computer writes its data onto YTD1. On the second week, it reads from YTD1 and writes on YTD2, thereby avoiding the necessity of prematurely erasing YTD1. Similarly, on the third week the computer could be instructed to read from YTD2 and write on YTD3, and so on until the fifty-second week, whereupon there are 52 files in the computer's memory.

If it is undesirable to have 51 obsolete files saved, the procedure can be modified one more time. Recognize that, in this example, the computer needs to have only two files available to it at once, one designated an "old" file from which to read, and another designated the "new" file on which to print. Therefore, the following rule can be adopted:

On weeks 2, 4, 6, . . .   write on YTD2, read from YTD1.
On weeks 3, 5, 7, . . .   write on YTD1, read from YTD2.

That is, alternate the roles of the files.

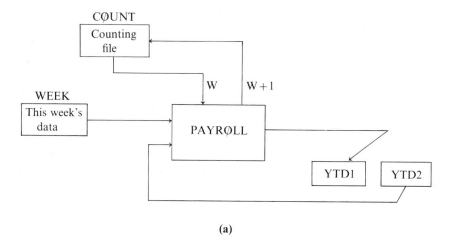

(a)

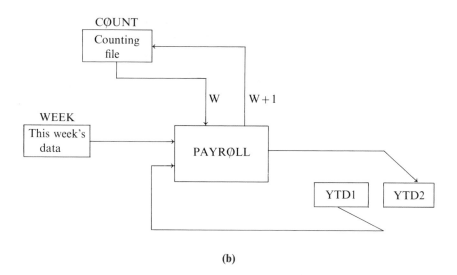

(b)

Figure 7.8 (a) The flow of data when PAYRØLL is executed on an odd-numbered week. The year's up-to-date accumulated record is written on YTD1. (b) The flow of data when PAYRØLL is executed on an even-numbered week. The year's up-to-date accumulated record is written onto YTD2.

How shall the computer be given the ability to decide which file to read and which to write? Shall the operator so instruct it each week? The risk of an error, coupled with the severity of accidental loss of the historical data, prompts one to look for an automatic, computerized, way of accomplishing the procedures.

To that end, the file named CØUNT, Figure 7.8, contains one piece of data—a single number that is incremented by one with each execution of PAYRØLL. The first week it is created with a "1." Refer now to Program 7.5. Its first activity is to read the number in CØUNT as the variable W, scratch CØUNT, and write a new value equal to $W + 1$ back on it (for example, on the first execution, a "2" is placed on the file). Then, in line 500, the computer detects whether W is even or odd. If even (i.e., weeks 2, 4, 6, . . .), the computer is diverted to line 1000 where W1 is set equal to 2 and R1 is set equal to 1. Then, in line 1200, file W1 is scratched; thereafter the computer reads from file R1 (i.e., file 1) and writes on file W1 (i.e., file 2).

On the second week of the year CØUNT contains "2," an odd number. Line 500 is passed and lines 700, 800 are executed. Ultimately, on odd weeks, file 1 is scratched and file 2 is read.

The technique described here, in Figure 7.8 and Program 7.5, is obviously extremely valuable to business applications, but it is also valuable to engineering applications where laboratory test data is to be updated, to manufacturing applications where production figures are to be updated, and many others. The reader should familiarize himself with the technique.

```
100 FILES YTD1,YTD2,COUNT
200 READ #3,W
300 SCRATCH #3
400 WRITE #3,W+1

500 IF W/2=INT(W/2) THEN 1000
600 LET W1=1
700 LET R1=2
800 GO TO 1200

1000 LET W1=2
1100 LET R1=1

1200 SCRATCH #W1
1300 READ #R1,N$,H,R,T
        .
        .
        .
8999 WRITE #W1,N$,Y,...
        .
        .
        .
```

Program 7.5 Illustrating the alternate selection of YTD1 and YTD2 as input and output data files.

SHARING DATA BETWEEN COMPUTERS

A BASIC program on the time-share computer may supply data for another program, on another computer, perhaps using another language. Or vice versa, another computer may generate data for a time-share program. To effect the transmission of the data from one computer to the other, output can be written onto a file, transferred to magnetic tape or punched card, and then rapidly fed into the other computer (see Section 8.7).

7.4   RANDOM-ACCESS FILES

The previous discussions have centered around "sequential" files—files which are read and written by beginning at the first element in the file and proceeding sequentially through the remainder. Random-access files are more convenient in some applications where the computer must manipulate the file in an unpredictable, randomly chosen,* sequence, or when the file must be both written and read. Depending on the computer being used, the implementation of random-access files can be quite complex. This is only a very simplified discussion, and the reader must research his supplier's manuals to actually use the feature.

Consider Figure 7.9a, which represents a file named XYZ containing ten lines of data. If the entries in each line are assigned the variable names A, B, and C, it is desirable to change the fifth, seventh, and ninth lines to A^2, $B/2$, and $C + 1$, and to do so without tampering with the other lines. Program 7.6 accomplishes the task. First, file XYZ is opened, and the computer is

12	3.4	6		12	3.4	6
13	6.6	8		13	6.6	8
4	−2.1	4		4	−2.1	4
10	5.5	3		10	5.5	3
9	4.4	3 ⟶		81	2.2	4
22	−1.6	4		22	−1.6	4
6	−3.4	8 ⟶		36	−1.7	9
5	1.1	9		5	1.1	9
90	3.1	6 ⟶		8100	1.55	7
20	4.4	5		20	4.4	5

(a) Before   (b) After

Figure 7.9   File XYZ before and after being manipulated by Program 7.6.

*Not to be confused with generation of random numbers. This only means in some sequence other than a sequential one.

```
100 FILES XYZ
200 RANDØM #1
300 FØR L1=5 TØ 9 STEP 2
400 READ #1 AT LINE L1,A,B,C
500 WRITE #1 AT LINE L1,A+2,B/2,C+1
600 NEXT L1
700 END
```

Program 7.6   Accessing XYZ at random points.

told that it is a "random-access" file (see line 200). Line 300 tells the computer which lines of the file are to be changed. Lines 400 and 500 are crucial—they permit the computer to access the file only at specific lines indicated by the variable L1, for the purpose of either reading or writing.

■ EXERCISES

7.1   Research your supplier's literature and determine exactly how (if at all) each of the features described in this chapter are implemented on your machine. If you wish, then, the problems below may be solved using that implementation rather than the one shown in this text.

7.2   License plate numbers, owners, and other information are stored in a data file named LICENS. Write two programs. One should ask the user to specify a license number and print the owner, color, year, motor number, and make of car associated with it. The other program should print the names of all auto owners between age 25 and 35.

Number	Owner	Make	Color	Year	Owner's age
ZSA018	J.T.ØWENS	CHEV	BLUE	64	32
WPY230	L.L.SMITH	FØRD	BLUE	69	19
AAA166	C.K.JØNES	CHRY	GREEN	70	38

7.3   A magazine company has its subscription data stored in a file—i.e., subscriber's name, address, and subscription expiration date. Write a program which (a) asks the user to specify a particular month and year and (b) writes onto another file the names of subscribers who expire during that month.

7.4   In the preceding problem, write a program which will add new subscribers to the file and delete old ones whose expiration dates were more than 90 days ago.

7.5   A file contains the following data on previous experiments: date of test, meter reading, number of trials made, experiment success or failure. A new experiment is performed. Write a program which will accept new data and add it to the file while deleting any existing data over six months old.

7.6   Two data files and one program must be written. The first file contains customer identification numbers, names, addresses, and cities. The second file contains customer number, item description, per-unit sales price, and number of units sold. All file entries are arranged in ascending customer number order. The program must (a) read a line from the second file; (b) find a matching customer in the first file; and (c) print out the appropriate customer's name, address, and total billing.

7.7   A real payroll program has many more things on which to keep records and make calculations than those discussed in this book. Name some of them. Break "this week's" file into two parts—one containing data which changes each week, such as hours worked, holiday pay, sick pay, etc., and the other containing unchanging data, such as hourly rate, number of tax deductions, credit union deductions, charity contributions, etc. Which data would you put in each?

*7.8   An input file contains the following names and salaries:

BRIAN MILLER	$326.18
HENRY SCHMØ	219.62
KIMBERLEY ANNE SHEA	136.42
BRETT MILLER	103.26
RØNALD R. PIEPER	256.00

Write a program to give a 10% raise to everyone, except to Kimberley Anne Shea, who gets a 15% raise. Write the names and new salaries onto an output file and print the names, old salaries, and new salaries onto the teletype.

7.9   An input file contains, in alphabetical order, the following part names and on-hand data:

Part	Quantity on hand
Capacitor #16A	416
Capacitor #49C	1532
Diode #821	700
Transistor #2N2120	3692

Write a program to read this data, add new deliveries to it, and write a new inventory record onto an output file. Have the computer ask the user to supply each part number and quantity delivered. Assume his responses are in alphabetical order.

7.10 There are three data files, illustrated in Figure 7.10. The first contains inventory item numbers, balance from the previous run, and the reorder point for each item. The second contains similar data for new items to be added to the list. The third file contains data on additions to, or withdrawals from, inventory—namely item number, quantity involved and a code "A" for additions, "W" for withdrawals. Write a program to read data from the first and second data files into a subscripted variable. Then, while reading the third file, alter the array as appropriate, determining new balance on hand as the additions/withdrawals are read. If an item is found in the third file which is not in the first or second file, print an error message on the teletype. After completing all readings of the third file, erase the first file and write the updated array onto it for use in the same manner later. If the balance falls below the reorder point of an item, print its inventory number on the teletype.

7.11 There are two data files. The one shown in Figure 7.11 is a permanent,

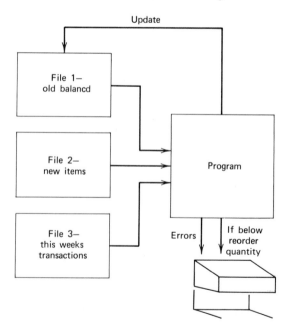

Figure 7.10

random-access, file which must be updated with new information, shown in Figure 7.12. Write a random-access program to read each line in NEWDATA, read the appropriate line in STATUS, add the new information to it, and write the updated data back on STATUS.

STATUS

CUSTØMER	NAME	ØWED
3140		400.00
8013	ATLAS MFG.	30.15
5144	AAA CØ.	0.00
4041	AJAX INC.	814.21
3141	ZANØU INC.	1320.00
6182	XYZ MFG.	619.23
4613	ZERØ INC.	408.12

Figure 7.11 Permanent file, STATUS, which must be updated with the receipts or invoices in Figure 7.12.

NEWDATA

5144	+ 32.16
4613	− 160.32
3140	− 200.00
4613	− 100.00

Figure 7.12 Invoices (+) and receipts (−) to be used for updating Figure 7.11.

8 COMPUTER FEATURES

"It's getting delusions of grandeur!.. Now it wants a goat sacrificed to it!"

*The "Grin and Bear It" cartoon above is printed here by courtesy of Publishers-Hall Syndicate.

330

The time-sharing concept offers many interesting and useful capabilities with which the programmer and his manager should both be familiar.

8.1   SHARING PROGRAMS BETWEEN USERS

It often happens that two or more users wish to share a given program or programs with each other. The cost of writing and storing the program is incurred only once; one user may not have a programming capability at his disposal; one user may charge another a fee for usage; etc. Most time-sharing computers permit such an exchange of programs under selective conditions which are controlled by the owner of the program.

The person under whose user number the program is stored must inform the computer that another is allowed to use his file. He must log in under his own user number and transmit to the computer the fact that a specific file is to be shared with another user, for example, the program PAYRØLL. Typically, he does this in one of the following ways:

■   Gives a command like

PERMIT,PAYRØLL,LZ402X

meaning, *"permit user LZ402X to use my program named* PAYRØLL.*"*

■   Places one or more "control characters"* somewhere in the name of the program. Such characters do not print, so accidental discovery by unauthorized persons is eliminated. Only the owner and the borrower know the specific characters and their locations.

After the owner has informed the computer that another person may properly use his program, the borrower instructs the computer to retrieve the program out of the owner's user number by the following typical sequence of computer and user dialog:

ØLD ØR NEW PRØGRAM———ØLD
ØLD PRØGRAM NAME———PAYRØLL,AX301GT

meaning, obviously, that the program to be used is one which has been saved under user number AX301GT and named PAYRØLL.

8.2   FILE PROTECTION AND DATA SECURITY

There are two kinds of file protection which the user can utilize—that which protects his programs from accidental damage, and that which prevents unwarranted access to private information.

---

*Generated by holding down the "CNTRL" key on the teletype while stroking the character—see Chapter 2.

DECLARED FILES

A department or company will often have several persons using the same user number, and this can lead to accidental destruction of programs. Typically, one or two persons in the department are proficient programmers, and they write programs which will be used by other, less proficient, members. Inexperience, hurriedness, or carelessness may occasionally lead to accidental erasure of an important program. The author has done it himself during moments of temporary lapses of intelligence. The results, of course, could be serious.

To avoid this, the user can use a statement similar to

DECLARE PAYRØLL,READ ØNLY

Afterward, even the user himself cannot accidentally erase the file. If the time should come when he wishes to erase it, he must first re-DECLARE the program to be a WRITE file. If he does re-DECLARE the program, he probably does so deliberately, minimizing the risk of accidental erasure.

ENCRYPTING FILES

For corporate security, client confidence, or other reasons, some data should be protected from accidental, unauthorized, or surreptitious disclosure. Company management personnel understandably feel apprehensive about putting such data into the computer for fear that it will somehow, by some error on the part of the computer or by an outsider's overt attempt, find its way into undesired hands. For this kind of data, some protection is offered by the **encryption** feature available on some computers. It works as follows: The user picks an eight-digit number, one known only to himself, and instructs the computer to "encrypt" one of his files by that number, with commands like these:

> ENCRYPT
> FILE NAME: PAYRØLL
> ENCRYPTING CØDE: 31498442
> READY

Upon receiving the encryption code, the computer "scrambles" the program by some manipulation which is dependent on the sequence of numbers given. If desired, the scrambled file may be rescrambled a number of times by other codes to further protect it. To use the program, it must be unscrambled by reversing the above procedure with a DECRYPT command.

In spite of this feature, the author recommends caution when deciding to put extremely sensitive data on the computer. The data is initially sent over the telephone lines and into the file in an unencrypted format, and telephone wires may be tapped. The file is also decrypted, and therefore vulnerable, while actually using it.

8.3 LIBRARY PROGRAMS

A major part of the cost of computing lies in the initial development of programs. Most programs are tailored by their user to meet his own needs, but there are many others which are common to a wide variety of other users. To avoid costly duplication of programming efforts, the supplier usually maintains a "library" of programs which he has developed for use by all his clients. These programs perform statistical analyses of data, evaluate complex mathematical functions, plot graphs and do a variety of other standard, universal, jobs. When the user wishes to borrow a library program, he simply instructs the computer to retrieve the program from a "LIBRARY" user number. It may be done in this manner: ∅LD PR∅GRAM NAME:STATAN, LIBRARY. Or, depending on the conventions adopted by the computer, the name of the library program may be identified with asterisks, quotation marks, or other symbols in the name. Once the program is brought into the user's memory, it is used as one of his own.

The supplier's library catalog or other manuals usually give a comprehensive set of instructions for running each library program—what kind of data it needs, how it must be organized, what options are available, what the printout represents, inherent limitations, etc. In addition, the manuals often provide a short lecture on how to apply the results to real-world problems and how the library program is structured.

8.4 COMMAND FILES

Once a program, or a series of them, is completely written and debugged, it may be turned over to many persons with absolutely no computing skill for repeated running on a daily or weekly basis. It may be desirable to avoid training these persons in all the intricacies of loading programs into working memory, saving them in permanent memory, executing them, and so forth, even though the necessary commands are entirely predictable.

On some computer systems the programmer is permitted to store the necessary commands in a file (in a manner quite similar to that for creating a data file). Let us say the file is named START. Thereafter the user can simply give the computer an instruction similar to

C∅MMANDS, START

whereupon the computer abandons its reliance on the user for its future instructions and begins taking them from START instead. Thus, execution of the programs does not depend on the skill of the operator.

8.5 OTHER LANGUAGES

Other languages besides BASIC are usually available on time-sharing computers. The most common are FØRTRAN, CØBØL, PL/1, and a variety of specialized languages tailored to electronic circuit analyses, civil engineering, finance, numerical control of machinery, and other fields. A manager who has people working for him who are already fluent in these languages will appreciate their existence on the same machine as BASIC. Sometimes customers or other factors may dictate going to one of these languages instead of BASIC.

8.6 EDITING

Very likely, the reader's computer has a flexible and highly useful set of commands available for editing and manipulating files of data. Whether these commands are thought of as a new language or a special part of the BASIC language depends on one's personal preference and on the computer's established conventions.

It is very difficult to generalize the format and uses of EDITØR commands. As with many of the features in the latter part of this book, the variety and implementation of these commands is not very consistent among computer systems, and not much is to be gained by trying to describe them in detail here. There are basically three kinds of EDITØR commands: those that operate on whole programs simultaneously, those that operate only on certain lines of the program, and those that operate on individual characters in a given line. The following discussion is very generalized and the reader is advised to secure a copy of appropriate manuals from his supplier to learn the detailed implementation.

FILE EDITING

These commands are used when manipulating whole programs or data files. They perform such functions as merging two or more programs together, extracting parts of a program, and listing the program in neat, organized $8\frac{1}{2} \times 11$ inch pages (numbered, with top and bottom margins, single or double spaced).

LINE EDITING

A line-editing command usually has associated with it some string of characters. A typical line-editing command takes the form

> READY.
> EDIT REPLACE/FØR I = 1 TØ N/,/FØR J = 1 TØ N/

This command instructs the computer to search through the entire program and replace the string of characters "FØR I = 1 TØ N" with the new string "FØR J = 1 TØ N." Variations also permit the user to stipulate that only certain of the occurrences be replaced. Line-editing commands can also be used to simply list all the variable names used in the program, print out certain lines for the programmer's examination, insert lines in data files, and edit certain characters in the middle of lines.

CHARACTER EDITING

Imagine a complicated line containing an error, as shown below, where the number "572" should have been "573":

> 10000   DATA 834.2,1949.4,572,1964,398.204,1632

To retype the line might lead to another error. The computer can be instructed to automatically copy parts of the line while the programmer alters only certain parts of it. The procedure begins with an EDIT command:

> READY.
> EDIT /572/
> READY.

meaning "edit the line with the string 572 in it." At this point, the computer is ready to copy parts of the line. The programmer issues the command "Z^c7"* (or mnemonically, "zo-o-o-m" to a 7). Then the computer copies over the line, through 7; the programmer types a "3" to replace the offending "2." Having corrected the line, the programmer can now type F^c, telling the computer to "finish copying the line." The whole procedure looks like

> READY.
> EDIT /572/
> READY.
> Z^c7 10000 DATA 834.2,1949.4,573F^c,1964,398.204,1632

---

*The Z^c means to depress the teletype's "Control" and "Z" keys simultaneously.

The programmer types only the underscored portion of the line; the computer types the rest, thereby avoiding the risk of another error.

Other control characters such as E^c to enter extra characters in a line or S^c to scratch characters from a line may also be available. Several control characters may be given in a line to incrementally space across it, correcting it in the process.

8.7 SERVICES PROVIDED BY THE SUPPLIER

The company which supplies computing time generally provides several valuable services, at varying charges (perhaps without charge), to which the user may avail himself. Among them are the following:

■ A reasonable amount of programming assistance for difficult problems, particularly for the new user.

■ Introductory and advanced programming classes.

■ Seminars to discuss new time-sharing applications and equipment.

■ High-speed line printers, punched card readers, card punch devices, and magnetic tape handlers. If a BASIC program generates a large volume of output data which would take a long time to print on the teletype, it might be written into an output data file. The computer center can then list it at a very high speed on a *line printer* or card punch.

8.8 TIME-SHARING CONTRACTS

Some large engineering companies have a dedicated time-sharing computer for the exclusive use of their personnel. However, most companies or individuals must sign a contract with a computer company in order to gain access to the computer. These contracts are not at all standardized from one company to another. Most contracts can be broken at the user's discretion with no more than a specified notice period.

There are a number of factors which may enter into the cost of the contract. Because of variations in charges that every company imposes for each of these factors, it is sometimes difficult to directly compare the cost of competing systems. However, one should expect to pay, on the average, about $10–20/hr of computer usage. This sum may be composed of individual charges for one or all of the following factors:

■ a service-initiation fee;
■ an hourly charge for time in actual contact with the computer (usually called *terminal-connect* time), measured in $/hr;

■   a charge, measured in ¢/sec, for the actual seconds (or fractions thereof) during which the computer actually works on the program (usually called CPU, or *central processor unit*, time);

■   a charge, measured in ¢/character/week (or month or day), for storing programs and data inside the computer (called a *storage charge*);

■   minimum monthly charges.

Ten to twenty dollars per hour is far below the amount usually associated with computer capabilities. This price range is the result of the fact that many persons are using the computer simultaneously and thus are able to share the cost.

■ EXERCISES

Your computer probably has a number of library programs available. Research and use them to solve the problems below. Also determine the language in which each is written, its data capacity, its optional printouts, and its limitations. Get a listing of the program, if possible. Add any data or parameters needed.

8.1   Given the following sales figures:

1963	3,139,000	1966	4,679,000	1969	6,600,000
1964	3,165,000	1967	5,051,000	1970	7,230,000
1965	4,664,000	1968	6,032,000	1971	7,617,000

determine (a) the rate of growth for the entire period and for the last five years, and (b) the annual sales in 1981 if the growth rate experienced for the past five years continues.

8.2   Your company has developed an activity network (Fig. 8.1) to show

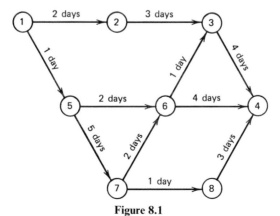

Figure 8.1

events that must take place while a design activity advances from event 1 (start) to event 4 (finished). The symbol Ⓐ $\xrightarrow{4}$ Ⓑ indicates the number of days required to advance from event A to event B. Find the "critical path" through the network—i.e., the path which determines the earliest completion. [*Note:* The network is interpreted as follows: The activity cannot begin progress from ③ to ④ until both ② and ⑥ are completed.]

8.3   Two factories must ship material to three warehouses. The costs of shipping each unit from factory i to warehouse j are shown in the lower triangles of Figure 8.2. Use the linear programming library program to determine the lowest-cost shipping mix (i.e., determine $Q_1,...,Q_6$ so that the objective function $0.30*Q_1 + 0.42*Q_2 + \cdots + 0.30*Q_6$ is minimized). Eleven constraints must be written and given to the computer. Write the appropriate constraining inequalities (or equalities) necessary to describe the following conditions:

■ $Q_1,Q_2,...,Q_6$ cannot be negative (six constraints);
■   the quantity of material delivered to each warehouse must exactly equal the requirements of that warehouse (three constraints);
■   the material shipped from each factory cannot exceed the capability of that factory (two constraints).

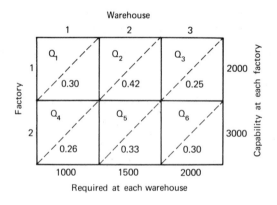

Figure 8.2

8.4   Perform numerical integration to determine y:

$$y = \int_0^{7.65} \log \frac{x^2}{10} \, 3x \, dx$$

8.5   Plot $R = \cos(3\theta)$ in polar coordinates.

8.6   Three reading tests are given to students in four different schools, with the following average scores:

School	Test 1	Test 2	Test 3
1	83	80	79
2	72	75	78
3	79	81	76
4	84	84	81

Perform a *two-way analysis of variance* to determine whether all tests produced statistically the same results, and if not, whether the difference can be attributed to differences in the schools.

8.7   Compute $\Gamma(-1.5)$, $\Gamma(-0.5)$, $\Gamma(2.3)$.

SOLUTIONS TO SELECTED EXERCISES

2.6   (a) LET $X = 3*A + 1$
     (d) LET $L1 = P\uparrow 3 + 2$
     (e) Okay

2.7   (b) LET $Y = X\uparrow 3 + 2*X\uparrow 2 - X + 1/X$
     (f) LET $X = (T-1)\uparrow(G-1)$
     (i) LET $I = Q - W + R$

2.8   (a) 13860000
     (b) 1.41E−2

2.10

```
100 LET F=2
200 LET Ø=4
300 LET Q=6
400 LET D=1
500 LET N=3
600 LET P=3
700 LET V=5*F+1*Ø+.25*Q+.10*D+.05*N+.01*P
800 PRINT "STUDENT HAS $";V
900 END
RUN

STUDENT HAS $    15.78
```

2.15
```
100 LET D1=35
200 LET D2=9
300 LET D3=8
400 LET W=(D1*D2*D3)*10.3
500 PRINT "WEIGHT =";W;" PØUNDS ØF WHEAT"
600 LET V=0.18*W
700 PRINT "INITIAL VALUE = $";V
800 LET A=169
900 PRINT "ADDED VALUE =$";A/W;" PER PØUND"
1000 PRINT "TØTL VALUE, AFTER SHIPPING = $";V+A
1100 END
 RUN
```

```
WEIGHT =      25956     PØUNDS ØF WHEAT
INITIAL VALUE = $       4672.08
ADDED VALUE =$       6.5110186E-03     PER PØUND
TØTL VALUE, AFTER SHIPPING = $      4841.08
```

2.17
```
100 LET L1=9
200 LET W1=20
300 LET L2=15
400 LET W2=20
500 LET C=8.32
600 LET C1=((L1*W1)/9)*C
700 LET C2=((L2*W2)/9)*C
800 PRINT "BEDRØØM",C1
900 PRINT "LIVING RØØM",C2
1000 END
 RUN
```

```
BEDRØØM           166.4
LIVING RØØM       277.33333
```

2.21
```
100 LET F=32
200 LET C=(5/9)*(F-32)
300 LET K=273.16+C
400 LET R=460+F
500 PRINT "FAHRENHEIT";F
600 PRINT "CENTIGRADE";C
700 PRINT "KELVIN";K
800 PRINT "RANKIN";R
900 PRINT
1000 LET F=212
1100 LET C=(5/9)*(F-32)
1200 LET K=273.16+C
1300 LET R=460+F
1400 PRINT "FAHRENHEIT";F
1500 PRINT "CENTIGRADE";C
1600 PRINT "KELVIN";K
1700 PRINT "RANKIN";R
1800 END
RUN
```

```
FAHRENHEIT    32
CENTIGRADE    0
KELVIN     273.16
RANKIN     492

FAHRENHEIT    212
CENTIGRADE    100
KELVIN     373.16
RANKIN     672
```

2.28

```
100 LET M=(6-2)/(4-2)
200 LET B=2-M*2
300 PRINT "M=";M,"B=";B
400 LET X=3
500 LET Y=M*X+B
600 PRINT "WHEN X=";X,"Y=";Y
700 END
  RUN
```

```
M=     2      B=     -2
WHEN X=   3    Y=    4
```

2.33

```
50 PRINT "CAR NØ.","MILES","GALLØNS","AVE. MPG"
100 LET M1=0
200 LET G1=0
300 READ N

400 FØR I=1 TØ N
500 READ M,G
600 PRINT I,M,G,M/G
700 LET M1=M1+M
800 LET G1=G1+G
900 NEXT I

1000 PRINT
1100 PRINT "TØTAL MILES =";M1
1200 PRINT "GALLØNS CØNSUMED =";G1
1300 PRINT "AVERAGE MPG, ALL CARS =";M1/G1

1400 DATA 4
1500 DATA 302,21.3
1600 DATA 418,25.0
1700 DATA 192,15.1
1800 DATA 225,14.8
1900 END
  RUN
```

CAR NØ.	MILES	GALLØNS	AVE. MPG
1	302	21.3	14.178404
2	418	25	16.72
3	192	15.1	12.715232
4	225	14.8	15.202703

```
TØTAL MILES =    1137
GALLØNS CØNSUMED =    76.2
AVERAGE MPG, ALL CARS =    14.92126
```

2.34
```
50 PRINT "YEAR","6% QUARTERLY","5-1/4% CØNTIN"
100 READ I1,I2
200 FØR T=1 TØ 20
300 LET V1=(1+I1/4)↑(4*T)*1000
400 LET V2=1000*2.71828↑(I2*T)
450 PRINT T,V1,V2
500 NEXT T
600 DATA .06,.0525
700 END
RUN
```

YEAR	6% QUARTERLY	5-1/4% CØNTIN
1	1061.3636	1053.9025
2	1126.4926	1110.7105
3	1195.6182	1170.5806
4	1268.9855	1233.6779
5	1346.855	1300.1762
6	1429.5028	1370.259
7	1517.2222	1444.1194
8	1610.3243	1521.9611
9	1709.1395	1603.9987
10	1814.0184	1690.4583
11	1925.333	1781.5782
12	2043.4783	1877.6098
13	2168.8734	1978.8177
14	2301.9631	2085.481
15	2443.2198	2197.8937
16	2593.1444	2316.3657
17	2752.269	2441.2236
18	2921.158	2572.8117
19	3100.4106	2711.4928
20	3290.6628	2857.6491

2.37
```
50 PRINT "TIME","DIRECTIØN","EAST","NØRTH","DISTANCE"
100 LET S=30
200 LET E=0
300 LET N=0
400 FØR T=0 TØ 3 STEP .5
500 LET E=S*T
600 PRINT T,"EAST",E,N,(E↑2+N↑2)↑.5
700 NEXT T
800 FØR T=3.5 TØ 7 STEP .5
900 LET N=S*(T-3)
1000 PRINT T,"NØRTH",E,N,(E↑2+N↑2)↑.5
1100 NEXT T
1200 END
RUN
```

TIME	DIRECTIØN	EAST	NØRTH	DISTANCE
0	EAST	0	0	0
.5	EAST	15	0	15
1	EAST	30	0	30
1.5	EAST	45	0	45
2	EAST	60	0	60
2.5	EAST	75	0	75
3	EAST	90	0	90
3.5	NØRTH	90	15	91.241438
4	NØRTH	90	30	94.86833
4.5	NØRTH	90	45	100.62306
5	NØRTH	90	60	108.16654
5.5	NØRTH	90	75	117.15375
6	NØRTH	90	90	127.27922
6.5	NØRTH	90	105	138.29317
7	NØRTH	90	120	150

2.45
```
100 LET X1=0
200 LET Y1=0
300 FØR I=1 TØ 5
400 READ X,Y
500 LET X1=X1+X
600 LET Y1=Y1+Y
700 NEXT I
800 PRINT "RESULTANT VECTØR IS ",X1;"+";Y1;"I"
900 DATA 10,3,4,5
1000 DATA -5,4.5,-3,-4
1100 DATA 10,-3
1200 END
 RUN

RESULTANT VECTØR IS        16    +      5.5  I
```

2.57
```
100 FØR I=1 TØ 5
200 READ S,L,W,H
300 LET G1=L+2*(W+H)
400 IF G1>72 THEN 700
500 PRINT "CARTØN STYLE";S,"CAN BE MAILED"
600 GØ TØ 800
700 PRINT "CARTØN STYLE";S,"CANNØT BE MAILED"
800 NEXT I
900 DATA 2044,36,2.5,8
1000 DATA 128,12,12,12
1100 DATA 1611,40.25,15,16
1200 DATA 9021,28,9,12
1300 DATA 4144,30,9,12
1400 END
 RUN

CARTØN STYLE    2044     CAN BE MAILED
CARTØN STYLE    128      CAN BE MAILED
CARTØN STYLE    1611     CANNØT BE MAILED
CARTØN STYLE    9021     CAN BE MAILED
CARTØN STYLE    4144     CAN BE MAILED
```

2.61
```
50 PRINT "ACCØUNT", "CHARGE"
100 FØR I=1 TØ 4
200 READ N,B
300 IF B>100 THEN 800
400 LET S=.04*N
500 IF S>.50 THEN 900
600 LET  S=.50
700 GØ TØ 900
800 LET S=0
900 PRINT I,S
1000 NEXT I
1100 DATA 3,96.00
1200 DATA 10,112.00
1300 DATA 23,16.00
1400 DATA 6,422.00
1500 END
 RUN

ACCØUNT         CHARGE
  1               .5
  2               0
  3               .92
  4               0
```

2.63

```
100 FØR J=1 TØ 8
200 READ V,I
300 LET R=V/I
400 IF R>10.2 THEN 700
500 IF R<9.8 THEN 700
600 GØ TØ 800
700 PRINT "RESISTØR";J;"IS ØUT ØF SPEC"
800 NEXT J
900 DATA 10,1
1000 DATA 10,.99
1100 DATA 10,.975
1200 DATA 10,.995
1300 DATA 10,1.005
1400 DATA 10,1.05
1500 DATA 100,10.34
1600 DATA 500,51.5
1700 DATA 100,9.79
1800 END
   RUN

RESISTØR     3     IS ØUT ØF SPEC
RESISTØR     6     IS ØUT ØF SPEC
RESISTØR     7     IS ØUT ØF SPEC
RESISTØR     8     IS ØUT ØF SPEC
```

3.2

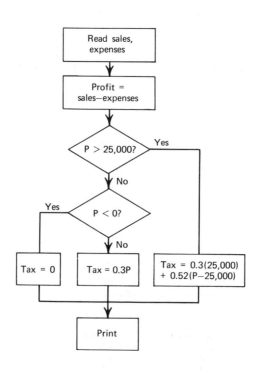

3.5

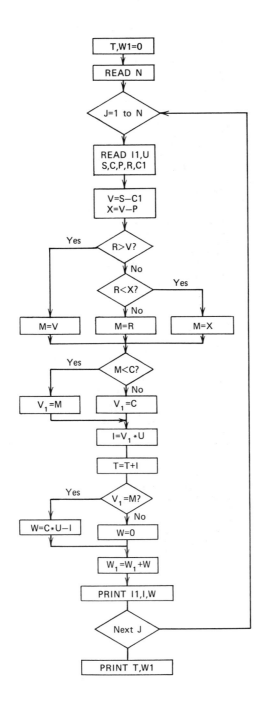

3.11

```
100 READ A
101 PRINT "FØR AMØUNT ";A
200 LET F=0
300 IF A<5.00 THEN 700
400 LET A=A-5.00
500 LET F=F+1
600 GØ TØ 300
700 LET Ø=0
800 IF A<1.00 THEN 1200
900 LET A=A-1.00
1000 LET Ø=Ø+1
1100 GØ TØ 800
1200 LET Q=0
1300 IF A<.25 THEN 1700
1400 LET A=A-.25
1500 LET Q=Q+1
1600 GØ TØ 1300
1700 LET D=0
1800 IF A<.10 THEN 2200
1900 LET A=A-.10
2000 LET D=D+1
2100 GØ TØ 1800
2200 LET N=0
2300 IF A<.05 THEN 2700
2400 LET A=A-.05
2500 LET N=N+1
2600 GØ TØ 2300
2700 LET P=0
2800 IF A<.01 THEN 3200
2900 LET A=A-.01
3000 LET P=P+1
3100 GØ TØ 2800
3200 PRINT "GIVE THIS CHANGE"
3300 PRINT "FIVE-$ BILLS";F
3400 PRINT "ØNE-$ BILLS";Ø
3500 PRINT "QUARTERS";Q
3600 PRINT "DIMES";D
3700 PRINT "NICKELS";N
3800 PRINT "PENNIES";P
3900 DATA 82.25
4000 END
RUN

FØR AMØUNT      82.25
GIVE THIS CHANGE
FIVE-$ BILLS    16
ØNE-$ BILLS      2
QUARTERS         1
DIMES       0
NICKELS     0
PENNIES     0
```

3.16

```
50 REM--AT YEAR 0, WØRLD PØPULATIØN
51 REM--IS EQUAL TØ "TØDAY'S" PØPUL.

100 LET P1=3.7E9
200 LET P2=P1
300 LET Y=0
400 LET C=0
500 LET I=.019

600 LET Y=Y+1
700 LET P2=P2+I*P2
800 IF P2<2*P1 THEN 600

900 IF C>0 THEN 1300
1000 PRINT "DØUBLE AT YEAR";Y
1100 LET C=C+1
1200 GØ TØ 600

1300 IF P2<3*P1 THEN 600
1400 PRINT "TRIPLE AT YEAR";Y
1500 END
  RUN

DØUBLE AT YEAR     37
TRIPLE AT YEAR     59
```

4.2

```
100 PRINT "METHØD 1,2 ØR 3";
200 INPUT M
300 PRINT "GIVE DEPRECIABLE VALUE AND LIFE";
400 INPUT V,L
500 IF M=1 THEN 1000
600 IF M=2 THEN 2000
700 IF M=3 THEN 3000
800 PRINT "SØRRY, YØU MADE AN ERRØR, TRY AGAIN"
900 GØ TØ 100
1000 REM BEGIN STRAIGHT LINE
1001 REM          •
1002 REM          •
2000 REM BEGIN SUM-ØF-YEAR'S-DIGITS
2001 REM          •
2002 REM          •
3000 REM BEGIN DECLINING BALANCE
3001 REM          •
3002 REM          •
 RUN

METHØD 1,2 ØR 3   ? 5
GIVE DEPRECIABLE VALUE AND LIFE   ? 100000,15
SØRRY, YØU MADE AN ERRØR, TRY AGAIN
METHØD 1,2 ØR 3   ? 4
GIVE DEPRECIABLE VALUE AND LIFE   ? 100000,15
SØRRY, YØU MADE AN ERRØR, TRY AGAIN
METHØD 1,2 ØR 3   ? 3
GIVE DEPRECIABLE VALUE AND LIFE   ? 100000,15
                 •
                 •
                 •
```

4.4

```
100 PRINT "HØW MANY SATELLITES";
200 INPUT N
300 IF N/2=INT(N/2) THEN 600
400 PRINT "ERRØR...MUST BE LAUNCHED "
401 PRINT "IN PAIRS, SØ YØU MUST ANSWER"
402 PRINT "WITH AND EVEN NUMBER"
500 GØ TØ 100
600 REM  BEGIN PRØGRAM
   RUN

HØW MANY SATELLITES  ? 5
ERRØR...MUST BE LAUNCHED
IN PAIRS, SØ YØU MUST ANSWER
WITH AND EVEN NUMBER
HØW MANY SATELLITES  ? 4
```

4.5   Solving only for the minimum of the triplet $(6, -16, 8.2)$:

```
50 REM SØLVING ØNLY FØR THE MINIMUM ØF
51 REM THE TRIPLET ØF NUMBERS

100 DEF FNA(X,Y)=(X+Y-ABS(X-Y))/2
200 READ A,B,C
300 LET M=FNA(A,B)
400 LET M=FNA(M,C)
500 PRINT "MINIMUM =";M
600 DATA 6,-16,8.2
700 END
   RUN

MINIMUM =   -16
```

or, replace lines 300, 400 with 300 LET $M = FNA(FNA(A,B),C)$:

```
100 DEF FNA(X,Y)=(X+Y-ABS(X-Y))/2
200 READ A,B,C
300 LET M=FNA(FNA(A,B),C)
500 PRINT "MINIMUM =";M
600 DATA 6,-16,8.2
700 END
RUN

MINIMUM =   -16
```

4.8   To determine the number of $5 bills and the number of $1 bills in X:

```
48 REM TØ DETERMINE JUST THE
49 REM  TØ DETERMINE JUST THE
50 REM NUMBER ØF $5-BILLS
51 REM AND $1-BILLS IN X:
98 LET X=49.24
100 LET F=INT(X/5)
200 LET Ø=INT((X-F*5)/1)
300 PRINT "$5-BILLS";F
400 PRINT "1$-BILLS";Ø
500 END
RUN

$5-BILLS     9
1$-BILLS     4
```

4.13
```
100 DEF FNS(A)=SIN(3.14159*A/180)
200 DEF FNC(A)=CØS(3.14159*A/180)
300 LET Y=FNS(30+15)*FNS(60)-FNC(30)*FNC(60)
350 LET Z=FNS(30)/FNC(30)
400 PRINT "Y=";Y
401 PRINT "Z=";Z
RUN

Y=    .17935824
Z=    .57734968
```

4.22
```
100 DIM C(23)
200 MAT READ C
300 LET T=0
400 FØR I=8 TØ 14
500 LET T=T+C(I)
600 NEXT I
700 PRINT "TØTAL ØF EIGHTH THRØUGH"
800 PRINT "FØURTEENTH 'C' =";T
900 DATA 32,44,26,16,55,32,49,51
1000 DATA 41,43,55,28,52,51,50
1100 DATA 39,53,47,62,59,66,37,29
1200 END
RUN

TØTAL ØF EIGHTH THRØUGH
FØURTEENTH 'C' =    321
```

4.25

```
150 DIM H(1:5,1:4)
200 MAT READ H
300 LET X=H(1,1)
400 FØR I=1 TØ 5
500 FØR J=1 TØ 4
600 IF X<H(I,J) THEN 1000
700 LET X=H(I,J)
800 LET R=I
900 LET C=J
1000 NEXT J
1100 NEXT I
1200 PRINT "SMALLEST NØ. IS ";X
1300 PRINT "AT";R;"DØWN"
1301 PRINT "AND";C;"ACRØSS"
3000 DATA  5, 4, 3, 2
3100 DATA  6, 9, 0, 4
3200 DATA 11, 9, 5,-1
3300 DATA 13, 5, 6, 9
3400 DATA 21, 6, 5, 0
3500 END
 RUN

SMALLEST NØ. IS   -1
AT     3    DØWN
AND    4    ACRØSS
```

4.28

```
100 DIM S(3,1),P(1,3),C(3)
200 MAT READ P
300 MAT S=ZER
400 READ N,S
500 IF N=0 THEN 750
600 LET S(N,1)=S(N,1)+S
700 GØ TØ 400

750 FØR I=1 TØ 3
800 LET C(I)=S(I,1)*P(1,I)
850 NEXT I

900 FØR I=1 TØ 3
1000 PRINT "SALESMAN #";I,C(I)
1100 NEXT I

1200 REM-PERCENTAGES
1300 DATA .14,.082,.11
1400 REM-SALES
1500 DATA 1,3428.00
1600 DATA 3,893.16
1700 DATA 2,1204.82
1800 DATA 3,1694.43
1900 DATA 1,342.08
2000 DATA 3,22.14
2100 DATA 2,648.24
2200 DATA 2,500.00
2300 DATA 1,1040.21
2400 DATA 3,988.43
2500 DATA 1,1204.32
2600 DATA 1,144.00
2700 DATA 2,3821.42
2800 DATA 0,0
2900 END
RUN

SALESMAN #    1   862.2054
SALESMAN #    2   506.30736
SALESMAN #    3   395.7976
```

4.30   Using only 11 data for illustration,

```
50 LET N=11
100 DIM N(11),P(11)
200 LET P1=1
300 LET N1=1

350 FOR I=1 TO N
400 READ X
500 IF X<0 THEN 900
600 LET P(P1)=X
700 LET P1=P1+1
800 GO TO 1100
900 LET N(N1)=X
1000 LET N1=N1+1
1100 NEXT I

1150 PRINT "POSITIVE NUMBERS ARE"
1155 FOR I=1 TO P1-1
1160 PRINT P(I)
1165 NEXT I
1170 PRINT "NEGATIVE NUMBERS ARE"
1175 FOR I=1 TO N1-1
1180 PRINT N(I)
1185 NEXT I

1200 DATA 44,76,-2,4,62
1300 DATA 23,-11,-42,16,4
1301 DATA -104
1600 END
RUN

POSITIVE NUMBERS ARE
 44
 76
 4
 62
 23
 16
 4
NEGATIVE NUMBERS ARE
-2
-11
-42
-104
```

4.36

```
100 DIM P(4,5),D(5,3),C(4,3)
200 MAT READ P,D
300 MAT C=P*D
400 LET S=C(1,1)
500 LET R=1
600 LET C=1

700 FØR I=1 TØ 4
800 FØR J=1 TØ 3
900 IF C(I,J)>S THEN 1300
1000 LET S=C(I,J)
1100 LET R=I
1200 LET C=J
1300 NEXT J
1400 NEXT I

1500 PRINT "LEAST PØSSIBLE CØST IS";S
1600 PRINT "PRØDUCTIØN METHØD";R
1700 PRINT "DISTRIBUTIØN METHØD";C
1800 PRINT
1850 PRINT "THE CØST MATRIX, WITH "
1860 PRINT "DISTRIBUTIØN METHØDS 1,2,3 ACRØSS"
1870 PRINT "AND PRØDUCTIØN METHØDS 1,2,3,4 DØWN"
1880 PRINT
1900 MAT PRINT C

1999 REM PRØDUCTIØN DATA
2000 DATA 100,100,100,100,100
2100 DATA  50, 50,200, 75,125
2200 DATA 150,150, 75, 75, 50
2300 DATA  75,125, 75,125,100
2399 REM DISTRIBUTIØN DATA
2400 DATA 5,3,7
2500 DATA 5,3,7
2600 DATA 5,7,7
2700 DATA 5,7,3
2800 DATA 5,7,1
2900 END
 RUN

LEAST PØSSIBLE CØST IS    2300
PRØDUCTIØN METHØD     3
DISTRIBUTIØN METHØD   2

THE CØST MATRIX, WITH
DISTRIBUTIØN METHØDS 1,2,3 ACRØSS
AND PRØDUCTIØN METHØDS 1,2,3,4 DØWN

    2500            2700            2500
    2500            3100            2450
    2500            2300            2900
    2500            2700            2400
```

4.51
```
100 LET R=RND(-1)
200 DIM A(10,10),B(10,10),C(10,10)
300 MAT A=ZER
400 MAT B=ZER
500 MAT C=ZER

600 PRINT "CARTØN","RØW","CØLUMN","LAYER"
700 PRINT

800 FØR B=1 TØ 4
900 FØR T=1 TØ 3
1000 LET R=INT(10*RND(0))+1
1100 LET C=INT(10*RND(0))+1
1200 LET L=INT(3*RND(0))+1
1300 IF L=1 THEN 1600
1400 IF L=2 THEN 1900
1500 IF L=3 THEN 2200

1600 IF A(R,C)>0 THEN 1000
1700 LET A(R,C)=1
1800 GØ TØ 2400
1900 IF B(R,C)>0 THEN 1000
2000 LET B(R,C)=1
2100 GØ TØ 2400
2200 IF C(R,C)>0 THEN 1000
2300 LET C(R,C)=1

2400 PRINT B,R,C,L
2500 NEXT T
2600 PRINT
2700 NEXT B
2800 END
  RUN
```

CARTØN	RØW	CØLUMN	LAYER
1	4	6	2
1	5	2	3
1	5	4	1
2	2	2	1
2	2	3	3
2	2	2	2
3	5	2	1
3	5	5	1
3	3	7	3
4	10	7	3
4	7	2	3
4	2	9	2

5.3

```
100 REM N1=#TIMES HE GETS HOME
200 REM N2=#TIMES HE GETS TO PUB
300 REM S=STARTING POSITION
310 REM B=CURRENT BLOCK
320 REM B1=MOVEMENTS: -1=TOWARD HOME
330 REM B2=         +1=TOWARD PUB
400 REM C=NUMBER OF BLOCKS MOVED

500 FOR S=2 TO 7
600 PRINT "IF HE BEGINS AT BLOCK ";S
700 LET N1=0
800 LET N2=0
810 LET C=0

900 FOR I=1 TO 1000
1000 LET B=S
1050 LET C=C+1
1100 IF RND(0)<1/3 THEN 1400
1200 LET B1=-1
1300 GO TO 1500
1400 LET B1=+1

1500 LET B=B+B1
1600 IF B=1 THEN 1800
1650 IF B=8 THEN 2000
1700 GO TO 1050

1800 LET N2=N2+1
1900 GO TO 2100
2000 LET N1=N1+1
2100 NEXT I

2200 PRINT "PROB. HE GETS HOME ";N1/1000
2300 PRINT "PROB. HE GETS TO PUB ";N2/1000
2400 PRINT "AVE. NO. OF MOVES ";C/1000
2500 PRINT
2600 NEXT S
2700 END
 RUN

IF HE BEGINS AT BLOCK    2
PROB. HE GETS HOME    6E-03
PROB. HE GETS TO PUB    .994
AVE. NO. OF MOVES    2.914

IF HE BEGINS AT BLOCK    3
PROB. HE GETS HOME    1.4E-02
PROB. HE GETS TO PUB    .986
AVE. NO. OF MOVES    5.43

IF HE BEGINS AT BLOCK    4
PROB. HE GETS HOME    6.9E-02
          .
          .
          .
```

5.8
```
100 LET L1=10000E-9
200 LET L2=16000E-9
300 LET L=17520
400 LET N=10000
401 LET M=0

450 FØR I=1 TØ N
500 LET T1=LØG(RND(0))/(-L1)
600 LET T2=LØG(RND(0))/(-L2)

700 LET X=MIN(T1,T2,L)
800 LET M=M+X

900 NEXT I
1000 PRINT "AVERAGE LIFE, ØR MTBF ="JM/10000
1100 END
RUN

AVERAGE LIFE, ØR MTBF =      14028.529
```

5.15
```
50 REM-MAT F IS THE CØEFFICIENTS ØF THE FIRST EQUATIØN
51 REM-MAT S IS THE CØEFFICIENTS ØF THE SECØND EQUATIØN
52 REM-MAT P IS THE CØEFFICIENTS ØF THE PRØDUCT EQUATIØN
100 DIM F(0:5),S(0:4),P(0:9)
200 FØR I=5 TØ 0 STEP -1
201 READ F(I)
202 NEXT I
203 FØR I=4 TØ 0 STEP -1
204 READ S(I)
205 NEXT I
206 MAT P=ZER

300 FØR I=0 TØ 5
400 FØR J=0 TØ 4
500 LET P(I+J)=P(I+J)+F(I)*S(J)
600 NEXT J
700 NEXT I
800 PRINT "PØWER ØF X","CØEFFICIENT"
900 FØR K=9 TØ 0 STEP -1
1000 PRINT K,P(K)
1100 NEXT K

1200 DATA 1,-3,6,12,1,-10
1300 DATA -65,-2,9,-4,2
1400 END
 RUN
```

PØWER ØF X	CØEFFICIENT
9	-65
8	193
7	-375
6	-823
5	-21
4	726
3	-7
2	-70
1	42
0	-20

6.1

```
50 PRINT "NAME","NØ.","SALARY","TAX","NET"
51 PRINT "----","---","------","---","---"
100 FØR I=1 TØ 6
200 READ N$,N,H,R,T
300 LET S=H*R
400 LET G=S*T
500 PRINT N$,N,S,G,S-G
600 NEXT I
700 DATA "ADAMS,JIM",40312,40,3.32,.103
800 DATA "SMITH,SAM",8140,42,5.25,.172
900 DATA "BARNETT,MIKE",31402,38,4.28,.145
1000 DATA "BARNETT,DEBØRAH",12440,40,2.13,.085
1100 DATA "RØBERTS,CLIFF",21443,40,6.28,.18
1200 DATA "JØNES,ALVIN",41102,41.5,5.03,.163
1300 END
 RUN
```

NAME	NØ.	SALARY	TAX	NET
----	---	------	---	---
ADAMS,JIM	40312	132.8	13.6784	119.1216
SMITH,SAM	8140	220.5	37.926	182.574
BARNETT,MIKE	31402	162.64	23.5828	139.0572
BARNETT,DEBØRAH	12440	85.2	7.242	77.958
RØBERTS,CLIFF	21443	251.2	45.216	205.984
JØNES,ALVIN	41102	208.745	34.025435	174.71957

6.4

```
100 PRINT "DØ YØU WISH TØ DØ PART 1":
200 INPUT A$
300 IF A$="NØ" THEN 5000
400 REM     START PART 1
401 REM        .
402 REM        .
5000 REM     START PART 2
5001 REM        .
5002 REM        .
 RUN

 DØ YØU WISH TØ DØ PART 1? "NØ"
```

6.13

```
100 READ M$
200 IF M$="STEEL" THEN 1000
300 IF M$="ALUMINUM" THEN 2000
400 IF M$="HØNEYCØMB" THEN 3000
500 IF M$="STAINLESS" THEN 4000
600 IF M$="TITANIUM" THEN 5000
1000 REM     BEGIN PRØGRAM
1002 REM        .
1041 REM        .
```

6.14

```
100 REM--THE COMPUTER SYSTEM ON WHICH THIS PROGRAM WAS WRITTEN
110 REM--PERMITS A 'STRING VARIABLE', SUCH AS MAT G$,  TO
120 REM--CONTAIN NUMERIC VALUES AS WELL.  HENCE, THE YEARS ARE
130 REM--MORE CONVENIENTLY TREATED AS NUMERICS BELOW.
140 DIM G$(-1:30,-1:50)
150 FOR I=-1 TO 30
160 FOR J=-1 TO 50
170 G$(I,J)=" "
180 NEXT J
190 REM--PUTTING IN THE GRIDS
200 NEXT I
210 FOR I=1 TO 50
220 IF INT(I/5)<>I/5 THEN 250
230 LET G$(0,I)="+"
240 GO TO 260
250 LET G$(0,I)="'"
260 NEXT I
270 FOR I=1 TO 30
280 IF INT(I/5)<>I/5 THEN 310
290 LET G$(I,0)="+"
300 GO TO 320
310 LET G$(I,0)="-"
320 NEXT I
330 REM--PUTTING ON THE SALES AND YEARS LABELS
340 FOR I=10 TO 31
350 READ G$(-1,I)
360 NEXT I
370 REM--MOVE SALES GRID, TO COMPENSATE FOR NO YEAR ON FIRST LINE.
380 LET G$(0,0)="        "
390 FOR I=1941 TO 1970
400 LET G$(I-1940,-1)=I
410 NEXT I
420 FOR I=1 TO 30
430 REM--READING THE DATA, PLOTTING IT IN THE MATRIX, AND THEN
440 REM--PRINTING IT OUT
450 READ S
460 LET G$(I,S)="*"
470 NEXT I
480 MAT PRINT G$:
490 DATA "S","A","L","E","S"," ","(","M","I","L","L","I","O","N","S"
500 DATA " ","O","F"," ","$","S",")"
510 DATA 3,5,7,10,11,9,13,12,10,15,20,18,19,20,18,18,17,19,21
520 DATA 23,25,24,29,29,28,32,30,29,27,29
530 END
```

6.18
```
100 :      'LLLLLLLLLLLLLLLLLLLLLLLLLLLLLLLLLLLLLLLLLLLLLLLLLL
200 :         'LLLLLLLLLLLLLLLLLLLLLLLLLLLLLLLLLLLLLLLLLLLLLLLLLLLL
300 :      'LLLLLLLLLLLLLLLLLLLLLLLLLLLLLLLLLLLLLLLLLLLLLLLLLLL
400 :            '##########              'LLLLLLLLLLLLLLLLLLLLLLLLL
500 :##### 'LLLLLLLLLLLLLLLLLLLLLLLLLLLLL  $$$.##  $$$$$.##
600 :                                      $$$$$.##
700
```

```
2000 PRINT USING 100,N$
2010 PRINT USING 200,A$
2020 PRINT USING 300,C$
2030 PRINT
2040 PRINT USING 400,N,S$
2050 PRINT USING 500,Q,D$,E,P
2060 PRINT USING 600,S
2070 PRINT USING 600,T
2080 PRINT USING 600,S−T
```

6.22   (a) P="I CAN BE PRØUD ØF MYSELF"
       Q="FATHER PRAISES ME"
       R="I DØ WELL IN SPØRTS"
       S="I STUDY HARD"
   (b) Therefore, the logic translation is
       (1) P IMPLIES Q
       (2) R ØR (NØT P)
       (3) S IMPLIES R
       (4) DØES (1 AND 2 AND 3) IMPLY [Q IMP (NØT S)]?
   (c) Alter Program 6.18 to include this logic statement, add a loop to
       vary S, and change the printed message appropriately.
   (d) The conclusion is valid.

7.8   100 FILES ØLD,NEW
      200 SCRATCH #2
      300 IF END #1 THEN 1100
      400 READ #1,N$,S
      500 IF N$="KIMBERLEY ANNE SHEA" THEN 800
      600 LET S=1.10*S
      700 GØ TØ 900
      800 LET S=1.15*S
      900 WRITE #2,N$,S
      1000 GØ TØ 300
      1100 END

INDEX